Selected Early Reviews:

"A practical, detailed, accessible and informative guide to wine for anyone caught up in the lure of the grape from beginners to advanced enophiles."

—Wine Journal, Pasadena, CA

"Provides a nice survey of the wine-making process along with a lot of information on wine appreciation. Miller ... provides just enough detail to educate without confusing. Her writing is very effective, straightforward, and unadorned, without a hint of rhapsody that seems to afflict many wine writers. This is a book that sneaks up on you —it doesn't seem to be going that deep but only when you've finished reading it do you realize just how much you have learned."

—Anthony Dias Blue, Syndicated Wine Writer

"A terrific no-nonsense book on wine ... discusses the significance of vineyards, vintages and vintners. There are complete chapters on identification, buying, storing, serving, tasting.

—Springfield Sun, Philadelphia, PA

"Here's an appropriate present for the would-be wine buff on your list: ... An entertaining primer that is loaded with useful information."

—Bon Appetit

"A broad survey [that's] useful for readers who want their facts straightforward and unadorned. To be fully appreciated, this book should be read slowly and the words tasted."

—Wine News, Coral Gables, FL

"Miller's no-nonsense approach should appeal to anyone who has ever been intimidated by the mystique often surrounding the selection of wine ... [She] presents the facts along with illustrative vignettes that add vitality to the text. The writing is agreeably free of confusing jargon. Types of wine are described in some detail as are wine-producing regions. A highly readable primer with sensible recommendations for storing, aging and serving fine wines."

—Booklist

Gloria Bley Miller

The Glory of Wine

*A straightforward approach to
the classic wine experience*

Ibrod Press

Ibrod Press
PO Box 24-Village Station
New York, NY 10014

Printed in The United States of America
Cover and book design by Joseph Macal Design, Inc.
Illustrations by Tomar Levine

The marble sculpture shown on the cover is by the French sculptor, Eugene Gillaume (1822-1905). It can be seen in the Orsay Museum in Paris. Photograph by Gloria Bley Miller.

An earlier version of this book was published in 1996 as "The Gift of Wine" by Lyons & Burford.

10 9 8 7 6 5 4 3 2 1

Library of Congress Cataloging-in-Publication Data

Miller, Gloria Bley
    The Glory of Wine: a straightforward approach to the classic wine experience/Gloria Bley Miller.
        p. cm.
     Includes index.
     ISBN 0-9679012-0-0 (paperback)
     1. Wine and winemaking
     2. Food and wine

For more information visit us at www.gloryofwine.com

CONTENTS

For my father, who once made wine

INTRODUCTION

This book is written for those who know a few things about wine and would like to know a few things more. It is meant for those who wish to become wine literate.

Encompassing history, geography, agriculture, and art, wine touches our lives in many ways. It is a gift of nature, modified by man. The uniqueness of this gift becomes evident as we follow the grape on its journey from vineyard to bottle. As we move ahead, we learn the significance of vintners, vintages, and grape varieties. We visit the world's major wine regions and the minor ones as well.

In these pages, you will discover what you need to know about the buying, storing, and aging of wines. You will learn to decipher wine labels, match wine with food, and know if —when and how— a wine should breathe. You can even set up your own wine tastings.

The basic information is here. Almost every conceivable question you might have on wine has been considered. The book is yours to celebrate and enjoy. Browse through its pages and explore to your heart's content. Then, with your greater understanding, you can proceed with confidence when confronted by a wine list in a restaurant, or when selecting a bottle for dinner at home.

The Old Testament has said that "Wine maketh glad the heart of man." May a heightened awareness of the glory of wine now gladden your own heart.

Gloria Bley Miller
New York City

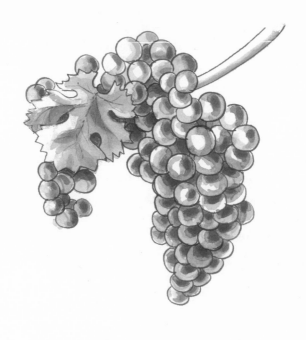

1

NATURE'S ROLE

Wine making is a collaboration between Man and Nature. Nature has generously provided the grape, soil, and climate as well as the key to wine making. This is Nature's gift. Man has his own role to play. He selects and cultivates the grape, then participates in its astonishing transformation from the sweet juice he has pressed to the exhilarating liquid known as wine.

THE GRAPE

The eventful journey of the grape begins in the spring. When average daily temperatures reach about 50°F, the vine begins its annual growth. Tender buds form on its branches and the sap rises, causing the buds to bulge and burst. This is the bud break. Downy shoots suddenly push out, becoming the spurs or fruiting units. Called canes when they mature, these will bear the grapes. Tendrils and leaves now appear. Trapping the sun's radiant energy by photosynthesis, they draw carbon dioxide from the air to produce the carbohydrates that will fuel the vine's growth and nourish the developing berries.

In early summer, when temperatures reach about 65°F, the vine begins to flower. Delicate green blossoms —looking like miniature grape clusters— appear. In Bordeaux, near the end of June, vintners celebrate this blossoming with a Fête des Fleurs (Feast of Flowers). Some ten days after pollination, the delicate blossoms wither, revealing in the center of each a hard green berry. This is the grape set. By late summer, the clusters are hanging plump and heavy on the vine. They begin to develop rich, lovely colors: crimsons, purples, and golds. Their once-opaque skins turn luminous and translucent.

Before the fledgling vine can bear suitable grapes for wine, it must first build a sturdy stalk to support the weight of the clusters. The vine must also develop a network of roots to extract nourishment from the soil. It needs at least three years to produce harvestable grapes and five or six years to be fully productive. (A premium plant needs a decade or more to produce first-rate fruit). Most vines reach their peak at about age fifteen; their productive life rarely extends beyond three decades. The older the vine, the more the roots will proliferate. Although its productivity decreases with time, the grapes are sweeter and more concentrated and the wines are much more intense. (Most vineyards replace their vines every twenty years or so, but in the Mosel Valley, some functioning vines are over fifty years old.)

The grape flourishes only in temperate climates; it is unable to survive in tropic heat or arctic cold. To be productive, the vine needs sunny days and cool nights, along with sufficient, but not excessive rain. The weather, however, should not be too compatible. Abundant quantity and high grape quality rarely coincide; bountiful vintages may produce good wines but never great ones. Harsh, difficult conditions seem to bring out the best in the developing grape.

Grapes can be grown successfully in the Northern Hemisphere, between the 30th and 50th parallels; and in the Southern Hemisphere, between the 20th and 40th. The most distinguished examples are cultivated in a band running along the 45th parallel. Included here are sections of France, Italy, Germany, Hungary, and the United States. Such grapes at their finest yield lively, complex and quite long-lived wines.

In the Northern Hemisphere, an imaginary line separates the growing areas into a cooler upper and a warmer lower zone. Characterizing the upper zone are four separate and distinct seasons. Its summers are warm and humid but not too hot, and its winters are quite cold. There is occasional frost in the spring and autumn, with rain falling throughout the year. During the growing season, gradually accumulating heat slowly ripens the grapes, giving them sufficient time to concentrate their sugars and develop their subtleties. The warmer lower zone, characterized by a Mediterranean climate, experiences essentially two seasons. Its long, hot, dry summers blend almost imperceptibly into mild and moist winters. Ripening rapidly under a constant sun, the grapes, grow fat and abundant, yielding robust and potent wines. But for the most part, these lack finesse and longevity.

Wine making's predominant grape is the *Vitis vinifera*, also known as the European or Old World grape. Characterized by a thin, easily bruised skin adhering firmly to a fleshy pulp, the vinifera grape is generally delicate and quite susceptible to biting cold, parasites, and disease. Yet the wines it yields are subtle, complex, and intense at their finest. The best-known red vinifera grapes are the cabernet sauvignon and pinot noir. The best-known whites are the chardonnay, riesling, and sauvignon blanc.

Hardier and more disease resistant is the *Vitis labrusca*, the New World grape. Indigenous to North America and generally grown east of the Rocky Mountains, the labrusca is also known as the slipskin grape because of its tough, sometimes inedible covering, which detaches easily from a slippery pulp. Labrusca wines are characterized by a grapy pungency, described as wild or "foxy." The red grapes include the concord, catawba and delaware. The white include the niagara and the diamond.

Hybrid grapes are also employed. Some varieties were bred to withstand cold climates and high humidity, while still retaining a European grape flavor. A number of hybrids are vinifera mixtures. Other varieties combine the vinifera's style and subtlety with the labrusca's sturdiness and disease resistance. (The latter are generally grown in cooler areas where the more delicate viniferas might perish.) The red hybrids include the ruby cabernet, chelois, baco noir, chancellor, maréchal foch, de chaunac, and léon millot. The white hybrids include the müller-thurgau, seyval blanc, and vidal blanc. (A number of these are named for the geneticists who developed them.)

NOTE: Some grapes are intended exclusively for wine making while others are meant mainly for eating. When serving both functions, the wines they yield are not very high in caliber as a rule .

Threats to the Grape

In its transition from flower to fruit, the grape faces a number of obstacles. Excessive rain may prevent its pollination. High winds may strip away the blossoms, while intense heat can wither them. Inclement weather may stunt the berries; drought may impoverish them. In spring and early summer, when good weather is essential, the tender vines are particularly vulnerable. Rain, suddenly becoming hail, can batter them, destroying their buds, and breaking off their shoots. Hail can bruise and ruin the developing berries. A harsh spring frost, wreaking havoc, can wipe out a vineyard overnight. Success is always dependent on the whims of the weather. As one grower pointed out, "This is not a business for the fainthearted to consider."

NOTE: During its winter dormancy, the vine can withstand the most disastrous conditions, even flooding.

Natural risks are always present in the vineyard. Even in ideal weather, a vineyard is never trouble free. Insects can defoliate the vines; predatory molds and mildews can attack the grapes. Rabbits and deer nibble at the tender shoots, while birds peck at the juicy berries. The most devastating threat of all has been the aphidlike and barely visible *Phylloxera vasatrix.* Piercing the roots of the vines with its sharp proboscis, phylloxera voraciously feeds on the sap, keeping the nutrients from reaching the grapes. At first, the clusters diminish; then the berries no longer ripen. Finally the aphid secretes a poison into the wound, killing the exhausted plant.

Phylloxera was apparently introduced into Europe from the New World. In the 1860s, it had turned up in a London botanical garden. English viticulturalists had sent to America for hardier cuttings while seeking ways to curb oïdium, a common and destructive fungus. (Grapes are generally cultivated from cuttings since their seeds do not pass the desired traits along as consistently.)

The prolific aphid, producing a dozen generations in a single year, spread like wildfire. No one knows exactly when it crossed over to France, but soon phylloxera was invading the finest vineyards of Bordeaux and Burgundy, attacking the soft fat roots of the vulnerable vinifera vines. Although the growers desperately tried to fend off the onslaught, nothing seemed to work. Spraying and burning had little effect. The aphids, operating underground, clung tenaciously to the deepest roots. Flooding damaged the soil but did not drown all the parasites. Uprooting the vines proved futile; once in the ground, the aphids could not be eradicated.

As the wine makers stood helplessly by, their losses mounted to the billions. Some, seeking a still-uncontaminated region, migrated across the Pyrenees from Bordeaux to Spain. Others retreated from the Rhône Valley to North Africa. Meanwhile the devastation continued, wiping out one wine region after another. The 1870s saw the invasion of Italy, Spain, Germany, Austria, Portugal, Greece, and Romania. By 1890, virtually every wine-producing region in Europe had been totally destroyed.

The relentless aphid crossed oceans as well, invading Madeira, the Canary Islands and Australia. Nor was California spared. In 1874, a Sonoma vineyard was found dying. In the Napa Valley, all but a few hundred acres were ruined. Sandy soil saved some patches of land in Portugal and Austria. (The aphid could not burrow deep enough to reach the roots.) Also spared were random sites in Champagne, Australia, Spain, and Cyprus.

Within three decades, phylloxera had brought virtually all of the world's wine making to a halt. Yet when the vine seemed totally doomed, French botanists found a way to save it. They had noted that the more fibrous roots of the tougher American plants seemed to heal quickly when pierced. Theorizing that coexistence might be possible between the parasite and a host with greater resistance, they grafted their vulnerable European vines onto the hardier American species, joining the scions of the viniferas to the sturdier, more resistant rootstocks of the labruscas. (The scion, or budwood, is responsible for the leaf-and-fruit-bearing structures and also determines the grape variety; the rootstock determines the character of the vine itself.)

Arduous trial and error was required to create phylloxera-resistant vines and to find matches that were compatible with the soil and weather. (France alone imported hundreds of thousands of rootstocks.) Slowly, painstakingly, and at great expense, the gigantic task of replanting was completed. Then there was the three-to five–year period of patiently waiting for the grafted plants to bear suitable grapes for wine. Eventually most of the world's vineyards —the great along with the commonplace— were returned to full productivity.

NOTE: Some experts have contended that the grafting process had diminished the wines, while others maintain the wines were better than ever. However, the rarity of prephylloxera examples precludes any useful comparisons.

Although most growers believed they finally had phylloxera under control, all but a few continued to graft their vines. Then, in the mid-1980s, a more aggressive mutant turned up in California's Napa Valley. The nonresistant rootstocks that had been inadvertently planted quickly succumbed to the predator. As yet no chemical or biological weapon has been found that can dispel the aphid. The only solution has been to uproot the infested vines, replant them with more resistant ones, and then wait for the replacements to mature. Thousands of vineyard acres have now been replanted in California.

SITE

Although the vine can adjust to many kinds of terrain, sloping land is best for the grape. Air circulation is always good on the slopes and brisk winds drying the grapes quickly after a rain, discourage mold and mildew. The soil on sloping land also drains well so the roots don't become waterlogged. (The vine doesn't like wet feet.) Most beneficial are mid-slope sites where warm air flows up. At the top, the grapes are too exposed to the elements, while at the bottom, cold air settles and the pools that form after a rain drench the roots.

South–facing slopes provide the best exposure. The vineyards on Burgundy's legendary Côte d'Or all face south. In Italy, the word *sori,* preceding a vineyard name, as in Sori San Lorenzo, indicates a beneficial southern exposure. Slopes facing east receive the morning sun and are second best. Least desirable is land facing north since its limited sunshine retards the grape's blossoming and ripening.

In the past, the choicest locations were discovered by trial and error with a bit of common sense thrown in. In the ninth century, Charlemagne observed that snow melted first on a south-facing site in the Rheingau. He ordered a vineyard planted there. That site, Schloss Johannisberg, continues active and productive to this day. In Germany's cool Mosel Valley, where the river executes a series of serpentine twists and turns, growers have shifted the siting of their vineyards from bank to bank to capture as much warmth from their thin northern sun as possible .

Beneficial too are large bodies of water. (The ancients said that a vine should look at a river.) The surface of the water reflects the sun's rays onto the grapes during the day, then retains its warmth at night, enhancing the ripening process. Rivers, lakes, and oceans also extend the growing season by moderating the temperature; dissipating excessive heat in summer and mitigating biting cold in winter. As one Long Island vintner, noted, "The surrounding ocean waters moderate the winter temperatures, then give us a very late bud break so we don't have to worry about possible frost." Some of the best vineyard sites are shielded by woodlands and mountains, inhibiting excessive rainfall and keeping the cold air away.

In site selection, scientific research has largely replaced trial and error. Viticulturalists now seek out microclimates, which are pockets of land created by a combination of elevation, exposure, fog intrusion, humidity, etc. (These range from less than a hundred acres to about three square miles.) For example, a too-warm site in California is cooled by a steady stream of air from San Francisco Bay, flowing in through a gap in the mountains. Even initially unpromising terrain can be reshaped to wine–making specifications. A California winery employed earth–moving machinery (previously used in building the Alaska pipeline) to create for itself a custom-made five-hundred acre vineyard. In recent years, urbanization and population growth have encroached on vineyard sites. Homes and grapes, it seems, are attracted to the same undulating terrain and are also partial to rivers meandering through.

SOIL

The grape finds its nourishment in a wide variety of soils: shallow and deep, coarse and fine, fecund and barren. One might assume that a fertile, well-endowed soil would be most desirable; but in fact, the richer the soil, the poorer the wine. In most vineyards, the soil (sandy, gravely, stony, or chalky) is so unfriendly as to be practically unfit for cultivation; most other crops would wither and die there. Yet the vine flourishes. Such soils force the plant to send its roots down to greater depths. (When the nutritive substances lie too close to the surface, the vine is not challenged.) Only when the roots have penetrated deeply in their search for minerals and other elements do finer and more subtle wines result.

It has often been said that "soil speaks" —that one parcel of land may yield a great wine, while a commonplace wine is produced only a few feet away. Vineyard soils themselves are rarely homogenous, consisting of various permutations of clay, sand, limestone, slate, gravel, etc. (Six distinct types of soil have been found in one Burgundy vineyard alone.) In the Médoc region of France, a deep layer of rocks and pebbles, brought down by the Gironde River over the centuries, covers the mineral-rich earth. Warming quickly and draining well even in the wettest years, this soil produces some of the world's most splendid wines. In Graves — whose name translates as "gravel bank"— a clay-and-limestone soil, topped by sand and pebbles, yields harmoniously balanced wines of great finesse. In the southern Rhône, smooth weathered stones carried down by the river absorb the sun's full impact during the day, then slowly release the heat back at night, giving the wine a rich, almost roasted flavor. In Germany's Mosel Valley, growers set slabs of slate beneath their vines to capture whatever beneficial warmth they can from the thin northern sun. Gradually disintegrating, the slate adds its own rich nutrients to the soil.

Volcanic soils give their wines a subtle aroma, an intriguing undertone and a slightly burned but attractive taste. They impart a gentle, bitter freshness to Orvieto wines and to those grown near Mount Etna. In Hungary, people once believed that gold deep in the earth was responsible for the excellence of Tokay wines. Investigating geologists found only volcanic rock.

Perhaps the most complex and extraordinary volcanic soil of all is seen on the island of Madeira. When the Portuguese discovered the island in the fifteenth century, they found it thickly wooded and uninhabited. The colonists set the forests ablaze to clear the land for farming and the woods, smoldering sporadically for years, added potash to the accumulated centuries of leaf mold. Madeira's wines are characterized by a refreshing acidity, a pungent nutlike taste, and the potential for great longevity.

In southern Spain, a chalky soil enables the sherry grapes to survive both the region's torrid heat and its virtually rainless days of summer. Hardening to a glasslike crust, the chalk beats back the fierce rays of the sun while sealing in the reserves of moisture below. Chalk also forces the vine to probe more deeply for its nourishment, while its natural acidity offsets the high grape sugars. The sherry makers, transporting their berries to the winery in open carts, noticed that the roadside dust blown onto their fruit added a stimulating tang to the wines. (The gypsum in the dust had increased the wine's tartaric acid.) The Jerez wine makers initially sprinkled some of the roadside dust directly onto their grapes, then eventually added the tartaric acid itself to their wines to create the same effect.

In the Champagne region of France, chalky soil gives its wines a crisp dry flintiness, a delicate bouquet and a tendency to sparkle. (Champagne's vast chalk deposit was formed when the primordial sea covered the land and the detritus of shellfish and other marine life gradually sank to the bottom.) This same chalk deposit —consisting mainly of fossilized seashells— extends to Chablis, where a layer of loam covering it introduces a fine earthiness to the characteristic austerity of the wine.

Clay soils in themselves are undesirably dense, but are more permeable and quicker warming when combined with sand. Sand alone is low in nutrients and too porous to retain much water. Vines planted in sandy soils must be set down deep to reach a more sustaining subsoil. In Portugal's Colares region, the vines are planted in vertical trenches dug thirty feet down. As they grow toward ground level, the sand is gradually returned to fill in the trenches.

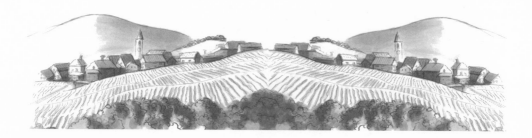

2

MAN'S ROLE

The Vineyard

Wine, according to an eminent vintner, "begins in the vineyard and always, always, we must come back to the vineyard." It has been estimated that vineyards occupy more than 25 million acres of the earth's surface, ranging from tiny plots consisting of a few solitary vines to vast expanses stretching farther than the eye can see. The vineyards, differing in the contours of their land and in their exposure to heat and cold, affect the development of their grapes and consequently the character of their wines.

Grapevines were once intermingled with trees, vegetables, and grain. (The Italians call this *coltura promiscua* or "indiscriminate cultivation.") The vines are planted more systematically now, set out in orderly rows, separated by wide "avenues," permitting tractors and harvesting machines to pass through.

For its proper development, the vine must be trellised and pruned. Trellising supports the vines and their clusters and also evenly distributes the bearing wood, exposing the berries more fully to sunlight and air. (Grapevines in the wild attach themselves to neighboring trees for support. In Italy, they can still be seen clinging to poplars, pear trees, and weeping willows.) Typically, a trellis consists of two more horizontal wires strung between wooden or concrete posts. Trellis styles vary with climate and custom. In the Galicia region of Spain, with its wet soil and elusive sunshine, the vines are trained on high wires for their maximum exposure to warmth and air.

Pruning cuts the plant back to guide its development and control its yield. Unlike most plants, the vine bears its fruiting units on a single year's growth. Pruning eliminates the canes that bore the previous year's growth since they won't be producing fruit again. Lesser plants are usually pruned to be as productive as possible, while the superior vines are cut back severely to reduce their yield. (When they concentrate their vigor on fewer berries, they produce more intense

and exceptional wines.) According to legend, a donkey was the first pruner. While its master was occupied elsewhere, the untethered beast was greedily nibbling away at the tender young shoots. The following year, the stripped-down plants yielded their best fruit and their most memorable wine.

Young vines are suckered in spring: their nonessential shoots rubbed off by hand. Mature vines are not cut back until winter when they are dormant. Since the sap has stopped flowing and their pruning cuts won't bleed, the pruner, wielding a knife or a pair of shears, can diligently clear away all counterproductive growth, removing the extraneous shoots and long trailing branches. He keeps only enough fruiting wood to ensure a proper crop level the next year. Should he retain too many buds, the shoots would be feeble and the canes unable to support the weight of their clusters. Should he let the plant blossom too freely, the fruit would set poorly and be low in sugar. Thinner, weaker wines would result.

THE HARVEST

The most hectic and critical time for the grape is the harvest. The French call it the *vendange,* the Italians the *vendemmia,* the Germans the *weinlese,* and the Americans the *crush.* Determining the starting date are the grape variety, site, soil, and previous six months of weather. In some places, an official decree or communal vote sets the date. In others, the individual grower decides for himself.

Anticipation is high as the harvest approaches. Dry, sunny weather is essential then. The French say, "August makes the grape and September the wine." An unexpected downpour —bloating the berries and diluting their sugars— can turn a triumphant crop into a disaster. Too much heat can lead to a surplus of fruit, known as a wine lake, while the grapes themselves can be so overwhelmed by their sugars, they produce dull and flabby wines.

Knowing when to pick calls for a mixture of instinct, temperament, science, and luck. One grower who brought his crop in before a heavy downpour said, "I felt in my bones we had better pick. Others were not so fortunate." To determine the ripeness of his grapes, the grower would crush a few berries between his fingers and know by the stickiness of the juice —which is called the must— when his fruit was ready to pick. Now he uses refractometers and hydrometers to monitor the shifting ratio of sugars to acids in his grapes. The refractometer, a hand-held prism, indicates the sugar's density by the amount of light the must bends or refracts. Since only a few drops are needed for each reading, this device can be used directly in the field. More precise is the calibrated hydrometer that floats correspondingly higher in the must as the density of the grape sugar increases.

The harvest may last days, weeks, or months, depending on the size of the vineyard and the number of pickers available. In early summer, as the clusters begin to form, the grower takes a bunch count and, by applying a certain formula, can estimate his potential tonnage with surprising accuracy. To recruit pickers, he will draw on family, friends, and neighbors, or hire migrants or other itinerants. In the Champagne region, families plan their annual vacations to coincide with the grape harvest. In Burgundy, foreign workers arrive for the picking each year. In Portugal, musicians playing pipes and drums are sent out to the hinterlands to attract pickers. In Andalusia, gypsies help to bring in the sherry crop.

The pickers do not pull the individual berries from the stems but use knives and shears to clip or snip the clusters. Often employed is a hooked knife that goes back to ancient times. Called a serpette, it features a curved blade that acts as an extension of the hand. Catching the clusters from below, the pickers gently drop them into boxes or buckets. Men, carrying back baskets with a hundred-pound capacity, collect the grapes at intervals. Or else the pickers deposit their fruit in gondolas, which are large containers set at the ends of the rows.

NOTE: For premium Champagnes, specially trained workers spread the grape clusters on trays and then, in a careful selective process known as *épluchage,* they discard the underripe, overripe, and blemished berries.

Ideally grapes are gathered under a blazing sun. Moving systematically up and down the rows, the pickers crouch over the vines or crawl beneath them to get at the fruit. The work is particularly backbreaking when the vines are trellised high or low, or when the terrain slopes precipitously. During a heat wave, the pickers

must scramble to collect the fruit before it spoils. A sudden rainstorm can drench them to the skin. Plummeting temperatures can freeze their hands and their feet. (Other occupational hazards include sore knees and scratched fingers.)

On average, an individual picker can harvest half a ton of grapes a day. Harvesting machines, widely used in large-scale operations, can collect anywhere from twelve to twenty-four tons an hour. Lumbering high above the ground, the machines shake the clusters loose with rods and paddles, catch them on a conveyor belt, then deposit them in the gondolas. A vineyard, once needing ten days of hand labor, can be picked clean in a matter of hours.

In the grape's development, the acids predominate at first, then as the sun stimulates the production of sugars, the berries begin to fill with their rich sweet juice. Grapes are generally gathered at their optimum ripeness: when the sugars are at their maximum and the acids at their minimum. Some growers prefer picking the fruit prematurely, while others deliberately delay their harvests. In warmer climates, earlier picking ensures a better acid balance, making for tarter, lighter, and livelier wines. For example, the Portuguese pick their berries prematurely for vinho verdes, as the French do for their Muscadets and the Californians for some of their Chardonnays.

Growers who prefer their berries riper than usual cut away some of the clusters to expose the remaining fruit more fully to the sun. This accounts for the generosity, richness, and sweetness of Italy's Amarone wines, also known as Reciotos. (The name derives from *recie* or "ears" in the Veronese dialect, because the remaining clusters stand out on the vine like ears.)

In the cooler, more volatile regions, growers sometimes leave their berries on the vine long after the normal harvest to obtain an extra measure of sun and so achieve a higher level of sugar. The heat absorbing the water in the grapes causes them to shrivel, concentrating their flavor and sweetness. In Alsace in good years, berries are left on the vine to reach their ultimate ripeness, becoming almost pure sugar, yet retaining enough acidity for balance. They yield sweet, intensely flavored wines with highly distinctive personalities. The Alsatians call their delayed harvest *vendange tardive*. White grapes —particularly the rieslings, chenin blancs, gewürztraminers and chardonnays— lend themselves best to this.

A rare few, late-harvest grapes are remarkably transformed by a unique fungus, called *pourriture noble* by the French and *edelfäule* by the Germans. In English, it is known as noble rot or noble mold. Its scientific name is *Botrytis cinerea*. Thriving in semisheltered environments near large bodies of water and encouraged by fog and mist, the botrytis appears in late autumn.

Assuming the form of an ash-gray film and attacking the grapes at random over a period of weeks, the botrytis pierces the berries with a series of microscopic holes which mottle, thin, and weaken the skins. Able to penetrate more readily, the sun, evaporates out 50 percent or more of the moisture, shriveling the grapes. (The remaining dense and concentrated juice ferments out slowly but not quite fully so alcohol levels can be as low as 7 percent.) However, the acids do not diminish as in normal ripening but remain to offset the wine's sweet intensity, and preserve it as well.

NOTE: The fungus requires alternating periods of humidity and warmth to flourish. It appears perhaps twice in a decade and only in the finest vintages. In years when it does not turn up, the grapes yield their usual wines.

Noble rot wines are splendidly smooth, luscious, and marvelously unctuous, displaying a fullness of bouquet, a subtlety of aroma, and a lingering freshness. Their extraordinary honeyed flavor is discernibly sweet yet never cloying; the wines might even seem dry on the palate..

Vineyards in both France and Germany have been credited with the discovery of noble rot. In any case, the harvest was inadvertently delayed one year, causing the grapes to shrivel and become progressively mold covered and mottled. When finally vinified, their wine was a splendid golden nectar, the best anyone had ever tasted. Sampling it the proprietor of Château d'Yquem in Sauternes supposedly said, "Never again will I let my grapes be picked until they are completely rotten."

Most vineyards are harvested once or at most twice to ensure ripeness. For botrytized berries, the pickers must make frequent forays into the vineyard so they can be gathered with the proper degree of rot. Methodically culling the affected grapes with long-bladed shears, the pickers collect them one by one if necessary. In Sauternes, between September and December, they go out six to twelve times over an eight-to nine-week period. Lesser makers, who can afford only three or four sorties into their vineyards, generally produce lighter bodied and less complex wines.

Included among the best botrytized wines are the sweet and luscious Sauternes and Barsacs of Bordeaux, the Auslese wines of Germany, and the Tokays of Hungary. Other late-harvested wines are produced in Austria, Switzerland, South Africa, Hungary, Australia, and the United States. (When the mold is not indigenous, it is introduced artificially by spraying.) Such wines, however, can never match the honeyed flavor and character of the prime examples produced in France and Germany.

NOTE: Because of the labor-intensive requirements and high cost of production, noble-rot wines are made more for prestige than for profit. Moreover, there is always the risk so late in the season of an unexpected rain bloating the berries or of a sudden frost decimating the fruit entirely.

The latest-harvested wine of all is Eiswein (ice wine), made from slow-to-ripen grapes left on the vine until they freeze. (The berries are not harvested until late December or mid–January.) Since all the grapes do not freeze to the proper degree at the same time, they must be gathered individually. The pickers, who cannot wear gloves even on the coldest days, collect only a handful at a time. The grapes themselves are crushed without thawing. Only the water in their juice freezes and it is discarded after pressing, leaving behind a highly intensified must, which ferments out slowly and becomes a rich, sweet, lovely wine. Although ice wines are as concentrated as the other late-harvest wines, they do not exhibit the same honeyed taste. Instead, they are characterized by an intense fruitiness and a vibrant acidity. Eisweins are produced in Germany, Alsace, Austria, and the United States.

(In warmer regions, the grapes are placed in cold storage for several months before crushing and pressing.)

NOTE: Grapes that lend themselves best to Eisweins are German and Austrian rieslings, Alsatian gewürztraminers, and vidal blancs from the Finger Lakes region of New York.

The Sugar–Acid Balance

The grape, more complicated than most fruit, possesses some three hundred components, including several sugars, (among them glucose and fructose), a number of acids, and a quantity of minerals. The fermentation process converts these sugars to alcohol, creating and then stabilizing the wine. (The alcohol content also limits the growth of destructive organisms such as mold.) A wine needs about 8 percent alcohol to survive, but most average 10 to 12 percent. (Those lacking a sufficient amount of alcohol will need some bolstering.) The wine's acids, meanwhile —the tannic, tartaric, lactic, malic, and citric— impart a lively, attractive tartness. More significantly, they give the wine the armature or structure required to preserve it and to extend its life.

Crucial to any wine is the proper balance of sugars and acids in the must. (The must is the fermentable grape juice itself, a complex solution composed primarily of water and grape sugars along with various substances of vegetable and mineral origin.) When the sugars outpace the acids in the must, the wine will be cloyingly sweet and flabby. (Low acid levels also mean that the wine will be ready to drink sooner.) When the acids overwhelm the sugars, the wine will be lighter at its best and thin and overly tart at its worst.

NOTE: Grape acids are measured in part by a pH rating that rises when the levels are down and falls when they are up. A pH of 4, for example, indicates an alkaline or a high-sugar wine, while a pH of 2.85 reveals a decidedly acid one.

The density of the grape's sugar is measured as degrees of *brix,* (Each degree represents 1 gram of sugar per 100 grams of must.) The brix reading helps the grower determine the ripeness of his grapes. Red grapes are considered in full possession of their character at 21 to 24 degrees brix, and white grapes at 20 to 23 degrees. The botrytized examples register considerably more. For sparkling wines the grapes may be picked sooner —at about 18 degrees brix— since such wines need a higher acidity.

Brix values also enable the wine maker to estimate the potential alcohol in his wine. Grapes harvested at 20 degrees yield wines with about 11 percent alcohol; at 22 degrees, 12 percent, etc. (Because every 2 percent of grape sugar converts out to about 1 percent of alcohol, the brix is multiplied by 0.55.) German and Swiss vintners use an Oechsle scale, which divides their readings by 8 so that the grapes

with a 73 Oechsle will produce a wine with 9.6 percent alcohol.

A number of factors can disrupt the grape's sugar-acid balance. A powerful sun, while burning out much of the acidity, can send the sugars soaring and coarsen the berries. (Grapes, subject to somewhat less sun, yield a better-balanced wine as a rule.) An insufficient sun can slow up ripening, as can excessive cold; in late summer, a heavy rain will dilute the grape sugars. Yet nature is ever resilient. While a chilly, rainy spring may cut the size of the crop, a bright sun emerging in autumn, followed by optimum weather conditions, may ripen the grapes properly and produce a respectable crop after all. Even vines hit by a spring frost can experience a hopeful second budding.

The grower will intervene if necessary to create a more felicitous balance of the grape's sugars and acids. In warmer regions, he can keep the sugars down and create a more stable acidity by trellising his vines higher, away from the reflected heat of the soil. Or he can cultivate hybrid grapes, capable of retaining acidity even under conditions of desertlike heat. Or he can gather his berries earlier in the season or perhaps in the coolness of the evening. And before crushing, he might add unripe, acidy grapes to his excessively sweet ones, or add alcohol to his inordinately high-sugar wines to stabilize them.

In cooler regions, the grower can increase his grape sugars by trellising the vines closer to the ground to let the soil's reflected heat warm them. Should the acids still outdistance the sugars, he can chaptalize his wines by adding cane or beet sugar to the must during fermentation. (The practice is named for Jean Chaptal, the nineteenth-century French chemist who devised it.) Converting out to alcohol while the natural sugar does, the added sugar strengthens the wine but does not sweeten it. (Wines made from grapes, rich and balanced in their essential sugars and acids, need neither enrichment nor adjustment.)

Certain natural processes also bring the young wine's acidity into better balance. One is malolactic fermentation, which is brought about by the lactic bacteria, widely distributed in nature and commonly occurring in grape musts. Slower growing than the yeasts responsible for normal fermentation, these bacteria consume the nutrients not of interest to the yeasts. Building up toward the end of fermentation, they attack the wine's harsh malic acid and break it down to a softer lactic acid. By reducing a young wine's excessive acidity, they smooth out its abrasiveness, increase its palatability, and add to its depth. In Champagnes, for example, malolactic fermentation will modify their taste from a green-apple tanginess to a buttery smoothness. The process also softens the flavor of California Chardonnays, and makes for rounder, fuller wines in Chablis.

Another acid reducer in the newly formed wine is detartration. Potassium bitartrate, which accounts for a good part of the must's acidity, isn't very soluble in alcohol. Detartration slowly crystallizes these tartrates, which then normally precipitate out of the wine. Some cling to the sides of the container, but most drift down to the bottom, forming the lees or sediment. This precipitation can be accelerated by lowering the temperature of the wine. Vintners once speeded things up by throwing their cellar doors open in winter. Now they employ cold stabilization which briefly but sharply chills the wine to about 50°F.

Some growers deliberately stress their vines to produce fewer berries and so concentrate the grape sugars to produce more intense wines. In a practice known as dry farming, they cut back on irrigation to deprive the vines of water. Or they space the vines in each row more closely, doubling or tripling their normal number. Some wine makers may concentrate the sugars in their grapes after the harvest by drying the clusters, suspending them on racks or stringing them from the rafters in airy attics. (This is done with Malvasia and Moscato wines.) The makers of sherries and Málagas heap their berries out-of-doors on straw mats to raisin in the sun, evaporating out as much grape moisture as possible and creating a greater sugar density. In Switzerland and in the cooler sectors of France, when the weather permits, the grapes are left out on straw mats until early winter. The resulting *vins de paille* (straw wines) are extraordinarily luscious and quite high in their alcohol.

CRUSHING AND PRESSING

After the harvest, the grapes are crushed and pressed. Crushing releases about 40 percent of the juice, known as the free run. Crushing also exerts just enough pressure to break the skins while leaving the grape stems and seeds intact. (These contain harsh concentrations of tannins and off-tasting oils.) Pressing, which follows, exerts a greater force to extract the remaining juice. That is known as the press run. Pressing, however, bruises the stems and seeds making for a harsher juice. As a rule, the free run and press run are combined for a better balanced wine.

The simplest form of crushing, known as bleeding the vat, piles the clusters one atop the other so that their accumulated weight can gently break the skins and let the juice ooze slowly out. (Bleeding the vat is associated with the finest rosés, rare Málaga wines and noble-rot Hungarian Tokays.)

The first instrument for crushing was the human foot, whose treading action brought out the grape's soft jelly while disturbing neither the tannic seeds nor stems. The foot's warmth also stimulated the onset of fermentation. In Portugal and elsewhere, barefoot men would climb into great stone troughs, called *lagares,* filled with freshly gathered grapes. Often spurred on by musical accompaniment, they would link arms while steadily and rhythmically stomping the berries, liberating the pulp and releasing the juice. Treaders in Jerez wore hobnailed clogs, which more quickly broke the skins, while leaving the grape seeds and stems intact. Crushing is now carried out in huge horizontal drums, equipped with high–velocity blades or paddles. These slap the berries from the stems and break the skins, while the must itself flows out serenely through perforations into a holding tank below.

The earliest presses were great, weighty stones raised up by ropes and long levers. Slamming down ferociously, they virtually demolished the grapes. Later, a giant wooden screw with a heavy lid was set in the center of the lagar. Several men, turning this screw, brought down the lid, pulverizing the grapes and expelling their remaining juice.

Presses are now either the batch type or the continuous type. The first must be cleaned after each batch is processed. The second runs at higher speeds without interruption and can recover a maximum of juice. The simplest batch press is the basket press, an upright cylinder of sturdy wooden slats with a solid-board plate attached to a screw at the center. Bringing the plate down expels the juice, which quickly gushes out through the slatted sides into a catch basin below. A mechanized batch press consists of a horizontal cylinder with a piston running its entire length. Plates at either end move slowly toward one another, pressing the grapes between them. A variant features a thick-walled rubber bag, which when inflated by compressed air, squeezes the berries and expels their juice.

The continuous press, a giant cylinder fitted with an auger, operates much like a meat grinder. The crushed grapes are fed in at one end and the solids are expelled out the other, while the juice flows out separately. The earliest continuous presses were crude and excessive in their friction, chewing up the grapes, browning the pulp and bruising the seeds. It is now possible to adjust their pressure much more precisely.

Pressing releases the grape juice fractionally; that is, there are several pressings. The first exerts the lightest pressure, affecting the center of the berry but not the seeds. The second has some contact with the seeds. The third, exerting the greatest force, releases the harshest juice. Because the third pressing includes proportionately more tannins and off-tasting oils, it is not generally used in wine making, but rather is distilled into brandy or an industrial alcohol.

Champagne was traditionally subjected to four pressings: *vin de cuvée, premiere taille, deuxième taille,* and *rebêche;* the last done on a smaller press. The makers of premium Champagnes once vinified only their first pressings, selling off their seconds and thirds to lesser firms. Now they may also include their second pressings. The same may be true of premium table wines, whose makers once used only the first pressings, but now may include their second pressings as well.

Crushing and pressing leaves behind a solid, pulpy mass of skins, stalks and seeds. Known as the pomace, this residue is not discarded but is used in various ways: its pigments are employed in the manufacture of inks and dyes. Its tannins tan leather. Its grapeseed oils are used in food processing and in the making of soaps and paints. Its residual alcohol is distilled into a coarse vigorous brandy, which the Italians call grappa, the French marc, the Spaniards aguardiente and the Germans tresterschnapps. The pulpy mass itself is dried as a fuel or pulverized into a mulch. After the growing season, the pomace can serve as a rich compost, spread over the vineyard to renew its depleted energies.

🍇 🍇 🍇

FERMENTATION

After the grapes have been crushed and pressed, fermentation —the heart of the wine-making process— occurs. Fermentation converts the grape sugar into alcohol through the natural action of yeast. It can occur within hours after crushing and continue for several days or for several months. How long the fermentation process lasts depends on the grape variety, the wine being made, the ambient temperature, and various other considerations.

Fermentation happens virtually by itself, needing no interference from man. First, a slight movement is seen in the juice, a bubbling around the edges. Then the must becomes agitated: fretting, frothing, heaving, and turning unpleasantly muddy. Gradually the liquid quiets down and becomes cleaner, clearer, more potent and vinous. The sweet mild grape juice has become raw wine.

Vintners once tipped their hats to their vats in deference to this strange and unaccountable phenomenon. The mystery was deciphered in the nineteenth century by Louis Pasteur, a French chemist. Through the lens of his microscope he could see strange single–celled creatures interacting with the sugar in the must. (These microorganisms are ever present in the atmosphere.) Pasteur called the creatures *Microbi vini*. We call them yeasts. Their scientific name is *Saccharomyces cereviseae*. Pasteur realized their life processes were intextricably linked with the conversion of the grape juice into wine. When he boiled the juice (pasteurization), he destroyed the *microbi vini,* and the liquid never became wine.

Like all living creatures, the yeasts need a source of nourishment which the sugar in ripe grapes provides. Irresistibly drawn to the sweetness inside, the yeasts settle on the grape skins by the millions, held fast by a whitish, waxlike bloom on the surface. When overripeness or crushing breaks the skins, the yeasts gain access to the sweet juice they crave. Once inside, they secrete an enzyme, triggering an intricate series of reactions, which split the sugar molecules in two; one half becomes a colorless, odorless, highly volatile liquid (ethyl alcohol), the other half becomes a gas (carbon dioxide or CO_2.) The gas, rising quickly to escape, pricks the surface of the liquid with countless tiny bubbles, creating the illusion of boiling. In fact, *fermentation* derives from the Latin *fermentare,* meaning "to boil."

Unlike most single-celled organisms, the yeasts do not divide in two but sprout vegetatively: small buds form on the mother cells, splitting off as daughter cells. Turbulently increasing more than fourfold in number, the yeasts greatly expand the volume of the liquid. Their violent molecular changes make the process hot and tumultuous. (The yeasts require heat as well as the sugar to function.)

Needing air to multiply, they find it in the open vats. But soon the buildup of carbon dioxide blankets the wine and excludes the outside air. No longer able to reproduce, the yeasts shift from their aerobic (oxygen-requiring) mode to an anaerobic (alcohol-producing) mode. Needing only a fraction of the grape sugar to function, they convert the remainder to alcohol and willingly secrete it back into the liquid where it accumulates. Fermentation in effect is a two-phase process: the yeasts multiply in the primary or respiratory phase and produce the alcohol in the secondary or airless, fermentative phase.

NOTE: Yeast strains vary in their tolerance for alcohol. Some strains can proceed no further after producing 12 percent by volume, while others are not perceptibly slowed down until the alcohol level reaches 14 or 15 percent. In the end, it is the alcohol —which the yeasts themselves have produced— that in effect becomes their undoing.

Ideally, fermentation temperatures should rise slowly to balance out the sugars and acids in the must and so produce fresh lively wines with a certain bite. Excessive heat accelerates fermentation, driving off the acids, destroying the wine's delicacy and rendering it dull, off-flavored, and rather short-lived. In warmer climates, must temperatures can rise more than a degree an hour, causing the liquid to boil over, damaging the yeasts and causing what is called a "stuck" or a halted fermentation.

To cool their feverish musts, vintners once lowered their casks into the sea, hosed them down with cold water, or surrounded them with blocks of ice. They also added cooler juice to the overheated must or used smaller vats with their higher ratio of heat-absorbing surface to liquid. Wine makers can now control their overly rapid fermentations with stainless steel technology, refrigeration and cold stabilization. The cold stabilization, chilling the must briefly but sharply to preserve a greater degree of acidity, has proved a boon in warm-climate countries, enabling vintners there to produce crisper, fruitier wines with more fragrance and flavor than were ever possible before.

NOTE: Fermentation can take place in wooden or stainless steel containers. (The best Burgundies are barrel fermented in small oak casks.) Stainless steel is generally preferred for white wines since it lets them retain the fresh fruity character that constitutes their distinctive youthful charm.

Left to their own devices, the yeasts convert out virtually all the grape sugar, leaving the wine bone–dry. (They generally proceed until about 0.2 percent sugar remains.) Vintners, who wish to make their wines sweeter than usual, can interrupt the process by stunning the yeasts with sulfur dioxide before they complete their task, or by adding more alcohol than the yeasts can tolerate, or else by filtering the yeasts out of the liquid entirely.

Vintners can also prolong the fermentation process so as to produce wines of greater richness and intensity. In Hungary, the makers of Tokay add botrytized berries to their must, measuring them out in seven-gallon tubs called *puttonyos.* (Puttonyos were the wooden hods, used in collecting the berries.) The more puttonyos added to the base wine, the finer and more luscious the results. In nineteenth century Hungary, some Tokays were enriched with seven to nine put-tonyos and reserved for royalty. Nowadays, five or six is the maximum employed. (The number appears on the label.) Lesser Tokays, trying to simulate the richness of the best examples, substitute grape concentrates for the botrytized berries.

After the turbulent expansion caused by the multiplying yeasts, the fermenting liquid cools down and contracts, creating a space or vacuum above the wine. Known as the *ullage,* the vacuum acts as a magnet, drawing in outside air and bringing with it spoilage organisms attracted by the wine's residual sugars and other substances. Most treacherous among these is the *acetobacter,* a microorganism that —by its own enzymatic action— dissolves certain minerals. The acetobacter forms various acetates including acetic acid, better known as vinegar. Acetic acid in minimal amounts enhances a wine's bouquet and flavor but its presence in excess makes the wine undrinkable. One Long Island vintner wryly described wine as "an intermediate stage between grape juice and vinegar."

Once the vinegar makers take over, there is no turning back. An early sign of their invasion is a reduction in the wine's alcohol content. As they convert more and more of the alcohol to acetic acid, the smell and taste of vinegar becomes apparent. At first, the wine is unpalatable; then it is completely ruined. It has become what the French call *vin aigre* (sour wine).

Unlike the beneficial yeasts, the spoilage organisms require oxygen to survive. While carbon dioxide blanketed the wine, the acetobacters were held in check, but once air entered the ullage, they could proliferate freely. Pasteur realized that an aerated wine was defenseless against these spoilers and knew that the way to repel them was to eliminate the air space or ullage in the vats and tanks. Teaching the French wine makers to top off their wines —that is to completely refill their containers with more wine— he helped put an end to sour wine. In wine-loving France, Pasteur had become a national hero.

Subsequently, more sophisticated methods were developed. An inert and color-less nitrogen gas, which did not interact with the wine chemically, was pumped into the casks to preempt the ullage. Another method was to float fiberglas lids on the surface of the wine. (These automatically dropped down as natural evaporation lowered the vat's liquid level.) More recently, German scientists have devised an elaborate system to seal off the entire wine-making process to protect everything from the air: the grapes, the wine, pumps, and even the bottling equipment. The system is quite costly, however, and beyond the means of most wine makers.

🍇 🍇 🍇

THE COLOR OF WINE

The color of the grape itself —specifically the pigments in its skin— determines in large part the color of the wine. (The pulp and juice are usually colorless.) The grape skins provide more than color; they are the source of tannins and other organic compounds that give the wine body, texture, balance, and structure, and that create its intensity and depth.

Since some grape varieties are more richly pigmented than others, the wines can be greatly diverse in color; ranging from pale straw to amber and from pink to ruby, on to garnet and beyond. Yet there are only two basic colors: red and white wines. (The rosés are a subcategory of the reds.)

The wine's color is produced by maceration, which ferments the skins with the juice. The newly formed alcohol, dissolving the pigments, makes them an integral part of the wine. Another factor in color is the degree of contact between the skins and the must. The more extensive the contact, the darker the wine. (When the skins are removed early, their pigments never get a chance to leach out, leaving the wine virtually colorless.)

NOTE: Red grapes need a warm but not an overly warm autumn to set their pigments properly. They tend to be lighter hued in the cooler regions and to lack color in the coolest areas. White grapes are generally golden in the warmer regions and paler in the cooler ones.

Red wines, depending on their desired style, are steeped on their color-laden skins from several days to two weeks. The more contact between the skins and must, the more multifaceted the wines become and the more complex their flavor and aroma. For white wines, the skins are usually separated out early to keep them light bodied and delicate. (White wines need only enough tannin to supply a little texture.) A few examples, however, are exposed to twelve-to twenty-four-hour skin contact, making them richer and more flavorful. These are closer in character to a red wine. (When fermented too long on their skins, white wines may become overly rich and heavy.)

NOTE: Although a white wine may appear to be milder than a red, it may in fact be stronger. (A wine's strength is based on its alcohol content, not on its color.)

Rosés remain on their skins just long enough to achieve the desired shade of pink. Classic rosés, pressed from lightly pigmented Mediterranean grapes, combine the richness of a red wine with the lighter character of a white. The best rosés are made by the *saignée* method (bleeding the vat). Their grapes are crushed, not pressed and macerated for twelve to forty-eight hours on their skins to let the juice pick up some color. Their still pale must is drained off and fermented like a white wine. (Most other rosés employ less intense grapes from younger vines.)

The simplest and cheapest way to produce a rosé is to blend a red and a white wine together. Inexpensive bulk wines are often made this way and are invariably innocuous and bland tasting. France bans such blending for its table wines but permits it for sparkling rosés or pink Champagnes, since such wines can undergo unpredictable changes of hue in the Champagne-making process, which creates an inconsistency of color from bottle to bottle.

A blush wine is somewhere between a white wine and a rosé. It's usually pressed from heavily pigmented grapes such as the zinfandel, whose skins are soon removed but a bit of their intense color inevitably leaches out, producing the pinkish tinge or blush. (A blush wine may also be made from unpromising grapes that lack enough color to produce a true red wine.)

As a rule, red and purplish grapes yield red wines, while white, yellow, and green grapes yield white ones. A canny vintner, however, can produce a red and a white wine from the same batch of red grapes. For the white wine, he immediately separates out half the juice and ferments it away from the skins. Then he processes the remainder as he would any other red wine. Or if he wishes, he can produce both a rosé and a red from the same batch of grapes, making an almost immediately drinkable rosé by tapping off the paler free-run juice from the just-crushed berries, and then pressing their skins and pulp for a darker, stronger, more concentrated wine that needs a year or more to mature.

Both red and white grapes can be used in the making of white wines. Champagne, for example, is pressed primarily from the pinot noir and the chardonnay. (The wine was initially tawny colored until its makers learned to exclude the skins.) Champagne's variations include a Blanc de Blancs (White of Whites) and a Blanc de Noirs (White of Blacks). The former, pressed exclusively from the chardonnay, is pale, delicate and light bodied but lacks the balance of the more typical red-and-white blends. The Blanc de Noirs, pressed from the dark purple, almost blackish, pinot noir grape together with the meunier, has had its skins removed early on. Slightly amber in color and somewhat fuller in body and flavor, this wine has more depth and richness than traditional Champagnes. Although sometimes bottled on its own, it is more often used as a blending wine.

During a red wine's fermentation, the skins and solids —buoyed up by the carbon dioxide— become densely packed, forming a thick crust known as a *chapeau* or "cap." The cap floats on the surface, while the liquid below generates great heat. Were the cap permitted to harden and float unbroken, it would seal in the heat and damage the yeasts, disrupting fermentation and ruining the wine. The cap must be moistened and dispersed if the yeasts are to be fruitful and multiply. Breaking it up will not only cool and aerate the liquid, but speed up the extraction of the pigments, tannins, and other beneficial substances from the grape skins.

To disperse the cap, barefoot men would sit on the rim of the vat, stomping the dense thick crust with their feet. Sensing the temperature with their feet, they knew exactly how much punching down was required. Some wineries now punch down the cap with a pneumatic device, consisting of a large paddle running on a track above the fermenting wine; its slow, gentle manipulation enables the vintners to get the best from their berries. Or they will use mechanical pumps to drain the cooler juice from the bottom of the vat and then spray it back over the top. Once the fermentation process is over and the production of CO_2 stops, the no-longer buoyant cap goes to the press, where its solids are broken down further and where the remaining juice is extracted. The pressing here also accelerates the release of the pigments, tannins, and other beneficial substances from the skins.

White wines, by and large, are not fermented on their skins. Their grapes go directly to the press after crushing. Since their solids have not yet been broken down, pressing is more difficult for them. Some white wines are sent to special dejuicers, whose tumbling action recovers more of their juice.

BLENDING

The wine is now ready for its blending. Of all the arts in wine making, blending is one of the most respected; it can serve many purposes. Blending can create a specific style of wine, ensure greater consistency, heighten desirable qualities; or produce a more complex and finer wine that is greater than the sum of its parts. Blending can also compensate for a wine's inadequacies and mask its flaws. And should the supply of certain popular grapes be limited, blending can "stretch" that supply by adding other grapes. Some of the world's greatest wines are blends, so are some of the most disreputable.

Swift transportation today enables the wine maker to transcend the limitations of his locale. He can draw his components from widely scattered sources. He can bring together grapes, musts, or wines from the same or different vineyards, from better or lesser soils, and from the same or different harvests. Blending also enables the vintner to counteract the vagaries of the weather. He can combine the acidy product of a rainy summer with the heavier one of a hot dry season. (Each wine may be unattractive in itself, but the blending improves them both.) As one wine maker said, "When nature doesn't come through, we blend."

If a wine is soft or indifferent, the blender can add a more tannic wine to create more body and structure. Or he can offset the cloying sweetness of one wine with another that is quite tart. Or he can strengthen a weaker product with a more vigorous and robust one. The vintner can also modify a coarser wine by adding one that's more delicate or speed up an immature wine's drinkability by combining it with a somewhat older example.

In blending, the human nose is an indispensable instrument. Relying on his nose, palate, and memory of other wines, the blender creates his own special harmonies. He may add one component for body, another for color, a third for dryness, and a fourth for fragrance. The more diverse his combinations, the more complex his results. The greater his artistry, the more splendid the wine. (Also influencing the blend are local custom and the house style of the winery.)

In Bordeaux at harvest time, the eminent estates separate their grapes according to their variety, age of their vines, and better or lesser sectors of their vineyards. After the wines have been vinified, the various batches are then blended together. For their premium wines, German wine makers vinify each day's pressings separately and then, at the end of the season, blend them together selectively. The makers of noble rot-wines also ferment each day's harvest separately, later blending their best batches together.

Burgundy uses the pinot noir for its red wines and the chardonnay for its white ones, but —because of the historic fragmentation of its land— draws the grapes from a number of vineyard sources. For its wines, Bordeaux traditionally blends together the cabernet sauvignon, merlot, cabernet franc and other varieties (the malbec, petit verdot, and perhaps a bit of the carmenère). The tannic cabernet sauvignon supplies the structure and elegance here; the other grapes soften the cabernet's austerity, while adding their own nuances to the wine. (Although each château follows a general formula in creating its blends, the wines may change somewhat from year to year, depending on the weather and how the various grape varieties fared.) In the Rhône Valley, more than a dozen varieties have gone into the Châteauneuf-du-Pape wines, and in Portugal as many as thirty go into the port wine blends. New York State combines three hybrids —the baco noir, chelois and maréchal foch— to produce a full-bodied red wine; while California creates rich, dark red wines by blending such Rhône Valley grapes together as the syrah, mourvèdre and grenache.

Champagne

The epitome of a great blended wine is Champagne, a blend created in the seventeenth century when the vintners of Épernay donated their wines to the church as tithes. Pressed from the pinot noir, chardonnay, and other grape varieties, these wines differed greatly. Some were tart and dry, others were soft and round.

Deciding to balance these out was Dom Pérignon, the cellar master at the Benedictine abbey of Hautvillers. The monk —who was blind and the possessor of a finely tuned palate— decided to combine the texture, headiness, and fruit of the Pinot Noirs with the delicacy, lightness and finesse of the Chardonnays and then to round out the mix judiciously with the other wines. (Some 60 percent were red wines and 40 percent white.) Dom Pérignon's blend proved so superior that few Champagnes remained vins de cru (wines of one location) after his time.

Champagne producers usually don't own any vineyards, but buy their grapes locally. Setting the prices is a rating system, based primarily on the region's vineyard soils. The finest grapes, rated 100 percent, go into the rarest blends. Top firms generally buy the grapes rated in the 90s, while the good smaller firms buy their grapes in the high 70s to low 90s.

The blend itself, known as the *cuvée* (translating as "batch" or "tubful"), is assembled in the spring after the Chardonnays, Pinot Noirs and Meuniers have been separately fermented. When these new wines have settled down sufficiently to be tasted, the wine maker selects samples from the various batches, then decides how much he wants of each and combines them on a small scale. When his assemblage is approved, the proportions of the components are then extrapolated to the proper scale for the actual production of the wine. (Champagne makers take special pride in their distinctive and unique house styles.) A typical Champagne usually combines anywhere from ten to thirty wines and represents a number of vintages. A Grand Cru cuvée may combine as many as forty to fifty wines, drawn from six to ten harvests. One Champagne blends a hundred and fifty wines. Another is drawn from twenty-five vineyards. Lesser Champagnes combine fewer wines from fewer vintages

NOTE: Many Champagne firms set aside their wines from good years to upgrade the blend. These are known as *vins de reserve* or correctives, The better houses keep at least a three-year supply on hand, while lesser ones may not employ any correctives at all.

Sherry

Another classic blend is sherry, which is simultaneously blended and aged. The process occurs in a solera, through which the wine gradually passes. A solera system can consist of anywhere from two dozen to several hundred casks, set out in equal rows and stacked one atop the other. Solera derives from suelo, translating as "foundation" and referring to the floor on which the casks sit. (The casks, each holding one hundred fifty gallons of wine, are known as *botas* or "butts.")

The simplest solera consists of three equal rows. The casks in the first row are filled with wine the first year; the next two rows are filled in the two succeeding years. At the end of the third year, wine is withdrawn from the bottommost casks usually no more than a third at a time. Those casks are then immediately refilled with a like amount of wine drawn from the row directly above. These in turn are replenished from the topmost row. Refilling the topmost row is a new wine that is similar in style and quality.

NOTE: Initially siphoned with hoses from cask to cask , sherry wines are now transferred by way of mechanical pumps.

Each solera has its own style and grade of wine. A typical system begins with a *criadera* (nursery solera) and ends with a shipping solera. Before a young wine is admitted to the solera proper, it may pass through two or three criaderas. Only wines of the properly developed style and quality are permitted to move ahead. As they slowly and gradually pass through the casks, the wines are continually blended and reblended. The older, more mellow wines "educate" the younger, transmitting to them their mature richness, subtlety, and depth of character. Meanwhile, the younger wines are refreshing their elders, giving them vivacity and tone. As the younger wines move progressively through several levels of increasingly older wines, they gradually become smoother and more complex, rounder and more mellow, while remaining remarkably fresh.

Such fractional blending ensures a uniformity of style and a consistency of wine quality year after year. And a solera system can be perpetuated indefinitely, guaranteeing a sherry as close as possible in color, flavor and character to one that emerged a decade before. Wines from top vineyards spend about nine years in the system. The more old sherries that pass through a solera, the better and more expensive the final blend. In really old systems, that go back more than a hundred years, a few drops of the original may still be dispersed among the casks.

NOTE: Madeiras are matured in a similar manner, with some of their components averaging eighty to a hundred years in age. Marsalas are also blended in solera systems.

AGING

Aging refers to the wine's slow aeration, to its gradual oxidation. To stand up to air, a wine needs enough tannin to hold it together. Tannin is an assortment of organic compounds found in the skins, stalks, and seeds of the grapes. Absorbed by the must during fermentation, these give the wine structure and backbone, helping to preserve it and lengthen its life.

The wine's tannin content determines its ability to age. Red wines, fermented on their skins, generate the most tannin and require the most aging. White wines, rarely fermented on their skins, exhibit relatively little and need virtually no aging at all. A wine's specific tannin is based on its grape variety, general growing conditions, and the weather that year. (Good vintages produce the highest tannins.)

Proper aging occurs under controlled conditions in wood and glass. Ideal for a wine's preliminary aging is a wooden cask. Although its construction is airtight, the porous staves let limited quantities of air enter and these gradually and evenly interact with the wine's organic constituents. The cask itself provides its own extractable elements, including tannins, vanillins, and various aromatic substances. As the wine absorbs them, the liquid nearest the staves becomes denser and heavier. Falling away, it is replaced by lighter liquid from the center of the cask. The circulation is constant; aerating the wine evenly and encouraging its slow and steady development.

The porosity of the wooden staves also causes some evaporation. Each year about 5 percent of the wine's volume is lost. This not only concentrates and intensifies the remainder, but creates an ullage, or air space, at the top of the cask. Were this ullage allowed to remain, the wine would be subjected to excessive oxidation, robbing it of its character and hastening its demise. To prevent this and ensure the wine's stability and soundness, the casks must be topped off at intervals with additional wine.

Best for aging is white oak. This wood not only imparts a vanilla-like flavor and aroma, but contributes its own tannins and organic compounds to the wine. Particularly prized is the French white oak from Limousin, characterized by a high porosity and rich vanillin and giving a soft, subtle quality to the wine. Other good oaks come from Nevers, Vosges, Allier, and Tronçais in France. Suitable oaks are also found in Germany's Black Forest, the former Yugoslavia, Mexico, and the southeastern United States.

Redwood and chestnut casks were once widely used in wine making. (Most other woods are either too resinous or insufficiently porous.) The towering redwoods, indigenous to California, permitted larger *cooperage* than oak. (Cooperage refers to any bulk wine container; the term deriving from *cooper*, the maker or repairer of barrels.) Redwood's extractable elements, however, are more limited than those of oak and impart little wood character to the wine. They preserve its fruitiness at the expense of its complexity.

Best for aging are new wooden casks, which possess fresh extractables. Vintners who can afford to, change their casks every year. Others keep some of their wines in new barrels and some in older ones. Still others age their less expensive products in used casks that once held premium wines. Another consideration is not only the cost of the barrels themselves, but the cost of maintaining the storage space. (While the wine matures slowly, the vintner gets no return on his investment.) This has led to various shortcuts designed to create an oaky quality artificially. Mesh bags holding oak chips have been suspended in the wine for days or weeks; or the wine has been forced through oak chips. Sometimes special concentrates simulate the aroma and the taste of oak.

NOTE: In recent years, stainless steel has generally been the material of choice for winery vats and tanks. Not as limited as wood in size, the metal is also much easier to clean and maintain. But since the stainless steel has no extractable elements, some wines are kept in it briefly, then complete their aging process in wood. Others never spend any time in wood, but are bottled and shipped out after six months or so in stainless steel.

Wood aging tempers a red wine's tannic astringency and gradually softens its initial rawness and harshness, rounding out the wine's character and making its complexity more apparent. Wood is generally not suitable for white wines. Lacking the preservative power of tannin, they are susceptible to overoxidation. Champagne, however, benefits from a brief stay in wood, acquiring a toasty flavor, a lovely bouquet, and a more complex roundness. Chardonnay wines also achieve a measure of roundness and complexity in wood, but are often overshadowed by too much oak. (This may be seen in some Californian and Australian Chardonnays, which end up tasting more like wood than like wine.)

NOTE: White wines are at their best when the wood flavors are sufficiently subdued to let their natural qualities come through. At one time, most white wines were aged extensively in wood. Absorbing too much of the cask's extractables, they often became heavy and assertive. Whatever aging these wines may need usually takes place in stainless steel now.

Wood-aging requirements for red wines vary from vintage to vintage. The more pronounced the tannins are, the more aging the wine needs. Customs change, however.

Long wood aging was once considered routine in Italy and most of Spain. Now about twenty-four months is often deemed sufficient. In Bordeaux, even the most prestigious châteaus rarely cask-age their wines more than eighteen months.

On emerging from its cask, a highly tannic red can still be quite raw and unyielding with the still-unresolved tannins masking its fruit and bouquet. Much too closed-in for immediate consumption, the wine needs additional aeration to smooth out its rough edges. The process by which a wine completes this maturation takes place in the bottle.

In the inert and neutral glass bottle, oxidation proceeds more slowly, enabling the wine to improve immeasurably. It was initially believed that some oxygen entered by passing through the cork. But the wine, enclosed in the sealed bottle, was breathing and absorbing a small amount of air already inside the bottle. (The air, in the form of a bubble, had inevitably been introduced at the time of bottling.)

The additional aeration allows the wine to expand and develop, to shed its youthful awkwardness, and gradually release its flavors. The wine also forms new compounds. Among them are esters —highly volatile combinations of acids and alcohol— which, although minor in quantity, are major in enhancing the wine's flavor, aroma, and bouquet. As it ages in glass, the wine develops depth and complexity, acquiring new and fascinating nuances. Growing supple, smooth, and fragrant, the wine takes on the splendid balance of maturity.

A key consideration is the size of the container itself. The larger the bottle, the better. A higher ratio of liquid to air will prevent excessive oxidation and allow the wine to develop at a more leisurely pace. The magnum is ideal, holding much more wine in proportion to air than a standard-sized wine bottle. A half bottle, on the other hand, ages the wine twice as fast as a standard bottle. The reverse occurs in wood aging: the smaller the cask, the better. Its higher ratio of wood surface to liquid exposes more of the developing wine to the porous staves, allowing it to breathe more evenly.

The cylindrical cork, sealing the bottle, protects the wine from outside air. The cork comes from the outer bark of a unique oak tree, which is stripped off and processed. Such trees are grown in the warm climates. They are to be found in Portugal, Spain, Algeria, and Morocco. (Portugal produces more than half of the world's cork supply.)

It takes some forty years for the oak tree to mature and about ten years for its stripped-off bark to regenerate. In recent years, poor harvesting practices have reduced the world's cork supply. Premium wines were once routinely fitted with two-and-a-half-inch stoppers but two-inch corks are now more the norm.

Faced with a shortage of good corks and a proliferation of bad ones, the wine industry has reluctantly sought out suitable alternatives. Wine meant for early consumption is now often sealed with metal or plastic caps or with stoppers combining cork, wood, and plastic. Metal screw caps —seen on soda bottles— have been associated with inexpensive wines, but are being used for some quality wines and have been accepted for use on airlines. (Such closures apparently can preserve the wine for years.) Advocates claim that they are more reliable than corks since corks can result in an inconsistency of wine from bottle to bottle. Yet, because premium wines have always been associated with corks in the public mind, there has been some experimentation with creating stoppers that look like corks and are extracted like them. The materials used are resilient cellulose and plastic resins, but these may affect the taste and aroma of the wine.

The practice of bottle aging began in the eighteenth century. Earlier glass bottles were squat with irregular apertures and could not be stoppered securely. Improved technology then made more uniform apertures possible, allowing the bottles to be corked tightly. The bottles also acquired straighter sides, enabling them to be stacked horizontally for long-term storage. The bottling process itself can be traumatic; a wine needs time to adjust to its confinement in glass. Some wines may become bottle sick and exhibit harshness and a loss of flavor. When allowed to rest before shipment, these symptoms usually disappear. Fine wines are binned away for several months; lesser wines for briefer periods.

Wines that lend themselves best to aging in glass are the more tannic reds. The most complex among them do not reach their ultimate development for years. Extended aging for the softer, less structured reds and rosés, which have lighter tannins, would cause their freshness to evaporate and their charms to decline.

Most white wines are reared in stainless steel, then bottled quite early to retain their fresh, crisp qualities. (Prolonged oxidation would produce disagreeable fuzzy tastes and off-flavors.) The more full-bodied white wines, however, can benefit from some time in glass, achieving greater vinosity and complexity with little loss of their freshness. Among them are the noble rots, the finest Chablis and the best German Rieslings. As the noble-rot wines age in glass, the luscious sweetness that initially obscured their flavor begins to subside, allowing their other delightful intricacies to come through.

Aging also transforms the wine's color. White wines, initially greenish or straw colored, head toward yellow, then darken and take on an amber hue. When overaged, they become brownish. Good red wines start out with a youthful purple that changes in time to a more profound garnet. (The French call the subtle russet of a fine old red wine *pelure d'oignon* or "onion skin.") As a red wine continues to age, its color progresses first toward orange, then toward brown. A brick color indicates that the wine has passed its peak. When the wine turns completely brown, it is most likely undrinkable. Both red and white wines eventually maderize, acquiring the brownish hue of Madeira, combined with a vapid odor and an acrid taste. White wines, less protected by tannin, tend to maderize more quickly.

A number of vintners are trying accelerate their wines' development and make them approachable sooner. They claim the public has neither the time nor the inclination to wait for a wine to mature slowly. Their motives are most likely economic, however. A winery has to be in good financial shape to let its wines age quietly for extended periods. A speeded-up wine, on the other hand, is not only less expensive to produce but provides a quicker return on its investment.

There are various ways to short-cut the aging process. Some vintners rely on stainless steel and vat their wines more briefly. They use less tannic, earlier-ripening grapes and include fewer varieties in their blends. (Châteauneuf-du-Pape once combined more than a dozen grapes, but now uses five or less.) Some remove the tannic stalks and stems before crushing (the French call this *égrappage*). They separate out the tannic skins within days or hours of fermentation; use hot pressing, a method that heats the skins and must briefly to accelerate the color's extraction; they filter the wine or dose it with sulfur dioxide; or they flash-pasteurize it to prevent spoilage and protect its color and aroma.

Red wines that are ready to drink in two to four years have been called "useful," or "accessible," or "transition" wines. The French describe them as *promptment buvable* (soon drinkable). Two-year-old reds from Bordeaux, suitable for immediate consumption, have been dubbed "supermarket wines" since this is where they are frequently found. Foreshortened wines have also been called "restaurant wines" since they can be added to a wine list as soon as they are delivered.

An abbreviated wine, however, can never compare with one that has evolved slowly. Lighter, paler, and more one dimensional, it lacks the intensity and complexity of the traditionally made wines, as well as their potential for further development. Such wines only become duller as they age.

After experimenting with various acceleration methods, some Rhône Valley vintners decided it was better for their wines to age naturally. As one said, "For the wine to grow old through some artificial process is not good for it at all." Echoing this sentiment, an American wine maker declared, "The minute you take a shortcut in the process, that's as good as your wine is going to be." And in parts of France, Portugal, and Italy, wine makers still toss the tannic stems and stalks into their vats, along with the grapes. As one Frenchman said, "Although this makes it more trouble, it gives the wine a richer body."

🍇 🍇 🍇

CLARIFICATION

As the wine ferments, it churns up a violent froth, containing bits of pulp, seeds, skins, and spent yeasts. These make up the sediment. At the end of fermentation, when the production of CO_2 stops and the heavier particles begin to settle out of the liquid, the wine is said to "fall bright". The muddy sedimentary deposit sinking to the bottom is called the gross lees. A volatile substance, it can reexcite fermentation, decompose, and encourage the vinegar-makers to proliferate. Because the gross lees threaten the wine's stability, they cannot be permitted to remain. Once they have settled out, they must be removed. Separating out the unwanted deposit from the liquid is known as clarification. The process involves racking and fining and —in the case of lesser wines— filtering.

Racking transfers the clear wine to another container by way of pumps and hoses, leaving the muddy sediment behind. Red wines, fermenting on their skins and generating the heaviest deposits, require the most racking. Red wines also need greater aeration since they possess more body and tannin, and racking enables them to pick up the oxygen that they require. Most white wines are racked early to preserve their fruit and delicacy. A few are steeped on their sediment for greater enrichment. Muscadet sur Lie, as it name implies, always ripens on its lees. Essentially neutral, this wine acquires a yeastier flavor, and a more pronounced aroma. In the process, it also becomes brisker, fruitier, and more full-bodied. Champagne benefits from some contact with its spent lees too. As it ages quietly, the wine achieves a greater fragrance, depth, and finesse. Although California Chardonnays are often reared in stainless steel, they spend some time steeping on their deposits to compensate for the metal's neutrality.

Wines from richer, riper vintages are racked sooner than those from poorer years. (Leaving the more meager examples on their gross lees longer makes up somewhat for their shortcomings.) Wines from warmer climates are generally racked as soon as possible to prevent any spoilage.

NOTE: A wine may be racked before and after blending, and while it's aging in wood. Red wines, which cast off soluble pigments along with their sediment, will lose some color in wood. The more often they're racked, the tawnier they become.

While the gross lees soon settle out of the liquid, the finer, lighter particles remain in suspension; clouding or "blinding" the wine and making for a certain harshness. Fining induces these particles to settle out as well by dispersing a coagulating agent through the wine. The agent creates a soluble filmlike net that drifts slowly downward over a period of days or months, capturing most of the particles that have not settled out by themselves.

Coagulating agents have included egg whites, skimmed milk, gelatin, boiled rice, beef blood, isinglass, plaster of paris, and casein. (Some Bordeaux wineries add six egg whites to each barrel.) The most powerful and fastest-acting agent of all is bentonite. A porous, expansive clay with phenomenal absorptive qualities, bentonite picks up the wine's finer deposits along with its sedimentary particles. Also removing valuable tannins, fruit acids, and mineral salts, this agent removes the elements responsible for much of the wine's flavor, character, and longevity. (Bentonite is never used for quality wines.)

As it ages in glass, the wine continues to precipitate out small quantities of its finer deposits. A teaspoon or two of sediment at the bottom of the bottle — provided the liquid itself remains clear— is a good sign, indicating that the wine has matured slowly. In a tannic red wine, the sediment may appear as a muddy deposit, brownish flakes, or a loose, murky film. (The French call the latter adhering to the bottle's interior, a *chemise*.) Although harmless, the sediment can display a texture that is sometimes disconcerting to the palate. (Decanting the bottle at serving time will leave this deposit behind.)

Vintage ports, aged primarily in glass, throw a series of precipitations, which cohere inside the bottle as a hard, clinging crust. The bottles must be handled with particular care to keep this crust intact; dislodging it would befoul the wine. To prevent this, the topside of each bottle is marked with a splash of white paint so that whenever the bottle is moved, that side can be carefully kept uppermost).

NOTE: Vintage ports are best left to "fall bright" on their own, but some producers fine them for export so they won't develop an interior crust that might become dislodged in shipping.

White wines and rosés throw only a negligible sediment. Their deposit, if any, appears as solitary crystals at the bottom of the bottle or looks like a few pale grains of sand. Neutral in taste and hardly evident in texture, this sedimentary deposit is easily ignored.

Filtering, a speedier form of clarification, forces the liquid mechanically through a series of porous layers or finely meshed screens. Removing the most infinitesimal particles, it ensures that a wine will not precipitate heavily during shipment or storage and also extends its shelf life. Although filtering creates bright, impeccably clear wines, it does so by stripping away the very compounds that sustain them and help them to develop. Since filtering thins and impoverishes the wines, it is mainly used for lesser examples.

*The enjoyment of a wine is not necessarily
in direct proportion to its price.*

—Anonymous

THE ECONOMICS OF WINE

The producers of wine range from small family-owned vineyards to vast industrialized empires. Between them are the boutique wineries, the estate, cooperative, and middleman wineries.

Family-owned vineyards —seen primarily in Europe— average little more than an acre and generally produce just enough wine for the grower, his family, and a few friends to share. Boutique wineries, associated mainly with California, are small-scale operations, specializing in highly individualized wines. Some produce only about three thousand bottles a year but their typical output runs from five thousand to twelve thousand cases. (In New York State, the boutiques are known as farm wineries.) The smaller establishments sell their wines on the premises, or send them through the mail.

Estate wineries concentrate on a few quality wines produced in lots of a few thousand gallons. Most of the famous châteaus in Bordeaux, produce between ten thousand and twenty thousand cases a year. (Elsewhere in Europe, and in the United States, many noted properties rarely produce more than twenty-five thousand cases a year.) Cooperative wineries consist of growers who pool their resources, not only to produce the wine but to market and distribute it. Some cooperatives are modest in size, others are mammoth. Middleman wineries do not deal with the public at all but sell their wine in bulk to others who blend, bottle, and distribute it under their own labels.

In recent years, a handful of giant corporations have absorbed many medium-sized wineries as well as the bulk processors. Their annual production starts at about three hundred thousand cases. (One huge establishment in California churns out some 9 million bottles annually.) Much of the activity here is mechanized and computerized. Harvesting machines gather the grapes, then transfer them to gondolas. The grapes, often traveling long distances to the winery, may be sprayed with sulfites or blanketed with nitrogen gas to prevent their oxidation or premature fermentation en route. On reaching the winery, the grapes go to powerful crusher-destemmers; their must is then inoculated with cultured yeasts. Workers sitting at computer keyboards continuously feed the must through a complex network of pipes. Fermentation takes place in huge stainless steel tanks, fitted with temperature controls. (Should the heat begin to climb dangerously, coolants will flow or alarms will sound.)

The raw wine flowing out is constantly monitored. High-speed centrifuges precipitate out its solids. Filtering clarifies the wine further. Blending occurs in quality-control laboratories, first in milliliters, then in gallons. Cellars are rare and aging times are brief. Fast-moving machines bottle, label, and pack the wines. (One giant winery can fill and cork three thousand bottles in an hour.) Some establishments even include their own barrel-making facilities and their own distribution companies.

NOTE: A number of wineries have no vineyards of their own. They purchase their grapes, either by establishing informal ties with independent growers or by signing them to multiyear contracts. Other wineries lease their vineyards on a long-term basis. In California, there are wine makers, who not only buy their grapes but rent out the space for producing and aging their wines; some even turn over the entire wine-making process to others.

Commercial wine making calls for a considerable outlay of capital. Many growers must borrow just to grow their crops each year. (They pay off their debts by selling their grapes, musts, or raw wines to others.) Various middlemen — négociants, shippers, and brokers— may lend these growers money and then act as agents to sell their products to the wineries. Shippers may buy raw wines throughout the region, then blend, bottle, and age them themselves in their own cellars. Others buy already bottled wines and simply affix their own labels.

In Bordeaux and Burgundy, local shippers stake out much of the crop — monitoring the fruit, sampling, judging, and choosing among the grapes they will acquire— then marketing and distributing the final product. Such middlemen often operate with borrowed funds and must juggle grape prices and market conditions in order to survive economically. The most successful middlemen persuade the growers to sell them their finest berries and so contrive the best blends. (Some have ended up owning the vineyards or parts of vineyards themselves.) In Burgundy, with its many small fragmented plots of land, the shipper's reputation usually carries as much weight as the wine itself. (One shipper blends the wines of three hundred vintners and fourteen cooperatives.) In Italy, Spain, and Madeira, foreign shippers operate extensively.

Tension is inevitable between the growers and the shippers. As one shipper asked rhetorically, "How many businesses are there that buy their raw materials for the entire year in a four-week period?" Meanwhile the growers, parting with their grapes for relatively little, see them disappear anonymously. "When I sold my grapes," one said, "they got blended into other people's wine and I didn't like that at all." Moreover growers don't profit if wine prices rise or if their wines become rare and quite expensive.

A number of small growers have found it psychologically and financially more satisfying to vinify, bottle, and market their own wines. Some in Burgundy sell the bulk of their grapes to shippers, while holding back a percentage for themselves. In Champagne, various growers are working through cooperatives to produce their own individualized sparkling wines.

In wine making today, mechanization has largely replaced human toil and primitive equipment. Vineyards have been replanted to increase their yields and to allow for more mechanical harvesting. Research, experimentation, and fast-changing technologies have made it possible to control virtually every aspect of the craft. The grower can plant higher-yielding, more disease-resistant vines. He can clone them to abbreviate the growing cycle. He can time his harvests scientifically and compensate for the vagaries of the weather in various ways. He can speed up the wine's development and accelerate its aging process.

A few traditional wine makers believe that too much technology leads to homogenized products. They rely on slower, age-old methods to preserve the flavors that Nature herself has provided. They seek to create an environment in which a wine can almost make itself. These traditionalists count on the natural yeasts to ferment their must spontaneously. Cultured yeasts, they maintain, will alter the wine. And they point out that the presence of wild yeasts is inevitable anyway, noting that the harsh processing needed to remove them only diminishes the wine's taste and character. As one vintner declares, "Each time you touch a wine, its quality decreases." Another says, "I call myself a noninterventionist. I let the fruit make the wine." And a third adds, "I let the wine be what it is."

Concentrating on limited production and high quality wines, these traditionalists do not use weed killers or chemical fertilizers, which they say destroys the soil's microbial and bacterial life. They continue to hand pick their grapes, pointing out that harvesting machines bruise and split the softest berries while indiscriminately gathering the defective fruit along with the good. They note that harvesting machines also pick up bits of foliage, imparting an odd, leafy taste to the wine. As one New Zealand grower said, "You get better grapes when you take the leaves off by hand and when you harvest by hand." Some high-caliber wines in Burgundy are still bottled and corked by hand.

A current trend is to combine the patient time-honored approach with new scientific methods. As one wine maker says, "I try to follow tradition with as much technology as possible." Another adds, "I believe in modern equipment and the latest machines but also in the old traditions." And a third declares, "If I have to use science, I use science, but my first preference goes to the art of wine making."

3

TYPES OF WINE

Wine is classified in various ways: by source (French, German, Italian, American, Swiss, etc.); by style (dry or sweet, light or full–bodied); by function (dinner, apéritif, or dessert); by color or CO_2 content. There are, however, only three basic types: still, sparkling, and fortified. Still or table wines are produced by the processes previously described. Sparkling and fortified wines begin as still wines but receive additional processing.

SPARKLING WINES AND CHAMPAGNE

Champagne, the prototype of sparkling wines, originated in France but is now made throughout the world. Some examples follow the original French method, while others do not. Yet all share the lively effervescence that enhances them visually and gives them their delightful piquancy. The source of their exhilarating bubbles is the carbon dioxide that fermentation generates. In still wines, the CO_2 escapes into the air and vanishes. In sparkling wines, this lively effervescence is always retained.

True Champagne captures its carbon dioxide in a remarkable manner. At the end of November, the winery's cellar doors and windows are deliberately flung open, admitting the chill autumn air. (This will send the yeasts prematurely into hibernation.) In the spring, when the wine settles down sufficiently to be tasted, it is blended, bottled and sealed with a temporary cork. A metal clamp securely anchors that temporary cork.

The dormant yeasts, awakened by the warmth of spring, resume their normal fermentation inside the sealed bottle, splitting the sugar molecules in two; generating both alcohol and carbon dioxide. The CO_2 —trapped in the bottle with no way of escaping— remains in suspension and is absorbed into the wine, becoming part of it. Uncorking the bottle eventually liberates the CO_2. Reexpanding quickly and rising through the liquid, the CO_2 forms the tiny bubbles that create Champagne's distinctive and exhilarating fizz.

Reactivated in the spring, the yeasts had created great carbon dioxide pressure inside the bottle, building up to more than a hundred pounds per square inch, and causing a number of the glass bottles to explode. Seeing the shards hurled throughout the cellars, people thought the wines were bewitched. Although thicker, more stress-resistant bottles were later developed, many still continued to shatter. The culprit was finally identified as the natural sugar in the must. The more sugar, the more carbon dioxide and the greater the pressure inside the bottle. Vintners realized they could keep this pressure at safe levels by controlling the amount of sugar in the wine. So they fermented out their wines completely dry and —just before bottling— stirred in a precisely measured solution of cane sugar. This produced the lively bubbles without any unwanted explosiveness.

Sparkling wines came into prominence in the eighteenth century. Credited in large part with their development was Dom Pérignon, the blind cellar master at the Benedictine abbey of Hautvillers. Dom Pérignon was the first to introduce cold air

into the cellars, the first to create the Champagne *cuvée* (or "blend"), and the first to bottle the still-fermenting wine. He also replaced the oil-soaked cotton wadding used to keep out the air with thick cork plugs, which sealed the bottles more tightly and were better able to withstand the fierce internal pressure of the CO_2.

In the classic Champagne method —the *méthode champenoise*— the wine never leaves its original container. (The consumer buys it in the same bottle in which secondary fermentation has taken place.) The steps in this intricate, labor-intensive Champagne-making process are: tierage, riddling, disgorging, adding the dosage, and recorking.

Tierage stacks the bottles in deep underground vaults, where the coolness and the quiet encourages the wine's gradual ripening. As the wine ages on its yeasty deposit for anywhere from one to six years or more, enzymes break down the yeast cells in a process called *autolysis.* This liberates various compounds in the wine while diminishing its acidity. The wine, initially hard and even thin, begins to fatten up, and develop a richness, lusciousness, and finesse. In the process, it acquires a depth of character and an extraordinary bouquet.

To ensure its stability, Champagne like other wines must be separated from its spent lees. Conventional racking and fining calls for opening the bottle which would soon dissipate the bubbles. Instead, an ingenious technique, known as *riddling,* was devised to spirit out the unwanted sediment but not the fizz itself. Its creator was Nicole Barbe-Clicquot Ponsardin, better known as Veuve Clicquot, the widow of a nineteenth-century wine maker, who had taken over the business after her husband died.

The original riddling method systematically rotated each bottle until its yeasty deposit gradually drifted down into the neck. The bottles were placed neck-forward in slotted A-shaped racks, given a quick quarter turn each day, then rapped sharply, tilted slightly, and put back into their slots. Expert bottle turners, using both hands and working with astonishing speed, could twirl about thirty thousand bottles a day. (More sophisticated racks increased these totals to some one hundred thousand bottles a day.) After three months, each bottle stood neck down in its slot; the yeasty sediment lodged compactly against the cork.

Disgorging, the next step, removes the sediment. The bottle neck here is dipped into a brine solution, which freezes the sediment into an icy lump. The metal clamp holding the temporary cork is then released and the internal pressure expels the cork. Flying out in one swift burst, it takes the congealed sediment with it. At the same time, a bit of wine is lost, creating an ullage or small air space at the top of the bottle. To protect the wine against excessive oxidation, the ullage is eliminated by topping off the wine with a *dosage* syrup (a mixture of wine, cane sugar, and brandy). The dosage not only keeps any viable remaining yeasts from going on with their fermentation, but enhances the taste of the wine as well. Once the dosage has been added, the bottle is swiftly resealed with a mushroom-shaped cork. Anchoring the cork firmly in place is a wire hood or muzzle. Champagne begins as a dry wine; its final style is determined by the dosage added. The five classifications of style in their ascending order of sweetness are: *brut, extra-sec, sec, demi-sec* and *doux*. Never having been standardized, these vary somewhat from one Champagne house to the next.

Brut translates as "unmodified" or "unrefined." The dosage here ranges from no sugar at all to about 1.5 percent. (*Extra-brut* denotes a sugar level below 0.6 percent while wines labeled *sans dosage, ultra brut, nature* or *naturel* usually have no sugar added at all.)

Extra-sec or *extra-dry*, often assumed to be the driest Champagne, may contain up to 2 percent sugar. *Sec*, despite translating as "dry," contains as much as 3.5 percent. *Demi-sec* has 4 to 6 percent sugar, while *doux*, the sweetest of all, contains 6 to 10 percent. (Because of the current preference for dryness, demi-sec and doux have virtually disappeared from the market.)

NOTE: To minimize any loss of fizz, the disgorging, adding the dosage, and recorking are carried out with dispatch as well as with dexterity. And these steps are scheduled as close to the shipping date as possible.

A sparkling wine, evolving in its closed container, needs enough acidity to keep from going flabby. White wines —inherently more acid than the reds— are best suited to the *methode champenoise*. Those that lend themselves to the process most successfully are the crisp, light, low-alcohol wines. In the Champagne region, they derive their acidity from a chalky soil and a cool climate, which ripens their grapes quite slowly and produces wines demonstrating both delicacy and breed.

Like the still wine from which it derives, Champagne develops best in larger sized bottles. Ideal is the magnum, although a standard 750-milliliter bottle is easier to handle. The sparkling wines sold in tiny splits or huge bottles are never fermented in these directly, but transferred there just before shipping.

In recent years, automation has modified the classic Champagne method. Mechanically operated or computerized riddling frames have replaced the hand labor of the bottle-turning workmen. (These devices can twirl as many as a thousand bottles at a time and work tirelessly around the clock.) Also introduced have been various assembly-line machines, which freeze the sediment, extract the temporary cork, add the dosage, and insert the shipping cork.

Other Sparkling Methods

True Champagne, made in the Marne Valley of France, accounts for less than 2 percent of the world's sparkling wine production. Other French sparkling wines made outside this zone may not be labeled Champagnes, but are called *vins mousseux* instead. (*Mousse* means "bubbles.") Hundreds of other sparkling wines are now made throughout the world, utilizing either the classic Champagne method or a faster, less expensive technique. The alternates include the Charmat method, the transfer method, and direct carbonation.

The Charmat method, also called *cuvée close*, or the bulk or autoclave method, is responsible for most low-priced sparkling wines. Invented in 1910 by Eugene Charmat, a French scientist, the wine here is fermented in huge pressurized tanks rather than in individual bottles. The yeasts are filtered out after anywhere from six weeks to three months, then the wine is bottled. The more costly transfer method is somewhat closer to the classic Champagne method. Employed by only a few wineries, secondary fermentation here takes place in the bottle; then the wine is transferred to a large pressurized tank, which preserves the fizz while filtering out its yeasty sediment. The wine is then transferred to fresh bottles. The cheapest sparkling method is direct carbonation, which quickly injects the wine with carbon dioxide in the manner of soda pop.

Wines made by the classic *methode champenoise* are more complex, significantly richer, and more profoundly flavorful than those produced by the alternate methods. Their bubbles are finer, tinier, and more persistent. Wines made by the other methods are generally simpler and less interesting, with quickly dissipating bubbles. Moreover, such wines in their transfers from bottle to tank and tank to bottle, undergo considerable oxidation, which darkens their color, affects their taste, and accelerates their aging process. (Sulfur dioxide may be added to counteract these unwanted effects).

A sparkling wine's effervescence is measured in units called *atmospheres*. In Champagne, these atmospheres range from 3 to 6; that is, the pressure inside the bottle is 3 to 6 times greater than that of the outside atmosphere. French wines with about half of Champagne's internal pressure are called *crémant* (creamy). Those with an internal pressure, measuring 2 atmospheres or less are called *pétillant*. They are characterized by a nice, delicate fizziness.

NOTE: A faint spontaneous prickliness can also be seen in wines that have spent some time on their lees and in wines bottled before malolactic fermentation has run its course. For example, a short-lived fizziness can be seen in the French Muscadets, the Portuguese vinho verdes, and the Italian Lambruscos.

Other Sparkling Wines

French sparkling wines grown outside the delimited Marne Valley, reflecting their own climates and locales, are as varied as their base wines. More than half come from from the area around Saumur in the Loire Valley. The best, generally a blend of the chenin blanc and the cabernet franc, are noted for their fine character and flavor. Vouvray, in the center of Touraine, is famous for its fruity, not-too-dry sparklers. Anjou to the west produces commendable sparkling rosés. The Côte de Blancs village of Cramant —just outside the Champagne zone— is known for its Crémant de Cramant, which employs the same grape varieties. St. Péray in the Rhône Valley yields a golden and substantial sparkling wine. Clairette de Die, produced to the south, is made both sparkling and semisparkling. Savoie is celebrated for its sparkling Seysalls; Alsace produces a dry and quite delicate Crémant with a lovely bouquet. Limoux, a town south of Carcassonne, blends the chenin blanc with local grapes to produces the fine Blanquette de Limoux.

In Italy, a fully sparkling wine is called a *spumante*. (spumante literally means "anything that bubbles"); a wine with a slight sparkle is called a *frizzante*. Best known is Asti Spumante whose finest examples, made by the Champagne method, are tart and dry. Most other Asti Spumantes are made by the Charmat process and tend to be on the sweet side. Spain's sparkling wines, called *vinos espumosos*, come from the Penedés region near Barcelona. Pressed entirely from indigenous grapes, these are typically fruity and full-flavored. The Spanish wines that follow the classic Champagne method are known as *cavas* and are aged at least nine months on their yeasts. The wines made by the Charmat method are the *granvas*. Portugal is best known for its fresh, slightly sparkling vinho verdes. (For export, these wines may be carbonated.)

Germany's sparkling wines are called *sekts* or *schaumweins*. The finest examples, pressed from the riesling, follow the classic Champagne method, and are fruity, flowery, and not too dry. Germany's lesser sparklers, made by the Charmat method, are often the overly acidy products of poor vintages, either chaptalized or bolstered with high-sugar wines. Most Russian sparklers are made by the Charmat method and are produced in Georgia and the Ukraine. (Some of the best originate in Odessa near the Black Sea.)

The United States, employing the classic Champagne method and its various alternates, relies on labrusca and hybrid grapes, as well as the viniferas for its base wines. New York State was an early leader in sparkling-wine production but California now dominates. Using typical Champagne varieties, California often harvests its naturally rich grapes early, while their sugars are still low and their acids are firm. (The wines typically tend to be more lush and fruity than the French.) American wine makers have appropriated the French terminology for dry, extra-dry, semidry and sweet, but have also indicated the absence of sweetness by labeling some wines "natural," "special reserve" or "*sehr trocken*" (very dry.)

NOTE: Sparkling wines elsewhere are often also pressed from early-picked grapes. Even when made by the classic Champagne method, they are usually bottled later and undergo their secondary fermentation at warmer temperatures. Since they spend less time on their yeasts, they don't undergo the enriching autolysis process to the same degree that Champagnes do. And those wines are usually fined and filtered as well.

Although a red wine can also be made effervescent, it requires a slightly warmer fermentation and greater oxidation than the white. It also needs a touch more sweetness as well to offset the slight bitterness created by the tannins in juxtaposition with the carbon dioxide. Best known among the effervescent reds are the sparkling Burgundies; the finest among them are pressed from the pinot noir. These follow the classic Champagne method and spend at least nine months on their yeasts. (A French rosé, made sparkling, is also known as a pink Champagne.)

Italy's best red sparkler is the Nebbiolo Spumante. More widely known is its Lambrusco, a somewhat sweet and spontaneously fizzy wine. For export, Lambruscos are generally made effervescent by the Charmat method or by direct carbonation. Portugal is celebrated for its naturally effervescent rosés. Some are carbonated for export to guarantee an animated display of bubbles.

FORTIFIED WINES

Fortified wines are generally high-sugar wines, preserved by the addition of alcohol. The idea of fortification came from the British and other Europeans, who imported rich, high-sugar wines from the Mediterranean region. Wanting them to withstand the rigors of sea travel, they strengthened these wines with alcohol. The additional alcohol, in the form of a high-proof spirit —usually brandy— not only stabilized the wines and prevented their spoilage, but greatly enhanced their character and extended their longevity. As they slowly assimilated the added alcohol, the wines acquired more body. They also went on to develop a more intense flavor, a vinous aroma, and a mouth-comforting warmth.

NOTE: Neutral spirits have also been used to fortify wines. Although more readily absorbed and faster acting, their wines are never as complex or interesting as those that were bolstered with brandy.

The point at which the additional alcohol is introduced determines the dryness or sweetness of the wine. Added at the start of fermentation, the alcohol inactivates the yeasts, leaving more residual sugar behind. Added midway, it balances out the sugars that have been converted with those that have not. Added after fermentation has run its course, it leaves the wine bone-dry.

Best-known among the fortified wines are ports, sherries, and Madeiras, along with vermouths and Marsalas. These all differ considerably in their base wines as well as in their processing.

Port

In the fifteenth century, Portuguese fishermen casting for cod off the coast of England bartered their red table wines for the sturdy British woolen goods they coveted. Those wines, produced under a strong Douro Valley sun, were fruity, full-bodied, and generous. When war with France deprived the British of their customary claret, enterprising English merchants purchased the Douro wines in bulk and fortified them for the voyage north. They named the wines "port" for Oporto, their town of origin.

Fortification not only made the port stout and bracing, but created an intensity of flavor, a delightful aroma, and a sweetness that did not cloy. Providing a perfect antidote to the damp, chilly climate of Britain, the wine soon became a national drink. George Saintsbury, a nineteenth-century wine enthusiast, defined its appeal when he said that port "strengthens as it gladdens as no other wine can do."

Port wines range from off-dry to sweet. After several days of fermentation, their still-active must is racked into casks containing a predetermined amount of brandy (usually one part brandy to four parts wine). This halts fermentation and retains some natural sugar. During the winter months, the wine precipitates out its heavier impurities as it settles down. Falling bright in the spring, it is racked into fresh casks and sent downriver to the shippers' lodges at Vila Nova de Gaia. (Picturesque sailing vessels, called *barcos rabelos*, once carried the wine there, but

trucks are the usual form of transportation now.) At the lodges, the port is tasted, blended, aged, and fortified further according to its type and style.

Although port wines vary considerably in their sweetness, color, and alcohol, there are only two basic types: those aged primarily in wood —constituting the majority— and those aged primarily in glass. Wooded ports are ready to drink when bottled. Bottle-aged ports usually require additional time to mature. Undergoing less oxidation as they age in glass, they are generally more subtle.

The basic wooded ports are ruby and tawny, both drawn from a number of harvests. Ruby, the simplest and least expensive blend, is made up of predominantly younger wines. Spending three years or less in wood, the wine retains much of its bright red color and exhibits a youthful aroma and a brash grapelike freshness. Ruby ports range from the dry to the semisweet.

Tawny ports, aged longer in wood, spend anywhere from three years to several decades in the cask. As they shed their pigment, their color gradually changes from a deep youthful ruby to a tawny golden brown. Slowly oxidizing, the wine becomes lighter, smoother, and more delicate, with a lingering aftertaste. A twenty-year-old may be light mahogany in color, with a bouquet reminiscent of hazelnuts. Becoming more complex and liqueurlike with time, the wine achieves an optimum balance of vivacity and flavor. Tawnies can differ widely. The best, aged in wood for up to forty years, acquire a truly memorable and nutty richness. Some resemble old sherries although somewhat richer in taste.

Tawnies may be aged separately, then have younger wines added to retain some of their original fruit flavor and to keep their color from fading too much. (The age on the label is the average age of the various wines.) Lesser tawnies are made by blending undistinguished ruby ports and white ports together.

NOTE: A rare variant is Colheita port, drawn from a single vintage and generally not released until it has spent at least seven —and as many as thirty— years in wood. (It carries a vintage date on its label.) Colheita port, moved less frequently from cask to cask than the tawny and so less exposed to outside air, combines the fruitiness of a vintage port with the nutty flavor of a tawny port.

Vintage port and its variants are the most complex of these wines. Dubbed the "queen of ports," vintage port is pressed from the grapes of a single, outstanding harvest. After spending its first two years in wood, it is then aged primarily in glass. In the bottle, its tannins slowly disintegrate, forming a heavy internal crust with the sediment. The wine ripens gently on this crust. It is coarse at first with an astringency masking its sweetness. Gradually gaining in character and subtlety, the wine attains a firmness of structure, an intensity of color, a concentrated fruity flavor, and a highly complex bouquet. The finest examples achieve lusciousness, balance and breed. Vintage ports need a minimum of ten years to mature. The best don't reveal their qualities for at least fifteen years. At the age of twenty, the wines are deep red in color and still redolent of fruit. Ideally, vintage ports should spend years in the bottle. Some have improved over three or four decades, while others have survived for more than a century.

NOTE: In Britain it was the custom to lay down some bottles at the birth of a son. Two decades later, when the lad had attained his majority, the vintage port had also matured and was ready to drink.

The most expensive and the most unusual vintage port accounts for only about 3 percent of the annual port production. However more affordable variants are available, which differ in their vintage requirements and in the time they spend in wood and glass. The variants are: late-bottled vintage port (LBV), vintage character port, port of the vintage, single-quinta port and crusted port.

The LBV and vintage character ports are ruby ports that strive to capture the flavor and style of a true vintage, but bear only a passing resemblance to it. LBV, the wine of a single year —although not of vintage quality— is good enough to merit a separate bottling. Aged in wood for at least four years, and for no more than six, it has precipitated out most of its sediment in the cask and is ready to drink when bottled. (Both the vintage date and the year of bottling appear on its label.) Vintage character port, a blend of LBV's, has thrown its crust in the cask and become ripe and flavorful there. Ready to drink when bottled, it's known as the "vintage port for the impatient." Port of the vintage is a single-vintage wine aged in wood. It's usually lighter and tawnier than either the LBV or vintage character port.

Single quinta port is aged primarily in glass. Grown in a high-quality vineyard and drawn from one or a number of harvests, it forms a crust in the bottle like vintage port. Still another variant is crusted port, which is drawn from several vineyards and from several vintages. After spending some three years in wood, it is aged in glass for another four and forms a heavy crust in the bottle. In effect, crusted port is a ruby port treated like a vintage port. (No longer a fashionable wine, its production is being phased out.)

Other wines are porto seco and white port. Porto seco is fermented out completely dry before fortification. White port, pressed from white grapes, is vinified bone dry or medium sweet and becomes amber colored after maturing in wood. Although usually reserved for blending, it has been taken up by the Scandinavians and other northern Europeans, who serve it chilled as an apéritif.

Sherry

The English discovered sherry while purchasing salt at the Spanish ports of Cádiz and Sanlúcar de Barrameda. After its fortification, the wine proved so suited to the British climate and temperament that, like port, it too became a national drink.

Sherry's vinification is unique. The wine is deliberately oxidized by setting it out-of-doors in loosely stoppered casks and never topped off at all. Siphoned from one cask to another in a solera, the wine is further exposed to the air. Such excessive aeration would ruin any other wine, but sherry is protected by a unique and remarkable yeast, called *flor* ("flower"). Indigenous to southern Spain and multiplying vigorously in the Andalusian warmth, flor forms a deep, soft, creamy crust, which floats on the surface of the wine like a water lily. Acting as a barrier against overoxidation and spoilage organisms, flor not only keeps the wine from turning to vinegar, but makes possible its slow and gradual oxidation. Because of flor, the wine acquires a delightful, nutlike flavor and aroma, a gently bitter or *rancio* taste, and quite a lovely bouquet.

Sherries are ruggedly individualistic. Some are affected by flor; others are hardly touched by it. In December, after most of the sugar has been fermented out, the wine is ready for its first classification (flor or nonflor). Those most affected by flor become the *finos;* those with scant flor or none at all become the *olorosos.* Because of flor's unpredictability, the wines must continually be classified and reclassified. Periodically sampling them, the blender chalks the appropriate symbol for each on the head of its cask. (Since the casks in a solera are not always stacked in chronological order, this form of identification is necessary.)

The finos, light in color and body, are divided into three subgroups: *manzanillas, finos,* and *amontillados.* The manzanillas, the crispest and lightest of the sherries, are grown in the vicinity of Sanlúcar de Barrameda, a fishing village on the Atlantic coast. Exposed to the bracing sea air, they are fresh, dry, almost salty tasting, and sometimes so pale as to be nearly colorless. The fino sherries —also light, dry, and delicate— range in color from white to pale gold, and on to amber. These are distinguished by a crisp, clean taste, a light but pungent nutty aroma, and a somewhat sharp, refreshing finish that has been described as "tongue-on-stone."

NOTE: When a cask of manzanilla is brought inland, the wine becomes less dry and austere. Conversely, when a Jerez fino is transferred to Sanlúcar de Barrameda, and exposed to the crisp sea air, it acquires the distinct, almost salty, manzanilla taste and aroma.

Amontillados are mature finos whose flor has mysteriously disappeared. Medium in body and topaz in color, they range from very dry to medium dry. Characterizing these wines is an intense vinosity, coupled with a robust, nutty flavor. They become more concentrated, darker, firmer and more pungently aromatic with age. And they acquire a rich, penetrating bouquet suggesting ripe tropical fruit, smoked almonds, and roasted walnuts.

NOTE: A number of sherries have appropriated the amontillado name but they are generally commonplace. They display none of the charm of the authentic amontillado examples.

Possessing less flor than the finos, the olorosos lack an effective shield against sherry's characteristic oxidation and so undergo greater interaction with the air. (They also pick up more color and flavor from their casks.) As a result, these wines are coarser, darker, and more full-bodied than the finos. The oldest, finest olorosos are dark, concentrated, and pungent, with richly satisfying flavors. They are also quite fragrant. In fact, they're the most aromatic of the sherry wines. (*Oloroso* translates as "agreeable odor.")

NOTE: While some olorosos are vinified completely dry, others are sweetened with an intense liqueurlike wine that combines brandy with the juice of raisined pedro ximénez (PX) grapes. Lesser olorosos are sweetened with *mosto apogado*, a boiled-down concentrate derived from lesser grapes.

Oloroso wines range in color from honey to rich, dark chestnut or mahogany. Some acquire an amberlike hue by the addition of a *vino de color*. (This is a thick, reddish black syrup, produced by slowly boiling down the juice of raisined PX grapes.) Ranging from dry to off-dry, the olorosos often seem sweeter than they actually are because their heightened levels of glycerin tend to create a somewhat opulent impression.

The oloroso group itself is subdivided into amoroso, brown, and cream sherries. Amoroso is medium dry and relatively light in body. Brown sherry is rich, walnut colored, and lusciously sweet with a full-bodied nuttiness. Cream sherry is golden brown, full-bodied, and vinous, with an almost viscous texture and a raisinlike taste. (The best examples are judiciously sweetened.) Other variants are palo cortado, pale dry sherry, pale cream sherry, golden sherry and solera sherry. Palo cortado, somewhere between an amontillado and an oloroso, combines the bouquet of the former with the fuller flavor of the latter. Although drier and leaner than the olorosos, it nevertheless possesses a full-bodied style and an aged nose. Pale dry sherry, a blend of fairly undistinguished wines, is not completely dry despite its name. Pale cream sherry is lighter in color than cream sherry and not very sweet, while golden sherry is decidedly so. Solera sherry is dark, heavy, and usually quite sweet. (Its name is misleading since true sherries always pass through a solera system.)

Madeira

In the eighteenth century, Madeira was a rough and ordinary fortified wine, serving as an item of sea trade. The wine of an unsold shipment, returned from the East Indies, proved surprisingly splendid. The long months at sea had transformed its character, improving the wine dramatically. The ship's rocking and pitching motion had accelerated its oxidation while the tropical heat had caramelized its residual sugars. Taking on a deep golden color and a wonderful softness, the wine acquired a smoothness of texture and an attractive bittersweet taste.

Madeira vintners began to send their wines to sea so they too could experience both the ship's rolling and pitching motion and the enveloping heat. (The casks of wine often served as ballast in transoceanic shipping.) Soon sailing vessels from England and the United States began making unscheduled stops at the island of Madeira to pick up the casks and stow them away in the holds to ripen in their own special way. Eventually the Madeira wine makers learned to re-create the seagoing conditions on land. Placing the new wine in specially heated chambers called *estufades,* they gradually increased its temperature to about 110°F, then slowly dropped it back to normal. This gave the wines the same desirable smoky quality and attractive caramel-like flavor they had acquired at sea.

Madeiras range in color from pale straw to an almost blackish brown. They differ not only in their grape varieties and degree of ripeness but in their vinification styles as well; they are either fermented quite dry or retain a degree of sweetness. The four types are: sercial, verdelho, malmsey, and bual. Malmsey and bual are the sweetest examples. They come from the lower warmer coastal vineyards where their early-ripening grapes are gathered at the start of September. Sercial and Verdelho come from a high volcanic plateau in the cooler north, where their grapes mature somewhat later. (Sometimes the grapes are also late harvested so as to concentrate their sweetness.)

Sercial, the leanest and lightest colored of the wines, is crisp and dry, displaying at its finest an extraordinary fragrance and bouquet. Verdelho, medium dry and a bit darker, is softer, more fruity, and quite fragrant, with a faintly honeyed sweetness. Rainwater, a variant, is a blend of fairly light verdelhos, developed in the nineteenth century by a Georgia wine importer. Pale in color, rainwater is vinified both dry and medium sweet. Bual (*boal* in Portuguese), a shade darker than verdelho is a sweeter and more full-bodied wine, combining a fragrant, lovely bouquet with a fresh, clean bittersweet aftertaste. Malmsey, the sweetest, richest, and darkest wine of all, is luscious and velvety with a great fragrant bouquet. It is also generously spirited and quite long-lived.

Vermouth

Vermouth is a flavored as well as a fortified wine. The idea of flavoring wines goes back to ancient times when flowers, leaves, roots, bark, herbs, and spices were added to improve the palatability of the coarse, rough, unaged wines then made. The Sumerians, Egyptians, and Greeks all flavored their wines. The Romans modified them with honey, spices, and roasted date pits.

Herb-infused wines have long been associated with the healing arts. Hippocrates administered such a wine in the fourth century B.C. In the Middle Ages, apothecaries dispensed a similarly prepare "hippocras." Flavored wines in the seventeenth century were taken as antidotes against the plague. And in the alpine regions of France and Italy, where herbs and aromatics grow in profusion, farm women still use such wines as home remedies.

Vermouth gets its name from one of its principal flavorings, wormwood (known as *wermut* in German), a woody herb with slightly aromatic blossoms that gives the wine a characteristically wry taste and a slightly bitter tang. Other flavoring agents include minty hyssop, bitter orange, angostura, cardamom, nutmeg, vanilla beans, cloves, allspice, cinnamon, cinchona bark, quinine bark, sweet marjoram, rosemary, sage, savory, thyme, hops, saffron, angelica, gentian root, cassia wood, linden tea, wild strawberries, and rhubarb.

Most vermouth formulas are privately held, some so closely guarded that they are handed down as proprietary secrets only within the family. For a typical vermouth, the formula calls for about fifteen flavorings although some have employed as many as fifty. Characterizing the best examples is a well-balanced flavor, rather than the predominance of any one ingredient.

Their bases —involving either white or red wines— are generally undistinguished since vermouth's character derives mainly from its botanical flavorings and aromatics, which are introduced either by maceration or infusion. Maceration slowly steeps the ingredients in a small amount of wine to produce a concentrate, which is added to the base wine. Infusion adds the flavorings directly to the wine itself. After flavoring several batches, the botanicals and aromatics are replaced by fresh ingredients (Lesser vermouths steep their aromatics in a high-proof alcohol, which speeds up the extraction of their flavors.).

NOTE: Quality vermouths are aged two to four years, while lesser vermouths are not aged at all but filtered or pasteurized instead.

Vermouths are vinified both dry and sweet. The drier and lighter-bodied examples contain 2 to 4 percent sugar; the sweeter contain as much as 14 to 16 percent. Dry vermouths are generally quite pale but this is not necessarily a sign of quality. (Charcoal filtering often lightens them.) France is generally associated with the dry vermouths and Italy with the sweet; although each country produces both. The French use rather dry acidic wines, such as thin Heraults from the Midi and lesser Sauternes as their base. They round out and enhance the best examples with mistelle, a sweet concentrate combining unfermented grape juice with brandy. The Italians, using muscat wines, produce somewhat rounder, more direct vermouths, which are made in four styles: *secco* (dry white), *bianco* (sweet white), *rosso* (semisweet red) and *rosé* (semidry rosé).

Ranging widely in their base wines and flavorings, vermouths are now produced all over the world: in Spain, Portugal, South Africa, Australia, South America, along with the United States.

Marsala

Marsala acquired its name from Mash-el-Allah —Arabic for "Haven of God"—the Sicilan port from which the wine was first shipped. (Sicily had long been under Arab rule.)

Marsala began as a potent but generally undistinguished Mediterranean wine. A Liverpool merchant, adding brandy to prevent its spoilage in shipping, commendably transformed the wine, giving it a rich full flavor and a sherrylike texture. The British, looking for alternatives to their more expensive ports and sherries, turned to this newly fortified wine and began importing it in quantity. In the process, they refined and modernized its production. By the mid-nineteenth century, Marsala had become another favorite British drink.

Traditionally, Marsala is fortified with *sifone* or *mistella*, a mixture of distilled wine alcohol and the must of nearly overripe grapes. The wine is then aged for several months in wood. Marsala is made in several styles: *fini, superiori,* and *vergini.* The fini and superiori Marsalas are sweetened with *mosto cotto,* a concentrated syrup of boiled-down grape must. The fini, containing 5 percent sugar, is aged in wood for at least a year and used mainly in cooking. The superiori is aged two years and may contain as much as 10 percent sugar. It's served as a dessert wine. (A special superiori, Vino da Meditazione, a full-bodied, semisweet, and silky blend, includes reserve wines dating back to the last century.) The highest quality Marsala is the unsweetened vergini. Brought up to 18 percent alcohol by fortification and aged at least five years, vergini owes its excellence in part to its passage through a solera system. (The wine is also known as *soleras* and *vino perpetuo.*) *Stravecchio* or *riserva vergini* has been aged in a solera for a decade.

4

HISTORY AND GEOGRAPHY

For thousands of years, wine has been part of the human experience,
a hallmark of civilization along with art, architecture, agriculture, and medicine.
It has occupied an important and honored place in history and literature as well.
Wine has also served as a focal point in religious services and in personal
celebrations such as birthdays, weddings, and anniversaries. Wine in fact is a
metaphor for the good life, a token of fellowship, and an expression of romance.

Historians have traced the grape to Asia Minor, to somewhere between the Black and the Caspian seas. They date wine's origins to some time between 6000 and 4000 B.C. The earliest known evidence has been found in the residue at the bottom of pottery jars discovered in the ruins of an ancient neolithic village, located in what is now Iran.

In Egypt, grape seeds and wine jars were found in tombs dating back to about 3000 B.C. (Apparently the wine was meant to refresh the pharaohs in their afterlife.) A Sumerian epic tells of an enchanted landscape, which yielded a wine that made the drinker immortal.

In ancient agrarian societies —involving the Mesopotamians, Hebrews, Egyptians, Phoenicians, Greeks, Etruscans, and Romans— the cultivation of vineyards, the art of making wine, and the appreciation of wine; were all held in high esteem. Both the Old and New Testament allude frequently to wine. In Judaism, wine consecrates the Sabbath. In Christianity, it sanctifies the Eucharist. (Although the Koran permits cultivating the grape, it forbids the drinking of wine.)

In the fourth century B.C., the Greeks were spreading wine making throughout the Mediterranean region. They introduced the practice to Sicily, Italy, the Iberian Peninsula, and southern Gaul. The Romans were especially influential. As their legions conquered lands as far north as the Rhine and eastward along the Danube, they planted vineyards wherever they went. Wine sustained the morale of their troops and and comforted their officials far from home. Virgil noted that the wines of Greece and Rome were "as innumerable as the grains of sand in the sea."

In their conquests, the Romans demonstrated that grapes could flourish in a wide range of climates and soils. In the process, they established the foundations of some of the greatest wine regions. By the second century A.D., the broad outlines of French and German viticulture were already evident.

During the Middle Ages, wine making was largely an ecclesiastic activity. Through decades of trial and error, the monks had developed great skill in cultivating and vinifying their grapes. It was said, "Wherever a monk may go, a vine will surely grow." The Church was to develop some of the world's finest vineyards in Burgundy and Germany.

The returning Crusaders planted the vines they brought back as souvenirs from the Middle East and so introduced new grape varieties to Europe. During the Renaissance, wine became the symbol of the power of the princes. In the seventeenth and eighteenth centuries, Europeans of considerable wealth acquired their own vineyards. Early in the nineteenth century, the rise of great banking and industrial fortunes, enabled the wealthy to invest in the châteaus of Bordeaux and to make them well known. Meanwhile, the less fortunate European citizens, seeking a better life, were migrating to North and South America, South Africa, Australia, and New Zealand, bringing their traditional wine-making skills to these new lands. In our own time, men who made their fortunes in business are establishing wineries in California, motivated not so much by financial gain but by the prestige and enjoyment of wine making.

Wine is now a vital element in the economy of many nations. The largest producers are Italy, France, Argentina, Spain, and Chile. (Italy and France alone account for about half of the world's production.) Other prolific countries are the United States and Portugal. Wine making also plays a significant role in the economies of Germany, Switzerland, Hungary, the former Yugoslavia, Romania, Greece, Bulgaria, and Israel. It is practiced as well in South Africa, Australia, New Zealand, Syria, Turkey, Algeria, Morocco, Egypt, Mexico, Russia, Brazil, and Uruguay, among others.

Largely European at the start, wine making has become global in scope. For a number of countries, national boundaries no longer contain their wine growing and wine-making activities. French Champagne makers are producing sparkling wines in Argentina, Australia, and California. Spanish firms are making sparkling wines in California. In the eighteenth and nineteenth centuries, the Germans had set up their own Champagne-producing establishments in France, creating the successful dynasties that continue to this day.

The Australians have acquired wineries in France and California. The owners of some Bordeaux estates are investing in Chilean and American wine production, while others in Burgundy have set up their operations in the American Northwest. (The French have also invested in Portuguese wine-making.) Meanwhile Italian wineries are buying vineyards in Eastern Europe; Californians are investing in Chilean wineries and acquiring vineyards in the south of France, while the Japanese have been buying wine properties in California and France.

FRANCE

The French produce some of the world's most magnificent wines and a number of commonplace ones as well. When the Romans arrived in southern Gaul, they found its people already engaged in viticulture. (The Phoenicians had planted muscat vines near what is now Marseilles.) Grape growing subsequently moved north through the Rhône Valley and into Alsace. Disseminating the grape further, the Romans planted vines wherever they went: in Burgundy, the Loire Valley, and Champagne. As admiration for the wines of Gaul grew, those of Rome began to lose favor. In A.D. 92 the Roman emperor Domitian issued an edict that called for the uprooting of all vineyards north of the Alps. His edict was only partially heeded.

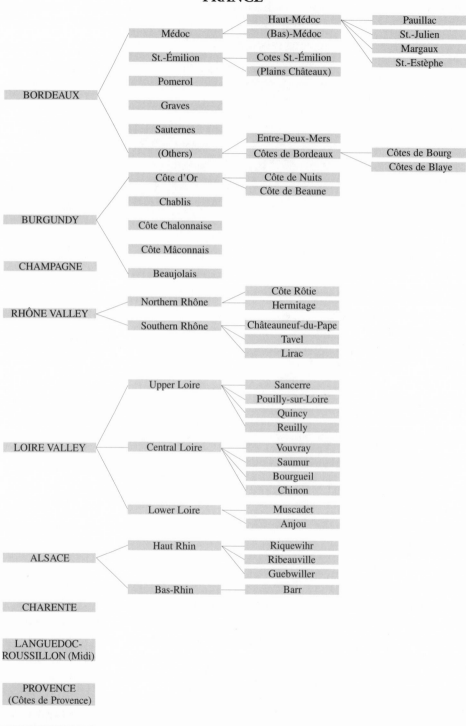

FRANCE

French wine growing now covers more than 3 million acres, stretching from the sunny south where it began, to the cooler regions northeast of Paris. (In the south, France is warmed by Mediterranean breezes; in the north, it's chilled by austere winds from the Atlantic Ocean.) There are seven major wine regions in the country: Bordeaux, Burgundy, Champagne, Alsace, the Rhône Valley, the Loire Valley, and the south of France.

Bordeaux

The largest and most important wine region is Bordeaux, located in the southwest, with more than two hundred thousand acres in vines. The Romans were the earliest champions of the region. Julius Caesar himself admired its wines and the poet Ausonius once owned a vineyard here.

Bordeaux takes its name from its port city, located on the banks of the Gironde River. (The Gironde, a broad estuary formed by the confluence of the Garonne and Dordogne rivers, flows in a northwesterly direction to the Bay of Biscay and then out into the Atlantic.) Although the city itself is located some fifty miles inland, the Gironde River enabled Bordeaux to become a major port, giving the residents easy access to the outside world and making the wines of Bordeaux widely known.

It was the English not the French, however, who were largely responsible for the fame of the Bordeaux wines. In 1152, when Eleanor, daughter of the French duke of Aquitaine, married Henry Plantagenet of England, her dowry included the province of Gascony, encompassing all of Bordeaux. Two years later, when Henry ascended to the throne of England, Gascony became a possession of the British Crown. The English, producing virtually no wine of their own, were enchanted by the red wines of Bordeaux. They admired their bright red ruby color and sumptuous bouquet, calling them *clarets*. (*Clairet* is French for "clear.") By the fourteenth century, nearly half the Bordeaux wines were shipped to England duty free.

When the French reclaimed their territory in 1453, some of the Britons stayed on as wine merchants and exporters. The French, however, tightly circumscribed their activities. They did not allow them to live inside the city walls or to establish offices there. Permitted to enter the city only between the hours of sunrise and sunset, the British set up their outposts on the Quai des Chartrons, a three-mile stretch along the Garonne River. (Some wine brokers still operate on the Quai des Chartrons.) Through their energy and enterprise, the British amassed considerable wealth and power. Through intermarriage, they acquired land of their own. By the nineteenth century, a number of Bordeaux vineyards were carrying such Anglo-Saxon names as Lynch-Bages, Talbot, and Langoa Barton.

The English influence extended to Bordeaux's law of inheritance, which was to have a great impact on the grape growing and wine making. According to French law, a father's property is divided among all his children, but English law passes the property on to the eldest child. Adopting the English law kept the region's large vineyards relatively intact and gave wine making here a greater continuity and consistency than elsewhere in the country. Many of the vineyards are still extensive, averaging at least one hundred to two hundred acres.

Covering a wide gamut, Bordeaux's wines range from the acclaimed offerings of the great estates to the uncomplicated and even the inconsequential. The region's northern sector specializes largely in red wines and the southern in white wines. The central sector produces both. The red wines blend the austere cabernet sauvignon with the merlot, cabernet franc, malbec, and petit verdot. Uncompromisingly rough when young, they possess at their finest the ability to age magnificently. At maturity, they can acquire a rich plummy depth of flavor, a black-currant bouquet, and a lingering aftertaste while retaining their basic austerity. The white wines —pressed from sauvignon blanc, sémillon and muscadelle grapes— are also full-bodied and flavorful. These wines range from the steely whites of Graves to the luscious noble rots of Sauternes.

Most significant of Bordeaux's thirty-five wine districts are the Médoc, St.-Émilion, Pomerol, Graves, and Sauternes.

The Médoc

A large peninsula on the west bank of the Gironde, the Médoc extends some fifty miles north of the city of Bordeaux, almost to the point where the river flows into the Atlantic Ocean. Well over half of the best vineyards in France are located here. The southern sector, a long strip of gently rolling land known as Haut-Médoc, is the source of some of the world's most elegant and complex wines which are characterized by great charm and finesse, rich fruit and fragrance. The smaller northern sector, the Bas-Médoc, with a flatter terrain, yields less concentrated and less interesting wines. ("Médoc" usually refers to wines from the Haut-Médoc.)

Of the twenty-eight wine-producing townships or communes in the Médoc, the largest and most prestigious is Pauillac, located some thirty miles north of the city of Bordeaux. Pauillac's red wines are notable for their subtlety, intensity, and elegance. The top estates here, sited on alluvial slopes above the Gironde River, include three world-famous châteaux: Lafite-Rothschild, Latour, and Mouton-Rothschild. Their wines, unsurpassed in magnificence and refinement, combine great generosity with an underlying intensity and the potential for great age. Traditionally, the Mouton wines are the most robust and the Latours are the softest, while the Lafites demonstrate a fine balance of powerful tannins and excellent fruit. Other major Pauillac estates are the châteaux Pichon-Lalande, Pichon-Baron, Clerc-Milon, Lynch-Bages, and Pontet-Canet.

The communes that follow Pauillac in their concentration of high-quality vineyards are St.-Estèphe to the north, St.-Julien directly to the south, and Margaux farther south.

St.-Estèphe, the northernmost township, brings forth on its claylike soil the Médoc's sturdiest and most robust reds. Harder and less yielding than the Pauillac wines, these are rough edged and tannic at the start, but acquire a superb concentration and a richness of flavor at maturity. They are also quite long-lived.

Margaux, the southernmost of the leading Médoc communes, features the thinnest soil and the highest proportion of rough gravel. Its red wines are remarkable for their delicacy and elegance. Silky, yet intensely powerful at their finest, they display a lovely ethereal quality, and a haunting violetlike bouquet. Margaux also produces small quantities of an exquisite white wine.

In St.-Julien, the smallest of the key communes, most of the vineyards face south. Grown here are some of the Médoc's most approachable red wines. Fuller than the Margaux and faster maturing than the Pauillacs, they are medium-bodied, well-knit and generous in their fruit. Never harsh or tannic, these wines are ready to drink at a fairly young age. St.-Julien's best-known vineyard is Château Ducru-Beaucaillou, which translates as "Beautiful Pebbles," a reference to its generally gravelly soil.

Other significant Médoc communes are Moulis, Cantenac, and Listrac. Moulis, located between Margaux and St.-Julien, produces dependable well-balanced red wines, which possess the ability to age well. The outstanding vineyard here is Château Chasse-Spleen, whose name translates roughly as "Chasing the Blues Away." Another is Château Poujeaux. Adjoining Margaux is the commune of Cantenac, whose wines share some of the same delicacy and grace. (These are often labeled "Cantenac-Margaux.")

Listrac, a few miles west of Pauillac, St.-Julien, and Margaux, had long been considered a backwater, associated with ordinary Bordeaux wines. It is now the site of Château Clarke, an estate created by Baron Edmond de Rothschild and his son Benjamin. Together they have transformed a virtually forgotten estate on unprepossessing acreage into an estimable and significant vineyard.

St.-Émilion

The most productive of the top Bordeaux districts is St.-Émilion, located on the right bank of the Dordogne, some twenty-five miles east of the city of Bordeaux. Its soil, a heavy and generally gravelly stretch of sand covered by clay and chalky limestone, is almost the reverse of the Médoc's. Its predominant grape is the softer merlot, not the more austere cabernet sauvignon of the Médoc. The region's commercial center is the city of Libourne.

St.-Émilion's wines, generally a blend of the merlot, cabernet franc, and bouschet, are the heartiest of the great red Bordeaux, Sturdy, supple, and generous, they are rounder and more approachable than the Médocs. At their finest, they display a great depth of color and a spicy fullness. Nicely balancing out their roundness is a degree of flintiness.

The region's relatively small vineyards are clustered around the ancient town of St.-Émilion. They are divided into an inner group called the Côtes St.-Émilion and an outer group called the Plains Châteaus. The inner Côtes St.-Émilion is situated on the mostly chalky slopes of a rocky plateau adjacent to the town. Its preeminent estate is Château Ausone, named for Ausonius, the fourth-century Roman poet who once owned the property. Other notable estates are the châteaus Canon, La Magdelaine, La Gaffliére, Pavie, Clos Fourtet, Bel-Air, and Beauséjour. The outer Plains Châteaus are located on a gravelly plain below the town. Their leading estate is the celebrated Cheval Blanc, whose wines at their finest display softness together with a fine bouquet, and exhibit an extraordinary distinction. Other notable St.-Émilion vineyards are the Châteaus Figeac, La Tour-du-Pin, Croque-Michotte, Corbin, and Dominique St.-Émilion.

Five small villages nearby and a portion of a sixth are legally permitted to append the St.-Émilion name to their own, although they share neither the same exposure nor wine quality. These are are St. Georges-St.-Émilion, Montagne-St.-Émilion, Sables-St.-Émilion, Puisseguin-St.-Émilion, Lussac-St.-Émilion and Parsac-St.-Émilion.

Pomerol

The tiny commune of Pomerol is the smallest of Bordeaux's fine wine districts, with only about two thousand acres in vines. Tucked in as an appendage of St.-Émilion, it was long considered its satellite, but early in the twentieth century Pomerol declared its autonomy and went on to become an official wine district of its own.

As in St.-Émilion, Pomerol's predominant grape is the merlot. Grown on sandier soil, it yields some of the region's most accessible wines. Although similar in structure, taste, and bouquet to the other Médocs, its wines at their finest are richer, more robust, rounder, and more plummy. The French say that the Pomerols have more gras (fatness). The wines also display a dark lustrous ruby color, a violetlike bouquet, and a remarkable trufflelike scent. Pomerol's leading estate is Château Pétrus.

Three nearby communes of interest are Fronsac to the west on the banks of the Dordogne, and Lalande-de-Pomerol and Néac to the north. Fronsac is known for its robust, deep-colored reds, which tend to display a great softness of body and considerable fruit. Notable properties here are the Côtes de Fronsac and Canon-Fronsac, the latter being best known for its Château Canon wine. Lalande-de-Pomerol, separated from Pomerol by a small stream, shares the same sandy soil but not quite the same exposure, making for somewhat lighter red wines. (They lack the concentration and consistent quality of their more esteemed neighbors.) Néac's wines are generally ordinary, but on occasion they bear a passing resemblance to those of Pomerol.

Graves

Graves, located directly south of the Médoc, is named for its characteristically gravel like soil. Although the grapes ripen earlier here, its wines are so similar in breed and finesse to the Médocs that they are often mistaken for them. Velvety and quite dry, they're remarkable for their dark brilliant color, their subtle character, and their long life.

The most outstanding Graves commune is Pessac, home of the estimable and world-famous Château Haut-Brion. Of almost comparable importance is Château La Mission-Haut-Brion, an estate located just across the road and under the same ownership. A vineyard to the southwest is Château Pape-Clément, known for its high-quality, but somewhat lighter-colored wines.

Graves also produces many fine white wines, ranging from the fairly dry to the medium sweet. The best examples display a richness and depth combined with a long lingering aftertaste. Further enhancing them is a faint yet distinctive metallic edge. The most celebrated white-wine estates in Graves are the Châteaus Carbonnieux and Olivier.

NOTE: Many of the notable vineyards here produce both red and white wines. Although Château Haut-Brion is best known for its reds, about a tenth of its output is devoted to whites. Château Carbonnieux is best known for its white wines while yielding good reds as well. Other red-and-white vineyards are located in Martillac, a commune to the south.

Sauternes

The southernmost of the major Bordeaux districts is Sauternes, located on the west bank of the Garonne River, about twenty miles south of the city of Bordeaux. An area of gently rolling hills and misty lowlands covering about forty square miles, Sauternes is named for one of its five top communes. (The other four are Barsac, Pommes, Preignac, and Fargues.) All five specialize in white wines and grow sémillon, sauvignon blanc, and muscadelle grapes.

Sauternes is particularly celebrated for its noble-rot wines, the quintessential example comes from Château d'Yquem, an estate situated on one of the region's highest hills. (The vineyards here descend to the river.) Château d'Yquem is a wine of luscious splendor. Described as "pure gold by the glass," it exhibits an astonishing fullness of body and a depth of vinosity. A subtle, lovely perfume balances out its opulent richness. Another outstanding botrytized wine comes from Château Rieussec in the commune of Fargues. North of Sauternes is the larger commune of Barsac, whose similar but somewhat more austere wines are a shade drier and a bit less concentrated. (The lesser sweet wines made here halt fermentation before all their grape sugar has fermented out.)

NOTE: In years when the Sauternes grapes don't achieve their botrytized ripeness and yield drier, more ordinary wines, Château d'Yquem labels them "Y" or "Ygrec" and Château Rieussec labels them "R."

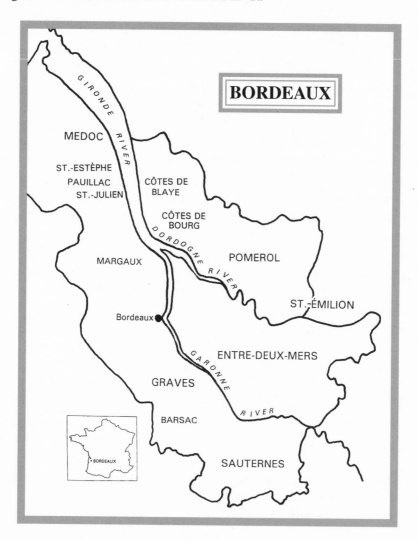

Other Bordeaux Districts

Located directly across the Gironde River from the Médoc are two districts: Côte de Bourg and the larger Côtes de Blaye to the north, producing red wines. Growing mainly the cabernet franc on their fertile high-clay soils, they yield unpretentious, light-colored, fruity, and quick-maturing reds. The Côtes de Blaye produces some white wine as well.

Across the Garonne River from Graves and Sauternes are a number of districts producing primarily white wines. Most notable is Entre-Deux-Mers (whose name translates as "Between Two Seas.") A large triangular wedge of land formed by the confluence of the Garonne and Dordogne Rivers, Entre-Deux-Mers grows sémillon and sauvignon blanc grapes. Its naturally sweet wine resembles a simple Sauternes, but is often vinified dry now to suit current tastes.

Across the river from Sauternes and Barsac are the Premières Côtes de Bordeaux, St. Croix-du-Mont, Loupiac, Cadillac, and Cérons. Their white wines tend to be sweet, pleasant, and generally not very full-bodied or intense. The Premières Côtes de Bordeaux —a narrow ridge of limestone cliffs extending about thirty miles on the east bank of the Garonne— produces decidedly sweet, small-scale white wines in its southern sector and quickly developing reds in its northern sector. Loupiac and Cadillac are also red-and-white wine producers. The tiny Cérons district north of Barsac is noted for its sweet white dessert wines, which range from light to medium in body. The wines of St. Croix-du-Mont are also quite sweet and high in their alcohol.

The Bordeaux Classifications

Most influential in establishing the current prices for Bordeaux wines is a classification system, casually introduced in 1855 at an exposition in Paris (the Exposition Universelle), which was designed to showcase French products. The Bordeaux Chamber of Commerce, wishing to promote the region's wines, decided to draw up a list of the region's leading vineyards to be featured at the exposition. The chamber established a committee, made up mainly of wine brokers, to do so. After some bitter infighting, the committee reached a consensus, basing its selections largely on the relative values of the vineyard soils and the prices their wines had fetched in previous years.

The 1855 list, known as the Classement des Grand Crus de la Gironde (Classification of the Gironde's Great Growths), included a number of red-wine vineyards in the Médoc and a number of white-wine vineyards in Sauternes. The wines themselves were called Crus Classés (Classified Growths).

Selected from the more than three thousand red-wine properties in Bordeaux were only sixty-one vineyards: they were divided into five categories; Premier Cru Classé (First Classified Growth) and Deuxième, Troisième, Quatrième and Cinquième Crus (Second, Third, Fourth and Fifth Classified Growths). Of the four estates awarded the Premier Crus, three were in the Médoc: Château Lafite-Rothschild, Latour, and Margaux; the fourth, Haut-Brion, was located in Graves. Fifteen of the remaining red-wine vineyards were classified as Second Growths, fourteen as Thirds, ten as Fourths and eighteen as Fifths.

NOTE: The 1980s saw the rise of Super-Seconds, the second-tier vineyards whose wines often matched the famous firsts and could be priced as much as 20 percent higher than their less-honored colleagues in the Second-Growth group.

Also established in 1855 were four lower-ranked red-wine classifications: Cru Exceptionnel, Cru Bourgeois Supérieure, Cru Bourgeois (CB), and Artisans et Paysans. Proprietors assigned to the lowest rank —and not pleased to find themselves there— appropriated the next higher classification, thus rendering their own category obsolete.

The white-wine listing included twenty-two Sauternes vineyards divided into three categories: Premier Grand Cru (First Great Growth), Premier Cru (First Growth) and Deuxième Cru (Second Growth). Awarded the highest rank was the estimable Château d'Yquem, granted a special category of its own. The Premier Cru went to nine others and the Deuxième Cru to another twelve.

In 1932, new classifications were established for nearly four hundred and fifty red-wine estates in the Médoc which had been excluded from the original listing. These categories were: Bourgeois Supérieur de Haut-Medoc, Bourgeois de Haut-Médoc and Bas-Médoc. Proprietors assigned the Bas-Médoc classification —and displeased with its lower connotation— featured only the "Médoc" on their labels, rendering their own category obsolete. Subsequently, a hundred other excluded Médoc vineyards formed their own syndicate, giving a Cru Exceptionnel to eighteen of its members and a Cru Bourgeois (CB) to sixty others.

Wine makers in St.-Émilion and Pomerol, rankled by their complete exclusion from the 1855 classifications, began to create their own. The St.-Émilion vintners gave themselves so many Premier Crus that their beleaguered Chamber of Commerce turned to the government for help. In 1958, four official St.-Émilion categories were created; the first two were the most significant: Premier Grand Cru Classé (First Classified Great Growth), awarded to twelve vineyards and Deuxième Grand Cru Classé (Second Classified Great Growth), given to seventy others. Transcending both was Hors Classé (In a Class by Itself), the equivalent of a Médoc First Growth. It was awarded to St.-Émilion's two preeminent estates: the Châteaus Ausone and Cheval Blanc.

Pomerol, not to be outdone, established its own three classifications: Premier Grand Cru, Premier Cru and Deuxième Cru, with the top rank going to ten vineyards.

Pomerol's most esteemed estate, Château Petrus, was declared Hors Classé. In 1959, Graves established classifications for thirteen of its own wines, giving Château Haut-Brion the same Premier Cru it had received in the original 1855 listing and elevating its neighboring estate, Château La Mission-Haut-Brion, across the road to the same prestigious rank. Château Carbonnieux was named the leading white-wine estate here.

NOTE: These various classified growths in Bordeaux represent only about 2 percent of the region's annual production.

The 1855 listing has proved to be an almost immutable force in setting the prices for Bordeaux wines. (The elite Cru Classés still command the highest prices.) The listing has wielded considerable influence on the international wine scene as well. Yet experts agree that Bordeaux's classification system is in need of a serious overhaul. They say that its rigid sequential structure invariably implies the inferiority of the lower-ranked wines, although in professional tastings, the so-called lesser wines have often scored higher than some top-ranked wines. (A second growth may outshine a first and a fifth can be the equivalent of a second, while a Cru Bourgeois may rival its more prestigious neighbors.)

Critics have also pointed out that of the original sixty-one Médoc vineyards, only thirty or forty still export their wines in significant quantities. (And they note that although St.-Julien contains more classified chateaus than any other Bordeaux commune, it cannot claim a single Premier Cru vineyard.) Moreover, certain châteaus have moved away from their original sites or have incorporated additional parcels of land into their estates. Nor taken into account have been the successive and inevitable changes of ownership. Some vineyards have deteriorated in the hands of indifferent or absentee owners, while others have been much improved by the change. Some owners have also introduced new grape varieties and modified their viticultural and vinification practices. In 1951, Château Prieuré-Cantenac consisted of some thirty-two acres of rundown vines. It now encompasses about one hundred seventy thriving acres. Some years ago when the Japanese took over Château Lagrange in St.-Julien, they not only restored its vineyards and its cellars but also modified the blend itself.

Vineyard names have been changed as well. Prieuré-Cantenac is now Prieuré-Lichine. Château Longueville au Baron de Pichon-Longueville has been shortened to Pichon-Baron, while Pichon-Longueville Comtesse de Lalande has been abbreviated to Pichon-Lalande. Château Mouton d'Armailhacq had been renamed Mouton-Baronne in memory of the wife of the owner, Baron Phillipe de Rothschild. After his death, his daughter restored the name to Armailhac, dropping both the final "q" and the Mouton prefix.

The owners of the high-ranking estates have continually blocked any attempt to update the 1855 listings, fearing a drastic overhaul might demote their properties or banish them entirely. In the 1950s, the owners of the classified châteaus established a committee to work on a revision, but its proposals created such a furor that any effort at reform was quickly dropped. So fixed have the Bordeaux classifications become that only one major change has occurred in more than a century. When Philippe de Rothschild took over Château Mouton-Rothschild in 1922, he vowed to have its status upgraded. After fifty years of active campaigning, he finally succeeded in advancing Mouton from a Second to a First Growth. (The Minister of Agriculture issued a special decree to that effect in 1973.) The château's motto had been: *Premier ne puis. Second ne daigne. Mouton suis.* (I cannot be first, I do not wish to be second. I am Mouton.) After its elevation, the estate's motto became: *Premier je suis. Second je fus. Mouton ne change.* (I am first. I was second. Mouton never changes.)

Today, three of the four of Bordeaux's most prestigious vineyards are owned by foreign interests or international families. Château Haut-Brion is the property of an American banking firm. Latour, having been run by a British food-and-beverage conglomerate for thirty years, has been returned to French ownership. Lafite has been acquired by another branch of the Rothschild family.

In the 1960s and 1970s, the French government, seeking to deter further foreign acquisition, declared that the important vineyard estates were the country's "national treasures." When the prestigious Château Margaux came on the market in 1974, the government turned down the bid of an American firm, wishing to purchase the estate and permitted the Greek-born owner of a French grocery chain to acquire that significant property instead.

In the 1980s, the French government shifted its position, declaring that long-term investments by foreign interests could contribute to the "dynamism" of the French wine industry. Since then, Japanese, American, Danish, Swiss, and German interests have acquired important vineyard properties. The winds seem to be shifting again; French banks and insurance companies are now competing to purchase a number of the leading wine estates. In recent years, several major châteaus, owned by French families, have been sold to large corporations.

Burgundy

Burgundy, in east-central France, is the country's second major wine region. Extending about one hundred and eighty miles between Chablis and Lyon, the region is less than a sixth the size of Bordeaux. Its administrative capital is Dijon; its wine capital is Beaune. Burgundy experiences generally volatile weather, with fog and wind roaring down from Alps, causing its vintages to vary greatly. (Usually about one year in three can be considered good.)

Wine making in Burgundy goes back to ancient times. The Gauls and Romans planted some of the first vineyards here. Today they are a patchwork of divided ownership, their fragmentation going back to the French Revolution when the big estates belonging to the Church and the nobility were parceled out to the people. The French law of inheritance split the land into even tinier plots through successive generations. (The law calls for a father's property to be divided among all his children.) As a result, many vineyards now average less than twenty-five acres; a number consist of only a few rows of vines. Some parcels in the famous vineyards consist of only half a row. (Traditionally the landowner and the wine maker divide up the vintage, with each receiving half of the wine.) Due to the fragmentation, shippers have long dominated the wine trade in Burgundy.

Despite sharing certain fundamental characteristics of site and soil, Burgundy wines vary substantially in style because the hundreds of small producers differ widely, not only in their individual approaches to pruning, harvesting, and vinification, but in their skills and experience. Wine quality even in the most famous vineyards, can vary considerably from one small parcel to the next.

Burgundy's wines are red, white and rosé, still and sparkling. The red wines account for about 75 percent of the output. Pressed primarily from the pinot noir, these are generous and full-bodied, less austere than those of Bordeaux. The wines are characterized at their finest by an intensity of flavor, a velvety texture, and a remarkably perfumed bouquet. They also display an unmistakable rich earthy quality, known as *goût de terroir* ("taste of the soil"). The finest examples demonstrate restraint and may seem dry and tarry at first, but exhibit a great intensity of fruit and a complexity of flavor. The whites, pressed primarily from the chardonnay, combine a rich fruitiness with a definite dryness. They demonstrate, an intensity of flavor, a somewhat spare elegance, and a touch of smokiness at their finest. (The region's other white varieties include the pinot blanc and aligoté.)

Burgundy encompasses five major wine districts: the Côte d'Or, Côte Chalonnaise, the Mâconnais, Beaujolais, and Chablis.

Côte d'Or

Burgundy's most important district is the Côte d'Or, whose name translates as "Golden Slope." (This derives from the burnished appearance the vineyards take on in autumn when the foliage blazes with color.) Covering some twenty-two thousand acres in central Burgundy, the Côte d'Or is in effect a limestone shelf, never much more than a mile wide. Beginning at Dijon and extending some forty miles southwest, it ends at the town of Santenay. The best vineyards here are located eight hundred to a thousand feet above sea level. Sited on a sunny southern slope, they're sheltered from the wind and rain sweeping in from the west. (Wines grown on the northern slope carry the lesser "Haute Côte de Nuits" label.)

The Côte d'Or is divided just about evenly in two. In the north is the Côte de Nuits, named for its principal city, Nuits-St.-Georges and extending from Dijon to Beaune. In the south is the Côte de Beaune, named for the city of Beaune, Burgundy's ancient capital, and extending from Aloxe-Corton to Santenay.

Côte de Nuits

The Côte de Nuits begins near the town of Fixin and ends some twelve miles south, near Prémeaux. Grown here on a soil of limestone, silica, and clay are Burgundy's greatest red wines. Deep colored, velvety textured, fruity, and delightfully tart, they combine a big mouth-filling flavor with a subtle, haunting bouquet.

The main Côte de Nuits communes or townships are Gevrey-Chambertin, Chambolle-Musigny, Vosne-Romanée and Nuits-St.-Georges. These are followed by Échézaux, Flagey-Échézaux, Morey-St.-Denis, Vougeot, and Fixin.

The uncontested leader of Gevrey-Chambertin's nine small vineyards, is le Chambertin, whose red wine is renowned for its magnificent character and power. Napoleon himself was partial to the wine and Alexandre Dumas said of it, "Nothing makes the future so rosy as contemplating it through a glass of Chambertin." Hilaire Belloc, in recalling a youthful idyll, wrote, "I forget the name of the place; I forget the name of the girl but the wine…was Chambertin."

Known for the splendor of its wine as well is the nearby Chambertin-Clos de Bèze vineyard. And across a narrow road is Charmes-Chambertin, whose admirable red wine exhibits only a touch less body and distinction than that of its two distinguished neighbors.

To the south are the estimable Mazoyères-Chambertin and Latricières-Chambertin vineyards, sharing much the same soil and exposure as le Chambertin and also producing rich, full-bodied, and distinguished red wines. Other Gevrey-Chambertin vineyards of significance are Mazis-Chambertin and the smaller Chapelle-Chambertin. Their wines too are notable for their strength and finesse. To the south, the commune of Morey-St.-Denis encompasses three outstanding vineyards: Clos de la Roche, Clos de Tart, and Clos St.-Denis. An underlying firmness distinguishes their sturdy and full-bodied red wines. South of Morey-St-Denis is the commune of Chambolle-Musigny, whose reds —lighter than the Chambertins— are considered the most charming and fragrant wines of the Côte d'Or. They display at their finest delicacy, refinement, and breed. Chambolle-Musigny's outstanding vineyards are les Musigny (whose ten owners share twenty-five acres) and the adjoining les Amoureuses to the east, along with les Charmes to the north and les Bonnes Mares still farther north and west. About four acres of Bonnes Mares are located in the Morey-St. Denis commune, while the remaining thirty-five acres are in Chambolle-Musigny. (A small amount of white wine is produced here as well.)

Directly to the south is the commune of Vougeot, the site of Clos de Vougeot, the Côte d'Or's largest and most famous vineyard. Consisting of about one hundred twenty-five acres, divided into sixty-five parcels, Clos de Vougeot is owned by about a hundred proprietors, including a number of syndicates. The vineyard owes much of its fame to the Confrérie des Chevaliers du Tastevin (Order of the Knights of the Tasting Cup), a celebrated eating-and-drinking society, founded in the 1930s, when a generally depressed economy and a series of poor vintages were battering the local wine merchants. Desperate to improve their lot, they initiated the confrérie (brotherhood) to promote the wines of Burgundy. They succeeded far better than they had ever imagined.

The confrérie's headquarters stands in the midst of the Clos de Vougeot vineyard and is housed in a magnificent structure built in the twelfth century by the Cistercian monks, who had planted the original vineyard. Held in this impressive building is a series of ceremonial dinners, whose ostensible purpose is to induct new members. Attending the ceremonies are hundreds of guests in formal attire. The presiding merchants wear sumptuous robes of crimson velour. During the elaborate rites, the initiates swear solemnly to empty their glasses whenever full, and to fill their glasses whenever empty. They vow that no wine other than a Burgundy shall cross their lips except under conditions of extreme duress; then they sip some of the Clos de Vougeot wine. The presiding officer, with equal solemnity, taps each initiate three times on the shoulder with a vine staff, then slips over the initiate's head a red-and-yellow ribbon to which a *tastevin*, a tasting cup, is attached. The tastevin, the symbol of the confrérie, is a small, shallow silver cup faceted with a row of indents around the bottom which reflect the light. (The cup is used in the dim Burgundy cellars to judge the wine's color and clarity as well as its taste.)

The elaborate Clos de Vougeot ceremonies and related promotional efforts have proven so effective that the confrérie now operates chapters in a number of countries and sells about 90 percent of the Clos de Vougeot wine abroad. Other French wine makers, impressed with the confrérie's success, have set up their own promotional activities, emphasizing pomp and circumstance and featuring festive rites, medieval robes, the sound of trumpets, and so on. In Burgundy, these groups include the Compagnons de Beaujolais and the Confrérie des Vignerons de Saint Vincent-et-Macon. In Bordeaux, there is the Commanderie du Bontemps de Médoc et Graves, the Jurade de St.-Émilion, and the Chevaliers des Lascombes de Margaux. (Sauternes and Barsac have their own commanderies.) In the Rhône Valley, wine merchants have established the Commanderie des Côtes du Rhône and in Alsace, the Confrérie de St. Etienne. Cahors in the southwest has created a Confrérie du Vin de Cahors to induct new chevaliers (knights) to its ranks. The idea has even spread to New York State's Hudson Valley, where a winery sponsors the Société de Vignerons, whose members help bring in the harvest and buy most of the wine that is produced.

South of Vougeot is the commune of Vosne-Romanée, much celebrated for its incomparable red wines. Preeminent among its forty-six vineyards is the prestigious Domaine de la Romanée-Conti or DRC, named for the Prince of Conti, who successfully outbid Madame Pompadour for the estate in the eighteenth century. The lady, once the favorite of Louis XV, had apparently lost her legendary charms by then and was unable to persuade the king that the property should be hers.

Considered Burgundy's greatest red-wine vineyard, the Domaine de la Romanée-Conti is little more than four acres, featuring a stony red soil made up of fragmented limestone with high levels of iron oxide. The wine it yields is perfectly balanced at its finest, and demonstrates a velvety texture, a great depth of flavor, and an extraordinary bouquet. (Since annual production here is less than seven hundred cases, the wine is sold by the bottle, not by the case.)

A few feet uphill and to the west is the tiny two-acre la Romanée vineyard, celebrated for its intensely perfumed, satiny wines. Two notable estates nearby are the thirteen-acre Romanée-St.-Vivant and the fifteen-acre La Tâche, both yielding finely scented wines. Characterizing these are a great depth of flavor and a long, lingering aftertaste. At the southernmost end of the Vosne-Romanée commune is Aux Malconsorts, whose wine also displays outstanding finesse, scent, and breed. And at the northern end, bounded by la Romanée-Conti and la Romanée, is le Richebourg, a vineyard, whose more deeply colored wines are generally sturdier and fuller-bodied than those of its more aristocratic neighbors.

To the north of le Richebourg are the vineyards of les Échézaux and les Grands-Échézaux. Their red wines, although not actually grown within the commune's borders, are close enough to the Vosne-Romanées in character to be grouped with them. Light colored, light bodied, and displaying considerable finesse, these wines are more remarkable for their subtlety than for their strength. The last major commune on the Côte de Nuits is Nuits-St.-Georges, situated at the southern end. The three leading vineyards here are les St.-Georges, les Cailles, and les Vaucrains. Their red wines are soft, generous, and well balanced, with a pleasant, slightly earthy flavor. Prémeaux, the southernmost commune here, is also known for its agreeable red wines. At the opposite or northernmost end of the Côte de Nuits is Fixin, whose outstanding vineyard is Clos de la Perrière. Noteworthy too is Clos du Chapitre to the east. Located at the northern end of the Côte de Nuits too is the little town of Marsannay-la-Côte, simply called Marsannay. The town is known for its delightful rosé, pressed from the pinot noir.

🍇 🍇 🍇

Côte de Beaune

The Côte de Beaune, the southern sector of the Côte d'Or, extends southward from Aloxe-Corton to Santenay. Much more prolific than the Côte de Nuits, it produces about twice as much wine. The Côte de Beaune also specializes in red wines, while producing excellent whites as well. The red wines, pressed from the pinot noir, are lighter in color and less robust and than their counterparts on the Côte de Nuits. The white wines, pressed primarily from the chardonnay, are characterized by a richness, floweriness, and a long, lingering bouquet.

The most important commune of the Côte de Beaune is Aloxe-Corton, known for its red wines although its whites are also highly regarded. Its leading vineyard is Corton, which produces a rich, dark red wine, considered one of the finest in the district. To the east is les Bressandes, a vineyard, sharing a similar soil and exposure and yielding full-flavored and scented wines. To the south and west is Corton-Charlemagne, renowned for its Chardonnays, which display at their finest depth, complexity, and a superb, unforgettable bouquet.

Tucked up on the side of the mountain behind the commune of Aloxe-Corton is the tiny village of Pernand-Vergelesses, primarily a red-wine producer. (White wines constitute about 10 percent of its output.) The red wine labels here read "Corton" and the white wine labels read "Corton-Charlemagne." To the south and west is Savigny-les-Beaune, another red-and-white-wine producer, but the red wines also predominate here.

Farther south, one hundred ninety miles southeast of Paris, is Beaune, the home of most of the Burgundy shippers. Like its neighbors, Beaune specializes in red wines while producing some white wines as well. Beaune is perhaps best known for its les Trois Glorieuses, an annual three-day harvest festival, culminating in a famous wine auction that is held on the third Sunday in November. (Dealers and wine enthusiasts from all over the world attend.) The significance of the auction extends far beyond the precincts of Beaune since the wines offered are a good indication of the size and character of the Burgundy crop. The annual prices established here indicate the market not only for the Burgundy wines but for the French wines in general.

The auction —initially organized in the fifteenth century to benefit a local almshouse— generates enough income to support the Hospices de Beaune, a local hospital that treats the city's sick and aged without charge. Over the years, its founders and patrons have donated vineyard properties to the hospital in addition to providing it with direct financial aid. Their donated parcels scattered among more than forty sites —and sometimes totaling no more than a quarter of an acre— represent nearly one hundred fifty acres of choice vineyard land. The wines they yield carry the Hospices de Beaune label.

NOTE: As has been the case with other successful wine promotions, the philanthropic auction idea has been adopted elsewhere. Beaujolais holds an annual auction for its Hospices de Beaujeau, while Nuits-St.-Georges holds one for its Hospices de Nuit. The Germans, inspired by the Trois Glorieuses event, honor the riesling grape during their *Glorreiche Rheingau Tage* ("Glorious Rheingau Days"), a harvest festival, featuring stylish dinners and wine tastings.

South of Beaune is the commune of Pommard. Produced here are some of Burgundy's most popular red wines. Fruity and not too deeply colored, they are celebrated for their scent and finesse, as well as for an unusual and gracious softness they demonstrate at an early age. Pommard's leading vineyards are les Épenots and les Rugiens.

To the south on a hilly slope is the commune of Volnay, producing both red and white wines. Volnay is best known for its red wines, which at their finest display breed, bouquet, and an intensity of flavor. The softest and most delicate of the fine red Burgundies, these —although light colored and light bodied— are nevertheless round and velvety. Volnay's most acclaimed vineyard is les Caillerets; others of note are les Champans and les Chevrets.

NOTE: The white wines of Volnay carry neither a commune nor a vineyard name, but are labeled "Meursault" instead, taking their name from a commune to the south which specializes in white wines.

The commune of Monthelie, southwest of Pommard, is known for its lightly scented reds, somewhat similar to the Pommard wines. Also to the south is the commune of Auxey-Duresses, which produces red and white wines, with the reds predominating. Still farther south is the hamlet of Blagny, which produces reds and whites, but is best known for its fine white wines.

Meursault, south of Volnay, has been called "The home of the great white Burgundies." (The wine output here is 90 percent white.) Dry and tangy, yet full in body, these wines display a remarkable softness, roundness, and scent; offering at their finest a luxuriously rich taste, a sumptuous texture, and a lingering hazelnut bouquet. Meursault's most notable vineyard is les Perrières; particularly admired for its central sector, Clos des Perrières.

NOTE: Held each November in Meursault is the *Paulée de Meursault*, a harvest celebration, at which a hundred or so producers assemble to exchange greetings and bottles of wine.

At the southern edge of Meursault are the adjacent communes of Puligny-Montrachet and Chassagne-Montrachet. Although producing almost twice as much red wine as white, these communes are known for their flavorful whites, which resemble the Meursaults in breed and class, but aren't nearly as soft or as round. The white wines here exhibit a certain firmness, a flowery richness, and an intensity of bouquet.

Burgundy's most celebrated white wine comes from the legendary le Montrachet vineyard, situated half in Puligny (where it's called le Montrachet) and half in Chassagne, (where it's called just plain Montrachet). A twenty-acre vineyard, it's shared by more than a dozen owners, whose parcels range from about a tenth to about five acres. (Only about three thousand cases are produced here annually.) Described as the "quintessential Chardonnay," the Montrachet wine is pale gold with a hint of green and dry, but not excessively so. Generous and smooth tasting, it combines great depth and complexity with an underlying soft-ness and succulence. In certain vintages, the wine attains an extraordinarily subtle flavor and a tremendous bouquet. Alexandre Dumas once said of le Montrachet, "I drink it only with head bared and on bended knee."

Two nearby vineyards are Chevalier-Montrachet, located on a slight slope to the west and Bâtard-Montrachet, on the slope below and to the east. Their pale gold, eminently dry wines also display at their finest an extraordinary wealth of flavor and bouquet.

Other notable white-wine vineyards on the Côte de Beaune are Bienvenue Bâtard-Montrachet and Criots-Bâtard-Montrachet, situated respectively in the communes of Puligny and Chassagne. At Chassagne's southern end is Morgeot, a ten-acre vineyard noted for its unusually deep-colored and long-lived red wines. Santenay, the southernmost of the important Côte de Beaune communes, is also known principally for its rather full-bodied red wines. While they register high levels of tannin, they are nevertheless quite soft and light.

Côte Chalonnaise

The Côte Chalonnaise, located at the southern end of the Côte d'Or, is a natural continuation of the Côte de Beaune. (Its name comes from the town of Chalon-sur-Sâone, which faces the Sâone River.) Although the region produces light, crisp, inexpensive white wines —both still and sparkling— it is mainly asso-ciated with some excellent red wines, a number of them pressed exclusively from the pinot noir. (Others are a blend of the pinot noir and the gamay.) These red wines, which are closely related to the wines of Beaune but usually lighter in body and shorter-lived, display considerable scent and charm.

The major Côte Chalonnaise communes are Mercurey, Rully, Givry, and Montagny. Mercurey to the south produces both red and white wines. Its dark colored, fruity reds are fragrant with an earthy component. Although the most structured of the Côte Chalonnaise, they are nevertheless rather quick maturing. The whites are quite light in character. Rully specializes in clean, fresh-tasting white wines, some made sparkling. At their finest, they demonstrate a surprising intensity of bouquet and flavor. (Rully's red wines are labeled "Mercureys.")

Givry, farther south, is primarily associated with red wines. The Rully and Givry reds often go into sparkling Burgundies. Montagny, the southernmost of the Côte Chalonnaise communes, is known for its fresh, light, and very dry white wines.

Mâconnais

Mâconnais is named for its capital city, Mâcon, another important Burgundy wine center. Many of its vineyards are sited on the rolling, often rocky hills facing the Sâone River. Because the region is to the south of Chalon-sur-Sâone, its climate is somewhat milder.

The Mâconnais, growing both red and white wines, has traditionally been the source of millions of gallons of moderately priced white wines. Pressed from the chardonnay —sometimes blended with the aligoté— these are fresh, fruity, engaging and well defined, with a certain touch of acidity. The reds, pressed from the pinot noir and gamay, are straightforward, pleasantly fruity and quite soft on the palate.

Best-known of the Mâconnais white wines is Pouilly-Fuissé, produced in the town of that name and in four small villages nearby: Solutré, Fuissé, Chaintré and Vergisson. Pouilly-Fuissé —crisp, dry, and fruity like the other Mâconnais whites— became popular in the United States, perhaps because of its strange-sounding name. (The French call it the "American wine.") A similar and less expensive wine is St. Véran, produced in six hillside villages to the south. Two other nearby communes, Pouilly-Loché and Pouilly-Vinzelles, are also known for their fresh, fragrant, and moderately dry white wines.

Two notable wine towns here are Vire and Lugny, both white-wine producers. (Their labels usually hyphenate the Mâcon name with their own.) Vire's leading vineyard, Clos du Chapitre, produces an excellent bone-dry, fragrant, fruity, and rather delicate white wine. Lugny's wines are quite engaging as well.

Also produced in the Mâconnais are a number of anonymous white wine blends, appearing under such names as Mâcon Blanc, Pinot Chardonnay de Mâcon, Mâcon-Villages and Aligoté. The latter, named for its grape, was initially an inferior acidy wine, but has lately been upgraded.

Beaujolais

On the west bank of the Sâone River is Beaujolais, located at the southern tip of Burgundy just below Mâcon. A strip of land about forty miles long and five to ten miles wide, Beaujolais takes its name from the little town of Beaujeu. This is red-wine country; the principal grape here is the gamay rather than the ubiquitous pinot noir seen elsewhere in Burgundy. (The blend, however, may include some pinot noir grapes along with such white varieties as the pinot gris, chardonnay, aligoté, and also the melon.)

Beaujolais is one of the most prolific regions of France. Its wines run the gamut from the rich and full flavored to the thin and acidic. The premier examples come from the region's northern sector, where the hills are rolling and the soil is largely granitic. Sharing some of the firmness, depth, and power of the better Burgundies, these are beautifully colored, well balanced, and relatively long-lived red wines, characterized both by warmth and intensity.

In this northern sector of Beaujolais are ten major communes, entitled to use their own names on the labels. These communes are: Moulin-à-Vent, Morgon, Chénas, Juliénas, Fleurie, Chiroubles, St. Amour, Brouilly, Côte de Brouilly and Régnié. The biggest and most full-bodied wines come from Moulin-à-Vent. Strong and solid when young, they open up beautifully with age, displaying considerable breed and a good depth of character. The wines of Morgon —similarly robust, but earlier maturing— exhibit a raspberrylike fruitiness. The wines of Chénas are soft, smooth, and comparatively full flavored, while those of Juliénas are characteristic-ally firm and generous. (Juliénas is named for Julius Caesar, whose legions once marched through the hills here.)

The other notable northern communes —Fleurie, Chiroubles, Brouilly, Côte de Brouilly, Régnié and St. Amour— produce more aromatic and delicate, but shorter lived wines. Fleurie's fruity, gentle reds combine body and breed with lightness, grace, and a wildflower bouquet. Similarly charming and scented is the wine of Chiroubles. Those of Brouilly and Côte de Brouilly are the most youthful; and although quite full-bodied, are endowed with a wonderful fruity softness. The wines of Régnié are light and berrylike, while the fruity, supple wines of St. Amour —the commune located farthest north— are particularly prized for their bouquet.

NOTE: Beaujolais also produces some white Chardonnays and an occasional rosé. The white wines, known as Beaujolais Blancs, come from the northern reach-es of the region, from the sector adjoining the Mâconnais.

The most typical Beaujolais wines, however, are light colored, supple, and fruity. Flowering rather quickly and soon fading, they come from thirty communes in the region's southernmost sector, the Bas Beaujolais, whose soil is primarily clay combined with limestone. Ready to drink about five months after the harvest, the greatest attraction of these wines is a disarming freshness and a general lack of complexity. After spending the winter and the early spring in wood, they are bottled and then shipped out.

These regular Beaujolais wines constitute about two-thirds of the Bas Beaujolais output. The remaining third are known as the Beaujolais Nouveaus (New Wines). Harvested in September and ready for sale some six weeks later, these are essentially half-finished wines; purplish in color, with a strong, youthful grapy flavor. Their greatest charm is a tingling freshness and a yeasty aroma, produced by the fermentation from which they have just recently emerged.

The early release of the Beaujolais Nouveaus began when local vintners brought casks of their new wines to the town square in mid-November for the villagers to sample. Subsequently, these wines were dispensed from their casks in local cafés and eventually were made available in heavy-bottomed forty-centiliter bottles, known as pots. The Nouveaus proved a boon to their makers. (They could sell them in November to pay off many of their debts by Christmas.)

The novelty of the Nouveaus' quick drinkability prompted a number of bistros and restaurants in Lyon and Paris to offer them to their patrons. This led to the promotional idea of organizing an annual "race" to see which establishment would receive its shipment first; the idea being to create a sense of anticipation and excitement about the wine. To generate as much publicity as possible, the "race" was extended to England, the United States, and Japan.

The Nouveau's official release date is now one minute after midnight on the third Thursday in November. (It had initially been scheduled a week earlier but the logistics of getting the wine to the restaurants and retail shops so quickly proved too daunting.) At the moment of release, trucks and helicopters speed shipments of the new wine to every point in France and to its channel ports and airports. A number of promotional bottles are shipped to the United States by plane for arrival the next day. They are known as the "Air Nouveau." (The bulk of the shipment, however, travels more slowly by sea, generally arriving by early December.)

These incomplete and vulnerable wines, traveling great distances, must often be toughened up to survive their long journey. Sugar may be added to boost their alcohol content, or sulfur dioxide introduced to discourage refermentation in the bottle. Some vintners speed up the wine's already abbreviated development with carbonic maceration, a process which blankets the uncrushed grapes with CO_2. Also known as whole-berry fermentation, this releases the wine's color, fragrance, and fruity flavor more quickly and preserves its freshness, but tends to make the wine less stable. Filtering or pasteurizing may be needed to compensate for this.

The successful marketing of the Beaujolais Nouveau has prompted winemakers both inside and outside France to produce their own accelerated wines by using earlier-maturing grapes or those harvested from younger vines. Some of these new wines are named for their grape varieties (Muscadet Nouveau, Gamay Nouveau); others for their locales (Bordeaux Nouveau, Côtes du Rhône Nouveau). The Italians call these wines *nuovos* or *novellos*.

NOTE: The attention that the Nouveaus attract in November has prompted the public to ignore the release of the regular Beaujolais several months later, causing marketing problems for their makers. Yet the regular Beaujolais are better balanced wines since they are allowed to mature more naturally.

Chablis

Chablis is usually considered a part of Burgundy although it's not geographically contiguous with that region. Situated forty miles northwest of the Côte d'Or and closer to Champagne than to Burgundy, Chablis is one of the country's most northerly wine-producing sectors.

The Chablis name applies both to a little village set in the hills and to a large crescent-shaped area surrounding it. Encompassed here are twenty communes. The best wines are produced in seven of these, which share a single south-facing, chalky slope on the Serein River. These communes are le Clos, Vaudésir, Preuses, Grenouilles, Bougros, Valmur, and Blanchots.

The Chablis region is subject to great vagaries of weather. Sudden frosts and devastating hail frequently buffet its vineyards, severely limiting their production of grapes. The wines themselves, pressed from the chardonnay, are pale straw with a hint of green. Magnificently crisp and dry at their finest, they are uniquely subtle in style. More austere than their counterparts in southern Burgundy, they combine a steely taste with a luscious nectarlike quality, endowing them with great finesse. (The wines have been likened to spring water in sunlight.) Lesser examples are produced on the outskirts of the town of Chablis and at the outer borders of the region.

The Burgundy Classifications

Because of the historic fragmentation of its vineyards, Burgundy's wines have been classified more by their vineyard quality than their geographic distribution. Its vineyards have been ranked according to variations in their soil, their terrain, and the exposure experienced by their *climats,* or individual parcels.

The Burgundian wines were first classified in 1861 when the Comité d'Agriculture de l'Arrondissement de Beaune (Agricultural Committee of Beaune) set up rankings for the red wines of the Côte d'Or. These rankings were Tête de Cuvée (Top Growth), followed by the Premier, Deuxième, and Troisième Crus (First, Second, and Third Growths). The four categories were subsequently simplified to two: Grand Cru (Great Growth) and Premier Cru (First Growth). The Côte d'Or's leading Grand Cru vineyard is the Domaine de la Romanée Conti (DRC), followed by les Bonnes Mares, le Chambertin, Chambertin Clos de Bèze, les Grands Échéchezaux, le Musigny, le Richebourg and la Tâche. Among the white-wine vineyards, le Montrachet was deemed to be in a class by itself.

In 1938, four other classifications were created for the wines of Chablis, based both on their vineyard locations and on their alcohol levels. The classifications were Grand Cru, Premier Cru, Chablis, and Petit Chablis. The Grand Crus, grown in the seven top communes on the north bank of the Serein River (le Clos, Vaudésir, Preuses, Grenouilles, Bougros, Valmur, and Blanchots) demonstrate the highest alcohol levels. The Premier Crus come from the town of Chablis and from a number of nearby villages. Chablis alone refers to the wines grown on the outskirts of the town of Chablis and in the communes whose soil is less chalky and whose exposure to sun is more limited. Such wines can vary in quality from excellent to indifferent. Petit Chablis, the lowest category, covers the rather acid wines drawn from the region's outermost boundaries.

In the classification of Beaujolais wines, a Grand Cru covers a whole commune rather than a *climat* or an individual parcel. Awarded Grand Crus have been the nine top northern-sector communes: Moulin-à-Vent, Morgon, Chénas, Juliénas, Fleurie, Chiroubles, Brouilly, Côte de Brouilly and St. Amour. In 1988, a tenth Grand Cru was awarded to Régnié.

While the Burgundy classifications demonstrate little of the rigidity that characterizes the 1855 listing in Bordeaux, they nevertheless have their critics, who contend that the ongoing fragmentation of the region's properties has made it virtually impossible to rank the individual vineyard plots with any degree of precision. The critics also point out that the problem is compounded by the differences between the individual proprietors, who share ownership in a given vineyard. These owners can differ markedly in their experience and skills and in their approaches to grape growing and wine making. Such a lack of consistency, the critics say, makes it difficult to create a uniform system that can set equal standards in the classification of Burgundy wines.

The Rhône Valley

The Rhône Valley —also known as the Côtes du Rhône— is an extensive strip of hillsides located south of Beaujolais and encompassing about a hundred thousand acres in vines. Running from north to south through the region is the Rhône River, which rises in the Swiss Alps, passes through Geneva, then travels almost due west, arriving in France where it is joined at Lyon by the Saône, one of its major tributaries. Then turning abruptly south, the river flows toward Marseilles and out into the Mediterranean Sea.

The Rhône Valley, experiencing a long growing season, produces vast quantities of wine, both red and white. The reds, among the fullest bodied and fullest flavored in France, are aromatic and heady at their finest; often suffused with the scent of peppers and blackberries. Many are noted for their longevity. The majority of these wines are fruity and uncomplicated, however; a bit like a typical Beaujolais although somewhat drier. The Rhône white wines are also big bodied and flavorful; some are crisp and clean, while others are broadly flowery with a marked spiciness. At their finest, they combine a rich nutty character and a refreshing dryness. A number demonstrate unusually high levels of alcohol; some are relatively long lasting for a white wine.

About twenty grape varieties are cultivated in the Rhône Valley, many indigenous to the region. Predominant among the red grapes are the syrah and grenache, followed by the cinsault, carignan, mourvèdre, picpoule, terret noir, and picardan. Significant among the white grapes are the marsanne, roussanne, clairette and the viognier.

The 45th parallel divides the Rhône into northern and southern sectors. The northern Rhône — geographically closer to Burgundy— experiences a generally more temperate climate, and yields the more elegant wines. The southern Rhône —closer to the Mediterranean Sea— is subject to a hotter, drier climate and produces bigger and warmer wines.

The Northern Rhône

The vineyards of the northern Rhone are concentrated mostly on the left bank of the river, beginning near Vienne and continuing on to St. Péray. The key districts here are the Côte Rôtie, Condrieu, Hermitage, Crozes-Hermitage, St. Joseph, Cornas, and St. Péray. Northernmost is the Côte Rôtie, which translates as "Roasted Hillside," deriving its name from the fierce sun beating down on the vineyards in summer. The best wines here are grown on the west bank of the river, on slopes that climb up precipitously from the valley floor. The Côte Rôtie consists of two sectors; each named for the color of its soil: Côte Brune (dark slope) in the north and Côte Blonde (fair slope) in the south. The darker soil soaks up the sun and retains the heat, enabling the grapes to mature more gradually. The fairer soil deflects the sun's rays back onto the grapes and so accelerates their ripening. Usually the yields of the two sectors are combined for a better balanced wine.

About four-fifths of the Côte Rôtie's wines are red. Pressed from the syrah, they are richly colored, robust, potent, and velvety at their finest; often demonstrating a ripe, raspberrylike flavor. Some of the reds are so intense that a white wine may be added to the blend to ameliorate their hardness. (As much as 10 percent is allowed by law although most producers rarely go above 5 percent.) The white wines are pressed mainly from the viognier grape; a number of them are splendid.

NOTE: Since the Côte Rôtie's entire annual output totals only about twenty thousand cases, the wines are available mainly in local establishments and served primarily in luxury restaurants.

Directly to the south is Condrieu, notable for its white wines. Pressed from viognier grapes, they range from the fairly dry to the moderately sweet, depending on the character of their vintage and the style of their vinification. Some display the mingled aroma of muscat grapes and violets. Condrieu is known for producing the most esteemed white wine in the Rhône Valley: Château Grillet. Grown in a tiny four-acre vineyard, and fermented slowly, this wine is not bottled for two years. Big, elegant, and redolent of spices, Château Grillet is high in alcohol yet its character is quite light and ethereal.

Farther south and across the river is Hermitage Hill, a steep, spectacularly terraced slope about half a mile wide and less than two miles long. (Its flinty bedrock soil is covered with a thin layer of chalk.) The hill acquired its name in the twelfth century when a returning Crusader halted wearily at a roadside shrine and decided to live out his life there as a hermit. Planting vines brought back from his pilgrimage, the hermit established the hill's first vineyard.

Hermitage wines are primarily red and the most deeply colored of the region. Fruity, substantial, and vigorous, with an almost overwhelming spicy scent, they are forthright in flavor when young and develop a degree of subtlety with age. The Hermitage whites are pressed from roussanne and marsanne grapes. At their finest, they are full bodied and dry, with a broad flavor and a definite aromatic character. Their intensity can sometimes surpass that of the Hermitage reds. Some of these white wines are also quite long-lived.

Encompassing the southernmost vineyards and known collectively as Crozes-Hermitage are eleven communes located at the base of Hermitage Hill. Because the soil here is much richer, the wines don't achieve the same distinction as those of Hermitage Hill. The soft, light reds are meant for early consumption. The white wines tend to be generally commonplace. Across the river is St. Joseph, stretching north and south from Condrieu and encompassing some twenty-three wine villages. The gentle red wines here are also generally accessible at an early age. Produced here too are sturdy white, and light fruity rosé wines.

South of St. Joseph is the smaller Cornas commune, whose red wines are sturdy and agreeable. The best examples, grown on steep hillsides, are dark and quite powerful, exhibiting a berrylike fragrance and a somewhat earthy quality. Farther south is the small commune of St. Péray, specializing in white wines, pressed from marsanne and roussanne grapes. A number are made effervescent. To the east is the township of Die, also known for sparkling wines, particularly its Clairette de Die, which is rather sweet with a pronounced muscat flavor.

The Southern Rhône

The southern Rhône, situated between the cities of Orange and Avignon, is subject to a hot, dry climate. Mistral winds temper its scorching sun, however. The vineyards here stretch for twenty to thirty miles on either side of the river. (By contrast, those of the northern Rhône cling to the riverbanks.) The region's coarse, alluvial soil is made up largely of stones and pebbles washed down over the centuries from the Alps. These stones, smoothed out by the flowing river, reflect the strong rays of the sun onto the vines during the day, then radiate the heat back at night. The grapes, developing inordinately high levels of sugar, yield big warm wines, rich in their fruit and considerable in their body. The southern Rhône cultivates about two dozen grape varieties, with the grenache leading and the other varieties including the syrah, cinsault, and mourvèdre.

The southern Rhône's leading districts are Châteauneuf-du-Pape, Côtes du Ventoux, Beaumes-de-Venise, Tavel, and Lirac. Châteauneuf acquired its name in the fourteenth century when the French popes, who dominated the Holy See, transferred the papacy to their own country and built an impressive enclave on the east bank of the Rhône in Avignon. This included a huge summer palace. (*Châteauneuf-du-Pape* translates as the "Pope's New Castle.") Pope Clement V, who was Bordeaux-born, encouraged the development of the region's viticulture and the labels of the estate-bottled wines here still feature the papal coat of arms.

There are now more than three hundred vineyards in Châteauneuf, covering some eight thousand acres and yielding primarily red wines. These are characterized at their finest by a deep, almost purplish color, a rich heartiness, and a great vinosity. Châteauneuf wines are produced in a number of styles, however, with their blends varying as to the grapes they include. Among the varieties employed are the grenache, syrah, mourvèdre and cinsault along with with muscardin, vaccarese, cournoise, picpoule, terret noir, and picardan. By law, the Rhône wine makers are permitted to employ as many as thirteen grapes in their blends but they now generally limit themselves to six or seven varieties. (Some use only four.)

Châteauneuf's white wines were initially made when the French popes found the red wines too heavy for morning mass. (The whites are still known as vins de messe.) Pressed from bourbolene, clairette, and roussanne grapes, these wines at their finest are full bodied and intensely perfumed with a clean finish. They are also capable of aging well.

North of Châteauneuf, near the city of Orange, is the Côtes du Ventoux, named for the six-thousand-foot-high Mount Ventoux, whose winds act to cool the vineyards here. As a rule, the Ventoux wines —red, white and rosé— are rough and uncomplicated, although a number of them are capable of some subtlety and smoothness. Located on the lower slopes of Mount Ventoux are the communes of Gigondas and Rasteau, whose red wines are solid, big and high in alcohol. Those from Gigondas are astonishingly dark, rich, and concentrated at their finest. They display a spicy, almost peppery flavor and are also quite long-lived. The Rasteau wines, grown farther north are big and intense as well, sometimes tasting of plums and spices. Rasteau is also known for its sweet, amber-colored Muscat wine which resembles a white port.

South of Gigondas is Beaumes-de-Venise, whose red wines are lush and peppery and whose full flavored white wines are relatively dry. Beaumes-de-Venise is best known, however, for its late-harvest Muscat, a deep golden, mouth-filling, lusciously sweet, and extravagantly perfumed wine whose nuances suggest apricots, orange blossoms, and honey.

Farther south and across the Rhône River are the sun-baked communes of Tavel and Lirac, celebrated for their full-bodied rosé wines. They range in color from pale orange to a deep, dark pink. Among the leading rosés of France, they are pressed from many of the same grape varieties as the Châteauneufs, with the grenache predominating. The rosés of Tavel, grown on a rocky, arid soil, are sturdy, warm, and vivacious, yet at the same time austerely crisp and clean. Exhibiting a tendency toward sharpness, they've been described as having "the taste of a rock warmed by the sun." The rosés of Lirac are somewhat softer. (Tavel and Lirac also produce other red wines and some white wines as well.) Nearby is the township of Chusclan, which is also known for its pleasant, warm rosés.

Champagne

Champagne, the northernmost wine-growing region of France, is located some ninety miles northeast of Paris. The Marne River runs through its center from east to west. Champagne is a largely flat plain, punctuated by a series of bunched-up hills. (*Champagne* literally means "open field.") Grapes have long flourished in its chalky soil, despite cold winds in winter and scorching heat in summer.

When Caesar's legions arrived in the region, viticulture was already thriving; the Romans soon were setting up vineyards of their own. When Emperor Domitian issued his infamous edict in A.D.92, most of the vines were uprooted, not to be replaced for another two hundred years.

Champagne's three principal areas are the Montagne de Reims, Vallée de la Marne, and the Côte des Blancs. Most important is Montagne de Reims, south of the city of Reims. (Reims, one of the region's major wine centers, was an important city in Roman Gaul. The other wine center is Épernay, a town on the Marne River.) Montagne de Reims, planted primarily with the pinot noir, yields rich, full red wines notable for their body and power. The Vallée de la Marne, farther south, also grows the pinot noir but produces softer, rounder red wines. Southernmost is the Côte des Blancs, growing chardonnay grapes. Characterizing its white wines are lightness, delicacy, and finesse. Usually the products of all three districts are blended together for a better balanced wine.

The Champagne region is celebrated for its exuberant sparkling wines. These range in color from pale gold to deep pink, and in style from light and sprightly to smooth, elegant, and complex. (Some Champagnes are big and fruity with plenty of flavor.) The region also produces red and white still or table wines. Initially called Vins Nature de la Champagne, they are now known as the Côteaux Champenois. Most noted among them is the Bouzy Rouge, pressed from the pinot noir, and named for its village in Montagne de Reims. The Vallée de la Marne produces a noneffervescent white wine, displaying a Champagne nose and a flintiness reminiscent of a fine Chablis. Saran Natur, another still white wine, is made from the second pressing of the chardonnay and other grapes.

The Loire Valley

The Loire River, the longest waterway in France, originating in the Massif Central southwest of Lyon, and travelling some six hundred miles north and west, finally arrives at the Atlantic Ocean. The valley itself is a vast expanse, encompassing half a million acres in vines. The Loire is known primarily for its great variety of white wines, although producing a few reds as well. The whites range from light, delicate, and short-lived to big, succulent, and long lasting. Yet all share a certain family feeling: a sprightly freshness, a lively fruitiness, a distinctly graceful charm, and a more or less floral bouquet. Often a hint of smokiness or flintiness is evident in their aftertaste.

Although the Loire Valley consists of twenty viticultural areas, it is perhaps best understood if divided into upper, middle, and lower sectors, based in part on their geography and in part on their predominant grape.

The Upper Loire

The Upper Loire is at the eastern end of the valley; its predominant grape is the sauvignon blanc. Its best known wines come from Pouilly-sur-Loire on the east bank of the river, and from Sancerre to the north on the west bank. Pouilly-sur-Loire is the source of Pouilly-Fumé, a wine also known as Blanc Fumé de Pouilly. (*Fumé,* the local name for the sauvignon blanc grape, translates as "smoky," and refers to the pale mist associated with the noble rot fungus which drifts over the vineyards at harvest time.) Pouilly-Fumé wines range from the sharp and acidic to the rich, full-bodied, full-flavored, and soft. In great vintages, the wines can acquire a fine botrytized sweetness.

NOTE: Pouilly-Fumé is often confused with the similar-sounding and better-known Pouilly-Fuissé. The latter comes from the Mâconnais region and is pressed from the chardonnay, not the sauvignon blanc grape.

The Sancerre district, characterized by slightly rolling hills and a chalky soil, encompasses fourteen wine-producing communes, which have some four thousand acres in vines. The leading communes are Chavignol, Bué, Champtin,

Crezancy, Amigny, Reigny, and Verdigny. The district's praiseworthy reputation is based on its straw colored or greenish yellow Sauvignon Blancs. Long the favorites of the bistros and brasseries of Paris, Sancerre's wines are generally fresh, sprightly, and bone-dry. Some of the best are austere, clean, and sharp, with a crispness that suggests a steely or a flinty edge; the other examples are somewhat fuller in body. (Also made is a late-harvest version.) Many of the wines, exhibiting a slightly vegetal or herbaceous quality, are redolent of new-mown grass. Sancerre also produces some sturdy red wines and good rosés.

Thirty miles to the southwest are the hamlets of Quincy and Reuilly, producing similarly fresh, dry, and slightly vegetal Sauvignon Blancs. Somewhat softer and more delicate than the Sancerres, these wines may exhibit an underlying flintiness, or else taste pleasantly spicy or tangy.

The Middle Loire

The Middle Loire, the valley's largest wine-growing sector, is also known as Coteaux de Touraine or simply Touraine. (The name derives from an ancient province surrounding the city of Tours.) Grown on its limestone slopes are red and white wines, with the whites being best known. Responsible for about half of these is the chenin blanc, known locally as the pineau de la loire. Its wines, charming, soft and not entirely dry, combine a fresh, fruity scent with an elusive flintiness. Other white grapes here are the sauvignon blanc, pinot gris, and arbois.

The most notable Middle Loire wines come from Vouvray, situated on the north bank of the river near the city of Tours. Vouvray encompasses eight communes within its borders. Its white wines at their finest are fresh, fruity, soft and scented; often displaying a delicate quincelike aroma. When the weather permits, they can acquire a great concentrated sweetness, offset by a fine acidity. Depending on the character of the vintage, Vouvray's wines may be vinified *sec* (dry), *demi-sec* (partially dry) or *molleux* (naturally sweet). Some of the wines are inherently sparkling, while others have their effervescence added.

On the south bank of the river —across from Vouvray— is the smaller Montlouis district, sharing a similar soil and also growing the chenin blanc. Its slightly softer and somewhat sweeter wines sometimes resemble a simple Sauternes. (A number have been vinified dry however to suit the current taste.)

The red grapes of the Middle Loire are the cabernet franc (which predominates) the grenache, and the gamay, along with the cabernet sauvignon, malbec, and meunier. The cabernet franc's fresh, fruity, light-colored wine may either resemble a typical Beaujolais or display the brisk, dry, slightly tannic character of a light Bordeaux. The most outstanding examples come from Bourgueil and Chinon, two villages facing each other across the river. (Bourgueil is on the north bank, Chinon on the south.) Bourgueil's best wine is characterized by a bouquet of wild raspberries, while the best Chinons display a violetlike perfume. To the northwest is St. Nicholas de Bourgueil, also producing a noteworthy red wine, pressed from the cabernet franc.

The Lower Loire

The Lower Loire is at the western end of the valley, closest to the Atlantic Ocean. Its key districts are Anjou, Saumur, Pays Nantais, and Gros Plant du Pays.

Anjou is the most versatile district, known for producing some of the most charming white wines in France, along with some excellent reds and rosés. The whites —fresh, fruity, and scented— are vinified both sweet and dry. Anjou is particularly celebrated for its rich yet delicate, late-harvest Chenin Blancs. Some of the most luxurious come from the slopes of Quarts de Chaume, a Coteaux du Layon vineyard, benefitting from a peerless southern exposure. It is best known for botrytized wines which, combining breed and a splendid texture, are comparable to the elegant late-harvest wines of Sauternes and Germany. The Bonnezeaux vineyards nearby produce similarly luxurious wines, pressed from partly dried chenin blanc grapes. Other Coteaux du Layon wines range from the fairly crisp and dry to the very sweet. Included among the latter are late-harvest wines, whose fruitlike, naturally honeyed flavors suggest nectarines and quinces.

One of Anjou's best red wines is a tender, fragrant Cabernet Franc, grown in the tiny village of Champigny to the south. (It is similar to, but a bit lighter than the Chinon wines grown upstream.) The Anjou rosés, pressed exclusively from the cabernet franc, are among the best rosés in the Loire valley. Most of the region's other examples are pressed from the gamay grape.

Saumur, on the south bank, produces almost equal quantities of red and white wines. Best known are its big, heady, long-lived Chenin Blancs, displaying an agreeable trace of sweetness. Some of these are also made sparkling. Saumur produces large quantities of rosés too, including the pleasantly fresh Cabernet Rosé de Saumur that is generally sweeter than most French rosés. On the north side of the river, not far from city of Angers, is Savennières, a tiny area known for its fragrant and excellent Chenin Blancs. These range from the delectably dry, tart and elegant to the late-harvested and sweet. The dry examples are similar to, but generally drier than, the Vouvrays; the sweet examples at their finest are evocative of honey and flowers. Savennières's most distinguished vineyards are Clos de la Coulée de Serrant and La Roche-aux-Moines; the former, a twenty-one acre estate, has been producing wine for some six hundred years.

Closer to the mouth of the river is the flat, windswept coast of lower Brittany, known as the Pays Nantais (the area around Nantes). A prolific district, it was producing mainly red wines until early in the eighteenth century when a disastrous freeze wiped out most of the grapes. According to legend, only the white muscadet survived. Known locally as the *melon de bourgogne*, because of its Burgundian origins, the muscadet went on to become the principal grape of the district.

In the Pays Nantais, chill air gusting in from the Atlantic keeps vineyard temperatures down and grape acids generally up. Microscopic salt crystals blown onto the grapes from the sea give the wines a slightly briny aftertaste. Varying from light to heavy, and from dry and steely to medium sweet, the Muscadets at their finest are pale, fruity, and light bodied; crisp, clean and tangy. Some are made *sur lie,* that is, steeped on their sediment for several months, giving them an extra measure of flavor and intensity. Others are bottled early to retain a slight, natural effervescence. (A number of the Muscadets are now carbonated for export.)

NOTE: Initially considered unimportant, Muscadet wines were consumed mainly by the district's poor. Quite fashionable now, they are produced in great quantities for domestic use and for export.

The Pays Nantais produces three types of the wine: Muscadet, Muscadet de Coteaux de la Loire, and Muscadet de Sèvres-et-Maine. Basic Muscadet is produced in the valley's westernmost reaches, nearer to the mouth of the river. Muscadet de Coteaux de la Loire is produced upstream and northeast of Nantes. The best examples come from Sèvres-et-Maine, some twenty-five miles east of the point where the Loire empties into the Atlantic. (Its hyphenated name derives from the two rivers that flow into the Loire near Nantes.) The largest wine-producing district of the Lower Loire is Gros Plant du Pays, located nearest the mouth of the river. Produced here in great quantities are fairly dry and acidic white wines, pressed from the folle blanche grape; these tend to be somewhat coarse and a bit short on fruit.

NOTE: Also considered part of the Greater Loire is Haut-Poitou, the district located between Nantes and Saumur. Produced here are nicely agreeable red wines pressed from the gamay grape, and crisp, solid, pleasant white wines pressed from the sauvignon blanc and the chardonnay.

Alsace

Alsace, a small region in northeastern France, extends from Strasbourg —its principal city— to the Swiss border. (Antedating Julius Caesar, Strasbourg was a crossroads settlement, which the Romans called Strateburgum or City of Roads.) The vineyards of Alsace are scattered through the gently rolling foothills of the Vosges Mountains. Three-to four-thousand foot high peaks shield them from the cold and harshness of the northern weather. Germany's Black Forest, located just across the Rhine, acts as a buffer as well.

Tucked in between the Vosges Mountains and the river, Alsace is geographically part of the Rhine basin. Throughout its history, the region has been closely linked with Germany. It was ruled by Teutonic princes until 1648. France then acquired the territory under the Treaty of Westphalia. The Germans retook it in 1870 and retained control until World War I, when France recovered the territory. German troops seized it once more during World War II. Not until 1945 was Alsace finally integrated as a part of France.

To keep the Alsatian wines from competing with their own, the Germans had dispersed the region's vineyard holdings, permitting only the most minor grape varieties, primarily the chasselas, to be grown during their various occupations. When the Alsatians retrieved their territory in World War I, they began to replace those vines with more noble ones. During World War II, the reoccupying Germans uprooted them once again, replacing them with lesser grape varieties. In effect, they turned the region into a source of cheap high-alcohol carafe wines to be served in the bistros and brasseries of Paris. The Germans also used some of these lesser wines in their own commonplace blends at home, such as the Liebfraumilchs. Not until the 1950s was Alsace able to restore its wines to the earlier quality levels they had attained nearly a century before.

Alsace is divided into the Haut-Rhin (Upper Rhine) and Bas-Rhin (Lower Rhine). Haut-Rhin, a twenty-five mile stretch of land between the towns of Hippolyte and Guebwiller, encompasses the region's central and southern sectors, and produces the best wines. Its famous towns are Riquewihr, Ribeauville, and Guebwiller. Other notable Haut-Rhin towns are Turckheim, Colmar, Éguisheim, Rouffach and Winzerheim. Bas-Rhin to the north produces generally less substantial wines. Its leading commune is Barr.

In many ways Alsace remains more closely linked to the German traditions than the French. Its wines, primarily white, are a combination of the Gallic and the Teutonic. Although slightly more alcoholic than the German, they exhibit some of the same lightness and grace; yet resemble the French in that virtually every bit of their sugar has been fermented out. Bone-dry and delicate with an engaging charm, they represent a remarkable balance between fragrance and fruit. Some examples are startlingly intense in their flavor. Noble rot wines are produced here too and, although characteristically unctuous, they demonstrate only a hint of sweetness despite their rich fruit and expansive bouquet.

Alsatian wines are named for their grape varieties. Most outstanding are the clean, crisp Rieslings, naturally high in acidity and hinting at sweetness, while being perfectly dry at the same time. Combining richness and depth with delicacy and aroma at their finest, they are endowed with elegance, complexity, and finesse. More characteristic of the region, however, are the fragrant and heady Gewürztraminer wines, which combine a mouth-filling richness of fruit with a pungent and distinctly herbal undertone.

NOTE: Riquewihr in Haut-Rhin is noted for its Rieslings and Gewürztraminers. Ribeauville is also known for its fine Rieslings, and Guebwiller to the south produces somewhat richer and distinctly softer examples.

Other Alsatian grape varieties are the sylvaner, pinot blanc, pinot gris, muscat, chasselas, and knipperle. The sylvaner —the region's primary grape until super-seded by the gewürztraminer— is responsible for soft, flowery, light bodied wines with a delicate flavor. (Barr in Bas-Rhin is noted for its refreshing Sylvaners.) The pinot blanc yields fresh, light, fragrant, but generally undistinguished wines. The pinot gris, known locally as the tokay d'alsace, produces austerely dry wines with good body and very round flavors. Wines pressed from the muscat grape are slight-ly drier here than elsewhere. The best known example, the Muscat d'Alsace, displays a fresh intense grapiness and aroma. (It is usually served as an apéritif.) A late-harvest muscat yields a wine of immense depth and power, balancing out its great natural sweetness with a high degree of acidity. The region's white peasant grapes —the chasselas and knipperle— are usually designated for miscellaneous blends. The red Alsatian grapes —the pinot noir and meunier— yield some good rosés but their wines otherwise tend to be light colored and undistinguished. Barr in Bas-Rhin is known for its commendable rosés, pressed from the pinot noir.

The Alsatian vineyard holdings are small, averaging only an acre or two. A number of growers cultivate grapes as a sideline to other crops or hold full-time jobs in factories or mills, tending their vines in the evening and on weekends. Some participate in cooperatives, but most growers sell their grapes to the big shippers and producers, who dominate the wine trade here. (Alsatian wineries depend heavily on these purchased grapes.)

The South of France

The south of France, bordering the Mediterranean, is made up of Provence (also know as the Côtes-de-Provence) and the Midi. A great variety of red, white, and rosé wines are grown here. Also grown are highly pigmented grapes, called *teinturiers*, which darken and enhance some paler northern French wines.

Provence, extending east from the mouth of the Rhône River to the Italian border, encompasses Marseilles, Toulon, Nice, and Aix-en-Provence. Its vineyards are sited between the foothills of the Alps and the Mediterranean. The white wines here are crisp and citric with plenty of body; the red wines are rich, dark, and somewhat herbal in flavor. Of particular interest are the rosés, pressed from the grenache and such other red grapes as the cinsault, syrah, mourvèdre, and cabernet sauvignon. The best rosés —grown between Aix and St.-Raphael— are fresh, light, fruity, and possess a delightful bouquet. Other good examples come from Bandol, some twenty-five miles southeast of Marseilles. Bandol is noted for its sturdy red wines and pleasant whites as well; the reds are pressed from the carignan and grenache, the whites from the clairette and ugni blanc. Produced in Palette, near Aix, are sturdy red and white wines, while Toulon specializes in red wines. The most famous Provençal wine is the crisp, white, delightfully dry Cassis, named for its village some twenty miles east of Marseilles. (Cassis serves as the base for the popular Kir apéritif.)

To the west of Provence is the Midi, a wide and prolific sweep of land with a hot climate, stretching westward toward Spain and the Pyrenees. An immense vineyard area since Roman times, the Midi is responsible for 40 percent or so of the total French wine output. For centuries, the region was better known for the quantity rather than the quality of its wines. After cultivating largely indifferent grapes used in bulk wines, the Midi has been gradually upgraded. Stimulated by the European Union and by French government subsidies, growers here have been encouraged to replace their lesser vines with better varieties. Uprooting thousands of acres, they have replanted them with such grapes as the cabernet sauvignon, merlot, and chardonnay. And employing modern vinification methods, the wine makers are producing wines with good fruit and bouquet, including fresh, clean whites and spicy, rustic reds.

The Midi itself is made up of two ancient provinces, Langedoc and Roussillon. Languedoc gets its name from an ancient Latin-based dialect, Langue d'Oc, spoken in the south of France. The largest producing areas here are Hérault, Aude, and Gard. Hérault is known for its white wines, including the sweet Muscats — grown in Lunel and Frontignan — and for its full-bodied Clairette du Languedoc, pressed from partially raisined grapes. Hérault also produces the thin white wines which provide the base for the best French vermouths. Aude produces a variety of red, white, and rosé wines.

Limoux, located near the ancient fortress town of Carcasonne, is known chiefly for its sparkling Blanquette de Limoux. Corbières, a district southeast of Carcassonne, produces Fitou, one of the Midi's best reds, a blend of the grenache and the carignan. Minervois, pressed from the same grape varieties and produced east of Carcassonne, is a big, heavy red wine with a ripe, earthy character. Gard, south of Nîmes, is noted for its fine Camargue rosé and for its soft, dry Clairette de Bellgrade.

Roussillon, a hilly district near the Spanish border around the city of Perpignan, is known principally for its fortified dessert wines. Produced here too is the acclaimed Banyuls red, pressed from late-gathered grenache grapes, and somewhat reminiscent of a tawny port.

Other French Regions

The Charente, a broad area north of Bordeaux, produces thin white wines which —although uninteresting in themselves— are distilled into the splendid spirit known as Cognac. Haut-Savoie, in northeastern France near Lake Geneva and the Swiss border, produces light-bodied, very dry white wines, often made sparkling. (Of particular interest are the wines of Crépy.) Another sparkling-wine producer is Seysell, set in the alpine reaches of the southeast, whose *vin mousseux* is considered one of the country's best. Also near the Swiss border is the Jura, celebrated for its late-harvest *vin jaune* (yellow wine), fermented for six years under a veil of flor. Dark and rich but austerely dry, vin jaune demonstrates legendary keeping qualities; some examples have remained drinkable for seven decades. Bugey, a little district in the foothills of the Alps —situated halfway between Haut-Savoie and Beaujolais— is noted for its good red wines, pressed from the gamay, pinot noir, and poulsard, among other grape varieties. Bugey is known for its rosé and Chardonnay wines as well. Ardèche, southwest of Beaujolais, a sparsely settled region on the west bank of the Rhône River, is notable for its red and white wines grown on chalky soil. A Gamay red here —also produced as a Nouveau— displays the freshness and uncomplicated grapiness of a typical Beaujolais, although it is sometimes a bit lighter. A Chardonnay, produced nearby, is fuller and richer than most Mâcon whites, yet exhibits a good acid balance.

Southwestern France, commonly known as Gascony, produces red and white wines. The reds, dark in their color and concentrated in their flavor, are usually hard when young. One example, Madiran, a blend of the cabernet sauvignon, cabernet franc, and tannat (a local variety) is so hard that —according to law— it must be wood-aged for at least twenty months before bottling. Gascony's white wines are primarily dry, but are on occasion sweet.

The southwestern wine-growing districts include Bergerac and the Côtes du Duras. Bergerac in the Dordogne Valley, almost sixty miles east of Bordeaux, produces wines similar enough to be grouped with those of Bordeaux. These include fruity, well-balanced reds (blends of the cabernet sauvignon, cabernet franc, and merlot) and whites (blends of the sémillon and muscadelle), which are somewhat drier than a typical Sauternes. The Côtes du Duras, situated between Bergerac and Entre-Deux-Mers, also grows the same grape varieties as Bordeaux and produces solid young red wines.

Gascony's sweet wines come from Jurançon and Monbazillac. The Jurançon vineyards, situated in the foothills of the Pyrenees near the Spanish border, were once known for their late-harvest wines, redolent of quinces, nectarines, and plums. The white wine of Monbazillac, grown on rolling hills, bears a passing resemblance to the wine of Sauternes. (Gascony mainly produces undistinguished white wines in large quantities now.)

Located some one hundred and twenty miles east of Bordeaux is Cahors, situated on the banks of the Lot River, which flows into the Garonne. One of the oldest French viticultural regions, Cahors is famous for its robust and inky *vin noir* (black wine). Pressed initially from the malbec grape, the wine was quite tannic and required about a dozen years of aging, exhibiting at maturity a rich concentration of fruit and a great fullness of flavor. Made now in a more rapidly maturing style (by including the merlot and other quick-ripening varieties) it is lighter in color and softer in texture. However, a number of Cahors vintners are trying to bring back the earlier, richer, and more slowly evolving version.

The island of Corsica in the Mediterranean, off the coast of Italy, had been engaged in viticulture since the ancient Greeks planted the first vines there. But the island did not become a notable wine producer until the 1960s. Algeria had then declared its independence from France and when the new Moslem-led government virtually put an end to its wine production, the Algerian wine makers were forced to leave North Africa and transferred their operations to Corsica. The island, acknowledging its proximity to Italy, now grows many Italian grapes but generally follows the Midi's style of vinification. Corsica's best-known wine is its full-bodied, high-alcohol red Patrimonio. The island also grows Beaujolais-like red wines as well as good rosés.

Although France has become synonymous with the world's most esteemed wines, more than four-fifths of its production consists of *vins ordinaire* or commonplace blends. In addition, France imports wines from Italy, Greece, Spain, Madeira, Tunis, and Morocco for blending with its high-acid, low-alcohol products. These blends are usually consumed locally.

France exports most of its best wines to western Europe, the United States, and Japan. (Foreign sales yield somewhat higher prices.) In Bordeaux, a number of the top estates will export anywhere from 50 to 80 percent of their annual output, while the proportion is even higher for some of the Burgundy vineyards. The French had traditionally shown little interest in drinking their own best wines but in recent years the emergence of a sizable middle class has created a larger domestic market for the country's finest wines.

❦ ❦ ❦

ITALY

Italy, growing grapes from virtually one end of the country to the other, from its northern Alpine valleys to its sunny southern shores, has been called a vast vineyard. A felicitous combination of soil and climate encourages prolific grape growing, making Italy one of the world's leaders in wine production.

Long casual about its wine making, the country has often been associated with flavorful but rather rough and somewhat overoxidized products. Seeking recognition as a serious producer, Italy began to upgrade its vineyards and to invest more heavily in its wineries. It is now the source of a number of elegant premium wines, while continuing to turn out great quantities of more commonplace ones.

Of the hundreds of grape varieties cultivated, the nebbiolo is preeminent among the reds, followed by the barbera, freisa, grignolino, lambrusco, dolcetto, sangiovese, and bonarda. (In recent years, French varieties have been introduced as well, particularly the cabernet sauvignon, merlot, and pinot noir.) Most widely planted among the white varieties are the trebbiano, verdicchio, pinot bianco, malvasia, cortese, tocai, and schiava, followed by the pinot grigio, chardonnay, sauvignon blanc, gewürztraminer, and riesling.

Italy literally makes thousands of wines: red, white, and rosé; still, sparkling, and fortified. Most outstanding are its robust and vinous red wines, vigorous at their finest with rich sustaining qualities. Italy's white wines, once undistinguished and characterized by a heavy, oxidized style, are now made fresher, leaner, and livelier by modern vinification methods. They range from the light, fruity, and crisp to the rich and full-bodied. A number of whites are made both sweet and dry, with the dry wines often intended for export.

Most significant among Italy's twenty major wine-producing provinces, are the Piedmont, Lombardy, Alto Adige, Friuli-Venezia-Giulia, Veneto, Emilia-Romagna, and Liguria in the north; Tuscany, Marche, Umbria, and Latium in the central sector and Campania, Apulia, and Calabria, along with Sicily in the south. The country's premier provinces are the Piedmont and Tuscany. The most prolific provinces are Veneto, Apulia, Emilia-Romagna, and Sicily.

The Piedmont

The Piedmont (Piemonte) is a small, somewhat austere province in northwestern Italy, bordered by the Alps and the Appennines. Its capital city is Turin. The Po and Tanaro rivers flow through the region, whose prime vineyards are sited on the banks of the Tanaro, around Alba. They lie in the low but steep foothills of the Alps.

ITALY

PIEDMONT

Barolo
Barbaresco
Gattinara
Barbera
Ghemme
Dolcetto
Freisa
Brachetto
Cortese di Gavi
Gavi dei Gavi
Asti Spumante

LOMBARDY

Valtellina: Sassella, Inferno
  and Grumello
Oltropo Pavese
Lake Garda: Chiaretto,
  Lugana

ALTO ADIGE

Terlano
Santa Maddelena
Kuchelberger
Lagrein

FRIULI-VENEZIA-GIULIA

Tocai Friulano
Picolit

VENETO

Bardolino
Valpolicella
Soave
Reciotos
Torcolato

EMILIA-ROMAGNA

Lambrusco
Sangiovese di Romagna
Gutturnio
Albano di Romagna

TUSCANY

Chianti
Brunello di Montalcino
Rosso di Montalcino
Vino Nobile de
  Montepulciano
Vernaccia di San
  Gimignano
Galestro
Vin Santo

LIGURIA

Cinqueterre
Dolceaqua

MARCHE

Rosso Piceno
Rosso Conero

UMBRIA

Orvieto
Rubesco
Torgiano

LATIUM

Frascati
Velletri
Albano
Marino
Grottaferra
San Giorgio
Est! Est! Est!

CAMPANIA

Lacryma Christi
Taurasi
Falerno
Gragnano

CALABRIA

Greco di Bianco
Ciro Wines

SICILY

Corvo
Faro
Etna
Malvasia di Lipari
Marsala

(*Piedmont* translates as the "Foot of the Mountain.") The region is celebrated for a host of outstanding red wines, pressed primarily from the nebbiolo. (Other grape varieties include the barbera, freisa, dolcetto, and grignolino. (Recent years have seen the introduction of the cabernet sauvignon and the merlot.) The Piedmont's premier wines are red: the Barolo, Barbaresco, Gattinara, and Barbera; the first three wines are pressed exclusively from the nebbiolo, while the fourth bears the name of its own grape variety.

Barolo, named for its village of origin southeast of Turin, is grown on chalky soil in steeply terraced vineyards. Known as the "king of Italian wines," it is deep ruby in color, robust, and brawny while nevertheless displaying a certain austerity. A rich memorable bouquet suggesting roses and faded violets serves as a counterpoint to its great, hearty pungency. Slow maturing and long-lived, Barolo acquires its delicious subtleties with age. Its greatest examples are among the world's finest and most complex red wines. Barbaresco, called "Barolo's younger brother" is somewhat similar in style but earlier maturing. Named for its village of origin and grown along the lower slopes near the Tanaro River, this is a lighter, rounder, slightly drier wine than the Barolo.

Gattinara, although less structured than the Barolo, is also slow maturing and long-lived. Grown in the Novarra Hills near Milan, it is a rich, robust red, exhibiting at its finest a fruity aroma and an attractive aftertaste, suggesting bittersweet almonds. Barbera, grown around the town of Asti, is a deep-colored, full-bodied, high-alcohol wine with a sturdy softness. (Asti, located between Turin and Milan, is an important Italian wine center.) Some Barberas are vigorous in their flavor and aroma, while others exhibit a lighter, fruitier style. (The barbera grape is now responsible for a number of high-quality wines.)

Also grown in the Piedmont are Ghemme, Dolcetto, Freisa, and Brachetto, all red wines. Ghemme, from the Novarra Hills, is powerful, full-bodied, and capable of considerable aging. Dolcetto is named for its grape. Depending on the character of the vintage and the style of vinification, this wine can range from the light and delicately dry to strongly flavored. There are in fact seven Dolcettos, each named for its commune of origin. Best known is Dolcetto d'Alba, a fresh-flavored, velvety dry, yet fruity red wine. The Dolcettos from Aqui and Ovada tend to be a bit more on the astringent side.

Freisa, also named for its grape variety, is vinified dry and semisweet. Particularly notable is Freisa di Chiera, grown near Turin; a light, dry, and fragrant wine with a raspberrylike aroma. (Freisas are sometimes also made sparkling.) Brachetto, named for its grape, is grown east of Barbaresco. Vinified both sweet and dry, this wine is also sometimes made sparkling.

The Piedmont is a region of intense white-wine production as well. The leading white grape here, the cortese, is responsible for the noteworthy Cortese di Gavi, a charming, crisp, aromatic, and somewhat flinty wine, named for the ancient village of Gavi. Its grapes are grown close enough to the Italian Riviera to benefit from the balmy Mediterranean breezes there. The wine itself demonstrates a fine balance between fresh fruit and acidity. Rarer still is Gavi dei Gavi, which displays an unusual richness and body for a white wine. The Piedmont is the source as well of the best Asti Spumantes, the country's noted sparkling wines. Produced here too are the lesser white wines, which provide the base for the better Italian vermouths.

NOTE: The red and white wines of Valle d'Aosta bear a certain resemblance to those of the Piedmont. Valle d'Aosta is an autonomous French-speaking district near Mont Blanc and the Swiss border. Its grapes are grown in alpine vineyards, perched more than two thousand feet above sea level.

❦ ❦ ❦

Lombardy

Lombardy in northern Italy —extending east from Lake Maggiore to Lake Garda— encompasses three widely separate and disparate wine districts: Valtellina, Oltrepo Pavese, and the southwestern shore of Lago di Garda (Lake Garda). The Etruscans and Romans planted the first grape vines here. Milan is its capital city.

Valtellina is an alpine district of rugged mountains and quiet lakes, not far from the Swiss border. Some of its best vineyards are located twenty-five hundred feet above sea level. The vineyards, sited on south-facing terraced land sloping down to the Adda River, are sheltered from the harsh winds blowing in from Switzerland to the north. Valtellina's red wines, pressed almost entirely from the nebbiolo, are deep colored, sturdy, and rather dry. Unattractively hard when young, they're capable of developing real delicacy and a pronounced bouquet with age. The district's best wines are Sassella, Inferno, and Grumello, grown in three hillside areas centered around the town of Sondrio. The Sassella wine is bright ruby red in color with a delicate, fruity bouquet. Inferno, named for the heat of its wind-sheltered vineyards in summer, is somewhat lighter in body while Grumello to a lesser degree shares the qualities of the other two. (Nearby Valgella produces a similarly sturdy and slow-maturing wine.)

Valtellina is celebrated as well for its Sfursat or Sforzato, a rare rich, concentrated, full-bodied red wine. Made from selected nebbiolo grapes left to dry in airy lofts, for about two weeks, Sfursat can attain unusually high alcohol levels for a table wine (about 14 percent by volume). It is also quite long-lived.

Oltrepo Pavese, extending south and west of Lake Garda, is a hilly area near the city of Pavia. Its wines are often named for their principal grape. The Barbera leads the red wines, while the whites are pressed from the pinot bianco, cortese, and riesling, among other grape varieties.

Grown on Lake Garda's western shore is the gentle Chiaretto rosé, which combines a delicate nose with a light attractive bitterness in its aftertaste. From the southern edge of Lake Garda comes Lugana, named for its tiny village. Pressed from the trebbiano, this white wine is agreeably light, dry, and delicately flavored.

Alto Adige

Alto Adige, the country's northernmost wine producer, is a three-thousand-square-mile stretch in the Italian Tyrol with its vineyards sited in the Dolomites, the foothills of the Alps. The capital city here is Bolzano. Once a part of the Austrian Empire, known as Sud Tyrol, Alto Adige became an autonomous region in 1919. The region is bicultural and bilingual; its official documents and wine labels are printed in both Italian and German. The northern sector, however, tends to be somewhat more Germanic in outlook, while the southern is more Italian in its language and culture. (Politically, the district is known as Trentino-Alto Adige.) Its grapes, grown along the banks of the Adda River, include a number of white varieties associated with Germany and Austria and a number of red varieties associated with Italy and France.

Among the white grapes are the riesling, sylvaner, gewürztraminer, and müller-thurgau; along with the pinot grigio, pinot bianco, sauvignon blanc, chardonnay, and muscat. The wines —some of the country's finest whites— are dry, aromatic, and fruity with a rich softness. (A notable example is Terlano, named for its village not far from the Austrian border.) Some of these white wines are made sparkling, while others are exported in bulk to Germany, Austria, and Switzerland for use in blending.

Alto Adige's red grapes include the pinot noir (here called the blauburgunder or blue burgundian), the merlot, and cabernet franc along with such local varieties as the friuli, lagrein, and schiava. Their wines, generally light in color, low in tannin, and early maturing, often display an attractive nutlike bitterness in their aftertaste.

Particularly noted for its fine red wines is the Lago di Caldaro district, called the Kaltersee in German. A prime example is the fruity, light, and delicate Santa Maddalena, grown on a mountain above Bolzano (Bozen in German). Northwest of Bolzano, the resort town of Merano produces Kuchelberger, another light, fragrant red wine. Noteworthy too is Lagrein, a light-to medium-bodied red, named for its grape variety. Its aftertaste displays a hint of bitter almonds. Alto Adige also produces rosé wines which are light, fragrant, and often intensely fruity.

Friuli-Venezia–Giulia

In northeastern Italy, wedged between the Alps and the Adriatic Sea, is Friuli-Venezia-Giulia, one of Europe's oldest wine regions; bordered by Austria to the north and Slovenia to the east. Its capital city is Trieste.

Friuli produces large quantities of light, refreshing, and generally quite dry red wines pressed from the cabernet sauvignon, cabernet franc, and merlot. The region is best known, however, for its delicate, dry white wines pressed from pinot bianco, pinot grigio, chardonnay, tocai, malvasia, and ribolla grapes, among others. The pinot gris yields smooth, round, mouth-filling wines; the wines of the chardonnay are clean and fresh tasting. Among the most appealing and popular of the white wines is the fruity but subtle Tocai Friulano, characterized by moderate acidity and a long finish. The region is particularly celebrated for its sweet golden Picolit, a legendary dessert wine.

Veneto

Veneto in the northeast, one of the country's largest and most varied wine regions, stretches from Lake Garda to the Adriatic Sea. Its capital city is Venice.

Premium wine production here is centered around the Adige River, which rises in the Alps near Austria, then travels south and east. After a turbulent descent, the river flows serenely through the city of Verona before emptying into the Adriatic below Venice. Veneto's wines are fruity, soft textured, and relatively low in alcohol. Best known among the reds are the light-bodied Bardolino and Valpolicella. Soave leads the white wines.

Bardolino, pressed from local grapes, is named for a pretty hill town on the eastern slopes of Lake Garda. Known as the "Italian Beaujolais," it's a fresh young wine that displays a charming fruity flavor, a faintly sweet character, and a refreshing sharpness. Hardly darker than a rosé, Bardolino is sometimes described as one. The Veneto region also makes a Chiaretto rosé.

Valpolicella, produced in the foothills of the Alps near Verona, is also pressed from local grape varieties. More deeply colored and fuller bodied than the Bardolino —although still light in alcohol— it's a smooth and supple red wine with a pleasant fruity flavor, a delicate bouquet, and a gently bitter aftertaste. Similar red wines are produced in nearby Valpantena, a district named for a valley north of Verona. The best of these are labeled "Valpolicella-Valpantena."

Veneto also produces the robust, powerful, and thickly textured Recioto della Valpolicella. Pressed from selected grapes which have been set aside to raisin for several months, this slowly vinified wine is a synthesis of astringency and richness. The Recioto at its finest is intense, lush, and complex, yet austerely dry with tremendous depth, exuding an aroma of violets and honeysuckle and displaying a long, lingering raspberrylike finish. (When aged for about three years, the wine is known as an Amarone.)

Veneto's white wines are pale, dry, and fragrant, with some of them made sparkling. Soave, the primary example, is pressed from the garganega grape, blended with either the trebbiano or the riesling. Soft textured, light, and clean on the palate, it is medium in body and fairly dry and zesty without being acid. A grassy or reedy undertone balances out its fruitiness, giving Soave a fresh piquant quality. The best examples come from the foothills of the Alps; those grown on the more prolific plain below are of a lesser quality. Adjoining the Soave district is Gambellara, cultivating the same grape varieties and yielding a similar but a generally lighter wine.

From the north of Venice comes Torcolato, a dessert wine, pressed from late-picked local grapes. At harvest time, the grapes are left on their branches, which are braided into giant corkscrewlike strands about twelve feet long. (Torcolato means "twisted.") The branches are hung indoors for about three months. After the dried grapes have been pressed, their wine is aged in small oaken casks for a year, then for another half-year in glass. The resulting wine is sweet, rich, vinous, and opulently mellow. Another sweet, rich Veneto wine is Prosecco, named for its grape variety. A dry Prosecco is also made, as well as a sparkling version.

Emilia-Romagna

Below Veneto —bounded by the Appenines on the south and the Po River on the north— is Emilia-Romagna, whose capital city is Bologna. Most of its grapes are grown here on a flat, fertile plain in the Po River valley. (Some are cultivated on the Appenine slopes above.) Varieties include the red sangiovese di roma, lambrusco, and barbera and the white trebbiano, albana, sauvignon blanc, and malvasia.

Extremely prolific, Emilia-Romagna produces vast quantities of red and white wines. Best known is the red Lambrusco, grown west of Bologna and named for its grape variety. Light colored and very fruity, this wine is somewhat on the sweet side and often naturally effervescent. The region's other notable reds are the dry Sangiovese di Romagna, produced near the Adriatic port city of San Marino, and the light red Gutturnio, produced in the hills south of Piacenza. Of particular interest among the white wines is the semisweet and excellent Albana di Romagna, produced near the town of San Marino and named for its grape variety.

Liguria

Liguria on the Italian Riviera is a remote and rugged arc of land, curving along the crescent of the Gulf of Genoa, and extending from Monte Carlo to just beyond Portofino. Steep, craggy cliffs run the length of the arc and strong retaining walls have been built at the water's edge to protect the terraced vineyards. Genoa is the region's geographic and economic center.

Liguria produces both red and white wines. Most celebrated is its white Cinqueterre, whose name translates as "Five Lands," and refers to the five wine-producing villages bordering the gulf between Chiavari and La Spezia. Known since medieval times the wine, pressed from raisined grapes, is golden and luscious with an intensely aromatic bouquet. To suit the current taste, Cinqueterre is often vinified crisply dry. Liguria's best-known red wine is the light, dry, ruby-colored Dolceaqua, produced near the town of San Remo.

Nothing more excellent or valuable than wine
was ever granted by the gods to man.
—Plato

Tuscany

Tuscany, a major wine-producing region in central Italy, is a rugged landscape of undulating hills and wooded valleys. Its capital city is Florence. Tuscany is celebrated for its red wines: Chianti, Brunello di Montalcino, and Vino Nobile de Montepulciano. The dominant grape here is the red sangiovese, along with its clone, the sangioveto. Tuscany also makes a few white wines.

The world-famous Chianti district —bounded by Florence, Arezzo, and Siena— includes seven separate wine-producing areas and covers about one hundred seventy-five thousand acres. Encompassed here are some seven thousand vineyards, a number having been passed down within the same family for as many as ten generations. (One Florentine citizen represents the twenty-sixth generation of his family in the wine trade.) At the center of the district is the Chianti Classico zone, a one-hundred-square-mile area deemed superior in its soil and climate. (The zone was officially delimited in 1716.)

Chianti Classico wines at their finest combine great character with a certain delicacy. Dark, tannic, rich and concentrated, with an attractive astringency that makes them lively on the palate, they display an enchanting violetlike bouquet and a lingering aftertaste. As a group, however, Chianti wines can vary greatly. Some are light and fresh; others are dark and heavy. Some are thin, some fat; some soft and others rough. Some are full-bodied and intensely flavored, while others are light bodied and uncomplicated. Some are soon ready to drink, while others need years of aging. Many are light, grapy, and unpretentious at their best, and harsh and acidic at their worst.

NOTE: The lesser examples may be bolstered by *il governo*, a richly sugared concentrate made by boiling down the grapes set aside at harvest time and allowed to dry before crushing. *Il governo* causes the new wines to referment, increasing their alcohol, body, and vinosity. This not only sweetens them perceptibly, but adds a fresh "burnt" quality to the taste of the wines. (Once commonly employed in the region, *il governo* has generally fallen into disuse.)

Chiantis have traditionally been a blend of red and white grapes. (The wines were initially called *vermiglios* because of their bright scarlet color.) The classic blend, codified in the late nineteenth century, combined the red sangiovese, canaiolo, and other varieties with the white trebbiano and malvasia. The official formula calls for 70 to 90 percent red grapes and 10 to 30 percent white. (By law, only the red wines meeting these requirements can be called Chiantis.)

In the 1960s, Tuscan vintners —seeking to produce darker, richer wines— began to place a greater emphasis on red grapes in their blends while reducing the proportion of white grapes or omitting them altogether. (Some of the wines are now 100 percent sangiovese.) The wine makers also began to use such atypical grape varieties as the cabernet sauvignon, cabernet franc, and merlot. Since the resulting wines did not meet Chianti's labeling requirements, they were given various other names, such as Solaia, Sassicaia, Carmagnano, Ornellaia, Pomino, Tiscvil, and Tiganello.

Tuscany's most complex wine is Brunello di Montalcino (named both for the sangiovese grape —known locally as the brunello— and for the hill town of Montalcino.) Produced beyond the southernmost reaches of the Chianti zone, Brunello di Montalcino was created in the nineteenth century when a particular sangiovese clone was isolated. Darker, richer, and more powerful than a classic Chianti, Brunello is a big, warm, deeply concentrated wine that at its finest displays a velvety texture, combined with rich fruit flavors and aromas. A subtle dryness balances out its intense richness. In good vintages, the Brunellos need decades of aging for their proper development.

NOTE: The growing demand for Brunellos has led to an expansion of their vineyard land, which had initially been limited to fifty acres. In some cases, the demand has led to vinifying the wines for their earlier maturation.

Tuscany also produces Rosso di Montalcino, known as "Brunello's younger brother." Pressed from the same grape varieties, but from the fruit of younger vines, the Rosso is aged more briefly in wood than the Brunello and is ready to drink at a much earlier age. Another outstanding Tuscan red is Vino Nobile de Montepulciano, named for its lovely hill town some thirty miles south of Siena. Pressed from the same grape varieties as traditional Chiantis, it is a full-flavored, medium-bodied, delightfully dry red wine with a good bouquet.

Tuscany is associated as well with generally fresh and agreeable white wines. Best known is its Vernaccia di San Gimignano, produced in the heart of Chianti country and named for a many-towered medieval city south of Florence. Pale gold in color and medium in body, the wine at its finest displays a delicate but penetrating bouquet, accompanied by a somewhat dry finish. One of Tuscany's modest little wines is Galestro, a pale, dry, crisp white that sometimes displays a slight and natural effervescence. A particularly celebrated Tuscan white wine is vin santo, a lusciously rich and very luxurious dessert wine.

Marche

Marche, in central Italy, extends from the Apennine Mountains to the Atlantic Ocean. It was once a medieval borderland (*a marca*) between the country's northern and southern sectors. The capital city here is Ancona. Marche is famous for its white Verdicchio, named for a local grape variety, which is blended with the trebbiano and malvasia. Light and fruity, with a delicate bouquet, Verdicchio is enhanced by a crisp, dry undertone and a pleasant bitterness in its aftertaste.

Among Marche's red wines are Rosso Piceno and Rosso Conero. Rosso Piceno, pressed primarily from the sangiovese grape, is soft and slightly dry, with a pleasant bouquet. Rosso Conero, pressed mainly from the montepulciano grape, is a robust and agreeably dry wine.

Umbria

The small landlocked region of Umbria is located, west of Marche between Florence and Rome. The capital city here is Perugia. In recent times, Umbria has come into its own as a source of reasonably priced wines. Although growing both red and white wines, the region is generally noted for its whites.

Best known is Orvieto, named for a famous cathedral town perched on a mountainlike outcropping of rock. Fruity with a slight, attractive bitterness in its undertone, Orvieto is vinified both semidry and dry. The semidry, delicate and fragrantly sweet, gives no hint of cloying, while the dry is usually fresh and crisp with a flowery bouquet. Best known among Umbria's red wines is Rubesco, pressed from the sangiovese, canaiolo, and other grapes. Deep ruby in color and excellent in body and bouquet, this wine takes well to aging. At its finest the Rubesco becomes soft, round, velvety smooth, and generous. Another noteworthy red is Torgiano, named for its town of origin, south of Perugia. A number of other Umbrian red wines reflect the current trend of including French grapes in Italian blends. Some of these are composed of half cabernet sauvignon and half pinot noir.

Latium

Latium (Lazio), located south of Umbria, lies between the Apennine Mountains and the Tyrrhenian Sea. Its capital city is Rome. The region is known for its fruity white wines, pressed from trebbiano and malvasia grapes. These range from the crisp and dry to the semisweet, on to the decidedly sweet.

Particularly noteworthy are the Castelli Romani (Roman Castle) wines, grown in a number of hill villages southeast of Rome. They include Frascati, Velletri, Albano, Marino, Grottaferrata, and San Giorgio.

Frascati, famous since the Renaissance, is a fresh, fragrant white wine, displaying a good degree of fruit combined with a touch of acidity and a slight attractive bitterness in its aftertaste. (An almost neutral version is made for export.) Velletri, produced nearby, is somewhat lighter in body and flavor. Grown in six communes in the fertile uplands of the Colli Albani (Alban Hills) is the modest white Albano, which is vinified both semidry and dry. North of Rome, from the slopes of Lake Bolsena comes Est! Est! Est! —a wine which acquired its curious name in the twelfth century. According to legend, a wine-loving bishop on his way to Rome would send his manservant ahead to scout out the best possible inns to stay the night. Whenever the manservant found a likely place, he would chalk the word *est* on the door, short for *vinum bonum est* (the wine is good). In the little village of Montefiascone, the white wine proved so splendid that the manservant enthusiastically scrawled *"Est! Est! Est!"* on the door of the inn. Apparently the bishop agreed. He never resumed his journey to Rome, but lived out his days in Montefiascone, happily savoring the pleasures of the local wine.

NOTE: Est! Est! Est! —initially pressed exclusively from muscat grapes— was light-bodied and semisweet. It is now a blend of trebbiano and malvasia grapes and vinified somewhat drier.

Campania

Campania lies on a fertile plain south of Rome. Hovering above is the volcanic Mount Vesuvius. The region's capital is Naples. Campania produces both red and white wines. Of particular interest is the white Lacryma Christi (Tears of Christ), whose dramatic name comes from the legend of Lucifer's expulsion from heaven. Lucifer apparently pulled off a piece of Paradise on his departure and descended with it to a spot near Naples. Witnessing this, Christ shed tears of sorrow, which fell to the ground, giving root to the vines. Fairly dry and somewhat aromatic, Lacryma Christi is pressed from the greco della torre grape, grown on the south-facing slopes of Mount Vesuvius. The best examples are full-bodied with a velvety texture, displaying a suggestion of fruit. (A richer, sweeter version of the wine is pressed from raisined grapes.)

NOTE: Although a number of Italian wines have appropriated the colorful Lacryma Christi name, only the authentic versions carry the phrase "del Vesuvio" on the label.

Among Campania's red wines are Taurasi, Falerno, and Gragnano. Taurasi, pressed mainly from the aglianico grape, sometimes blended with the barbera or sangiovese, traces its lineage back to the Greeks. Robust and full of complex fruit, it is a splendid and intense wine. (Taurasi has been called the "Barolo of southern Italy.") Falerno, a medium-bodied and singularly fragrant wine, is often vinified semidry. The Gragnano is a soft, light, fruity wine.

Offshore from Campania are the islands of Capri and Ischia, facing each other across the Bay of Naples. Capri produces a number of clean, dry white wines and other whites which are somewhat sweetish. Ischia, known for its good reds and whites, has often appropriated the Capri name for its wines, as have a number of other wine makers from the nearby mainland. Perhaps they wish to take advantage of Capri's association with fantasy and romance.

Apulia

Apulia (Puglia) is located in the heel of Italy's geographic boot; its regional capital is Bari. A rugged, prolific land with a rich, claylike soil, Apulia is Italy's largest wine producer. The region is best known for its strong, hearty, uncomplicated wines, both red and white. Of special interest is the red Torre Quarto, a wine from the Castel del Monte district, with a good bouquet, Also noteworthy are the sturdy reds and rosés of San Severo.

As a rule, the wines of Apulia lend themselves best to blending; the medium-to full-bodied reds usually serving as body builders for the thinner wines of the north, the whites providing the base wines for the Italian vermouths. Employing modern vinification methods now, Apulia has been improving its red wines and producing clean, fresh-tasting white wines as well.

Calabria

Another prolific province is Calabria, located in the toe of the Italian boot. Its capital city is Reggio. Characterizing the region are a rough terrain and a hot, dry climate, yielding generally coarse wines. These are best suited to blending. The heavy reds are shipped out in bulk to strengthen the thinner wines of northern Italy and France; the full-bodied whites provide the base for Italian vermouths. Calabria also produces medium-bodied, dry red wines and sturdy, flowery whites. Of particular interest is the white Greco di Bianco, along with the red, white, and rosé wines of Ciro.

NOTE: Basilicata, a region north of Calabria, is known for its dry, intense, bold red wines, and particularly for its Aglianico del Vulture.

Sicily

Lying offshore from Calabria, almost within sight of North Africa, is the island of Sicily, whose capital city is Palermo. Seven centuries before the birth of Christ, the Greeks and Carthaginians were planting muscat vines here.

Sicily's volcanic soil and warm climate yield full-bodied, high-alcohol wines. Best known are the Corvos grown near the little town of Casteldaccia, south of Palermo. The red Corvos are fine, soft, and velvety, yet almost austerely dry; displaying an abundance of fruit, a mouth-filling flavor, and a berrylike bouquet. The white Corvos, although somewhat more ordinary, have been made crisp and clean by modern vinification methods. From Sicily's northeastern sector near Messina, comes the ruby-colored Faro, which exhibits unusual qualities for a warm-climate wine; a lightness of body, a dryness of flavor, and a delicate nose.

From eastern Sicily come the Etna wines, named for the great volcano that towers over the city of Catania on whose slopes they grow. The red Etnas are full-bodied and not too alcoholic with a good acidity, making them pleasantly dry. The white Etnas are straw colored and intensely aromatic.

Sicily is particularly known for its sweet, luscious, and aromatic dessert wines, pressed from raisined grapes. Especially celebrated are the wines of the small Lipari Islands lying off its northern coast. Of special interest is the deep-colored Malvasia di Lipari, which at its finest possesses a ripe velvety taste and a rich aroma, suggesting ripe apricots. (The wine is reminiscent of a good Sauternes.) From the torrid expanses of Sicily's west coast come the world-famous Marsala wines, which are generally dark and sweet with a raisiny flavor. Among the fine rich, heady Muscat wines of the island's southeastern sector is the Moscato de Siracusa.

NOTE: Sicily ships many of the wines it produces out in bulk, often sending the reds to Germany to strengthen the paler red wines there. The Sicilian white wines usually remain at home to serve as the base for Italian vermouths, or else they are distilled into brandies.

Sardinia

Some one hundred and twenty-five miles away from the Italian mainland, in the Tyrrhenian Sea just below Corsica, is the island of Sardinia. The regional capital here is Cagliari.

Grown on a mountainous terrain are many of the same grapes as on the mainland. The island is best known for its white wines, vinified both sweet and dry, but red wines are also produced. One notable example is a full, intense, beautifully balanced cabernet sauvignon, enhanced with an aromatic touch of oak.

NOTE: Other Italian wine regions of note include Abruzzi (Abruzzo) and Molise. Abruzzi in central Italy is known for its lusty red wines —including Montepulciano d'Abruzzo— and for its complex dry white wines —including the Trebbiano d'Abruzzo. Molise on the Adriatic coast produces clean, dry white wines, along with sturdy reds and rosés.

SPAIN

Spain, like Italy, is largely mountainous, but devotes more of its acreage to grape growing than either Italy or France. Although Spain currently has more than four million acres under cultivation, it produces relatively less wine than the other two.

Much of its land is arid, the vine density is quite low, and many vineyard owners lack the equipment that is needed for greater productivity.

The Phoenicians had planted the first vines here. The Romans found an already thriving viticulture when they arrived. Iberia soon became an important wine supplier to Imperial Rome. When the Roman emperor, Domitian, sought to suppress competitive wine growing in A.D. 92, he singled out Iberia as one of his major targets.

For centuries, Spanish wine making had remained essentially unchanged. (The vintners would toss their tannic stalks and stems into the vats and age their wines in a leisurely manner.) In recent years, however, Spain —seeking to expand its wine industry beyond a largely domestic market— has begun to promote and export its wines in earnest. Vineyards have been upgraded, a number of wineries have been modernized, and some are now capable of immense production.

Spanish wines range from the simple and uncomplicated to the more formal, subtle, and sophisticated. Reflecting the generous warmth of their southern climate, they are characterized by a distinctive lushness. Red wines are predominant; Spain produces good rosés as well. The white wines run the gamut from the light and aromatic to the full-bodied and floral.

Among the red grapes grown are the indigenous tempranillo, parellada, garnacha (grenache), graciano, cariñena, mazuela, and xarello, along with the French cabernet sauvignon and cabernet franc. The white grapes include the native viura, verdejo, and albariño, along with the French chardonnay.

Comprising Spain are seventeen wine-producing regions. The major ones are Rioja and Catalonia in the north and Andalusia in the south. Other notable regions are La Mancha, the Levant, Castilla-Leon, and Galicia. There has also been an expansion into new regions like Ribera del Duero.

Rioja

Rioja, lying along the banks of the Ebro River in north-central Spain, is the country's premier table-wine region. The river is joined near Pamplona by a smaller tributary, the Rio Oja, whose name in shortened form became the name of the region. Rioja is a small and largely treeless area of chalky white cliffs and terraced vineyards; some sited more than fifteen hundred feet above sea level. (The Pyrenees shelter the region from the cold winds of the north.) A long spring with abundant rainfall gives way to a relatively gentle summer, encouraging the slow and gradual ripening of the grapes. Autumn is warm and quite prolonged.

The Romans made wine here in the first century. Six centuries later, the Moors conquered the territory and, following the teachings of the Koran, forbade the making of wine. Benedictine monks restored wine production in the Middle Ages. In the nineteenth century, when phylloxera was devastating nearby France, many Bordeaux vintners fled over the Pyrenees to Rioja, greatly influencing its wine making and helping to establish the region's notable reputation.

NOTE: Because Rioja is essentially landlocked, its wines were little known to the outside world at first. (Those that had been exported were used primarily in blending.) Extensive road building after World War II created a greater access to the region and to its admirable wines.

About three-fourths of Rioja's wines are red. The main grape varieties are the tempranillo and garnacha (grenache), followed by the mazuela and graciano. More recently, the French cabernet sauvignon has been added to the blend. The wines themselves range from the darker, fuller-bodied Tintos —displaying a strong tannic backbone and intense berrylike flavors— to the lighter-colored, lighter-bodied, velvety Claretes. Classic Riojas, reflecting the French influence, are matured extensively in wood and exhibit the body and much of the elegance of a good French Bordeaux, combined with a deeper, more assertive Spanish bouquet. Under the influence of American importers, however, many of the red wines have now been vinified for earlier maturation. Made less tannic and oaked more moderately, they are softer and more supple, but lack the solid structure and potential for development which their French prototypes have shown.

Rioja's white grape varieties include the viura, malvasia and calgrano. The white wines, like the reds, were traditionally fermented as well as aged in wood.

Only when quite oxidized and tasting heavily of oak were they considered at all drinkable. Vinified in stainless steel now and bottled while still young, Rioja's white wines are lighter, fresher, and ready to drink in about six months. Most are vinified dry, but a number are made semisweet.

Rioja encompasses three subregions: Rioja Alta, Rioja Alavesa, and Rioja Baja. Rioja Alta to the west, is subject to a moist, cool climate, and grows its grapes about twelve hundred feet above sea level. (The vineyards are clustered around the city of Haro, the center of Rioja's wine trade.) Some of Spain's best table wines are produced here. They're characterized by good acidity and a great potential for aging. The finest demonstrate both elegance and distinction.

Rioja Alavesa, located at the tip of the Basque province of Alba, shares the terrain, climate and soil of Rioja Alta, but the sheltering mountains keep its vineyards warmer and drier. The wines here are richer, fruitier and softer, and as a rule, show less capacity for aging. The climate in Rioja Baja, the vast lower sector, is hotter and its wines are somewhat heavier and coarser. For better balance, the products of all three sectors are usually blended together; the house styles of the individual producers determine their relative proportion in the blends.

NOTE: Another important Spanish wine producer is Navarra, situated just east of Rioja. (It is also the site of Pamplona and the running of the bulls.) Extending from the Pyrenees to the Ebro River basin, Navarra produces some excellent white wines but is known primarily for its reds and rosés. Many are pressed from such Bordeaux grapes as the merlot, cabernet sauvignon, and cabernet franc as well as from native varieties. A rosé is made from the garnacha (grenache).

Catalonia

Catalonia, east of Rioja on the Mediterranean coast is in Basque country. Its principal wine districts are Penedés, Alella, Tarragona, and Priorato.

Penedés, a wedge-shaped area of chalky hills sloping down to the sea, is about twenty-five miles west of Barcelona. A center of wine production under the Romans, it fell into disuse under the Moors and did not re-emerge until the late nineteenth century when it became a substantial producer of wine. The Penedés district (Panedés in the Basque language) is celebrated for its surprisingly light, dry white wines, grown in the mountains along the coast. Relatively high in acidity and low in alcohol, they are particularly well suited to sparkling wine production.

The traditional Spanish white grapes grown here are the parellada, macabeo, viura, and cariñena. Cultivated now as well are the muscat, riesling, gewürztraminer, sauvignon blanc, and chardonnay. The Penedés red wines are robust, lush, and velvety, displaying at their finest a rich texture and a fruity aroma. Included in their blends are such traditional grapes as the tempranillo and garnacha along with the French cabernet sauvignon, cabernet franc, pinot noir, and carignan.

One of Spain's smallest producers, the Alella district north of Barcelona, grows its grapes on granite slopes. Four-fifths of its wines are white. Usually vinified semisweet, these are considered some of the best whites that Spain produces.

Southwest of Barcelona is Tarragona, once a supplier of wine to Imperial Rome. Produced here are red, white, and rosé wines. Best known among the reds is the sweet, full-bodied Tarragona; among the whites are the sweet Muscatels. A number of the Tarragona wines are fortified. (France employs them in its apéritif blends.) To the north is Priorato, a small area specializing in strong dry red wines, which are characterized by a lush, blackberrylike fruitiness.

RIOJA	Penedés
	Allela
CATALONIA	Tarragona
	Priorato
ANDALUSIA	Sherry
LA MANCHA	Valdepeñas
GALICIA	
THE LEVANT	Alicante
CASTILLA-LEON	Ribera del Duero

Andalusia

Andalusia in southern Spain is the home of the world-famous sherries. Many invaders had marched through the region: the Phoenicians, Greeks, Carthaginians, Romans, Visigoths, Vandals, and Moors. Some three thousand years ago, the main town here, Jerez de la Frontera, was a Phoenician outpost called Zera. The Greeks modified its name to Shera, the Romans to Serit. The Moors, crossing over from North Africa, called it Sherez, later to become Jerez (pronounced *hair-ETH*). Grape cultivation continued during the five centuries of Moorish occupation but most of the berries were consumed as raisins. (Some were vinified and the wine was sold to the infidels.) In the thirteenth century, the Moors were ousted. By the fifteenth century, Jerez had become a fortress on the Christian-Moslem border and the phrase *de la Frontera* ("of the Frontier") was added to its name. The sherry zone, known as the "Golden Triangle," is bordered by rivers on two sides (the Rio Guadalquivir and Rio Guadelete) and by the Atlantic Ocean on the third side. Located within its twenty-mile radius are the towns of Jerez de la Frontera, Puerto de Santa Maria, and Sanlúcar de Barrameda.

Low, hilly, and treeless, Jerez experiences cool winters, rainy springs, and fiercely hot summers. (Temperatures can rise to 100°F.) Mitigating the intense heat are gentle breezes and dry winds blowing in from North Africa across the sea. Andalusia produces low-acid white wines, ideal for sherry making. The grape varieties grown here are the palomino, pedro ximénez (PX) and, to a lesser extent, the moscatel. (The palomino is responsible for the delicate finos and the pedro ximénez for the fuller-bodied olorosos.)

Three distinct types of soil characterize the sherry district: albariza, barro, and arenas. The albariza soil is lime rich and chalky; its name derives from *albero*, meaning "white" and it rich wines demonstrate the greatest finesse. The denser, more claylike barro produces heavier wines, while the sandier, more prolific arenas produces somewhat thinner ones. For better balance, the wines of all three soils are generally blended together.

Northwest of Jerez and about one hundred miles inland is the province of Córdoba, encompassing the vineyards of Montilla and los Moriles. The Montilla-Moriles wines, also grown on an arid chalky soil, bear a strong resemblance to the sherries of Jerez and are often confused with them. Subject to cooler upland conditions, however, they usually demonstrate less bouquet and breed than a first-rate sherry. Nevertheless they display at their finest, exceedingly delicate flavors and aromas. Since their natural alcohol levels reach as high as 16 percent, the wines receive little or no fortification.

About a hundred miles east of Jerez, on Spain's southern coast, is Málaga, celebrated for the fortified wines which bear its name. Pressed from PX and muscat grapes, these wines are rich, raisiny, and quite intense.

La Mancha

South of Madrid in central Spain is La Mancha, the country's largest wine producer. (The hot, dry climate here is comparable to that of California's Central Valley or the French Midi.) A vast province with more than a million acres in vines, La Mancha accounts for about half of all Spanish wine production.

The region is best known for its red wines, many of them light, fruity, refreshing, and not much darker than a dark rosé. They have been called the "Beaujolais of Spain." (The more tannic among them are usually marketed as Spanish Burgundies.) Of La Mancha's five wine-producing villages, Valdepeñas, located in rolling upland country near Andalusia, is the most important. (The name Valdepeñas translates as "Valley of Stones.") The red wines of the other La Mancha villages tend to be more ordinary. White wines are also produced here; some are now vinified crisp and dry to suit the current taste.

The Levant

The Levant, another vast wine-growing area, is situated on the country's east coast and subject to a hot, dry climate. Produced here are both red and white wines. The reds, heavy and high in alcohol, are made in great quantities and usually exported for blending. The medium-bodied whites are generally consumed domestically as bar wines. The region's best-known wines come from Valencia, famous for its orange groves. Alicante, located farther south, is another noteworthy producer, known for its full-bodied red wines, light rosés, and rather bland white wines, together with some sweet Moscatels.

Castilla-Leon

Castilla-Leon is in northern Spain. The Duero River runs through it, becoming the Douro as it flows almost due west into Portugal. Grapes have been grown on the banks of this river and wines have been made here since Roman times. The region includes the newly demarcated Ribera del Duero district near Valladolid, the source of dark, fruit-filled, well-structured red wines which are succulent at their finest. Legendary among them is the rare and expensive Vega Sicilia, a blend of local grapes —primarily the tempranillo— combined with such classic French varieties as the cabernet sauvignon, merlot, and malbec. Made only in exceptional years and aged extensively in oak (sometimes for more than a decade), the intensely rich and densely textured Vega Sicilia demonstrates a great subtlety of flavor and aroma. Another noteworthy red, grown near Valladolid, is the Pesquera del Duero. Made almost entirely from the tinto del pais, a local grape, and aged extensively in wood, this is a rich, dark and brawny wine, which is concentrated in its fruit. The Pesquera exhibits at its finest the intensity and elegance of a high-caliber St.-Émilion or a Pomerol from France.

Galicia

Galicia, on the Atlantic Ocean in northwestern Spain, is the country's coolest and wettest province. Produced in this land of green hills and deep forests are red, white, and rosé wines. The whites, pressed from the albariño grape, are similar to the Portuguese vinho verdes from across the border. Smooth textured and somewhat acid, vinified either bone-dry or near dry, they exhibit an applelike crispness and a rich fragrance at their finest. Galicia's red wines include Vino de Riverso and Ribeiro del Avia. The former is pleasant and fruity with a pronounced flavor; the latter is big and rough. Galicia also produces good rosé wines.

NOTE: The Canary Islands, which lie in the Atlantic Ocean off the northwest coast of Africa, were much celebrated in Shakespeare's day for their extraordinary Malvasia wines, grown on a volcanic soil. In the nineteenth century, when phylloxera had wiped out its vineyards, the wine industry never quite recovered. Although the Canaries have continued to produce some wine, little of it is exported.

PORTUGAL

Portugal, sharing the Iberian Peninsula with Spain, experiences virtually the same kind of climate and soil, but relies much more on hand labor for its wine making. (Many of the wines are still fermented in the same stone lagars in which the grapes are crushed.) Portugal is best known for its fortified port wines, rosés, and slightly sparkling vinho verdes. Less familiar are the table wines. Its noteworthy reds range from the fruity and light to the bold and deep bodied; displaying at their finest a subtlety, complexity, and rare distinction. Its substantial and aromatic white wines have been made crisp and clean by modern vinification methods.

Most of Portugal's wine growing is concentrated in the northern and western sectors of the country. The main regions are the Douro, Dão, and Minho.

DOURO	BUCELAS
DÃO	TAGUS VALLEY
MINHO	SETUBAL
COLARES	CARCAVELOS
BAIRRADA	

The Douro

The rugged Douro Valley in northeastern Portugal, near the mouth of the Rio Douro ("River of Gold"), is the source of the world-famous port wines. The river, a great waterway rising in the mountains north of Madrid (where it's called the Duero), runs for some seventy miles in a westerly direction before turning abruptly south at the Portuguese border. After plunging more than a thousand feet in a series of gorges and rapids, the river again turns westward and flows swiftly toward the Atlantic Ocean.

The wines for port are grown in the Alto Douro (Upper Douro), a bleak, mountainous, almost inaccessible area extending some thirty miles on either side of the river. (The Douro region was officially delimited in 1756.) Terraced vineyards line and cling to its steep, precipitous banks. (Many of the vineyards were created here by blasting the rugged rock with dynamite.) Winters are severely cold and frequently experience heavy frost. Summer temperatures often exceed 100°F and the rainfall is sufficient, but not excessive. A long growing season with a blazing sun ripens the grapes intensely. (This season extends from April through October.) The Douro's wines are red, ranging from youthful rubies and tawnies to splendid and elegant vintage ports. The region's grape varieties include the indigenous touriga, tinta, bastardo, and alvarelhão. (Anywhere from seven to several dozen grape varieties go into the blends for port wine.)

The Douro's traditional wine centers are Oporto, the hillside city for which the celebrated wine is named, (it is called Porto by the Portuguese) and Vila Nova de Gaia downriver, where the young wines are taken in spring for blending and aging. Some eighty port wine lodges are located along the waterfront here. (Until 1987, it was illegal to bottle or ship the port wines from anywhere in the country but from these lodges in Vila Nova de Gaia.)

The Douro is also the home of another prestigious red wine: the full-bodied, long-lived, and richly flavored Barca Velha. (Its predominant grape is the tempranillo.) Developed in the 1950s, this wine is made only in exceptional vintages. Also noteworthy is the red Ferreirnha, grown at the region's northern edge. Somewhat fruity rosés are produced in the Douro as well.

Dão

Dão, a small mountainous area with a hard granitic soil, located some fifty miles southeast of Oporto, is known for its red table wines, which range from the soft, fruity, and easy to drink to the robust, intense, and full flavored. Some exhibit a berrylike taste, a slightly puckerish quality, and a long, tart, pleasing finish reminiscent of a Bordeaux wine. Other Dãos display the spicy aromas and flavors associated with Rhône Valley wines. The finest examples, pressed from the same grape varieties as port, are noted for their longevity. The Dão region also produces firmly structured and not–too–dry white and rosé wines.

Other Portuguese Districts

Minho, in northwestern Portugal, is known for its naturally effervescent white wines, particularly for its vinho verdes. (These are pressed from the alvarinho grape.) Other Portuguese districts of note are Colares, Bucelas, the Tagus Valley, Setúbal, and Bairrada. Colares is on the Atlantic coast, west of Lisbon. Its vines proved to be phylloxera resistant; having been planted so deep in the sandy soil that the destructive aphid could not get at their roots. They are among the very few vines in the world that have remained ungrafted. Colares wines are dark, tannic, and unappealingly harsh when young, but can acquire a soft, flowerlike bouquet with age. Salt air blowing in from the Atlantic Ocean gives them a certain piquancy.

North of Lisbon is the hill country of Bucelas, known for its white wines. Some are dry, fresh, and lively, while others are quite sweet. The Tagus Valley, northeast of Lisbon, is noted for its deep-colored red wines which demonstrate soft, smooth flavors with age. Immediately south of Lisbon is the Setúbal peninsula, celebrated for its sweet white Moscatel de Setúbal. This wine, fermented on its skins, acquires a honeylike taste, an almost overwhelmingly rich bouquet, and a definite potential for aging. Also south of Lisbon is Carcavelos, known for its sweetish, almond-flavored red wine, high in alcohol and served as an apéritif. Bairrada in the west-central sector, near Coimbra, has been called the "Bordeaux of Portugal" because of the finesse and ageability of its excellent red wines.

GERMANY

Germany, Europe's most northerly wine-growing country, shares roughly the same latitude as Newfoundland. Moderating its relatively harsh climate are great rivers, forests, and mountains. Despite a short growing season, the grapes here are able to ripen properly. The Romans cultivated their vines in the first century and by the third century, the Mosel Valley had become the northern frontier of the Roman Empire. In the ninth century, Charlemagne was setting up his own vineyards. By the tenth, Germany was exporting some of its wines to Britain.

About 85 percent of the German wines are white; the best of them are among the world's most splendid wines. Rich, flavorful, and ripely scented, they are able to achieve a remarkable balance between natural sweetness and high fruit acidity.

The grape varieties grown include the riesling, müller-thurgau, sylvaner, rulander, gewürztraminer, gutedal, kleinberger and kerner. The riesling is responsible for the most elegant wines, which are quite light in alcohol as a rule. Possessing less body, they are able to reveal their subtle nuances more distinctly and brilliantly. The most widely distributed wines, however, are the commonplace Liebfraumilch, Moselblumchen, Zeller Schwartze Katz, and Niersteiner Domtal, usually characterized by blandness and an often cloying sweetness. Germany's few red grapes include the spätburgunder (late-ripening Burgundy), portugieser, and dornfelder, whose relatively low-tannin, and generally soft, thin wines are often in need of bolstering. Strengthening them are robust high-alcohol wines imported from other countries.

Germany's wine regions are the Rhineland and its subdivisions, along with the Mosel-Saar-Ruwer, Franconia, and Baden, followed by Nahe, Hessiche

Bergstrasse, and Württemberg. The regions of greatest viticultural importance are the Rhineland and the Mosel-Saar-Ruwer.

The Rhineland

The Rhineland, the country's most valuable wine region, encompasses the valleys of the Rhine River and its tributaries. The preeminent district here, the Rheingau, is followed by the Rheinpfalz (Pfalz) and Rheinhessen. The other districts are the Mittelrhein, Ahr, and Assmannhausen.

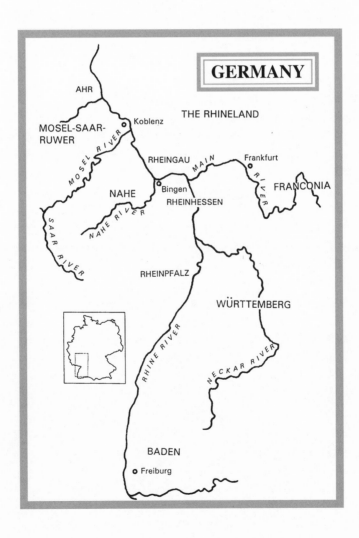

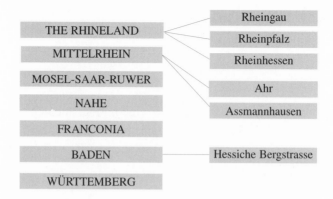

The Rheingau

The prestigious Rheingau is situated on the north shore of the Rhine River, which —after following a long impetuous course down from Switzerland— is deflected by the Taunus Mountains when it reaches Mainz. This causes the river to turn briefly westward. The Rheingau is located on this straight and narrow stretch of land running from east to west, beginning near Hochheim and ending just to the west of Rüdesheim. The Rheingau is only some twenty miles long and two to five miles wide. Encompassed in the region are many of Germany's greatest vineyards. Sited on steeply terraced slopes, they enjoy an incomparable southern exposure, while the Taunus Mountains shield them from the cold, harsh winds of the north. The grapes themselves are often grown a thousand or more feet above sea level; some of the vineyards have names ending in *berg*, meaning "mountain," as in Steinberg and Ruppertsberg.

Four-fifths of the Rheingau wines are Rieslings. Austere, but mouth filling, these are generous, well-rounded wines, which are firm and complex. A definite crispness offsets their fruity, flowery flavors. They exhibit at their finest extraordinary grace and breed, amazing vitality and stamina. The fine acid balance that even the richest among them possess gives them an unusual capacity for aging.

The Rheingau's great wine villages include Rauenthal, Eltville, Erbach, Hattenheim, Hallgarten, Oestrich, Winkel, and Geisenheim; some are sited on the banks of the river, while others are set farther back in the hills. Erbach is celebrated for its fruity, scented wines, especially those grown in the Marcobrunn vineyard. Distinguishing Hattenheim's wines are a grace and elegance. Oestrich's heavier soil yields wines that are fuller in body. Rauenthal's finely scented wines demonstrate a certain spiciness. Those of Hallgarten are often the most pronounced in flavor, while Eltville's wines are consistently charming.

One of the Rheingau's leading estates is Schloss Johannisberg. Sited on a high slope above the river, its wines are particularly prized for their concentration and scent. Charlemagne himself established this vineyard when he observed that snow melted here in the spring sooner than elsewhere. In the nineteenth century, the Congress of Vienna ceded Schloss Johannisberg to the Austrian emperor, who in turn deeded it to Prince von Metternich. The von Metternich family still maintains a degree of ownership in the property.

Another estimable Rheingau estate is Schloss Vollrads, nestled in the hills above Winkel. (It has been in the hands of the same family for six centuries.) At its finest, the Vollrads wine displays a great fruity character and impeccable balance. Situated directly behind the village of Hattenheim is the notable Steinberg vineyard, established by a monastic Cistercian order in the twelfth century and secularized some seven hundred years later. The vineyard is now the property of the Staatsweingut or State Domain. (The original monastery, Kloster Eberbach, adjacent to the vineyard, has become a wine museum.) The Steinberg Rieslings, demonstrating a great deal of breeding, are typically fruity and powerful.

On reaching Rüdesheim, the most westerly village of consequence, the Rhine River shifts abruptly from its straight east-to-west course and resumes a generally northward direction. To the east, where the Rhine is joined by one of its tributaries —the Main— is the village of Hochheim. Its wines, although technically produced outside the Rheingau, are so similar in style and character as to be generally grouped with the Rheingaus. Hochheim's most notable vineyards are Kirchenstuck and Domdechaney.

NOTE: The Hochheim wines have long been popular with the British, who shortened their name to *hock*, which became the generic name for Germany's white wines in England .

At the western end of the Rheingau, between Rüdesheim and Lorch, is Assmannhausen, responsible for Germany's best-known red wines. An eighty-five-acre tract growing spätburgunder grapes, it produces wines which are velvety and fiery in some vintages and not very powerful in others. Assmannhausen produces some noteworthy late-harvest rosés as well.

Rheinpfalz (Pfalz)

The Rhineland's next important subdivision —and the vastest wine-producing region in the country— is Rheinpfalz or the Pfalz; also known as the Rhenish Palatinate, having been named for one of Rome's seven hills. Located south of the Rheingau, on the left bank of the Rhine River, the Pfalz is a fertile plain about fifty miles long and two and a half to four miles wide. Its vineyards, sited along the lower slopes of the Haardt Mountains (a continuation of the French Vosges), are shielded and protected by those mountains. Spring arrives here early and a strong sun during the growing season makes the Pfalz one of the country's warmest and driest areas. Grown on its better soils is the aristocratic riesling but the predominant grape varieties cultivated here are the müller-thurgau and sylvaner, followed by the rulander, tokayer, traminer and muscat. Pfalz wines range from the mild and thirst quenching to the big, heavy, and robust. They display at their finest bouquet and breed, coupled with a definite but unobtrusive sweetness.

The Pfalz is divided into three sectors: the Ober, Mittel, and Unter Haardt ("Upper, Middle and Lower Haardt"). The Upper and Lower Haardt are areas of large production, yielding generally undistinguished wines. (Many are not bottled but served directly from the cask as carafe wines, or else consigned to commonplace blends.) The most favored sector is the Middle Haardt, which shares the climate but not the soil of the other two. The soil in its best vineyards is a schistous, sandy basalt. The most notable wine estates in the Middle Haardt are Diedesheim, Forst, Ruppertsberg, and Wachenheim.

Rheinhessen

Rheinhessen, also known as Rhenish Hessia, is located on the west bank of the Rhine, north of the Pfalz. Running parallel to the Rheingau across the river, the region begins near the city of Worms, continues north as far as Mainz, then extends west to Bingen. A plateau with a few wooded areas, it is sheltered from the harsh weather by a series of hills. Because its characteristically heavy soil contains a dark, reddish sandstone,vineyards here are called Rotenberg (Red Mountain) and Scharlachberg (Scarlet Mountain).

Only about a fourth the size of the Pfalz, Rheinhessen devotes almost as much acreage to grape growing, making it Germany's largest wine producer. Its subdistricts are Nierstein, Wonnegau, and Bingen. Most important is Nierstein, whose sunny vineyards yield full, fruity, and fragrant wines. Nierstein's leading wine towns are Nackenheim, Oppenheim, and Dienheim. The village of Ingelheim to the north —the site of Charlemagne's palace— specializes in white wines but is known for its red wines as well.

In Rheinhessen, the riesling grape yields full-bodied, vigorous, and fragrant wines, characterized by great fruit. (As a rule, they don't age as gracefully as their more austere counterparts in the Rheingau.) However, the bulk of the wines, pressed from the sylvaner and müller-thurgau, are soft and moderately dry. Grown in heavier soils, they acquire an earthiness and a sweetish quality. Often lacking in real character, they are generally consigned to commonplace blends.

Rheinhessen's most widely exported wine is Liebfraumilch. Initially pressed from the riesling and produced in a monastic vineyard near the city of Worms, the wine was mild, fragrant, and delicate, with a light earthy taste reflecting its alluvial soil. Primarily pressed now from the sylvaner grape, Liebfraumilch has become a haphazardly blended and somewhat sweetish wine over the years. More representative of the region are the wines produced in three vineyards at the site of the original monastery: Liebfrauenstift, Liebfrauenstift Klostergarten, and Kirchenstück. Another commonplace and widely exported wine is Niersteiner Domtal, which isn't a Niersteiner at all, but a miscellaneous blend drawn from various vineyards, which may or may not be located in Rheinhessen.

Other Rhine Districts

The Mittelrhein, situated north of the Rheingau, is an eighty-four-mile stretch of gentle slopes with a slatey and claylike soil. Traversing the region is the Rhine River, which has resumed its generally northward course after passing through the Rheingau. The Mittelrhein wines, full-bodied, vigorous, and hearty, are more pronounced in their fruit and acidity than those of the Rheingau.

Farther north and across the river is Ahr, named for its own river, which joins the Rhine north of Koblenz. The Ahr, Germany's largest continuous red-wine region, cultivates spätburgunder and portugieser grapes. Its wines —more pink than red— are generally light and for the most part are consumed locally. The Ahr also produces steely white wines, pressed from müller-thurgau and riesling grapes.

Mosel-Saar-Ruwer

The Mosel-Saar-Ruwer, located north and west of the Rheingau, is made up of three interconnecting river valleys: the Mosel and its tributaries, the Saar and the Ruwer. The region currently has some three hundred thousand vineyard acres under cultivation.

The Mosel Valley

The Mosel River rises in the Vosges Mountains of France (where it is known as the Moselle), then sweeps northward toward Lorraine and skirts Luxembourg before entering Germany at Trier. Until it joins the Rhine River at Koblenz, the Mosel meanders capriciously in a northeasterly direction for nearly a hundred miles, following a twisting serpentine course and executing a bizarre series of hairpin turns, which encompass a number of microclimates. The vineyards here are sited wherever exposure to the sun is favorable; sometimes on the left bank, sometimes on the right. The vines themselves are grown on the incredibly steep terraced slopes lining the river.

More than half the Mosel wines are pressed from the riesling. Other grape varieties include the müller-thurgau, kerner, and bacchus. The Mosels, generally airier and more delicate than most German wines, are characterized more by their bouquet than their body. At their finest they display a great but unobtrusive sweetness, combined with a tart, refreshing bite. The wines have been described as a "mingling of honey and steel: honey in the scent and steel in the finish." Responsible in part for their delightful freshness and unique flowery scent is the region's characteristically slate-strewn soil.

The Mosel Valley is divided into upper, middle, and lower sectors. The Upper Mosel is situated at the southern end of the valley and the Lower Mosel is located where the river runs a straighter course. These two sectors produce generally undistinguished wines. Of greatest viticultural importance is the Middle Mosel, where the river is at its most serpentine. The notable wine towns here are Piesport and Bernkastel, followed by Wehlen, Zeltingen, Trittenheim, and Graach.

Piesport's south-facing vineyards are sited on one hundred twenty acres of steep, rocky terrain, rising some five hundred feet above the river. Their wonderfully light, delicate, and subtle wine is known as the "queen of the Mosel." Preeminent among the vineyards here is Piesporter Goldtröpfchen, whose name translates as "Golden Droplets." Across the river is another notable wine town, Bernkastel, dominated by the Doktorberg (Doctor Hill). Its most celebrated vineyard is Bernkasteler Doktor. The vineyard acquired its name in the fourteenth century when, according to legend, the Prince-Bishop of Trier was stricken with a mortal illness and, when all other treatments failed, he drank some of the Doktorberg wine and was miraculously cured.

Other light, engaging wines are produced in Trittenheim, south of Piesport. while those of Wehlen, north of Piesport, are also prized for their delicacy. North of Wehlen is Urzig, whose brick-red soil yields interesting and spicy wines, which are among the longest-lived of the region. Zeltingen, farther north and across the river, produces some of the fullest bodied of the fine Mosel wines. North of

Zeltingen is the village of Erden, famous for its Treppchen vineyard, whose name translates as "Little Staircase." (Steps cut into the stony slope provide access to this steeply terraced vineyard.) South of Zeltingen is the tiny but well-known village of Graach, noted for its fine Himmelreich and Josephshofer wines.

Saar

The Saar River also rises in France and, flowing in a generally northern direction, joins the Mosel a few miles west of Trier. While some sectors of the Saar Valley are warm and well protected, others are vulnerable to the harsh winds from the north. Frost in May is not uncommon and hailstorms are always possible during the summer season.

The Saar's prime vineyards, sited on steeply slanted slopes, are known for their slatelike, crumbly soil. The riesling grape, higher in its acidity here than in the Mosel, yields generally more austere wines, which at their finest display an especially firm, elegant character and a great depth of flavor. The wines of the Saar have been likened to a "steel fist in a velvet glove."

The region's largest and most important wine town is Wiltingen, located southwest of Trier. Some three hundred and thirty acres of vines are cultivated here on a few south-facing and incredibly steep hills. Wiltingen's most notable vineyard, Scharzhofberg, occupies about seventy acres and is shared by a number of owners. Its wines, pressed from the riesling, are complex in character and finely scented. The Riesling wines from the adjoining town of Oberemmel, are somewhat similar. From the west, in Kanzem, come wines also closely resembling those of Wiltingen, but generally a bit fuller in their body.

Other Saar communes of note are Ockfen and Ayl, situated on opposite banks of the river. Ockfen is known for its great Bockstein vineyard, much celebrated for its scented, well-balanced Rieslings. Ayl's eminent vineyards are Herrenberg and Scheidterberg. Another noteworthy Saar vineyard is Vogelsang, situated in the village of Serrig.

Ruwer

A few miles downstream from Trier is the much smaller Ruwer region. (It's only about six miles long.) Ruwer's typically light, dry wines are closer in character to those of the Saar than to the Mosels. Gently subtle with a bit of spice, they combine at their finest considerable bouquet, together with a delicate floweriness and a certain elegance. A number of famous vineyards line the slatey banks of the Ruwer River, most notably Maximin Grunhaus (in Mertesdorf) and Karthauserhofberg (in Eitelsbach). Maximin Grunhaus, which was the property of the St. Maximin monastery in the tenth century, is now owned by the family that acquired it in the nineteenth century. Karthauserhofberg, once operated by Carthusian monks, is a much subdivided vineyard now.

Nahe

Nahe, west and north of Rheinhessen, is another of Germany's smaller wine regions. The Nahe River, running in a generally northeasterly direction for some eighty miles, joins the Rhine after passing through Bad Kreuznach. Located between the cities of Bingen and Bingerbruch, the Nahe's open, undulating valley encompasses some eight thousand acres in vines.

Nahe's climate is mild, dry, and generally sunny. Spring arrives here early and the autumn season is long. The soil on its often steep hillsides, is diverse, consisting of slate, gravel, fertile loam, igneous rock, and sandstone. The grape varieties grown are the riesling, sylvaner, and rulander. Nahe's wines are somewhere between those of the Mosel and the Rhine in character. They range from the markedly flowery, fragrant, and delicate to the full-bodied and powerful.

The Nahe region is divided into upper, middle, and lower sectors. In the Upper Nahe, the soil —consisting of slate and igneous rock— produces fresh, lively Rieslings and other good wines. In the Lower Nahe, where the river assumes a predominantly northern course, the vineyards are confined to the left bank and yield somewhat fuller bodied wines.

Chiefly responsible for the region's fine reputation is the Middle Nahe, whose most famous vineyards are Kreuznach and Schloss Bockelheim. The Kreuznach wines —fresh, clean tasting and well balanced— display a soft fruity charm, while those of Schloss Bockelheim are somewhat on the lighter side. Other Nahe towns of note are Roxheim, Niederhausen, and Norheim.

Franconia

Franconia, east of Rheinhessen, is situated in the upper valley of the Main River. The river, winding its way through the Franconian hills in an erratic series of turns, bends and loops, creates a discontinuous region characterized both by desirable microclimates and patches of land not at all suited to the grape. Spring is generally short here and frost always a possibility, even in mid-May. The summers, however, are long and dry.

Franconia grows sylvaner, müller-thurgau and riesling grapes on a generally heavy soil. Its wines —sturdy, full-bodied, and lower in acidity than those of the Rhine— are dry and well balanced at their finest; exhibiting an earthy firmness, unsuspected alcoholic strength, and great keeping powers.

Franconia's principal town and main wine center is Würzburg. (Other villages of note are Randersacker and Escherndorf.) Würzburg is celebrated for its prestigious Stein vineyard, whose chalky slope is known as the Steinmantle. The Steinweins, largely riesling in composition, are among the longest lived in Germany. (They bear a greater resemblance to the drier wines of France than to the sweeter wines of the Rhine and the Mosel.)

NOTE: Steinweins are bottled in distinctively shaped *bocksbeutels* or "goat pouches." These are rounded glass flasks with flat sides. Although other Franken and German wines have borrowed both the Steinwein name and the bocksbeutel's shape, authentic examples come only from the famous Stein vineyard.

Baden

Baden, Germany's most southerly wine region —situated in the foothills of the Alps— is subject to a rather dry climate. Its wines, primarily white, range from the gentle, low in acid and low in alcohol to the full-bodied and robust. They are pressed from rulander, sylvaner, gutedal (chasselas), riesling, and gewürztraminer grapes. About a fourth of Baden's wines are red. Pressed primarily from the spätburgunder, they range in character from velvety to fiery.

Baden's prize district is the Kaiserstuhl ("King's Throne"), a small cluster of low volcanic hills rising from a plain northwest of Freiburg. The Kaiserstuhl became a viticultural area in the nineteenth century when a German army surgeon, visiting Italy, observed vines flourishing on the slopes of Mount Vesuvius. He thought a vineyard might also thrive on the volcanic soil of Baden. The Kaiserstuhl, with its warm climate and great productive capacity, is known as the "Kitchen of Bacchus," named for the Roman god of wine. Baden's best wines, grown on the southern slopes, are pressed from the rulander grape.

A subregion of Baden is Markgräfler, located between Freiburg and Basel near the Swiss border. Its principal grape, the gutedal —known locally as the markgräfler— yields a pleasant but short-lived white wine. Situated across the Rhine from Strasbourg is Ortenau, which cultivates the gewürztraminer grape as does its French counterpart in Alsace. Ortenau's wines can sometimes achieve an Alsatian charm. Nearby is Breisgau, growing a noteworthy weissherbst (rosé) wine. And close to the French border on the north shore of Lake Constance is Bodensee, noted for its light red Seewein (Lake Wine) pressed from the spätburgunder grape.

❦ ❦ ❦

Hessiche Bergstrasse

Across from Rheinhessen on the east bank of the Rhine is Hessiche Bergstrasse, a thirty-three-mile stretch of vineyards running between Heidelberg and Darmstadt. Its climate is one of Germany's mildest; its soil is extremely fertile. Hessiche Bergstrasse's wines have long been grouped with those of Baden. Although quite heady, they are generally drier than the Rhine wines, displaying less bouquet but enlivened by a certain refreshing acidity. Most are consumed locally.

Württemberg

Württemberg is located in the Neckar Valley, east of Baden. Its principal city is Stuttgart. Primarily a red wine area, Württemberg grows the spätburgunder and the portugieser among other grape varieties. Its red wines are fruity and hearty with an earthy, attractive aftertaste. Its white wines, pressed from the riesling, sylvaner, müller-thurgau, and traminer are somewhat robust in character as well. Württemberg also produces a light red Schillerwein which blends both red and white grapes. Most of its wines are consumed locally.

NOTE: Germany imports a number of warm-climate wines from Europe and elsewhere as well so as to strengthen its paler reds and to fill out its sparkling wine blends.

THE UNITED STATES

America has had knowledgeable wine collectors since the eighteenth century when the squires of Virginia, like their English counterparts, appreciated good wines. In his travels, Thomas Jefferson had visited the wine regions of Bordeaux, Burgundy, Champagne, and Alsace as well as those of Italy and Germany. Asking questions, taking notes and tasting the wines, Jefferson went on to acquire a formidable and famous wine cellar for his home in Monticello.

NOTE: In the colonies, Madeira was generally a popular drink among the elite, in part because it wasn't taxed like other imported wines. By order of the Crown, the wine could be shipped directly to the colonies without going first to England and being subject to an import tax when shipped from there.

The United States, spanning three thousand miles from the Atlantic Ocean to the Pacific, produces wine in more than forty of its fifty states. Commercial production however is concentrated mainly on the East and West coasts, with California alone accounting for about 90 percent of the country's output. Other major western states are Washington and Oregon. The leader in the East is New York, followed by Virginia, Florida, Pennsylvania, Arkansas, New Jersey, and Ohio. Other notable wine states include Idaho, Connecticut, Michigan, Illinois, Missouri, Arizona, and Texas.

NOTE: Vinifera grapes are cultivated west of the Rocky Mountains, while the labruscas —supplemented by hybrids— predominate in the East. The cultivation of viniferas in the eastern part of the country has been increasing in recent years.

New York and the Northeast

In the eleventh century, the Vikings landed near what is now Massachusetts. Finding wild grapes growing in abundance there, they called the place Vinland the Good. Five centuries later, the English colonists had domesticated the native grapes, but the resulting wines were quite unlike any they had known at home. They displayed an unfamiliar pungency, a certain "foxy" flavor.

Trying to create the more familiar Old World wines, the colonists began to import vinifera cuttings from France, Germany, and Italy. They also recruited European wine makers for their expertise. But all such efforts failed. The northeastern growing season was too short for the tender viniferas and the climate fluctuations too extreme for them. (Intense heat marked the summers, while winter temperatures could plummet below 17°F. And ever present was the threat of mold, mildew, and other vine diseases.)

In the nineteenth century when phylloxera was decimating the vineyards of Europe, the wine makers there became interested in growing the hardier, more resistant American vines, whose transplanted rootstocks were to save the viniferas from extinction. American vintners themselves began to single out and cultivate their own premium labruscas; finding that, despite the persistence of a definite foxy character, they could subdue some of the wine's excessive pungency.

Yet despite the then-accepted wisdom that only indigenous grapes and sturdy hybrids could withstand the harsh northeastern winters, efforts continued to produce more "European-tasting" wines. In the 1950s, some wine makers thought that with proper care the viniferas could survive and began to grow these grapes again, employing more advanced methods of cultivation and grafting. Since the 1970s, more and more growers have been planting the viniferas although they continue to cultivate the sturdier native grapes and winter-hardy hybrids as well.

With its somewhat short growing season, the northeastern United States is generally best suited to growing white grape varieties. Cultivated among the viniferas now are the riesling, chardonnay, sauvignon blanc, gewürztraminer, aligoté, and muscat. Although red grapes experience more difficulty here, the pinot noir, merlot, and cabernet sauvignon are also grown. Among the native American varieties are the white diamond, dutchess, aurora, diana, elvira, and ives and the red concord, catawba, and delaware. Joining them are such hybrids as the white seyval blanc, seibel, cayuga, vidal blanc and ravat and the red alden, baco noir, bath, beta, buffalo, chelois, clinton, de chaunac, chancellor, léon millot, maréchal foch, schuyler, van buren, and yates.

New York State

In the Northeast, New York State is the major wine producer. Its white wines, naturally high in acid, proved particularly suited to the production of sparkling wines. (At the time of the Civil War, New York State accounted for about half of all American sparklers.) In the early 1900s, the emphasis was on growing indigenous, high-sugar concord grapes and on fortifying their rich, sweet, syrupy wines. The subsequent interest in cultivating viniferas, in addition to the labruscas and hybrids, led to the production of a wide variety of good red, white, and rosé table wines.

New York State's major viticultural regions are the Finger Lakes and Long Island, the Hudson Valley, and Lake Erie.

The Finger Lakes

The Finger Lakes, New York's premier wine-producing region, is a compact eighty square miles of rolling countryside situated between Rochester and Syracuse. The lakes themselves —long, narrow bodies of water— moderate the chill of the northern climate and encourage grape growing. Of greatest importance is Lake Keuka near Hammondsport, the site of the first vines, planted in 1812. By 1860, Keuka's wines —and particularly its sparkling wines— were widely known. Other Finger Lake areas of note are Canandaigua, Seneca, and Cayuga. The region is a good source of cool-climate white table wines, vinified dry, semidry, and sweet. In addition to riesling and chardonnay grapes, the cabernet franc and clones of the pinot noir are cultivated here.

Long Island

Although Long Island was producing wine as early as the seventeenth century, commercial-scale operations did not start until the 1970s. (They began with an experimental vineyard planted in what had been a potato field.) The eastern end of Long Island is divided into North and South Forks, and of the more than a dozen vineyards now operating in the region, most are concentrated on the North Fork, between Mattituck and Southold. Located between a bay and a sound, the area experiences a moderate maritime climate, which extends Long Island's wine-grow-ing season somewhat further than that experienced by the state's other districts.

The region specializes in vinifera grapes: white varieties include the chardonnay, gewürztraminer, johannisberg riesling, fumé blanc, chenin blanc, and pinot blanc. (The Chardonnays at their finest here display a rare crispness and delicacy.) Long Island has proved suitable for red grapes as well. The merlot, a consistent performer, has emerged as the leading red varietal, yielding a medium-bodied wine with lively flavors and aromas. The cabernet franc also produces appealing red wines, while the cabernet sauvignon is beginning to make substantial gains. (Since the Long Island growers don't always grow enough grapes to meet their own needs, they may purchase additional berries, buying these primarily from California and Oregon.)

The Hudson Valley

The Hudson Valley, north of New York City, is one of the oldest wine-growing areas in the country. In 1677, French Huguenot refugees were planting vines near New Paltz. Before the Civil War, a Croton Point winery was selling its products in New York City. In recent years the valley, particularly in the lower sector, has seen considerable expansion of its vineyard acreage. The grape varieties grown include the chardonnay, cabernet franc, and seyval blanc. A number of wineries are now active in Ulster, Dutchess, and Orange Counties. Wine making, however, continues as a cottage industry here .

Lake Erie

Westernmost in New York State is the Lake Erie region, beginning at Buffalo, stretching along the southern border of Lake Erie and continuing over the Pennsylvania line into northern Ohio. The Lake Erie region accounts for about 50 percent of New York's vineyard acreage. Growing concord grapes in abundance, it is mainly grape-juice country, while also producing some red and white wines. Among these is a late-harvest dessert wine, made from the delaware grape.

The Prohibition Era

In 1919, an amendment to the United States Constitution virtually brought all American wine making to a halt. The Eighteenth Amendment —better known as Prohibition— banned the sale of alcoholic beverages throughout the country. Although essentially aimed at hard liquor, it forced nearly all of the nation's wineries to shut down. The handful that survived were producing sacramental wines and medicinal spirits. (The latter euphemistically described as "tonic medicines" required a doctor's prescription and were dispensed by pharmacists.) As one wine maker commented at the time, "You would not believe the number of customers who said they were doctors and priests."

Although described by some as a noble experiment, Prohibition in effect ushered in an era of organized crime and political corruption. Illegal sales, known as bootlegging, flourished. Dealers often resorted to violence to obtain and sell the illicit beverages. (The amendment, in effect, worsened the problem it was intended to solve.) In 1933, after more than a decade, the Prohibition amendment was finally repealed and the right was returned to the states to regulate the sale of alcoholic beverages within their own borders.

Prohibition had caused many fine vineyards to be neglected or uprooted and their grapes were largely replaced by fruit trees, corn, and other crops. The few vintners still working were cultivating table grapes or selling grape juice. (The labels on the grape juice warned that adding yeast could result in fermentation. Many purchasers saw this as a recipe, rather than as an admonition.)

When the repeal of Prohibition finally came, most of the wineries had fallen into disrepair, their equipment had rusted away or was sold for scrap. Skilled wine makers had drifted into other occupations; cooperage and storage facilities were inadequate. There was no system for marketing or distributing wine. Total reconstruction of the industry was needed. Yet just as the growers were beginning to replant and the wine makers to retool, the economic Depression of the 1930s struck, followed by the upheavals of World War II. American wine making was not to come into its own for another three decades.

California

California is a vast state, stretching more than seven hundred miles from north to south and, extending two hundred miles from east to west at its widest. The state exhibits an astonishing diversity of topography, soil, and climate. The weather along the cooler shores of San Francisco Bay is somewhat reminiscent of the northern Rhône, while the torrid conditions in the Central Valley, resemble those of the Mediterranean region. Southern California too, is relatively hot.

In the seventeenth century, Spanish missionaries, moving north from Mexico planted the first vines in California. (Earlier, a Jesuit priest, Juan Ungarte, set up a vineyard in Baja, California.) Needing wine to celebrate mass, the missionaries found that the process of importing the wine from home was slow and uncertain. By 1769, Padre Junipéro Serra, a Franciscan monk, had established the Mission San Diego, the first American settlement, planting vines around its tile-roofed adobe buildings. The grapes, which flourished, were called mission grapes.

Under Padre Serra's direction, the Franciscans gradually moved north toward the state's cooler valleys, setting up a chain of twenty-one missions in the five hundred miles between what are now the cities of San Diego and Sonoma. (Each mission was located one day's journey from the next by horseback.) Linking them together was the Camino Real, the "King's Highway." Many important California cities were to spring up around these missions: Santa Barbara, Santa Clara, San Luis Obispo, San Gabriel, San Miguel, and San Francisco.

Eventually the missions were secularized and subsequently shut down. Private citizens began to take over the abandoned vineyards and to set up vineyards of their own. (The Franciscans had inadvertently stimulated a local interest in wine making by bartering their excess wine for needed supplies.) The first major secular pioneer was Bordeaux-born Jean-Louis Vignes, who planted more than a hundred acres of imported French vines in the pueblo of Los Angeles. Vignes should have been named the "father of California viticulture" but that title went to Agoston Haraszthy, a flamboyant Hungarian with an engaging manner and a knack for self-promotion. Haraszthy, who claimed to be an aristocrat and later took to calling himself "Colonel," had set up his first vineyard near San Diego in 1852, then he gradually moved north as the Franciscans before him had done. By 1857, he had established one of the state's largest wineries in Sonoma.

Haraszthy proved to be a first-class wine promoter, convincing the newly formed state legislature that California could produce some of the finest wines in the world. He also persuaded the governor to send a commission abroad to study wine making, with himself named as its head. Visiting France, Italy, Germany, Spain, and Russia, the commission acquired some two hundred thousand cuttings that represented nearly five hundred vinifera grape varieties. Haraszthy planted some of these in his own vineyard and handed out the others on a random basis to his fellow growers. (His disorganized method of distribution was to create great viticultural confusion in the state for many years to come.)

The nineteenth-century Gold Rush gave California's fledgling wine industry a boost. The prospectors, thirsty for wine, encouraged the expansion of vineyards to the foothills of the Sierra Madres, virtually next door to the mines. Further impetus to the wine industry came at the turn of the century when Italian immigrants arrived, bringing with them their wine-drinking and wine-making traditions. (A number of the state's major wineries trace their origins back to this time.) Many progressed from bulk sales to jug wines, and then moved on to quality wine production.

Prohibition had devastated viniculture in the West as it had in the East. Fine California vineyards were converted to fruit orchards and cattle pastures. Only six or seven wineries escaped dismantling because they were producing sacramental wines and medicinal spirits. Yet the demand for California's wine grapes continued, coming primarily from the European immigrants who had settled in the

East. Accustomed to taking wine with their meals, they began to make it at home. (Then, as now, the U.S. government permitted one-adult households to make one hundred gallons a year for their personal use tax free.) The new immigrants were buying thin-skinned California viniferas, but the grapes didn't hold up very well when shipped across country by rail. The sturdier, more durable varieties that were substituted yielded heavier-bodied, more sugary wines that often needed fortification to preserve them.

Characterizing the state's early wine industry were huge vineyards growing lesser grapes, and giant wineries producing sweet wines in bulk (generally intended for fortification). After the repeal of Prohibition, the California wine makers began to rebuild. Less bound by tradition than their European counterparts and stimulated by ongoing developments in enology, agricultural research, and industrial methods, they became experimenters and innovators. Applying new technologies, the United States became the world's leading nation in the scientific approach to wine growing and wine making.

For instance, studies undertaken by scientists at the University of California greatly influenced the wine makers. The scientists had analyzed the state's viticultural characteristics and divided California into a number of climate zones based on the weather and the degree-days of heat they experienced. Championed then was the idea that climate and weather were the main quality factors in wine making. (On the other hand, the Europeans, have always stressed the primacy of the soil.) More recently, however, the Californians have shifted their focus to soil and plant culture and are now adapting their various grape varieties to local conditions.

California now grows more than one hundred twenty-five viniferas commercially, most of them meant for wine; the others serve as table grapes or raisins. Leading the red grapes are the cabernet sauvignon, zinfandel, pinot noir, and merlot. Other reds include the gamay beaujolais, grenache, petite sirah, barbera, charbono, grignolino, carignane, and ruby cabernet. Leading the white grapes are the chenin blanc, chardonnay, and johannisberg riesling. Other varieties include the sauvignon blanc, pinot blanc, traminer, sémillon, gray riesling, sylvaner, colombard, folle blanche, emerald riesling, green hungarian, muscat, málaga, aligoté, gewürztraminer, müller-thurgau, palomino, pedro ximénez (PX), and thompson seedless. There has also been an increasing emphasis on such Rhône Valley varieties as the syrah, cinsault, and mourvèdre. (The general climate is considered closer to that of the Rhône than to Burgundy or Bordeaux.) There has been a greater emphasis on Italian grapes as well, particularly the sangiovese.

California now produces a wide array of red, white, and rosé wines —still, sparkling and fortified. The best examples come from the more northerly regions, where morning fog and sea breezes mitigate the heat of day. Most of the wine, however, comes from the hotter and drier central and southern sectors in the state.

California's wine growing encompasses some two hundred and thirty districts, beginning at the Mexican border and extending north to Mendocino. Major among them are Napa, Sonoma, Mendocino, Lake County, Monterey County, and the Livermore Valley. California's wine growing can perhaps be best understood by dividing the state into four geographical areas: North Coast, Central Coast, Central Valley, and southern California.

North Coast

The North Coast, fanning out beyond the upper reaches of San Francisco Bay, includes Napa, Mendocino, and Sonoma Counties. (The actual boundaries have never been officially drawn up.)

Because of its various microclimates, the North Coast is subject to widely different growing conditions. Its northern end is warm enough to grow robust zinfandel grapes, while its southern end —cooled by the fog and breezes from San Francisco Bay— is better suited to the white chardonnay and riesling grapes and the red cabernet sauvignon and pinot noir. The wines here at their finest display a full lush finish, while they retain an underlying tannic structure that endows them with elegance and strength.

NOTE: California's grapes, generally high in sugar and low in acid, yield richer wines than their counterparts in Bordeaux and Burgundy. Earlier harvesting and other modifications, however, have adjusted the sugar-acid balance.

The prime North Coast area is Napa Valley, set between the Mayacamas and Howell mountain ranges. About thirty miles long and five miles at its widest, Napa stretches north from Carneros at the northern tip of San Francisco Bay to Calistoga. Napa's main subregions are Rutherford and Stag's Leap. Also considered a subregion is Carneros, a cool, foggy district, which straddles the southern end of both Napa and the adjacent Sonoma County.

Sometimes called the "American Médoc," Napa is celebrated for its well-balanced, plummy wines, pressed mainly from the cabernet sauvignon, which is cultivated in the cooler upland areas. Some of the best examples come from Rutherford —and specifically from Rutherford Bench— a three-mile stretch whose topsoil sits on a gravel bed deposited by an old stream. (Bench indicates the low slopes of a ridge.) The majority of the cabernets, however, are grown on the floor of the valley below. Napa is also noted for its outstanding sparkling wines.

NOTE: While the city of Napa is situated east of the Mayacamas range, the vineyards themselves and the wineries are located farther north (near Yountville, Oakville, Rutherford, St. Helena and Calistoga).

Sonoma, known too as the "Valley of the Moon," is directly to the west. Running virtually parallel to Napa and separated from it by the Mayacamas mountains, Sonoma is large and sprawling, almost seventy-five miles long and about fifteen miles at its widest. Bordering the Pacific, the district is subject to morning fog but also to a warmer afternoon sun than Napa. Its wine output averages about twice as much. Sonoma's wines are generally softer than those of Napa; its Cabernet Sauvignons often more defined by their fruit than by their tannins.

Sonoma's subregions are Russian River, Dry Creek, and Alexander Valley. Russian River is best known for its chardonnays and Dry Creek for its zinfandels, while the versatile Alexander Valley grows the cabernet sauvignon, chardonnay, riesling, gewürztraminer, and chenin blanc. (Carneros, straddling the southern end of both Napa and Sonoma, grows the chardonnay and the pinot noir.)

NOTE: In recent years, the Napa and Sonoma vineyards have attracted the interest of foreign investors —French, Spanish, English, and Japanese— who have made substantial purchases here. Much of Napa's wine making, now under corporate ownership, is largely high-tech in character although a few small vintners continue to operate in the traditional way.

Directly above Sonoma is Mendocino, another coastal area. Located twenty miles north of San Francisco, this is the most northerly of the North Coast counties. Heavily forested, Mendocino limits grape cultivation to its inland valleys. (Most of the vineyards are centered around the town of Ukiah.) Spring is warmer here than in Napa but the summers are somewhat cooler. The Russian River rises in the eastern half of the district, while the cooler western half —the site of Anderson Valley— more subject to fog and frost, has proven ideal for sparkling wine production. Its cool nights and foggy mornings have also been good for cultivating such grapes as the pinot noir.

Mendocino's primary red grapes are the cabernet sauvignon and zinfandel; the latter producing the district's best wines. The primary white grapes are the chardonnay, colombard, and sauvingon blanc. Produced in great quantities here are red and white wines, including a large share of the state's jug wines.

Other North Coast districts are Lake and Amador counties. Lake County, east of Mendocino and Sonoma, is known for its rounded red wines. Amador, a hundred or so miles east of Napa, specializes in full, rich zinfandels, while growing cabernet sauvignon and chardonnay grapes as well. Amador's wines generally tend to be less elegant than those of Napa and Sonoma. Also considered part of the North Coast are El Dorado, Calaveras, and Nevada counties.

Central Coast

In the 1960s, population growth and accelerating real estate values forced many North Coast wine makers to move to previously undeveloped areas, south and east of San Francisco Bay. Encompassing thousands of acres in vines, these areas are sometimes now considered part of the North Coast but more properly should be classified as Central Coast, whose boundaries are also vaguely defined. The Central Coast has been variously described as extending from Monterey to Santa Barbara, or from south of San Jose to Santa Ynez, or —at its most extreme— as beginning just below San Francisco and stretching all the way to Los Angeles. The region does however encompass Monterey, Santa Cruz, and Alameda counties, along with Santa Barbara, San Luis Obispo, and the Sierra foothills.

The hot, dry climate of the Central Coast was once considered most suitable for growing alfalfa and grazing cattle. Yet the fog and cool breezes blowing in from the Pacific reduce the intensity of the sun and temper its heat. Scientists, armed with sophisticated soil and weather data, have located a number of microclimates suited to the grape here. Grown now are the red cabernet sauvignon and pinot noir and the white chardonnay and sauvignon blanc, among others. There has also been a recent emphasis on cultivating such Rhône Valley grape varieties as the grenache, syrah, mourvèdre, and cinsault.

Some of the best Central Coast vineyards are situated between San Francisco and Monterey. Monterey —the most extensive wine-growing county— features granite slopes, sandy soil, hot springs, and a long growing season. It has been most successful in cultivating the white johannisberg riesling, chardonnay, and gewürztraminer. (Also grown here are the sauvignon blanc, chenin blanc, and riesling.) Monterey's red grapes have proven somewhat more difficult to cultivate. The cabernet sauvignon's wines often exhibit vegetal flavors and odors, suggesting cabbage or green peppers. Improved by modifications in trellising now, the wines are becoming leaner and sharper. The pinot noir grape, grown in the chalky soil of the Gavilan Mountains high above the Salinas Valley here, has been achieving a considerable degree of success.

On the eastern shore of San Francisco Bay is Alameda County, including Livermore Valley. The growing of grapes began here more than a century ago, when a Frenchman, finding the sea breezes salubrious, planted the cuttings he had brought from his native land. Grown now are the sauvignon blanc, sémillon, and chardonnay, along with the pinot blanc, ugni blanc, and gray riesling. Livermore's generally gravelly soil is similar to that of Graves; its white wines are among California's best. The red wines of Alameda are soft and early maturing.

A subregion, known as the South Central Coast, encompasses San Benito County and stretches south to San Luis Obispo and Santa Barbara. (Most of its vineyards were planted in the early 1980s.) The limestone soil here, resembling that of Burgundy's Côte d'Or, is hospitable to the pinot noir grape. Nearby growing areas of note are the Templeton district, the Santa Ynez and Santa Maria valleys in Santa Barbara County, and the Edna Valley in San Luis Obispo. Santa Ynez is the southernmost of the important Central Coast wine areas; Edna Valley is particularly known for its Chardonnays. York Mountain, situated in the vicinity, and seven miles from the Pacific Ocean, is subject to a moist maritime climate of fog and rain. Its vineyards are sited high, at sixteen-hundred to eighteen-hundred feet above sea level.

Central Valley

The Central Valley is a vast hot, fertile region lying between the Sierra Madre and the Coast Ranges and extending from San Joaquin in the north to Bakersfield in the south. A highly industrialized and intensively cultivated agricultural region, it accounts for more than half of the state's wine production.

Summers in the Central Valley are cloudless with temperatures hovering at more than 100°F for days at a time. Mountains block the rainfall, making the humidity negligible. The soil, baking in the blazing heat, forms a hard clay surface which must be broken up periodically and irrigated constantly. Grapes grow here in abundance, yielding high-sugar and low-acid wines. The region has long been known for its heady, fortified wines, made in port and sherry styles. But the Central Valley, having adopted modern vinification methods in the 1960s and 1970s, now produces table and sparkling wines as well. (These wines outnumber the fortified wines by a wide margin.) Cold stabilization has helped some of them achieve a lighter, fresher style, but most are meant for wine coolers and for various other inexpensive blends.

The leading red grape cultivated here is the carignane (spelled with an *e*), followed by the zinfandel, barbera, grenache, petite sirah, alicante bouschet, and mission. White grapes include the french colombard, thompson seedless, palomino, muscat, and chardonnay. Also grown are such hybrids as the ruby cabernet and carnelian, both designed to retain as much acidity as possible under the dry growing conditions and intense heat of the region. And the search goes on for new varieties capable of withstanding the torrid climate, while still producing distinctive wines.

Southern California

Southern California, situated between Los Angeles and San Diego, is also relatively arid and in need of extensive irrigation. Its climate is too hot and its soil too rich for quality grape production. Many of the same varieties are cultivated here as in the Central Valley, but with a greater emphasis on grapes of Italian origin. The wines themselves —big, pronounced, and best suited to fortification— are made primarily in the port and sherry styles. The finest growing district here is Temecula in Riverside County, sixty miles north of the Mexican border. It is especially noted for its sparkling wines.

The Pacific Northwest

The increasing cost of California real estate in the 1970s spurred on the expansion of America's viticulture to the Pacific Northwest. Vintners were discovering that that the region's northern light and volcanic soil made it a fine place for growing grapes. Although subject to mercurial weather, the Pacific Northwest enjoys enough sunshine to encourage the slow ripening of the grapes; and the rainfall, although heavy, generally occurs during the winter months when the vines are dormant. The first wines to gain attention here were the Rieslings and the Chardonnays. There has also been consistent acclaim for the Merlots and Cabernet Sauvignons of Washington State, and for the Pinot Noirs of Oregon.

Oregon

In the nineteenth century, Oregon was producing folk wines pressed from various fruits and berries. Despite the assumption that grapes could not flourish in its volatile, fog-shrouded climate, newly arrived European immigrants began to establish vineyards here. Encouraged by a felicitous combination of soil and weather, the Oregon grapes were soon thriving. (Protecting them from the cold air blowing down from Canada were the Cascade Mountains located to the east and the Coast Ranges to the west.)

The state now cultivates a number of varieties with great success. Among the red grapes grown, the temperamental pinot noir does particularly well here, producing a world-class wine. (California vintners have been purchasing the Oregon grapes for their own wines and a number of Burgundian wine makers have set up shop in the state.) Other thriving red grape varieties are the cabernet sauvignon, merlot, and zinfandel. Among the white grapes cultivated are the chardonnay, riesling, sauvignon blanc, pinot gris, and gewürztraminer. Oregon's wines in general are soft, fruity, and accessible.

The state's wine regions are in the Willamette, Rogue and Umpqua valleys. Willamette, the major region, is a strip of land about one hundred forty miles long and forty miles wide that begins northwest of Portland and follows the Willamette River south to Eugene. Nestled between two mountain ranges, it enjoys a long growing season. To the south are the warmer Umpqua and Rogue districts. (Rogue Valley is just north of the California border, while Umpqua is between Rogue and Willamette.) Of particular note is Roseburg in the middle of the Umpqua district. Another notable wine area is the Hood River valley near Portland, whose weather is slightly warmer and more consistent than that of Willamette.

NOTE: Since 1980, Oregon's viticultural acreage has increased tenfold, with the success of its small wineries attracting the interest of several corporate investors.

Washington State

Washington State, with its moderate climate, is the second-largest wine producer in the United States. Long, warm days help to ripen the grapes here, while cool nights preserve their fragile acidity. Most of Washington's vineyards are concentrated in three valleys east of the Cascade Mountains: Yakima, Columbia, and Walla Walla. Yakima accounts for about 85 percent of the state's wine production.

Although Washington has grown grapes for decades, serious wine making did not begin here until the 1970s. A number of premium French and German grapes are successfully cultivated now. The state's reputation rests largely on its white wines, the best of these pressed from riesling and johannisberg riesling grapes. The wines, characterized by a buoyant fruitiness and a distinctive acidity, are typically quite heady; often reaching alcohol levels of 13 percent or more. Other white varieties include the sémillon, sauvignon blanc, chardonnay, gewürztraminer, chenin blanc, müller-thurgau, and muscat canelli.

Washington is also becoming known for its red wines. The Cabernet Sauvignon here is leaner and more restrained in its fruit and bouquet than in California. The best examples are characterized by good structure and balance, displaying at their finest both nuance and complexity. The merlot is a popular grape here. The concord accounts for about half of the state's grape production but is primarily used for juices and for jellies

Other American States

American growers located away from the country's East and West coasts are generally part-time wine makers, who earn their livelihoods at other pursuits. Most of their wines are consumed locally.

In colonial Virginia, the earliest attempts at wine making were hampered by disease and insects. In the nineteenth century, German settlers brought back grape growing, but the first commercial winery wasn't established until 1970. (Most of the wineries here are small and family owned.) Virginia is known for its white wines, pressed variously from the riesling, chardonnay, gewürztraminer, sauvignon blanc, chenin blanc, and seyval blanc. Its red grapes —the cabernet sauvignon, pinot noir, merlot, and barbera— yield somewhat soft and easy-to-drink wines.

In nineteenth century Ohio, Nicholas Longworth planted vines in the hills overlooking Cincinnati. German settlers also established vineyards here, cultivating their vines on the banks of the Ohio River. Subsequently, large-scale plantings were seen on the south shore of Lake Erie and on the Lake Erie islands. Before the Civil War, Ohio had produced the country's first commercial sparkling wine: an

effervescent Catawba. Currently more than two dozen wineries are operating in the state. Grape varieties now grown include the chardonnay, johannisberg riesling, gewürztraminer, seyval blanc, cabernet sauvignon, and pinot noir. Ohio also makes a number of fruit-based wines.

In the seventeenth century, Franciscan missionaries were producing sacramental wines in the El Paso Valley of Texas. The state now grows a wide variety of grapes: the red merlot, ruby cabernet, barbera, zinfandel, grenache, and petite sirah; the white johannisberg riesling, sauvignon blanc, chenin blanc, sémillon, and emerald riesling. One example, a blend of sauvignon blanc and sémillon grapes, yields a fresh flavored wine with a fruity bouquet.

Idaho's climate is similar to that of Oregon, but the state does not receive as much rainfall because of its inland location, some four hundred fifty miles from the ocean. Idaho grows the johannisberg riesling and the chardonnay, while purchasing about half of its wine grapes from nearby Washington State.

Wine making in New Mexico dates back to the seventeenth century. The conditions on a thirty-five-hundred-foot-high plateau here, with warm days and cool nights, are ideal for grape growing. Among the varieties cultivated are a number of French-American hybrids. The state produces sparkling and still wines.

Most of the wineries in southeastern New England —in Connecticut, Rhode Island and Massachusetts— generally specialize in Chardonnay wines. Those that do not grow enough grapes to meet their own wine making needs purchase them from New York vineyards, in the Finger Lakes and on Long Island.

Hawaii cultivates grapes on its volcanic slopes and has most recently been experimenting with the carnelian, a hybrid grape originally developed in California for the torrid climate of the Central Valley.

NOTE: In addition to its own great domestic output, the United States imports wines from all over the world, purchasing more premium wines from France than any other country and accounting for some 20 percent of all French wine exports.

Other Wine–Producing Countries

Algeria

While Algeria made wine in Roman times, little was produced between the eighth and nineteenth centuries, when the country was under Arab rule. In the nineteenth century, France annexed the country and went on to restore its viniculture. Then, when phylloxera decimated the vineyards of Europe, Algeria became an important source of wine. By the end of World War II, nearly a third of its labor force was engaged in the wine industry. After Algeria had won its independence from France in 1962, the country reasserted its Moslem traditions and most of its vineyard acreage was again uprooted.

The grapes had been grown on a coastal Mediterranean plain, rising to a high plateau. The French had planted such commonplace varieties as the carignan, alicante bouschet, and clairette blanc, which yielded hearty, generally rough wines, much more notable for their strength than their finesse. These were used in strengthening the French vin ordinaires and apéritifs and in bolstering the lesser Bordeaux and Burgundy wines as well.

Subsequently, Algeria cultivated better grape varieties, producing improved red and white wines, with the reds more noteworthy. The most outstanding examples came from the western sector, near Oran, and from the uplands around the cities of Mascara and Tlemcen. The Coteaux de Mascara was famous for its deep-colored, full-bodied reds, while Tlemcen produced rich reds and good whites as well. Médéa, south of Algiers, was known for its red and white wines too.

NOTE: Other wine-producing countries in North Africa are Morocco and Tunisia whose high-alcohol, low-acid wines are best suited to blending. Adopting modern vinification methods, both countries now produce soft pleasant red wines and dry, fruity rosés along with refreshing white wines.

Argentina

Argentina is South America's largest wine producer. In the sixteenth century, Jesuit missionaries planted vines here that the Conquistadors had brought from Spain. (Many of the early colonists were from southern Spain.) In the nineteenth century, a great wave of Italian immigration transformed the country's wine making from a casual pastime to a full-fledged industry.

Argentina's wine growing now extends some seven hundred miles, stretching southward from the Cafayate region of Salta to Mendoza and beyond. Its wine regions are: the Northwest, including the province of Salta; the Central West, encompassing Mendoza province; and the southern region and San Juan, including the valleys of the Rio Colorado and the Rio Negro. Mendoza —located some six hundred miles west of Buenos Aires— is the main province, accounting for more than 90 percent of the country's vineyard acreage. Mendoza is known for its huge vineyards and its large wineries. The vineyards themselves (some located fifty-two hundred feet above sea level) are sited in the foothills of the Andes, where the days are warm but the air is cooled by mountain breezes. The Andes also block rainfall, making the land arid. However, the vineyards are irrigated by a remarkable series of dams and reservoirs, which channel melted snow down from the mountains —on a fixed schedule — during the growing season.

Argentina was initially known for growing commonplace grape varieties: the criolla and pedro ximénez. In 1853, a French specialist —commissioned to upgrade the country's winegrowing— brought in the red cabernet sauvignon, malbec, merlot, and pinot noir, and the white sauvignon blanc and sémillon, among other varieties. (Since phylloxera never reached South America, most of the vines are cultivated on their own rootstocks.)

Argentina produces red, white, and rosé wines. Its vintners at first were not overly concerned with quality and produced immense quantities of simple, inexpensive, high-alcohol wines, meant for a huge domestic market and for export in bulk to France, Spain, and Scandinavia. (Argentina also sells great quantities of grape concentrates to Japan.) Most widely planted now are the red barbera and the white chardonnay and riesling. The introduction of these new grape varieties, together with stainless-steel technology and cold stabilization, has led to an improvement in wine quality, particularly in the wines designated for export.

Australia

Australia has made wine since its early days as a penal colony. The first attempt to grow grapes was a failure, however. The vines, imported from South Africa and planted near Sydney, proved incompatible with the soil and climate there. In the nineteenth century, an expedition that had been sent to Europe to acquire better vines returned with about twenty thousand cuttings drawn from the leading vineyards of France and Germany. Representing hundreds of grape varieties, the cuttings became the foundation of modern Australian viticulture. The predominant red grape now is the red hermitage (syrah); others are the cabernet sauvignon, pinot noir, and shiraz. Among the white grapes grown are the chardonnay, sémillon, riesling, fumé blanc (sauvignon blanc), marsanne, and muscat.

Experiencing generally warm, dry conditions during the growing season,

Australia produces high-sugar, low-acid wines on large stretches of dry land made usable by irrigation. The earliest examples were often fortified and the country was known for its cheap port-and sherry-type wines intended for export to Europe. In the 1960s, technological advances and the development of cooler growing sites made possible lighter, drier, and more subtle wines. Strong in premium wine production now, Australia is known for a wide range of red, white, and rosé wines, along with sweet Muscats and botrytized Sémillons.

Australia's vintners, unhampered by any previous wine-making tradition and free to be innovative, are especially noted for their Shiraz and Shiraz-Cabernet wines, which combine at their finest the richness of a Rhône with the elegance of a Bordeaux. The Cabernet Sauvignons here are somewhat similar to those of California: rich flavored, smooth textured, and easy to drink.

Australia's main wine-producing regions extend in a twenty-five-hundred-mile arc across the southern half of the country. They are South Australia, New South Wales, Victoria, and West Australia.

South Australia, which includes Adelaide and its environs, is responsible for about two-thirds of the country's wines. The prime districts here are Barossa Valley, Coonawarra, McLaren Vale, and Clare. Barossa Valley, situated about thirty-five miles north of Adelaide, is subject to a hot climate, but its vineyards are sited in the hills about fifteen hundred feet above sea level. Silesian immigrants, settling here in the mid-eighteenth century, made German-style wines. Their descendants continue to produce Rieslings which are remarkable for their acidity and delicacy. Other white wines combine the richness of the chardonnay with the fruitiness of the sauvignon blanc. Barossa Valley, also the home of some great red grape vineyards, is known for its Hermitage and Cabernet-Shiraz wines which exhibit considerable tannin and a fine fruity character.

The small, cool Coonawarra district —considered one of Australia's best— is notable for its late-ripening red grapes, including the cabernet sauvignon, malbec, merlot, and shiraz among others. (Particularly celebrated are its Cabernet Sauvignon wines.) The white grapes grown include the riesling, chardonnay, and gewürztraminer. McLaren Vale, south of Adelaide is cooled by gentle sea breezes and specializes in chardonnays, while producing some good red wines as well.

New South Wales, one of Australia's oldest producers, encompasses Hunter Valley, the site of the big wineries. Best known for its white wines, Hunter Valley grows the sémillon (here called the Hunter Valley riesling) and the riesling itself (called the Rhine riesling), along with the chardonnay and traminer. The region also produces excellent red wines, pressed from the shiraz grape, along with highly esteemed rosés.

The country's southernmost region is Victoria, whose principal city is Melbourne. Victoria is known for red and white wines. (Some outstanding reds are grown on the lime-rich soil of the Yarra Valley.) The small Goulburn Valley is also notable for its excellent red wines.

Rutherglen, northeast of Melbourne, is known for its red and white wines too, and especially for its sweet Muscats. Red grape varieties here include the cabernet sauvignon, pinot noir, and shiraz; the whites are the chardonnay and sauvignon blanc. Margaret River, a newly developed district near Perth in West Australia, specializes in red wines, pressed from the cabernet sauvignon.

NOTE: Australia has been increasingly selling its wine overseas and now exports about a fourth of its production, primarily to Britain and the United States.

Austria

It is believed that five hundred years before the Christian era, the Celts planted grape vines in what is now Austria. When the Holy Roman Empire collapsed, the vines disappeared, not to be replaced until the tenth century when German settlers moved into the territory. Austria now devotes about one hundred thousand acres to its vineyards, which are concentrated in the eastern third of the country, where the climate is sunny and ideal for grape growing. Austrian vineyard plots are generally small, ranging from twelve to fifty acres. About four-fifths of the wines are white. Fruity with a flowery fragrance and a good bouquet, they are similar to their German counterparts, but a bit lower in acidity and somewhat higher in alcohol because of their warmer growing conditions. Generally dry, the Austrian wines are more like those of Alsace than those of the Rhine or the Mosel Valley.

The country's predominant white grape, the indigenous grüner veltliner, yields marvelously fresh, fruity wines which display a spicy, almost peppery flavor. Other white grape varieties, deriving mainly from German and Alsatian sources, include the müller-thurgau, sylvaner, gewürztraminer, chasselas, rheinriesling, wälschriesling, weissburgunder, muskat-ottonel, pinot gris, rotgipfler, furmint, and sauvignon blanc, along with the chardonnay.

Austrian red wines tend to be light bodied and short-lived. (They may be bolstered with imports from Italy or the former Yugoslavia.) The country's primary red grape variety is the pinot noir, variously known as the spätburgunder, blaufränkisch, and blauerburgunder. Other red grapes cultivated here include the blauer portugieser and the st. laurent.

The country's key wine regions are Vienna, Lower Austria, Burgenland, and Styria. Wine growing was once extensive in Vienna and its environs but urbanization has preempted most of the vineyard land within the city limits. (Little more than fifteen hundred acres remain and these are preserved and protected by law.) The wine villages near Vienna include Grinzing in the suburbs, Sievering, Nussdorf, and Kahlemberg.

Lower Austria, extending north along the Danube from Krems to the border of the Czech Republic, produces Gumpoldskirchen, the country's best-known white wine. A blend of the grüner veltiner and rotigipfler together with the riesling, gewürztraminer and other grapes, Gumpoldskirchen ranges from light, dry, and charmingly scented to full-bodied and fruity. The main white-wine area in Lower Austria is Wachau in the Danube Valley. Krems, located on a steep hillside, is the most important town here, celebrated for its light, fresh, fragrant, and gently rounded wines, pressed from riesling, grüner veltliner, and sylvaner grapes. Other notable wine towns are Durnstein to the west and Loiben to the south.

Burgenland, southeast of Vienna, surrounds the Neusiedler See, one of Europe's largest lakes. Experiencing a moist, sunny climate with warm autumns, Burgenland is a largely red-wine area, best known for its dry, dark, heady Vöslauer wines. It also produces high-quality white wines, including deep golden Ausleses, Beerenausleses, and Trockenbeerenausleses, which aren't as sweet as their German counterparts. The village of Rust on the gentle western slopes of the Neusiedler See, is famous for its Ruster Ausbruch, a sweet, almost syrupy wine, pressed from late-harvested furmint and muscat grapes. Across the border from Slovenia is Styria, which produces good red and white wines.

Much of Austria's wine is consumed domestically; some of the wines are not bottled, but dispensed directly from their casks in special taverns called heuriges. Heurige, a dialect word meaning "this year," refers to the new wines of the season or to wines less than a year old. Every tavern calling itself a heurige possesses its own vineyard in the surrounding hills and makes its own wine. Located primarily around Vienna, the heuriges originated in the eighteenth century when Emperor Joseph II permitted vintners to sell their wine directly to the public on their own premises. The heurige taverns typically feature modest interiors with whitewashed walls and plain tables. The wines themselves are served in viertels (fourths), thick glass mugs with a quarter-liter capacity. Accompanying the wines is a selection of smoked meats and sausages, fresh vegetables, and good bread.

Bulgaria

Wine growing in Bulgaria goes back two thousand years, to the time when the country was known as Thrace. Subsequent Turkish domination and Moslem rule banned wine making here; the Islamic influence prevailed until the nineteenth century. After World War II, the country was socialized and huge vineyards were set out on flat blocks of land for machine cultivation; industrialized too was the wine-making process itself.

Most of the country's vineyards are located on a central plain east of Sofia. In the northeast, the coastal region of the Black Sea is known for its white wines, pressed from the local misket grape, along with the chardonnay and the aligoté. The southern and western sectors produce red wines, ranging from the light and dry to the sweet and heavy. (The south is especially noted for its sweet, rich Muscats.) Of interest too are the red wines, grown in Sukhindol, north of the Balkans; pressed from the cabernet sauvignon and merlot, among others,

NOTE: Opening its markets to Western investors and entrepreneurs, Bulgaria has become one of the world's leading wine exporters. The country now ships out most of the wine it produces.

Canada

Canada concentrates about 90 percent of its wine growing on the Niagara Peninsula, a neck of land in southern Ontario, separating Lake Erie and Lake Ontario. The lakes moderate the northern climate, making grape growing possible. Although active since the mid-nineteenth century, Canada's wine industry has only recently begun to recruit expert wine makers from Germany and Austria, as it seeks to upgrade its production. (Of the more than two dozen wineries now in operation, most have been established since 1979.)

Ontario's growing conditions are much like those of New York's Finger Lakes. Labrusca grapes have traditionally been cultivated here, but French-American hybrids and vinifera grapes have also been grown in recent years. The viniferas include the white chardonnay and riesling, and the red pinot noir, cabernet sauvignon, cabernet franc, and merlot.

In addition to producing red, white, and rosé wines, Canada makes a winter-harvested ice wine that's available in two versions: the more expensive employs the riesling; the less expensive uses the vidal, a hybrid grape. Wine is also made, in the Okanogan Valley of British Columbia, which grows vinifera grapes imported from the Mosel region of Germany. British Columbia is noted for its good sparkling wines as well.

NOTE: Canada domestically consumes most of the wine that it produces.

Chile

Chile is a narrow strip of coastal land, situated across the Andes Mountains from Argentina. It's about twenty-eight hundred miles long and two hundred miles wide at its widest. Spanish missionaries, accompanying the Conquistadors, planted the first vineyards here. German immigrants colonized the southern farmlands early in the nineteenth century, introducing their own styles and methods of vinification. At the end of the nineteenth century the country, seeking to reorganize and expand its wine industry, recruited French experts as advisers. Chile has largely followed the

French approach ever since. Its grapes, reflecting the French influence, include the cabernet sauvignon, merlot, malbec, and pinot noir among the red varieties, along with the cabernet franc and petit verdot. The white varieties include the sauvignon blanc, riesling, sémillon, and chardonnay, along with the pinot blanc, pinot gris, gewürztraminer, and sylvaner.

NOTE: Chilean vines, protected by vast stretches of sandy soil and the Andes Mountain range, are among the few purebred descendants of the vines that date back to pre-phylloxera times.

Much of the country's early production was in jug wines. Often overripe and heavy with a decidedly baked character, they were either sold locally or exported to Chile's Latin American neighbors. Using modern fermentation methods now and aging their wines in small French oak casks, the Chileans have made them more supple and attractive.

The country's grape growing is divided into six regions. Of greatest importance is the Maipo Valley, south of Santiago, whose soil is largely volcanic and alluvial. Maipo experiences intense sunshine during the day and chilly conditions at night; the growing season ends with minimal rainfall. Produced here are red, white, and rosé wines. Particularly outstanding is a powerful and concentrated Cabernet Sauvignon with plenty of character, which at its finest is well balanced and elegant. Other Chilean reds display modest fruit and soft tannins. Among the white wines, the Chardonnays and Sauvignon Blancs do especially well. Also produced in the Maipo Valley are sparkling wines and generics such as Borgana (Burgundy), Sauterne, Chablis, and Rhin (Rhine) wine.

In recent years, investors from France, the United States, and Spain have updated and modernized the country's wine industry and expanded its wine growing to the cooler regions south of the traditional areas. These foreign investments —along with government tax breaks designed to encourage entrepreneurship— have made Chile one of South America's leading wine producers. The country is also a major exporter of wine, particularly to the United States. (Some Chilean wines are shipped in bulk to California for bottling there.)

NOTE: In the past, the larger wineries were responsible for the exports, with the smaller Chilean establishments, which have been making wine for more than a hundred years, serving mostly as suppliers to the larger enterprises. The smaller wineries are now intent on gaining a share of the export market for themselves.

China

Although grapes are believed to be indigenous to China, wine making was largely a foreign affair. (Wine has never been a part of the Chinese diet.) The Chinese themselves prefer a high-alcohol Shaoxing (Yellow Wine), which is technically not a wine at all. Made with rice, wheat, water, and yeast, Shaoxing is similar in character to a sherry and ranges in color from pale apricot to dark umber and in taste from semidry to very sweet.

In the nineteenth century, Catholic monks made wine for the observance of Mass in Beijing. In the twentieth century, French missionaries set up a winery there. Subsequently, a small quantity of wine was produced commercially both for the foreign community in China itself and for export to the Chinese overseas.

The early Chinese wines had been unappealing and cloyingly sweet, but beginning in the 1970s, increased contact with the West and a burgeoning tourist trade stimulated an interest in creating wines that were more "European" in flavor. The government began to sign contracts with various specialists from France, England, and Austria: the Chinese were to supply the land, the grapes, and the labor; the foreigners were to provide the wine-making technology, equipment, and skills. China is currently producing wines east of Beijing, near Tianjin, and in Shandong Province along the northeastern coast. Available in shops catering to the tourist trade is a light, dry, fruity white wine with a delicate bouquet which is reminiscent of a Chenin Blanc.

Some of the country's best wines are now produced in Shazikou, an eastern coastal city, some twenty-five miles from Quindao. Characterizing the area are a lime-rich soil and south-facing slopes. The grapes here are grown in a vineyard established in the 1980s by a Briton, who had transplanted chardonnay and riesling cuttings from Europe on his own.

Cyprus

The island of Cyprus in the eastern Mediterranean is said to have made wine centuries before the birth of Christ. Grapes are grown here in the mountains of the southern sector, at elevations of nearly three thousand feet.

Cyprus makes a variety of red and white wines, with the reds predominant. Especially esteemed is the red Commandaria, dating back at least to the twelfth century. (The Crusaders are said to have introduced the original vines.) Initially sweet, pungent, liquorous and heady, Commandaria is now generally vinified lighter and drier. Cyprus also makes sparkling wines and quantities of sweet and semisweet fortified wines, including flor-style sherries. Most are produced by four modern wineries. Several mountain monasteries are also making wine.

NOTE: Because its vines were never exposed to phylloxera, Cyprus cultivates only native grape varieties to avoid contamination.

❦ ❦ ❦

Czech Republic

In the Czech Republic, the Moravian region and Slovakia are noted for their red and white wines. The whites, which are best, reflect the influence of nearby Germany and Austria; their main grapes being the German riesling —rizling or risling rinkski (Rhine riesling), and the Austrian veltlinkski (grüner veltliner). Other white varieties are the traminer and sylvaner, the müller-thurgau, and sauvignon blanc. Red grapes include the blauburgunder and the portugieser.

Many Czechoslovakian wines are served in special restaurants, accompanied by simple foods. Called *vinarnas*, these establishments are similar to Austria's *heurige* taverns and serve their wines by the glass as well as by the bottle.

Great Britain

The British have long grown grapes; monasteries were maintaining vineyards here in the Middle Ages. The Norman invasion brought with it French abbots accustomed to drinking good wine. In the twelfth century, when Henry Plantagenet married Eleanor of Aquitaine, the English literally acquired all of Bordeaux along with the Charente and the Loire. Becoming a world power with easy access to the great wines of Europe, the English lost interest in producing their own and abandoned most of their vineyards. Although wine growing continued on a small scale into the nineteenth century, various mildew diseases killed off the remaining vines.

The 1930s saw a resurgence of grape growing, which gained some momentum after World War II. In 1946, Britain opened its first modern viticultural research station in Surrey. In the 1970s, with the introduction of modern wine-growing practices and carefully selected clones, small-scale wine making resumed, particularly in Wales and in the south of England. White grapes fare best in Britain's short growing season and include such early-ripening varieties as the müller-thurgau and seyval blanc. (Their light, fruity wines sometimes demonstrate a touch of earthiness.) Few observers, however, expect English wine making to become much more than a marginal activity.

While producing no significant wines of their own, the British have been tremendously influential in the wine world. (Wine has long been considered a gentleman's calling here.) The English more or less invented the practice of drinking fine wines and were the first to write about and to romanticize wine.

The British had acquired French wines ever since Roman times. During Henry Plantagenet's reign, England became a land of Bordeaux connoisseurs and was the largest consumer of premier clarets. When war and import taxes cut off their French wine supply, the British turned to Spain and Portugal, seeking out alternatives. In the process, they helped to "invent" fortified ports and sherries. These wines provided an appealing antidote to the country's chill climate. (It has been wryly noted that in the nineteenth century, the British considered port wine a substitute for central heating.)

In the fifteenth century, English wine merchants sensing the commercial possibilities of sherry, settled in Jerez. Investing time, labor, and capital in the production of sherry, they ensured its distribution to the major wine markets. (The British also married into local wine-producing families.) They called sherry *sack*, a term deriving either from *sacar*, meaning "to export," or *sec*, translating as "dry." (Shakespeare's Falstaff expressed his fondness for sherry by declaring that the first principle he would teach his sons would be to "forswear thin potations…[and] addict themselves to sack.") Because England imports about 60 percent of all the sherry produced, the wine is sometimes considered more British than Spanish.

The English dominated the port-wine trade as well. Some three hundred years ago, they were setting up shipping houses in Portugal's Douro Valley. Although conglomerates began to buy up the British firms after World War II, the names of many English families are still linked to port wines. The British have been similarly influential in the wine trade of Madeira. (Of the handful of families controlling the island's large wine interests, a number of these are Anglo-Madeiran.) The British have also played a significant role in encouraging the development of fortified Marsala wines and have demonstrated great enthusiasm and support for Rhine and Mosel wines. They call the latter *hocks,* an abbreviation of Hochheim, a notable German wine town.

NOTE: Despite their association with fine wines, the British also import great quantities of commonplace red and white wines in bulk from Italy, Spain, Germany, and the south of France. They call these ordinary products "plonk," thought to be a corruption of *vin blanc*.

Greece

Greece has grown grapes for some three thousand years. Among the varieties cultivated are the indigenous red xinomavro (a deep purple grape), the pinkish rhoditis, and the white assyrtiko. Other varieties grown include the muscat and cabernet sauvignon.

Countless vineyards dot the Greek mainland and its nearby islands. The greatest concentration is on the Peloponnesus, the large southern peninsula which is separated from the mainland by the Gulf of Corinth. Its climate is typically Mediterranean, its soil is largely volcanic. The Peloponnese is celebrated for its dark red Mavrodaphne (mavro translates as "black"). Full-bodied, richly flavored and sweetly aromatic with a velvety taste and an almost burnt aftertaste, this is quite a potent wine, ranging from 15 to 20 percent in alcohol. (Macedonia, to the north, is celebrated for its Mavro of Naoussa, a dry, dark red wine, pressed from the xinomavro grape.) From the mountain vineyards of the eastern Peloponnese comes the full-bodied, deep-colored red wine grown in Nemea. And produced around Athens, where the vineyards are cooled by mountain breezes, are rather subdued red and white table wines. Greece also produces some Bordeaux-style red wines.

The Greek islands produce a variety of wines. From Crete comes a fruity white vin de pays; from Corfu, a stout sturdy, red Robolo. Samos is famous for its late-harvest Muscat, a sweet golden brown wine that is also made in a dry version. Santorini grows good white wines; some slightly acid, others semisweet.

Most widely exported are the Greek retsinas or resinated wines, characterized by the unmistakable pitchlike taste of pine needles. Produced mainly in the Attica region north of Athens, the wines may be red, white, or rosé. (Usually quite light, they average no more than 9 percent alcohol.) The practice of resinating wines goes back to ancient times when the Greeks fermented, stored, and shipped their wines in amphorae, the two-handled porous clay vessels that taper to a point at the bottom. The vintners had coated the interiors of these porous vessels with a pine-sap resin, which reduced the wine's oxidation and evaporation and also inhibited the growth of bacteria, preventing the wine from turning to vinegar. The permeating pungency of the resin gave the wine a pronounced flavor that people came to expect. (Modern vintners have re-created the taste by adding some resinated flavoring to their wines during fermentation.)

In recent years, the Greeks have applied high-tech methods to their winemaking and sought out the advice of foreign enologists. The country now produces a variety of wines ranging from crisp whites to robust and claretlike reds. Most of the wine is consumed domestically; about 15 percent or so is exported.

NOTE: The better Greek wines are mainly made by a handful of family-owned enterprises. The bulk wines are usually produced by cooperatives and shipped out to France, Switzerland, and other northern European countries, where they're used to bolster red wines on the thin and pale side.

Hungary

Thousands of years ago, Magyar tribes pushing out of Central Asia found grapes growing wild in the foothills of the Carpathian Mountains. The Roman legions introduced other varieties when they arrived. By the time of the Crusades, Hungarian wines were quite well known. In the Middle Ages, vast quantities of these were exported to Poland and Russia.

Hungary's major wine district is on the Duna, a great plain extending over much of the country's middle sector. Most of its wines are sturdy whites, pressed from furmint and olaszrizling grapes among others. Generally characterizing them is an intense grapiness and a certain headiness or fieriness; some of the wines display a touch of sweetness. Also produced are distinctive red wines, pressed from the indigenous and widely planted kadarka grape, along with the merlot, pinot noir, and other grape varieties.

Hungary's most celebrated wine comes from Tokay, a one hundred fifty square-mile district in the northeast, which encompasses twenty-eight villages. (Tokay takes its name from one of its hill towns.) Sited along the low-lying slopes of the Carpathians are some twelve thousand vineyard acres. A sunny climate and a largely volcanic soil make the region ideal for grape growing; the main grape variety cultivated here is the furmint.

Tokay wines range from the dry and ordinary to the sweet, rich and celebrated. The basic types, in their ascending order of sweetness are: Furmint, Szamorodni, Aszu, and Essenz or Esszencia. Furmint is the driest of all. The Szamorodni wine is dry or semidry. (When full in body, it is quite similar to a light sherry.) Some Szamorodnis display a fresh flavor and bouquet while others tend to be rather harsh and heavy. Although these are unfortified wines, their natural alcohol level is rarely less than 13 percent.

Tokay Aszu, produced only in the best vintages, combines noble rot grapes with normal ones. (The proportion of the botrytized grapes is indicated as puttonyos on the label.) The grapes here are late-harvested, then fermented separately according to their variety. Added to a dry neutral wine of the same vintage, they cause it to referment. The resulting Aszu is a rich, full-bodied, and heavy wine with a degree of residual sugar. Dark gold or amber in color, sweet and luscious but never cloying, the wine is similar to, but somewhat spicier than, the rich botrytized French and German examples. The Aszu also possesses a highly perfumed bouquet, reminiscent of a fragrant green tea, while a lingering hint of dryness offsets its intensely honeyed richness. Louis XV of France called Aszu the "wine of kings and the king of wines." Before World War II, the finest examples were aged for at least ten years in wood. Now the wine is vinified to age for six years or so.

The extremely rare Tokay Essenz or Esszencia is ranked among the world's finest dessert wines. Pressed exclusively from noble rot grapes, culled from special vineyards, the wine is made from their free-run juice and left to ferment for years. The natural sugars here are so concentrated that the wine doesn't ferment out fully, leaving the alcohol level quite low. (Although unfortified, it is more like a liqueur than a wine.) The legendary Esszencia is renowned for its splendid bouquet, concentrated honeylike flavor, and great longevity. (Some examples are known to have survived for two centuries.)

NOTE: Esszencia was never sold on the open market, but reserved for Hungary's Imperial Court. Since World War II, the little produced has been used primarily in sweetening Aszu wines. (Wines now sold under the Essenz or Esszencia label are at best diluted and unaged versions of the original.)

Other Hungarian white wines —often highly potent, fiercely dry, flowery, and scented— come from the north shore of Lake Balaton, Europe's largest fresh-water lake. Among them is Kéknyelü, pressed from furmint and olaszrizling grapes. Similar wines, pressed from the same grape varieties, are produced in Somlo, farther north. Also grown on the north shore of Lake Balaton, in the Badacsony hills, is Szürkebaràt, a medium-dry white wine with an earthy undertone. Another white wine is the semidry and mellow Hàrslevelü.

Hungary's principal red wine, Kadarka, is grown on the central Duna. More widely known however is Egri Bikavér, whose name translates as "Bull's Blood." Grown in the Eger Valley, a hilly district of volcanic soil in the northeast, the wine is celebrated for its aroma and richness of flavor. Stout, sturdy, rich colored and full-bodied at its finest, the wine is also fiery, dry, and velvety smooth with a touch of spice in the taste and a fine bitterness in the aftertaste. The Egri Bikavérs differ widely. (Lesser examples may include wines from Algeria, Morocco or Bulgaria in their blends.) Another Hungarian red wine is Nagyburgunder, grown in Villany, a small region along the Austrian border and pressed from the pinot noir grape.

NOTE: Hungary heavily subsidizes its wine exports and sells about 40 percent of its production abroad on the world market.

Israel

Wine is said to have been produced in what is now Israel as early as 3000 B.C. During the centuries of Saracen and Turkish domination, wine making had largely disappeared and did not reemerge in earnest until the early 1900s. European vines were then imported and the first modern winery was built south of Tel Aviv under the sponsorship of Baron Edmund de Rothschild of the French wine-making family. (Another branch of the Rothschilds built a winery near Haifa.)

Planted at the time were commonplace vines, which proved to be prolific bearers, yielding heavy, undistinguished wines, somewhat on the sweet side and best suited to fortification. Aided now by modern viticultural methods, Israel is cultivating premium wine grapes, including the red cabernet sauvignon and the white riesling. Other white varieties are the colombard, sauvignon blanc, sémillon, and chenin blanc. Produced are a wide range of red, white, and rosé wines; still, sparkling, and fortified, with the red wines outnumbering the whites.

Three-fourths of the country's wine growing is concentrated on a hot, semiarid coastal plain, close to the Mediterranean Sea. Other vineyards are scattered around Jerusalem, near Beersheba and most recently in the Golan Heights. The Golan, a relatively new growing area, is characterized by a volcanic soil, much cooler temperatures, and more plentiful rainfall than the coastal plains. (Its vines, cultivated some eight hundred to eighteen hundred feet above sea level, are sheltered from the hot lowland winds.) The main Golan grape variety is the sauvignon blanc, which yields a crisp, dry, and elegant wine here with a clear fruity character. Also grown in the district are the chardonnay and the cabernet sauvignon. Much of the Golan's wine output is sold abroad.

Japan

Most of the Japanese vineyards are located in Yamanashi province west of Tokyo. Because of the country's limited land mass and its great demand for table grapes, only a sixth of the crop is devoted to wine making.

In the late nineteenth century, the Japanese, wishing to upgrade their wines, traveled to Bordeaux to study vinicultural methods there. Grown now along with native koshu and Chinese grapes are other varieties imported from Europe and America. These include viniferas, such as the cabernet sauvignon and sémillon, and labruscas such as the concord and delaware. For its wine making, Japan also purchases from France, Germany, Italy, Algeria, Argentina, and other countries large quantities of frozen grapes and grape juice concentrates. In addition to producing a wide range of its own red, white, and rosé wines, Japan imports a million gallons of wine or more annually for blending and bottling.

NOTE: Since the 1970s, Japanese interests have been purchasing vineyard properties and wineries around the world. They have recently acquired an interest in the French shipping firm which holds the distribution rights to the most prestigious Burgundy wine, that of the Domaine Romanée-Conti.

Madeira

Madeira is a small island in the Atlantic Ocean, only about thirty-five miles long and twelve miles at its widest. Situated some three hundred and fifty miles west of Morocco, Madeira occupies the same latitude as Casablanca. The island rises so abruptly from the sea that there are no natural beaches. A long-extinguished volcanic range runs through its center. The rugged terrain here is marked by ravines and deep valleys.

When discovered by the Portuguese in the fifteenth century, the island —covered with deep woods— was uninhabited. The Portuguese named it Madeira ("Island of Trees"). To farm the land, they burned off the forests, further enriching the soil. Along with other crops, the colonists planted grapevines imported from Portugal, Spain, Crete, and Germany. The grapes thrived in Madeira's mild climate where year-round temperatures range from the 60s to the 70s and where rain is plentiful in the spring when it is most needed.

Madeira is best known for its fortified wines. These date back to the eighteenth century, when the island served as a victualing station for clipper ships sailing around the Cape of Good Hope. Taking on supplies at the port city of Funchal, the ships also took on casks of the local wine, which had been fortified for the voyage. Rocking and rolling about in the holds of the ships as they sailed through tropical seas, the wine had acquired a bittersweet taste and a wonderfully smooth texture. (To duplicate these characteristics, the Madeira wines were subsequently baked in special estufa ovens.)

In the nineteenth century, oïdium, a mildew disease wiped out virtually all of the island's vines. Twenty years later, phylloxera struck. Although some of the premium vines were replanted, many of them were replaced with cheaper varieties. Madeira's main grapes include the sercial, bual, verdelho, and malmsey. Among the lesser varieties is the tinta negra mole, whose wine is shipped in bulk to France for use in cooking.

Mexico

Mexico is believed to have produced the first wine in the New World in the sixteenth century. Two centuries later, Spanish missionaries were moving on to Baja California, where they applied their skills to grape-growing and wine-making.

Much of the Mexican climate was too hot for quality grapes. (The sweet, heavy wines produced were most often distilled into brandy.) Aided now by the selection of better grape varieties, cold stabilization and other modern vinification methods, Mexico is producing much-improved wines. The best reds, pressed in part from the cabernet sauvignon grape, are somewhat claretlike in character. Among the best white wines are fruity blends of the chenin blanc and the ugni blanc.

NOTE: Mexico has also expanded grape growing to its largely mountainous north-central sector, to the states of Durango, Chihuahua, and Coahuila, where cooler weather prevails. The country domestically consumes most of the wine that it produces.

New Zealand

Early in the nineteenth century, European colonists established the first vineyard at Hawke Bay in eastern New Zealand, planting cuttings they had imported from France, Spain, and Central Europe. Under cultivation now are some three thousand acres in vines, most of them in the cooler areas not far from the sea. Initially, nearly four-fifths of New Zealand's wines were fortified and port and sherry types still predominate. Aided now by stainless-steel technology, the vintners have also been able to produce a good share of table wines.

Because of its generally cool climate, New Zealand is better suited to the production of white wines than to red wines. The whites, pressed from such classic vinifera grapes as the chardonnay, sauvignon blanc, riesling, semillon, and müller-thurgau, are generally lighter and somewhat more acid than their Australian counterparts. Fresh, sometimes intensely flavored and relatively low in alcohol, these at their finest demonstrate a certain austerity and reserve. The red grapes grown are the pinot noir and merlot.

In addition to Hawke Bay, New Zealand's principal wine districts are Gisborne to the north and Auckland to the northwest. On Cook Strait, the Marlborough area experiences the country's sunniest and perhaps driest weather, making its sauvignon blanc grapes high in both their sugar and their acidity.

Romania

The best Romanian wines come from the foothills of the Carpathian Mountains which curve through the country. The growing season here is warm and sunny with sufficient rain, followed by a long, dry, mild autumn.

Primarily a red-wine country, Romania grows the cabernet sauvignon, pinot noir, and merlot as well as several indigenous varieties. The white grapes include the riesling, chardonnay, furmint, pinot gris, sylvaner, aligoté, traminer, and muscat. Produced here are a number of table wines, including sweet Muscats, along with various sparkling and fortified wines.

In the southeast is the Dealul-Mare region, an important producer, known for its red wines. The country's largest region is Foçsani, located east of the Carpathian Mountains; growing both red and white wines on its sandy soil. From the cool mountain plateaus of Transylvania come white wines, pressed from the sauvignon blanc and indigenous grape varieties. And from the temperate coastal province of Moldavia in the northeast comes Cotnari, one of the country's best white wines, finely scented with a great depth of flavor. Somewhat reminiscent of the sweeter Hungarian Tokays, Cotnari is served as a dessert wine.

NOTE: Romania consumes most of its wine domestically.

Russian Federation

The Russians have long had an affinity for wine. Despite the country's northerly location, it has been producing wine since ancient times. Peter the Great brought French vintners to Azerbaijan to plant vines there. In Czarist Russia, the famous French Champagne houses found enthusiastic buyers, many of them attached to the Court in St. Petersburg.

In addition to its native grapes, Russia grows the red cabernet sauvignon, merlot, and malbec and the white aligoté, riesling, sylvaner, pinot gris, and muscat, along with various hybrids. In the 1950s, the wine industry underwent an enormous expansion: cultivating its grapes on huge collective farms and processing its wines in giant wineries.

The country's largest viticultural region is in the south, on the Crimean Peninsula bordering the Black Sea. Produced in the arid subtropical climate here are rich, high-sugar wines. Since the late nineteenth century, the region has specialized in dessert wines and in fortified wines, including flor sherries, made more or less sweet. Produced as well now are red and white table wines and sparkling wines, the latter are made near Odessa. Wine growing is also seen in Georgia, Armenia, and Moldova. Georgia has been producing a variety of wines for nearly five thousand years. Its red and white, sweet, and dry wines enjoy special cachet in Russia and in much of central Europe, being much admired for their variety, character and warmth.

NOTE: One of the world's top producers, Russia not only consumes most of its own wines domestically, but imports millions of gallons more from Eastern Europe, particularly from Hungary.

South Africa

In the seventeenth century, French Huguenots established the first vineyard in South Africa, in the Franschhoek Valley some forty miles east of Cape Town, planting cuttings they had brought from Europe. Other viticultural pioneers were the Dutch, who arrived late in the seventeenth century and set up a trading post at the Cape of Good Hope to supply food and wine to ships sailing to and from the East Indies. By the eighteenth and early nineteenth centuries, South African wines were among the best known in the world. A particularly notable example was Constantia, the legendary sweet Muscat from the Cape of Good Hope. (Louis XVI's wine cellar was said to contain more Constantia than claret.)

South Africa's vineyards extend some two hundred miles north and east of Cape Town. The Cape region itself has more than a dozen officially designated wine districts. Best known are Paarl, Franschhoek, Constantia, and Hermanus. The greatest concentration of wineries is in Stellenbosch, thirty-five miles east of Cape Town and not far from the site of the country's original vineyards. The riesling once predominated, but white grape varieties now also include the steen (chenin blanc), clairette blanc, gewürztraminer, sauvignon blanc, sémillon, palomino, and muscat. A recent addition is the chardonnay. Red grape varieties include the cabernet sauvignon and shiraz (syrah), along with the cinsault, merlot, grenache, gamay, cabernet franc, hermitage, and pinotage.

Growing high-sugar grapes, South Africa has traditionally specialized in port- and sherry-style wines and shipped out its mostly inexpensive table wines in bulk. Modern viticultural and vinicultural methods have now made the production of quality wines —still and sparkling— possible. The country's current reputation is based on its dry reds, ranging from those wines which exhibit a pronounced rusticity to quite elegant examples. Among the best is a Burgundy-style Pinot Noir. The country also produces a variety of white wines, ranging from the crisp and dry to the semisweet and sweet. (Among the latter are a number of late-harvest wines.)

NOTE: Most of South Africa's grapes are cultivated on small farms whose growers sell their crops to others rather than producing the wines themselves. And, according to informal estimates, about 40 percent of the output goes into the production of commercial alcohol. (Many of the growers plant high-yielding grapes, knowing that much of their crop will be used in this way.)

Switzerland

Switzerland produces wine primarily in its western and southern sectors. Most of its vineyards are tiny; their sites range from warm valleys to colder mountain areas that sometimes grow their grapes four thousand feet above sea level. (The vines cling to south-facing Alpine slopes whose lofty peaks protect them from the harsh northern weather.) Many of the best vineyards are sited along the banks of the Rhône River, which flows down from the Alps to Lake Geneva, then continues on its way to France.

Four-fifths of the Swiss wines are white. Their grape varieties include the riesling, pinot gris, chasselas, sylvaner, müller-thurgau, marsanne, chardonnay, gutedel, rauschling, muscat, and petit arvine. The riesling accounts for the finest wines, which are sprightly, fruity, and crisply dry. More widely cultivated is the productive chasselas grape, whose wines are sturdier and lower in acid. The country's red grape varieties are the pinot noir, gamay, and merlot. (The pinot noir produces lighter, fruitier wines here than it does in Burgundy across the border.)

NOTE: Swiss grape names often vary from region to region: the chasselas is also known as the dorin or fendant; the sylvaner as the johannisberg; the marsanne as the ermitage; the pinot gris as the malvoisie. The pinot noir is variously called the blauburgunder, spätburgunder, clevner, and schwartze klevner.

Switzerland produces wine in nineteen of its twenty-three cantons. About three-fourths of its output comes from Valais and Vaud, which are primarily white-wine districts featuring the chasselas grape. Other significant Swiss cantons are Ticino and Neuchâtel, both primarily red wine districts.

The country's oldest and largest wine district is Valais in the upper Rhône Valley not far from the Italian border. A stable climate with plenty of sunshine makes this district one of the warmest and driest. Both red and white wines are produced here. Of particular interest is the white Fendant from Sion, the district's capital and principal wine center. Pressed from the chasselas grape, the Fendant is an impeccably light and dry wine. Other white wines from Valais include the Johannisberg, Ermitage, and various muscat blends. The district's leading red wine is Dole, a blend of the gamay and the pinot noir. (When pressed exclusively from the pinot noir, the wine is known as the Petit Dole.) Fruity and generally dark colored, Dole ranges in body from light to full. Valais also produces some good rosé wines.

The canton of Vaud on the north shore of Lake Geneva consists of La Côte, west of Lausanne (producing especially light white wines) and Lavaux to the east (producing somewhat fuller ones). The wines are generally known by their village names. Most celebrated is Dézaley, grown in steeply terraced vineyards on the outskirts of Lausanne. Pressed from the chasselas, Dézaley is fine, fruity and generally dry. Another fine white wine comes from St. Saphorin near Montreux. To the southeast are the wine towns of Aigle and Yvorne, whose white wines are fairly full-bodied, yet somewhat flinty.

North of Vaud and less than twenty miles from the French border is the canton of Neuchâtel, also known as Suisse Romande. Situated on the shores of the lake from which it takes its name, Neuchâtel grows red and white wines on a chalky soil. Among them is Cortaillod, pressed from the pinot noir; fruity, agreeable, and quite pale. Virtually a rosé wine, Cortaillod is often labeled "Oeil de Perdrix" (Eye of the Partridge) because of its pinkish hue. Neuchâtel's white wines, pressed from the chasselas, are light, dry, and fragrant. Some are naturally pétillant (displaying a slight sparkle) while others have their effervescence added.

NOTE: Switzerland's most northerly wines are produced near Zürich, not far from the German border; the white wines pressed from müller-thurgau and rauschling grapes and the reds from the schwartze klevner (pinot noir).

Ticino, in southern Switzerland, is a warm, sunny region, situated on the slopes of the Italian Alps near Lakes Lugano and Maggiore. Featuring the merlot, and producing highly palatable light-to medium-bodied wines, the canton is best known for its Merlot di Ticino, a fruity, robust red wine with an attractive bouquet. The more ordinary reds are usually served directly from their casks.

NOTE: The Swiss consume domestically almost all the wine they produce and import another 60 percent, mainly red wines, from Burgundy, Bordeaux, and Italy.

🍇 🍇 🍇

Turkey

Historians believe that the Hittites first made wine in Anatolia, now Turkey, around 4000 B.C. Half the country's wine output now comes from state-run wineries, the remainder from smaller producers. Turkey's red and white wines, little known outside the country, are generally light and agreeable. Included among them is a crisp, bone-dry Muscat.

(Former) Yugoslavia

Yugoslavia is said to have its feet in the Balkans and its head in the Alps. In the Mediterranean sector to the south, the grapes ripen earlier, yielding sturdy full-flavored wines. In the northern sector, which experiences a more typically Central European climate, the later ripening grapes yield generally lighter and more aromatic wines.

In addition to the indigenous prokupac, malic, and plavic grapes, other varieties cultivated here include the white riesling, sylvaner, sauvignon blanc, and traminer, along with the sémillon, muscat, malvasia, and pinot blanc. Among the red grapes are the merlot and cabernet sauvignon, along with the pinot noir and the gamay.

Yugoslavia's principal wine regions are the hilly landscape of Slovenia in the north, the rugged Dalmatian coast of Bosnia-Herzegovina in the east and mountainous Serbia farther inland. Slovenia, bordering Italy and Austria and growing grape varieties associated with both countries, yields the best wines which are white. Dalmatia, on the shores of the Adriatic, produces a variety of red, white, and rosé wines, including deep-colored, full-bodied, high-alcohol reds. From the Neretva Valley northwest of Dubrovnik come the strong, full, red Blatina and the dry, white, fruit-scented Zilavka. Serbia and Macedonia are known for their fruity, rather emphatic red wines and their good rosés. A distinctive Yugoslavian specialty is a sweet and potent golden brown dessert wine called Prosek.

Therefore God gave thee of the dew of heaven
and the fatness of the earth with plenty of corn and wine.

—Old Testament

5

IDENTIFYING WINES

Different countries identify their wines in different ways; relying to some extent on the shapes of the bottles, but depending more on the labels. The information the label does or does not provide offers some insights into the character and temperament of the country that issues it. In Europe, place names predominate, while in America the names of the grapes are often employed.

BOTTLE SHAPES

The shape of the bottle is one indication of the wine's type and origin. The basic bottle shapes are the Bordeaux, the Burgundy, and the German flute. The Bordeaux bottle features straight sides, clearly defined shoulders, and a concave indentation —known as a punt, kick, or pushup— at its base. (This holds back the

Bordeaux   Burgundy   Flute   Champagne

sediment during pouring.) The somewhat stouter Burgundy bottle features gently sloping shoulders, while the German flute also displays sloping shoulders, but a longer and more graceful neck.

The Italians call their Bordeaux bottles *bordoleses* and employ them for their classic Chiantis; the Spaniards use them for their lighter Riojas and sherries. The French put their Champagnes, Rhône, and Loire wines into Burgundy-style bottles, while the Italians use them for their Barolos and the Americans for their Pinot Noirs. The Alsatians and Austrians bottle their white wines in German flutes, while the Italians employ them for their Soaves.

Note: A number of variants in these basic shapes include a Burgundy bottle that flares out at the bottom for Spanish sparkling wines and a Bordeaux bottle for port wines that features a slightly bulbous neck.

Other bottle styles include the bocksbeutel, clavelin, amphora, fiasco, and carafe. The bocksbeutel, a rounded pouchlike flask with flat sides, is used in Germany for Franconian wines and in Portugal for some rosés. The squat clavelin, with its squared-off shoulders, is associated with the vin jaunes of the Jura. The slender, vaselike amphora, which is tapered at bottom like its ancient Greek prototype, is employed for the Verdicchios of Italy and the rosés of Provence.

The fiasco, a round-bottomed flask with a woven straw or plastic covering, is associated with the lesser Italian Chiantis. The style originated with Tuscan farm workers, who —taking wine with their lunch in the fields— wrapped their bottles with straw to prevent their breakage. (The covering also protected the wine from the heat of the sun.) A squatter and more truncated variant is the pulcinella, used for Italian Orvietos. And seen primarily in California is the carafe-style bottle, whose wide neck is sealed with a thin metal lid.

The glass of the bottle is usually tinted green or brown to keep out the harmful rays of light. For Bordeaux, Burgundy, Champagne, Alsatian, Austrian, and Mosel wines, it's tinted green and for Rhine wines, brown. White wines and rosés, meant for immediate consumption, are sometimes bottled in untinted glass to show off their clear, fresh brightness.

An increasingly popular variant is not a bottle at all, but a sturdy rectangular cardboard container. Known as wine-in-a-box and pioneered in Australia, this holds a plastic bag filled with wine which is dispensed through a built-in spigot. As wine is withdrawn, the bag collapses correspondingly, eliminating the air space inside and preventing excess oxidation. Once opened the container needs to be refrigerated. (The wine will keep for a few weeks.) Available in three-to five-liter sizes, the wine-in-a-box is not only less expensive to produce, but requires less storage space and eliminates the breakage problems of bottles.

NOTE: This container is intended for soon-to-be-consumed wines, which will keep unopened for six months or so.

READING THE LABELS

Wines were first identified by the writing on their stone jars. Such jars, discovered in Egyptian tombs, bore the name of the owner and grower, and the date. The Greeks would stamp the wine's place of origin on their clay amphoras. Paper labels didn't arrive until the mass production of glass bottles in the eighteenth century. These labels eventually included information as to the wine's style or quality, its alcohol content, and the amount of wine in the bottle. Introduced later were neck labels carrying a vintage date and back labels, which provided simplified maps, background facts, anecdotal information, regulatory details, etc.

NOTE: For quality wines, the corks are usually stamped as well with the name of the vineyard and the wine maker.

The Place–Name Concept

The place-name indicates a wine's origins. This form of identification was introduced in France early in the twentieth century as a way of combating fraud. Unscrupulous vintners in Reims and Épernay had been using cheap grapes from the South of France and calling their wines Champagnes. The actual Champagne growers —threatened with economic ruin— rioted, forcing the government to send in the troops. Protective legislation, subsequently passed, delimited the region's boundaries to the Marne Valley. To be called "Champagne," the wine had to be pressed from grapes grown in that clearly demarcated region around Reims and Épernay. This was the start of the Appellation d'Origine Contrôlée (Controlled or Protected Place Name) or AOC system, covering specific geographical areas. Its basic premise was that the more precisely a wine's origins was pinpointed, the more authentic and better that wine is likely to be.

The AOC provided not only the legal authorization for a regional, district, or a vineyard name, but sought to raise wine standards as well. The place-name regulation spelled out which grapes could be planted, how the vines were to be grown, how many grapes could be picked, and the quantity of wine that could be pressed from those grapes. Also specified might be the method of vinification, the wine's characteristics, the proportions of the various grapes in the blend, the requirements for aging, etc. Wines that do not meet the standards of their locales are declassified, losing the right to their appellations. Although authentic products of their region or district, they are no longer permitted to carry their geographic name.

NOTE: In France, wines covered by such appellations constitute a relatively small proportion now of the country's output, representing only about 30 percent.

The place-name concept has been adopted in varying degrees throughout the world. The minimum standards and controls that are set differ greatly from country to country and even within sectors of the same country. In some places, government agencies regulate labeling, while in others, the wine producers and merchants police themselves. In still others, a coalition of private and public interests supervises the regulation and labeling of the wines.

Estate–Bottling

Estate-bottling is the most precise form of labeling. Associated with quality wines and specifying the smallest and most localized growing areas —the vineyards — this designation not only indicates that the grapes come from the owner's parcel of land but that he himself is responsible for the vinification and bottling of the wine. The estate-bottled label is based on the premise that in order to protect his own reputation a producer will do his utmost to guard the individuality, distinctiveness, and quality of his wine and will pay close personal attention to every phase of the grape-growing and wine-making process carried out on his property.

Second Labels

Second-label wines originated when the famous Bordeaux vineyards began to bottle separately the earlier-maturing products of their younger vines. Second-label wines have included Carruades de Lafite (Château Lafite), Pavillon Rouge du Château Margaux (Château Margaux), Les Forts de Latour (Château Latour), Hauts de Pontet (Château Pontet-Canet), Bahans Haut-Brion, (Château Haut-Brion), Château Potensac (Château Léoville-Las-Cases), Comtesse de Lalande (Château Pichon-Longueville), Château Marbuzet (Cos d'Estournel), Château Malmaison (Château Clarke), Les Fiefs de Lagrange (Château Lagrange) and Château Haut-Bages Averous (Château Lynch-Bages).

NOTE: In the Bordeaux trade, it is said that the wine from twelve-year-old and older vines goes into Château Lafite-Rothschild, while the wine from seven-to twelve-year-old vines goes into Carruades de Lafite. Another château uses the top 45 percent of its production for the first label and the second 45 percent for its second label; selling off the remainder to others for use in inexpensive blends.

A number of California wineries have adopted the second-label idea, applying it to wines that do not measure up to the more demanding standards of their main label. Hawk Crest is the second label of Stag's Leap Wine Cellars. Liberty School comes from Caymus Vineyards, while Beaulieu Vineyards second-labels a trio of its wines: Georges de Latour Private Reserve, Beaulieu Rutherford, and Beau Tour. Some wineries even offer a third label to take advantage of surplus grapes or of grapes purchased from others. (The third label of Château Lafite-Rothschild is simply called "Pauillac," the name of its commune.)

Varietal Labeling

A varietal wine is named for its principal grape. (This designation is particularly useful when the wine retains the distinctive character and aroma of that grape.) The best varietals are pressed from such premium grape varieties as the cabernet sauvignon, pinot noir, chardonnay, and riesling.

Since there were few geographical appellations in the United States until fairly recently, varietal labeling was the main means of identifying American wines. A wine here can be named for its grape if the blend includes at least 75 percent of that grape variety. (An earlier minimum called for 51 percent.) Some vintners, seeking to create wines of greater uniformity and overall quality, go well beyond the required minimum, including as much as 90 to 100 percent of that varietal grape in their wines.

Some California wineries have sought to have the grape minimum raised to 85 percent, while others object, claiming this would interfere with their blending options and curb their creative impulses. (Oregon requires a 90 percent minimum for its chardonnay and pinot noir varietals.) One Long Island winery, employing 58 percent cabernet sauvignon for a Bordeaux-style wine (the merlot and cabernet franc make up the rest) does not meet the minimum and so cannot use the varietal name. The wine is labeled "Select Reserve" instead.

NOTE: When an abundant vintage yields a substantial grape surplus, the wines are offered at lower-than-usual prices and are known as "Fighting Varietals."

Other countries have adopted varietal labeling; among them are Australia, New Zealand, Chile, Argentina, and South Africa. In Europe, where geographic names are usually employed and where law and tradition determine which grapes can be grown in the fine-wine districts, varietal labeling is infrequently seen. Alsatian wines are an exception. Because of the region's intermittent occupation by Germany, Alsace remained outside the French tradition of relating a wine's name to its place of origin. Instead its wines were named for their predominant grape. Varietal labeling is also seen in Austria, where the wines carry such indigenous grape names as Veltiner, Rotgipfler, and Walschriesling.

Some European wine makers have been turning to varietal labeling to circumvent the tougher appellation laws of their countries. A French wine can carry a varietal label as long as it is pressed 100 percent from the grape named. Yet these grapes may be grown anywhere in the country. (The quality of the wine here depends largely on the individual producer.) In Burgundy, for example, an Aligoté may be attractive in one place and coarse and acidy in another. In the South of

France, a recent trend has been to identify wines by their grape names rather than by their geographic locales to make them seem more distinctive. And in Italy, a winery has dropped the custom of using local denominations on its labels, deciding to emphasize the grape names instead.

Proprietary Labeling

A proprietary label, featuring a brand name, trade name, or winery name, offers the vintner the greatest degree of flexibility. He is completely free to alter his blend at will. He can use whatever grapes in whatever proportions he chooses and can blend his wine in whatever way he sees fit. The wine maker does not have to identify his grapes or their source. He can draw the grapes from widely divergent sources, representing several sectors of a country or perhaps more than one country. (Grape availability and price are usually the determining factors.) Whatever the components, the vintner can adjust the blending and other cellar treatment to create a uniformity of style so that his wine displays the same taste and aroma year after year. (In exchange for such flexibility, some producers readily forgo the right to identify their wines as varietals.)

Proprietary labeling in Europe enables the wine maker to get around the tougher appellation restrictions. In France, a number of the proprietary wines are inexpensive blends produced by famous châteaus. Carrying such names as Mouton Cadet and Maître d'Estournel, they almost suggest Second Labels. A wine in Bordeaux, initially made in Pauillac, became so popular that its producer had to reach for his grapes not only beyond Pauillac itself but beyond the larger Médoc region. An even more extreme example was a white wine sold in England with a French–sounding name. Its components had initially been French, but as grape prices rose, the makers turned first to Italian sources and then to Austrian vineyards. Although the character of the wine kept changing, neither its name nor its label was altered.

In the United States, proprietary labeling allows the vintner to bypass varietal requirements. American proprietaries have become popular, in part perhaps because brand–name recognition is a key characteristic of the culture. Some proprietary wines, however, are moving into the premium field. For the upscale market, Californians have developed wines with such names as Opus One, Dominus, Rubicon, Trilogy and Insignia. This prestigious top–quality group whose overall name is Meritage, signifies that the wines are blended only from premium grapes. Since the makers can blend these quality wines as they please, they may meet the varietal requirements in some years, but not necessarily in others.

🍇 🍇 🍇

Generic Labeling

Technically, generic labeling indicates the type or class of the wine. More commonly, the term refers to wines that have appropriated the name of a European wine (claret, Chianti, port, Rhine wine, or sherry) or that of a European locale (Beaujolais, Burgundy, Champagne, Chablis, and Sauternes.) These borrowings began innocently enough in the nineteenth-century, when newly arrived immigrants in America, used familiar Old World names for the wines they were making. The custom was subsequently perpetuated in commercial wine production since the immigrants, who then made up the bulk of the American wine market, were most familiar with such names.

Generics, with few exceptions, are little more than routine jug wines, bearing little if any resemblance to their namesakes. Rarely do they use the same grape varieties and production methods, and when they do, they cannot duplicate the climate conditions or the soil quality of the original wines.

For example, a true Burgundy is pressed exclusively from the pinot noir, while a California generic may rely on such hot-climate varieties as the zinfandel, grenache, barbera, ruby cabernet, and carignane. A true claret is a rich yet austere Bordeaux while the generic can be a dry, sometimes tart red wine which is usually quite light in body. (American wine makers have been known to bottle their generic clarets and generic Burgundies from the same vat.) True Sauternes, pressed from noble rot grapes, is richly luscious. The generic (dropping the final *s*) never uses botrytized grapes and is more likely to be a dry wine than a sweet one.

A true Chablis is characterized by crispness, flintiness, and bite. In the United States, "Chablis" is synonymous with an inexpensive and generally undistinguished white wine. Usually soft and slightly sweet, these may be red or pink as well as white, and can even be slightly fizzy. A true Rhine wine is known for its splendid sugar-acid balance; the generic is generally quite tart. And although Mosel wines are celebrated for their delicacy and fragrance, wines calling themselves "Moselles" are usually quite bland and commonplace.

A generic sherry, like its nominal prototype, may be pressed from raisined grapes and may even be inoculated with flor. Many, however, are baked at high temperatures to approximate the original's nutlike "rancio" taste. Such wines may also be filtered through wood chips to simulate the slow aging process that occurs during the solera blending of true sherries in oak.

Generic ports are often lamentably raw; they may be pressed from low-quality berries or even culls. While a true tawny port acquires its color through wood aging, the generic may combine red and white wines, employ less pigmented grapes, or use coloring agents. And generic Tokays, often bear a closer resemblance to generic ports and sherries than to their original Hungarian namesakes.

In the United States, generics have become a way for American producers to market their surplus grapes or wines. Only the vaguest regulations cover generics; the use of borrowed names is permitted as long as the label indicates the wine's general place of origin —as in a Napa Valley Chablis or a New York State Burgundy. Generics are also seen in Europe, Australia, South America, and South Africa. Chile uses label designations such as Tipo Borgana (Burgundy Type) and Tipo Chablis (Chablis Type), but sometimes confusingly employs Bordeaux grapes for its Burgundy-type wines. The Australians make a variety of generics, including Moselle, hock (Rhine wine), Chablis, Sauterne, claret, and Burgundy, as well as port-and sherry-type wines. A number of other countries —including the USA and Russia— also produce generic ports and sherries.

European vintners have long sought to prevent the exploitation of their wine names. In 1916, an agreement between Britain and Portugal defined port as "a wine produced in the delimited Douro region," and specified that a wine could not be sold as port in England unless it was produced within those delimited boundaries. (Britain does, however, allow the sale of generic ports, provided they specify their country of origin —as in "Australian port" or "South African port.") Portugal itself hoped to set true port apart from its imitators by creating an official "Oporto" designation, but since most of the wine is shipped out in bulk for bottling elsewhere, foreign shippers continue to use the more familiar "port" designation.

Other attempts have been made to restrict wine names to their original locations. Early in the twentieth century, the Madrid Convention gave wine sources the sole right to their own geographic names. In the 1970s, the Common Market required that wines shipped by its member nations be accompanied by certificates of origin, spelling out the source of their components. (When the wines of more than one country are involved, the label reads "Countries of the European Economic Community.") Yet attempts by France and other wine-producing nations to have the California jug-wine makers end their use of geographic names have generally not succeeded.

The most freely appropriated name is "Champagne," which is applied to white, red, and pink wines, pressed from a variety of grapes and made sparkling by the classic méthode champenoise or one of its alternatives. Trying to maintain the exclusivity of that name, the Champagne industry has spent millions on lawsuits; fighting successful legal battles in Australia, Germany, Spain, and Italy. By international agreement and Common Market regulation, the name is now restricted in Europe to French sparkling wines, grown in the delimited Marne Valley region. Even the term "méthode champenoise" has been banned outside of that region.

The United States has never been a signatory to such agreements. American courts have consistently rejected the French claims, stating that the French producers waited too long to sue and that in the meantime, the Champagne name had found its way into common usage. American vintners can still call a sparkling wine Champagne, provided they indicate its place of origin —as "New York State Champagne" or "California Champagne."

Some people believe that generic labeling should be discontinued. They say it misrepresents and debases the unique identity of the original and deceives the consumer. Recommendations have been made in the United States that generic labels calling wines Barolo, Beaujolais, Frascati, Rhône, Rioja, and Mosel be eliminated, while those for Champagne, Chablis, Madeira, Málaga, port, and sherry be retained. (These recommendations have not been carried out.) Some American vintners are phasing out their generic labeling to a degree. A number of wineries in the northeast have combined varietal and generic names, as in: "Diamond Chablis," "Duchess Rhine Wine" and "Delaware Moselle." Other American wine makers are turning to proprietary or varietal names for their wines, or simply labeling them "red" or "white." (Some California wines are called "Rosso" for red and "Bianco" for white.)

NOTE: When Australian producers replaced the familiar generic names with varietal ones, domestic sales fell. The Australians now use generic labels for their wines at home, while employing varietal labels for those shipped abroad.

Vintage–Dating

A vintage date refers to the year the grapes were harvested and made into wine. Any wine —good, bad, or indifferent— can carry a vintage date if made from the grapes of a single year.

Vintages first came into prominence with port wines and Champagnes. Port shippers would declare a vintage in years of splendid weather, when the crop was excellent enough to stand on its own and when the wine showed a fine potential for aging. Each firm made this decision individually. Some vintners would wait eighteen months after the harvest to see how their wines were coming along; others waited thirty-four months before declaring a vintage. (A port vintage is declared only three or four times in a decade.)

Declaring a vintage in the Champagne region is often based on the recommendation of a local growers' organization, the Comité Interprofessionel du Vin de Champagne (Interprofessional Committee of Champagne). Individual producers can follow suit if they wish since the region's variable weather gives them some leeway. Vintages in Champagne would appear only in those years when the producers knew their wines would be especially good. Now more and more vintages are being declared there. (The prices fetched by vintage Champagnes are generally 25 to 50 percent higher than the nonvintage ones.) Yet, while a vintage Champagne is the wine of a single harvest, a nonvintage Champagne —which represents the blending and reblending of a number of wines— may be a better-balanced product. (The best firms combine as many as fifteen wines, drawn from four or five harvests, in order to create and maintain their unique house styles.)

The vintage dating of table wines did not begin until the eighteenth century, when glass bottles were mass-produced and wines could be aged in them. (The bottles, with their uniform apertures and straight sides, could be securely corked and stored away for extended periods.) Vintage dating was a way for the winemakers to differentiate between their production of various years and also provided the consumer with the key to storing his wines, while helping him avoid wines that were too old.

Vintage dating differs with location. In the Northern Hemisphere, the grapes are usually gathered between September and November. Below the Equator they're generally harvested six months earlier. (Southern Hemisphere wines may already be on the market while their Northern counterparts have not yet been vinified, yet the labels of both will carry the same year.) German Eisweins carry two dates, indicating the crop was harvested in one year but not vinified until the next. Since sherries, Madeiras, and Marsalas are all blended in soleras —and so combine a number of vintages— the dates on their labels generally indicate the year when the solera began, not the year when the wines were harvested.

Vintage dating is most significant in Northern Europe, particularly in regions of uncertain weather, such as Bordeaux and Burgundy in France, and the Rhine and Mosel Valleys in Germany. For most other table wines, vintage dating was not considered important until the twentieth century when a date on a label came to suggest status and prestige. This was due in part to an association with the laying down of fine wines and in part to advertising. In the public mind now, vintage dating has become synonymous with superior quality. Many producers have capitulated to the consumer's insistence that a year be indicated on the label and are now vintage dating their entire production regardless of its quality. The majority of wines, however, are nonvintage leaving their makers free to blend the products of two or more years for maximum effect.

FRENCH LABELS

Charlemagne introduced laws to regulate French wines in the eighth century. Charles VI specified where Burgundy wines could be grown in the fifteenth century. The nineteenth century saw the start of the appellation contrôlée, or controlled place-name system designed to certify specific areas of production. In the twentieth century, a semiofficial regulatory agency was created to bring order to French grape growing and wine making. Composed of civil servants and wine-industry representatives, it was called the Institut National des Appellations d'Origine Contrôleé, or INAO. Its purpose was to classify the country's wines and to determine which growing areas should receive their own appellations.

The INAO established three basic French classifications: Appellation d'Origine Contrôlée (AOC), Vins Délimités de Qualité Supérieure (VDQS) and Vins de Pays (Country Wines). There was also a catch-all group, Vins de Table (VDT), which included vins ordinaire, or ordinary table wines.

The highest ranking AOC covers wines from the better regions, guaranteeing that their grapes are grown in a specific locale and that the wines themselves are made under fairly strict conditions. The VDQS, the next level down, covers regional and district wines. (These are inexpensive blends, produced mainly in the Midi, Provence, and Corsica.) Once an honorable category, the VDQS has become a stepping-stone to an AOC. The Vins de Pays, or Country Wines, covers the blends from small, off-the-beaten-track regions; many in the south of France. (These may bear the name of their village, county, or grape variety or be given such elegant-sounding names as Côtes du Rhône and Langue d'Oc.)

The French appellation system in effect is a series of geographical groupings, narrowing down to smaller and smaller areas. Wines from the largest and least-precise areas are labeled "Produce of France," followed by such regional appellations as Bordeaux, Burgundy, Rhône Valley, Loire, Alsace, etc. Next come the districts within the regions, the villages within the districts, and finally —and most specifically— the individual vineyards.

The broadest grouping, the VDTs or vins ordinaire, are mostly nondescript jug wines which carry no geographic designation at all other than France itself. They may come from almost anywhere, including other countries. Among them is the *gros rouge* (fat red) of the Midi, once a staple of the workingman's diet. (Its cost is based on its alcohol content.) Included here too are the "zip-code wines," whose only indication of origin is the postal zone in which they were bottled.

The AOC regulations are periodically revised, with new appellations created from time to time. In 1936, St.-Émilion was recognized as an official wine district with its own Appellation d'Origine. Muscadet's appellations include Muscadet de Sevre-et-Maine, Muscadet des Côteaux de la Loire, Muscadet and Muscadet Côtes de Grand Lieu. Among the more recent AOCs are the Côte de Bourg and Côte de Blaye, Cahors, St. Véran, and Côtes du Ventoux along with Minervois and Côtes-de-Provence. For the Rhône Valley, a separate Gigondas appellation was established to distinguish its wines from the more routine Côtes-du-Rhones. And a special appellation sets Savennières apart from the Côteaux de la Loire sector surrounding it. In Burgundy, a les Maranges appellation was created to cover the marginal areas on the periphery of the famous Côte d'Or communes. (The AOC here includes three small communes at the region's southern tip.)

The French appellations do more than indicate geography; they may specify production standards, crop yields, and minimum alcohol levels. A wine that does not meet its AOC requirements is declassified and must be sold under a lesser label, either with a commune name or with an even broader district name. Also declassified is the overproduction of a given wine.

NOTE: Growers who overcrop, who push their vines beyond their allotted limits or who squeeze more wine out of a given quantity of grapes usually end up with products that are thin, weak, and watery. But growers who limit their yields are able to further concentrate the flavors in their grapes and produce generally more intense and richer wines.

To bear the name of a vineyard, a French wine must achieve a certain level of alcohol. Wines registering less than the minimum level must carry a lesser name. If the alcohol drops below a certain point, the wines must carry a more general regional appellation. (If they contain slightly more alcohol than their classification requires, they may add the term, "Supérieure" to their labels.)

In poor years, French estates sell off the wines that do not meet their standards. They sell them to shippers and others who blend them with the discards of other estates and label them as regional wines. (When the grapes are completely anonymous, their wines are classified as "Vins de Table.")

Although the AOCs strictly limit wine output, some growers in the traditionally famous locations have exploited their marginal areas —by creating new vineyards; bulldozing trees and smoothing out fields— while still remaining within the delimited boundaries. In little more than a decade, the Champagne region has just about doubled in size while the success of the Beaujolais Nouveaus has led to huge plantings in the less favored Bas-Beaujolais sector. An increased demand for white wines in general and for Chablis in particular has caused that region to expand the limits of its legal acreage and to incorporate once-banned grape varieties into its blends. Chablis is now three times larger than it was in 1960. In the Rhône Valley too, the delimited Côte Rôtie district has almost doubled in size, with new vineyards now sited at the less desirable top of the slopes.

NOTE: Nature as well as law limits the production of wine. The French —having developed virtually every spare inch of their land in choice viticultural areas— have gone abroad to extend their wine-making activities; purchasing vineyards, building wineries, and participating in various joint wine-making ventures in a number of other countries.

❦ ❦ ❦

Bordeaux Labeling

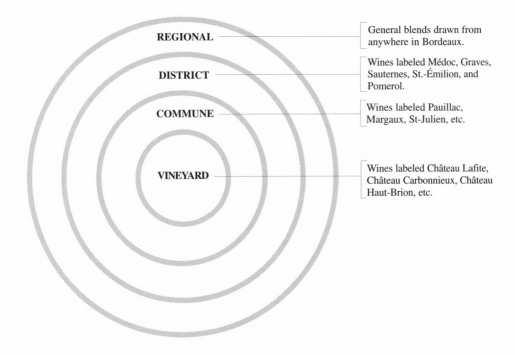

REGIONAL	General blends drawn from anywhere in Bordeaux.
DISTRICT	Wines labeled Médoc, Graves, Sauternes, St.-Émilion, and Pomerol.
COMMUNE	Wines labeled Pauillac, Margaux, St-Julien, etc.
VINEYARD	Wines labeled Château Lafite, Château Carbonnieux, Château Haut-Brion, etc.

The three appellations in Bordeaux are Regional, District, and Subdistrict (Commune). Regional applies to wines from any sector of the entire region. District applies to wines from the five main areas (Mêdoc, Graves, Sauternes, St.-Émilion, and Pomerol.) Subdistrict applies to wines grown in specific communes within the five districts. The smallest and most precise locations are the individual vineyards, whose wines carry a vineyard name rather than an AOC as such.

Bordeaux labeling is perhaps best understood if visualized as four concentric circles, with the outer circle representing the most general area: the regional AOC which encompasses all of Bordeaux. Labels here read "Appellation Bordeaux Contrôlée." Its wines, which can be drawn from anywhere within the vast Bordeaux region, are generally undistinguished and include the millions of gallons produced by cooperative wineries.

The second circle encompasses the five main Bordeaux districts and draws its wines from several communes within each district. The labels here read "Appellation Médoc Contrôlée," "Appellation Graves Contrôlée, etc. (Second-label wines may also use this designation, but third-label wines must carry the broader "Bordeaux" appellation.)

The third circle, encompassing the subdistricts, draws its wines from a number of vineyards within the borders of a single commune. Labels here read "Appellation Pauillac Contrôlée," "Appellation Margaux Contrôlée," etc. (For example, more than thirty Pauillac communes are entitled to carry the "Appellation Pauillac Contrôlée.")

Wines from the the smallest and innermost fourth circle carry the name of their vineyard along with that of their commune or village. Labels here read: "Château Lafite-Rothschild, Appellation Pauillac Contrôlée;" "Château Carbonnieux, Appellation Graves Contrôlée." (An exception is the prestigious Château Haut-Brion in Graves, whose illustrious vineyard name is permitted to stand alone.)

To summarize: Four red Bordeaux wines, representing the four concentric circles, would be labeled "Bordeaux AOC" (region), "Médoc AOC" (district), "Pauillac" (commune) and "Château Lafite-Rothschild" (single vineyard).

NOTE: The bulk of the Bordeaux trade, however, is in shippers' wines, which are mostly anonymous blends. (The shippers usually buy their wines by the cask from a given region or township, then blend, finish, and bottle the wines themselves.) These are sold under the shipper's label, which generally carries his name along with the wine's source of origin.

Because the Médoc is known primarily for its red wines, white wines —even from the top estates— carry only the wider "Bordeaux" appellation. Conversely Graves, generally associated with red wines, must use a subappellation for its white wines. As a result, Château Margaux's exquisite white wine cannot carry the name of that celebrated vineyard, but will use a proprietary name instead. Red wines, grown in the primarily white wine regions, are subject to the same restrictions. For example, the red wines of Entre-Deux-Mers must carry a wider "Bordeaux" designation.

The finest Bordeaux wines, the Vins de Château, come from officially demarcated vineyards under a single ownership. (The vineyard itself must possess the building and equipment to press the grapes and store and bottle the wines.) Although *château* translates as "castle," only a few of the buildings here are actually palatial structures. Just about any wine-making operation in Bordeaux — regardless of its size or character— can call itself a château. The building may be a cottage, farm house, warehouse, or even a shed. Most are little more than modest vineyards with wine cellars. And of the seven thousand or so châteaus, only about two hundred produce quality wines. (The legendary estates represent less than 2 percent of Bordeaux's acreage and produce less than 1 percent of its wine.)

NOTE: Located on the fringes of the fine-wine districts are the *Petit Châteaux,* which are small, little-known vineyards situated at lesser sites and on lesser soils. The wines that they produce are usually simple and early maturing.

The term "Château-Bottled" or "Estate-Bottled" refers to a wine vinified in a structure attached to a specific vineyard, provided that the structure and the vineyard are mutually engaged in the production of the wine. (Although French producers and shippers outside Bordeaux have appropriated the "Château-Bottled" designation, it has no legal status elsewhere in the country.)

In Bordeaux, these phrases establish the authenticity of estate-bottled wines:
• *Mis* (or *mise*) *en bouteilles au* —or *du*— *château* (Château-bottled)
• *Mise du château* (short form)
These, along with the château name, may also be branded on the cork.

The following designations have no legal standing in Bordeaux:
• *Mis en bouteilles dans nos caves* (Bottled in our cellars)
• *Mis en bouteilles dans nos chais* (Bottled in our warehouses)
The cellars and warehouses can be located anywhere in the country.

Other designations without official standing are:
• *Mis en bouteilles dans Château* so-and-so
• *Mis en bouteilles en Bordeaux*
• *Mis en bouteilles dans la region de production*
The first does not mean the bottler owns or controls the vineyard's production, while the other two don't claim very much.

   NOTE: Bordeaux wines meant for export often carry the initials ADEB (Association pour le Dévelopement du Vin de Bordeaux), indicating that their maker has voluntarily submitted his wine to a panel of experts for their approval.

Burgundy Labeling

Burgundy's labeling system is based more on quality levels than on geographic distribution. The scattered parcels in the region's fragmented vineyards are classified down to and including the tiniest parcels of land. The four classifications here are: Region, Commune, Premier Cru, and Grand Cru. These too are perhaps best understood if seen as four concentric circles, narrowing down from the largest, most general growing area to the smallest, most precise parcel of land.

   The outer or regional circle encompasses general blends whose grapes can be drawn from anywhere in Burgundy. Labels here read: "Appellation Bourgogne Contrôlée." The second or commune circle includes the ordinary wines drawn from two or more vineyards within a given village or commune. Its labels read: "Pommard," "Nuits-St.-Georges," "Volnay," "Côte de Beaune," etc. (When preceded by a village name —as in "Santenay-Côte de Beaune" or "Monthélie-Côte de Beaune"— the wine comes from that village.) Also included in the second circle

Burgundy Labeling

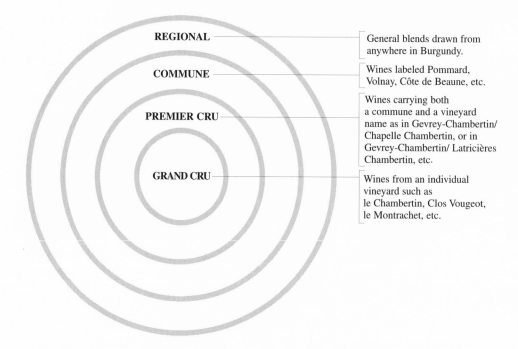

REGIONAL — General blends drawn from anywhere in Burgundy.

COMMUNE — Wines labeled Pommard, Volnay, Côte de Beaune, etc.

PREMIER CRU — Wines carrying both a commune and a vineyard name as in Gevrey-Chambertin/ Chapelle Chambertin, or in Gevrey-Chambertin/ Latricières Chambertin, etc.

GRAND CRU — Wines from an individual vineyard such as le Chambertin, Clos Vougeot, le Montrachet, etc.

are wines from secondary communes situated at either end of the Côte de Nuits — such as Fixin— along with the wines coming from single, but from generally undistinguished vineyards.

NOTE: By law, the Côte d'Or red wines must be pressed from the pinot noir and white wines from the chardonnay. Wines employing other grape varieties cannot carry such a second-circle designation but must use the broader "Appellation Bourgogne Contrôlée" instead.

The third circle represents the Premier Cru wines (First Quality Growth), grown in the better vineyards of each Burgundy commune. These carry both the commune and the vineyard name. For example, the village of Gevrey-Chambertin encompasses twenty Premier Crus, including Chapelle-Chambertin, Chambertin Clos de Bèze, Latricières-Chambertin, Charmes-Chambertin, and so on.

NOTE: When a third-circle vineyard, known primarily for its white wines, also produces red wines, the reds must carry the less specific second circle designation.

The fourth and innermost circle represents the highest-quality Burgundy Grand Crus (Great Growths). Grown mainly on the Côte de Nuits, these come from vineyards of superior soil and exposure. So esteemed are they that their Grand Cru label need only carry the name of their eminent vineyard. Included here are Clos Vougeot,

Chambertin, Montrachet, and Musigny. (The smallest Grand Cru vineyard is the tiny two-acre Romanée-Conti, also known as the Domaine de La Romanée-Conti or DRC.)

To summarize, Burgundy's quality levels are: 1) Regional, 2) Commune, 3) Premier Cru, and 4) Grand Cru. For example, the lowest category of a Gevrey-Chambertin wine is the regional "Appellation Bourgogne Contrôlée." The next level is the commune name: "Appellation Gevrey-Chambertin Contrôlée;" then comes the Premier Cru, whose label reads "Gevrey-Chambertin/La Combe-aux-Moines" (the commune name and vineyard name). The highest-ranking Grand Cru carries the name of an estimable vineyard, such as "Le Chambertin."

In Burgundy, a wine estate is known as a *clos* or a *domaine*. Only a few Burgundian parcels of land are large enough to produce estate-bottled wines. Their labels carry not only the vineyard name but the name of the owner, followed by the term *"Viticulteur"* or *"Propriétaire."*

The following phrases establish the authenticity of estate-bottled wines here:
• *Mis* (or *mise*) *en bouteilles au domaine* (Bottled at the estate)
• *Mis au* —or *du*— *domaine* (short form)

Less frequently used but nevertheless authentic are:
• *Mis en bouteilles par le propriétaire* (Bottled by the proprietor/grower)
• *Mis par le propriétaire* (short form)
• *Mis en bouteilles à la propriété* (Bottled on the property)
• *Mis à* —or *de*— *la propriété* (short form)
These designations must appear in French and on the main label. (If they appear in English or on the neck label, they are not valid.)

Often seen on the labels of Burgundy shippers but lacking official standing are:
• *Mis en bouteilles au mes caves* (Bottled in my cellars)
• *Mis en bouteilles dans nos chais* (Bottled in our wineries or cellars)
• *Mis en bouteilles à Beaune* (Bottled in Beaune)
The first may be the product of more than one vineyard and the shipper's cellar might be located anywhere. The second may be bottled in a shipper's cellar located some distance from the vineyard. And although the third provides a commune name, it does not indicate where the grapes themselves were grown.

Vaguer still are the following designations:
• *Mis en bouteilles sous nôtre garantie* (Bottled under our guarantee)
• *Mis de l'origine* (Bottled at the place of origin)
• *Mis en bouteilles par les vignerons* (Bottled by the growers)

Although using uniform and logically based standards applicable to the entire region, Burgundy's labeling has rightly been called a jungle. Much of the confusion began in the nineteenth century when some Côte d'Or vintners — wishing to increase the sale of their wines— decided to associate them with the most prestigious vineyards in their village. With official approval, they added the name of a prestigious vineyard nearby to the name of their village, separated only by a hyphen. These composite names seemed to suggest that the village wines had come from a quality location when in fact they were drawn from a much wider area. The public was beguiled by these hyphenated labels and sales figures began to show a marked increase. Other Burgundy villages soon followed suit.

Gevrey rechristened itself Gevrey-Chambertin; Chambolle became Chambolle-Musigny. Morey-St.-Denis expanded its name with a nod to Clos St.-Denis. The little village of Aloxe appended the illustrious Corton name to its own, becoming the impressive Aloxe-Corton. Vosne-Romanée renamed itself for the eminent Domaine de la Romanée, while the adjacent communes of Puligny and Chassagne claimed the Montrachet name for themselves since that prestigious vineyard straddled them both, becoming Puligny-Montrachet and Chassagne-Montrachet.

Adding to the confusion were other vineyards which decided to append to their own names, the names of the most notable vineyards nearby. In Gevrey-Chambertin, for example, eight vineyards appropriated the illustrious Chambertin name; becoming Chapelle-Chambertin, Chambertin-Clos de Bèze, Latricières-Chambertin, Charmes-Chambertin, etc.

Since the commune names and vineyard names are now so similar, it is often difficult to distinguish between the two. Yet the difference between the wines themselves can be enormous. A Vougeot wine is a commune wine bearing little resemblance to the outstanding wine grown in the prestigious Clos Vougeot vineyard. A wine labeled "Beaune AOC" can easily be mistaken for a Côte de Beaune Villages. (The former comes from the fine and closely delineated commune of Beaune; the latter derives from farther afield and is a blend of two or more wines drawn from secondary communes.)

Compounding the confusion has been the ongoing fragmentation of the vineyards themselves. As their proprietors died off, the land was divided into smaller and smaller plots. Yet anyone owning a parcel in a given vineyard can name his wine for that vineyard, whether his plot is at the top, bottom, or middle of the slope. And each owner cultivates his parcel in his own way and makes his own special style of wine. The variations are many. The same vineyard might yield three distinct wines: one from a grower who produces, bottles, and sells his own wine; another from a shipper to whom the grower has sold his raw wine; and a third from a shipper, who owns a parcel in that vineyard and blends his wine with the wines of others.

In Burgundy, the maker or shipper is as important as the wine itself. Depending on his experience and skills, he may assemble a blend that is better than the wine made from a single parcel owned by one wine maker. (The shipper who blends the wine of several owners may use the vineyard name if all the parcels are located there, but not if he has drawn the wine for his blend from several vineyards.)

Chablis Labels

Chablis wines are categorized as: Petit Chablis, Chablis, Chablis Premier Cru, and Chablis Grand Cru. Most modest is Petit Chablis, also known as *Bourgogne des Environs de Chablis* (Burgundy from around Chablis). This is a shipper's blend from lesser vineyards, which attains at least 9.5 percent alcohol and may include wines from outside the Chablis district. The next category, Chablis alone, possesses slightly more alcohol and richness, while the Premier Cru, produced in nearly two dozen small vineyards around the town of Chablis, must reach at least 10.5 percent alcohol. (Several Premier Cru vineyards have been legally permitted to add the name of a famous vineyard nearby to their own name, as in Chablis-Vaudésir, Chablis-Grenouilles, etc.)

Grand Cru is reserved for Chablis wines grown in the region's seven leading vineyards: Les Clos, Blanchots, Bougros, Grenouilles, Les Preuses, Valmur and Vaudésir. (These wines must attain a level of at least 11 percent alcohol.) Their labels carry the vineyard name, often with the "Grand Cru" added.

Beaujolais Labels

Only red wines pressed from the gamay grape may legally be called Beaujolais. Although the Chardonnays wines grown in the region have been called Beaujolais Blancs, they are not —strictly speaking— true Beaujolais.

The appellations here are: Beaujolais, Beaujolais-Villages, and Cru Beaujolais. Beaujolais alone comes from Bas-Beaujolais, the region's southern sector, where the terrain is flatter and the soil is a sedimentary clay. These wines are required to attain at least 9 percent alcohol and may be chaptalized to achieve that strength. (For export, their alcohol may be increased to 11 or 12 percent and more.)

Beaujolais-Villages wines are drawn from thirty-nine communes in the Haut-Beaujolais sector. Sturdy and dependable, they usually demonstrate more character than Beaujolais alone. (Adding "Villages" to an appellation indicates a somewhat better product.) Although generally higher in alcohol, these wines are often chaptalized too.

The top-ranking Cru Beaujolais are invariably darker, richer, and fuller than the other Beaujolais wines. Produced in the top nine northern sectors and bearing a commune name rather than a vineyard name, they are: Moulin-à-Vent, Morgon, Chénas, Brouilly, Côte de Brouilly, Fleurie, Juliénas, Chiroubles, and St. Amour. A tenth cru, Beaujolais-Régnié, added in 1988, is known simply as Régnié. All the Cru Beaujolais, whether grown on the largest vineyard estate or on the smallest parcel of land, are entitled to bear the name of their prestigious communes.

NOTE: Beaujolais Nouveaus are drawn from Beaujolais wines alone or from Beaujolais-Villages, never from the top-ranking Cru Beaujolais.

Champagne Labels

The Champagne name in France constitutes a guarantee of authenticity in and of itself. To bear the name, the wine must be grown in the strictly demarcated Champagne Délimitée zone of the Marne Valley and must follow the *méthode champenoise*. Since these wines are pressed from purchased grapes, they do not carry a vineyard name but are known by the name of their maker instead. The prestige Champagnes, labeled either *Grand Cuvée* (Great Blend) or *Tête de Cuvée* (Top of the Line), are usually made from the first pressings of the highest-rated grapes and often sold in elaborately decorated bottles. Other Champagnes may combine several pressings but never the third or the fourth alone. Speciale Cuvée indicates a producer's best wines, while Premier Cuvée refers to the best wine of a given commune.

Champagnes are also characterized as Vintage or Nonvintage (NV). Only about 3 percent bear a vintage date. To ensure their proper aging the Vintage Champagnes are not sold until two years after the harvest. (Most of the better makers keep them in their cellars for five years or more. Some prime examples are not released until they're at least eight to ten years old.) NV Champagnes can include wines from as many as ten previous years to achieve their desired style. (The minimum aging time is one year before release.) Grand Cru refers not to the wine itself but to a quality vineyard in a famous village whose grapes have fetched the highest prices. RD stands for *Recemment Dégorgé* (Recently Disgorged) and refers to particularly fine Champagnes, which have been allowed to rest on their yeasty sediment several years longer than the others, rendering them fuller and more flavorful. (The British equivalent is LD or late disgorged.)

RM stands for *Recoltant Manipulant* ("grower and wine maker"), CM refers to *Coopérative de Manipulation* (a cooperative that makes wine from its members' grapes), NM stands for *Négociant-Manipulant* (a Champagne house that buys grapes and makes wine) and MA for *Marque Acheteur* (purchaser's mark). Meaningless label terms for Champagne are: Réserve, Privat, and Speciale.

NOTE: Authentic Blanc de Blancs Champagne comes from the delimited Côte de Blancs zone. Elsewhere in the country, *Blanc de Blancs* simply indicates a white wine made from light-skinned grapes. Although the term is meaningless and redundant, producers outside the Champagne region often use it, hoping it will give their wines some elegance and prestige.

Rhône Valley Labels

The Rhône Valley's classifications are: 1) Côtes du Rhône, 2) Côtes du Rhône-Villages, 3) Côtes du Rhône with a district or a village name, and 4) Rhône wines with their own appellation. Côtes du Rhône refers to the region's simplest and least expensive wines. Covering the entire Rhône Valley, this label encompasses some one hundred and twenty communes, producing literally millions of gallons of wine annually; many made by cooperatives. Most of these wines are sturdy and tasty, but rather undistinguished. Slightly better are the Côtes du Rhône-Villages, produced mainly in the region's southern sector and representing blends drawn from one or several villages. Usually, these are also produced by the cooperatives.

NOTE: Because the southern Rhône is best known for its red wines, the highest appellation permitted its white wines is Côtes du Rhône-Villages.

Côtes du Rhône with a district or a village name covers wines drawn from a delimited and specified locale such as Côtes du Rhône-Chusclan and Côtes du Rhône-Ardèche. The highest-quality Rhône wines carry their own appellations. Numbering less than twenty, these include Côte Rôtie, Condrieu, Châteauneuf-du-Pape, Château Grillet, and Hermitage. (The Hermitage AOC covers only the prestigious Hermitage Hill; wines from the surrounding area carry a lesser Crozes-Hermitage designation.)

NOTE: Single vineyard names are rare in the Rhône, but a number of producers are beginning to engage in estate-bottling and to feature vineyard names.

Alsatian Labels

Most French wines are named for their place of origin but —because of the recurrent German occupation of Alsace— its wines did not come under the French labeling laws until the 1960s. As a result, the best Alsatian wines carry a varietal name rather than a place name.

The Alsatian wine categories are: Grand Vin d'Alsace, Edelzwicker, and Zwicker. Grand Vin, also known as Grand Cru or Grand Réserve, applies to wines grown in the best vineyards of the leading villages. To qualify, these must be made 100 percent from the specified grape variety (riesling, gewürztraminer, tokay d'alsace, or muscat), they must employ only the first and possibly the second pressing of the grapes and must attain a minimum alcohol level of 11 percent. A Grand Vin will carry a commune name or a village name —Guebwiller,

Ammerschwir, Ribeauville, etc.— along with the shipper's name and address.

NOTE: Grand Vin or Grand Réserve has no official significance elsewhere.

Edelzwicker (Blend of Noble Grapes) refers to wines, combining two or more of the better grape varieties. Made from the second and more likely the third pressings, these are generally served as carafe wines. The more commonplace Zwicker (Blend of Grapes) combines lesser grape varieties: the chasselas and sylvaner.

Cru Exceptionnel or Réserve refers to an Auslese wine, while Vendange Tardive or VT translates as "late-harvest wine." Selection du Grains Noble or SGN (Selection of Only the Ripest Grapes) refers to those rare wines pressed from individually picked noble-rot berries. (They are somewhat similar to the German Trockenbeerenausleses.)

NOTE: Since few Alsatian vintners own enough land to produce single-vineyard wines, a shipper's name or a brand name is more common than a vineyard name. Some Alsatian wine makers, however, are beginning to engage in estate-bottling, and to feature vineyard names on their labels. Such single-vineyard wines are known as Special Reserve Selection. (To merit the designation, the wine must derive 100 percent from the named estate.)

Miscellaneous French Labels

Authentic Pouilly-Fuissé always carries a vineyard name. When grown outside its delimited zone, the wine must be labeled "Mâcon-Fuissé." A relatively recent appellation is St. Véran, encompassing the wines of eight nearby Mâconnais villages. (They previously carried only a Beaujolais Blanc or a Mâcon Blanc designation.) Côte Châlonnaise wines of officially recognized quality are labeled Premier Cru (First Growth). In the Côtes de Provence, the wines of officially recognized quality are labeled Cru Classé (Classified Growth) and carry a vineyard name. Although the South of France is now making more varietal wines, some producers who believe that grape names lack personality are giving their wines more impressive labels like Château de Jonquierre and Domaine Pujol.

In water you see your own face;
in wine the heart of another.

—Old Proverb

ITALIAN LABELS

Italy has named its wines for their place of origin (Chianti, Orvieto, Bardolino); for their grape variety (nebbiolo, sangiovese, dolcetto); or for a combination of the two (Dolcetto d'Alba, Sangiovese di Romagna, Brunello di Montalcino). Other wines carry their winery name or their shipper's name, and still others have been given such fanciful names as Lacryma Christi and Est! Est! Est!

In 1963, Italy instituted its appellation system, the Denominazione Controllata (Controlled Place Name), which designated some two hundred fifty wine zones. Although nominally supervised by the Ministry of Agriculture, the system is in fact administered by a committee consisting of wine growers, producers, dealers, members of professional wine associations, state experts, and others.

Italy's appellation system sets up three categories: 1) Denominazione Semplice di Origine (Simple Place-Name), 2) Denominazione di Origine Controllata or DOC (Controlled Place-Name) and 3) Denominazione di Origine Controllata è Garantia or DOCG (Controlled and Guaranteed Place-Name). In addition, there are the vinos de tavola, the ordinary table wines.

The Simple Place-Name, covering about 12 percent of the country's output, indicates the wine's general place of origin. The DOC, or main category, covers more than one hundred fifty wines from about seventy districts and designates their legally defined viticultural areas; specifying that a wine may not be sold under a given name unless produced in the defined area. The wine must also be pressed from specified grape varieties, and bottled according to certain regulations. (The DOC controls the wine's production, not its quality.)

The DOCG, the highest category, concentrates on the finest wines and covers specific vineyards in nine districts. It establishes, controls, and guarantees their territorial zones of production, specifies which grapes can be grown, and sets their yields. Among the DOCG wines are: Chianti, Albana di Romagna, Vino Nobile di Montepulciano, Brunello di Montalcino, Barolo, Barbaresco, Gattinara, Carmagnano, and Torgiano.

To earn this appellation, the wine maker must submit the wine to a panel of his peers, who set the standards for taste, flavor, bouquet, color, acid content, etc. Panel members periodically retaste the DOCG wines, declassifying those that do not measure up to their standards. (The DOCG is meant to verify the quality of the wine as well as its authenticity.)

Before Italy instituted its nationwide labeling system, local conzorsios (associations of growers) established their own regulations. Operating on a self-policing basis, each conzorsio created a quality-control system for its area; establishing basic wine styles and setting production standards, along with alcohol levels and minimum aging requirements. The conzorsios also monitored the cellars of their members. They still oversee some of Italy's strictest labeling regulations.

Best known is the Conzorsio del Chianti Classico (Consortium of Classic Chianti Producers), formed in 1920. The conzorsio determined whether or not a given parcel could be turned into a vineyard, drew up the boundaries of the district, and established Chianti's Zona Classico (Classic Zone). The association also issued a neck seal for the bottles of its members, featuring the Gallo Nero or Black Rooster (the symbol of the Chianti League, formed in 1376 to defend the Florentine Republic against Siena). The conzorsio's standards were enacted into law in 1933 and Chianti's Zona Classico was officially designated in 1976.

NOTE: Although more than two hundred classified vineyards produce classic Chianti wines, the conzorsio currently represents only about a fourth of the famous ones; the others believe that their own names are a sufficient guarantee of quality.

Growers in the immediate vicinity of the Zona Classico established their own conzorsio; setting their own standards and issuing a special neck seal for their bottles. (The seal depicts a della Robbia cherub.) Several districts, adjoining the Zona Classico, are permitted to combine the Chianti name with their own: Chianti Montalbano, Chianti Rufina, and the Chiantis Colli Fiorentini (Wines from the Florentine Hills). The latter include Colli Pisane, Colli Senesi, and Colli Arentini.

The Chianti blend, codified in 1967, consists of 50 to 80 percent red sangiovese, 10 to 30 percent red canaiolo, and 10 to 30 percent white trebbiano. In 1984, the white wine component was reduced to 2 percent and the red-canaiolo component reduced to 5 percent, while up to 10 percent of nontraditional grape varieties could be included in the blend. Some Tuscan vintners, seeking to create richer, smoother, and more velvety wines, have further altered the blend by eliminating the white grapes entirely and employing either 100 percent sangiovese, or its close relative, the sangioveto grosso. It is also fashionable now to include French grape varieties, such as the cabernet sauvignon, merlot, and cabernet franc along with the principal Chianti grapes. These special blends — although grown in the delimited Chianti district and of high quality— are not permitted to carry the Chianti name because they do not conform to the Chianti formula. Instead, they have been given such names as Carmagnano, Solaia, Tinscvil, Tiganello, Sassicaia, Ornellaia, and Pomino. Classified at first as *vinos de tavola* (table wines), they have recently received a new designation: the Indicazione Geographica Tipica or IGT, in acknowledgment of their Tuscan origins.

NOTE: Only red Tuscan wines may be called Chiantis. The whites must be labeled Bianco Toscano (Tuscan White) or Colli Toscani (from the Tuscan Hills).

Veneto has set up a Zona Classico for its Soave wines. (The acreage, initially quite small, has been extended to meet the demand for white wines.) Marche has established a Zona Classico for its Verdicchios and the designation, Conzorsio dei Verdicchio dei Castelli di Jesi guarantees their authenticity .

Estate-bottling, something of a rarity in Italy, is mainly practiced by a few vintners in Chianti and Lombardy. Their labels read:

• *Imbottigliato al tenuta*
• *Imbottigliato al castello*
(A single-vineyard estate is known as a *tenuto* or *castello.*)

Much vaguer designations are:

• *Imbottigliato ne'l origine* (Bottled at the place of origin)
• *Imbottigliato nella zona di produzione* (Bottled at the zone of production)
• *Meso en bottiglia del produttore al'origine* (Bottled with products from the place of origin)

The better Italian wines usually carry a vintage date. Other label terms used to indicate age are Vecchio (old) and Stravecchio (older still). The labels may also carry such age designations as Riserva or Riserva Speciale. (These, however, differ in significance from wine to wine.) For a Chianti, Barolo, or Barbaresco, "Riserva" indicates that the wine has spent three or four years in wood and another half year or so in glass; "Riserva Speciale" is a few years older. (A Brunello di Montalcino must be aged at least five years to be called a Riserva, with four and a half years spent in wood and the additional time in glass.)

"Superiore" refers to a wine with a higher-than-normal level of alcohol. To qualify, Bardolinos and Soaves must register at least 11.5 percent alcohol, while Valpolicella Superiores must reach 12 percent. "Liquoroso" indicates a wine whose alcohol content has reached 16 percent or more.

A red seal, affixed to the cork and bearing the words *Italia Marchio Nazionale* (National Italian Trademark) guarantees that the wine comes from where the label says it does. Also attesting to a wine's authenticity is a red seal, bearing the initials INE. Issued by the Instituto Nazionale per l'Exportazione (National Institute for Export), this seal is affixed to the bottles of wine that are shipped abroad.

🍇 🍇 🍇

SPANISH LABELS

For its labeling, Spain relies on geographic names. It has had an appellation system in place since 1933, but bases much of its approach on brand names or producer's names. The Spanish appellation system, known as the Denominación de Origen (Name of Origin) or DO, is administered by the Instituto Nacional de Denominaciónes de Origen (National Institute of Place Names). Encompassed here are twenty-seven appellations; most notable among them are Rioja, Jerez, Montilla-Moriles, and Málaga.

Working through the Ministry of Agriculture, the Spanish government has also created a self-regulating control board for each of its delimited regions, a Consejo Regulador de la Denominaciónes de Origen (Regulatory Council of Place Names). These boards set nominal vineyard standards for their regions and collect wine samples for analysis. The approved wines then receive an official Denominación de Origen number, which usually appears on the back label. Those wines approved for export receive a Garantia de Origen (Guarantee of Origin) designation, which appears as a paper sticker on the cork.

Rioja's regulatory council, applies somewhat stricter standards to its wines than do most of the other regions. The council allows only a handful of grape varieties to be cultivated and sets specific requirements for aging. Rioja classifies its wines as Viños de Crianza (with breeding) or Viños sin Crianza (without breeding). The wines with breeding, usually designated for export, must spend at least one year in wood and one in glass. Those "without breeding" are regional wines, subject to neither barrel-aging nor bottle-aging requirements. (They are generally consumed locally.) In Jerez, the *consejo regulador* subjects sherries to special regulations, defining the zones of production, specifying the grape varieties which may be grown, and setting the minimum alcohol levels for the wines.

NOTE: As a rule, the Spanish regulatory councils lack any capabilities for strict enforcement.

Estate-bottling, known here as *Embottelado de Origen* or *Gengarrafado de Origen,* is rarely practiced in Spain, although it's occasionally seen in Rioja, where only a few of the better wines are actually drawn from single estates. (The majority are blends drawn from a number of vineyards, generally combining the grower's or producer's grapes with those purchased from other sources.) Although *viña* stands for "vineyard," its appearance on the label does not necessarily mean the wine was bottled from a single vineyard. Vineyard names are more like brand names in Rioja. And in Jerez, sherries never carry a vineyard name since they are blends drawn from a number of vineyards.

Reserva in Spain generally refers to a red wine of a good vintage, aged at least three years. A Gran Reserva, made in exceptional vintages, is also aged a minimum of three years. A Reserva designation in Rioja is based on the individual producer's assessment. If he doesn't think the wine merits that designation, he will bottle it after some wood aging and ship it out forthwith. (Some of the older establishments age their Reservas for at least six years.) Gran Reservas spend a minimum of two years in wood and three years in glass. (Some older Rioja establishments age them for at least eight years.)

The Spaniards do not take vintage dating very seriously. (The year on the label may reflect only the age of the oldest wine in the blend.) For sherries, the vintage date refers to the year the solera began.) *Cosecho* and *vendimia* both translate as "vintage" but are used quite loosely. *Años* (years) preceded by a number refers to the time the wine has spent in wood. *Vieja pasada* means "old" and *escogida,* "very old" or "selected." (*Pasada,* for sherry, refers to superior old finos or amontillados.) When Spanish sparkling wines, known as *viños espumosos,* meet certain production standards, they receive a Denominación Especifica. Wines made by the classic Champagne method are known as the *cavas;* those made by bulk fermentation are called *granvas.*

Portuguese Labels

Regulating Portuguese wines is a semiofficial agency, the Junta Nacional de Vinho, which has established a number of officially recognized regions and indicates a wine's authenticity by giving it a Denominacao de Origen (Place Name) or a Selon de Origen (Seal of Origin). These, however, are not consistently applied.

The strictest regulations are seen in the Douro, the only region where *vinho do porto* (port wine) can be produced. There, the Instituto do Vinho do Porto (Port Wine Institute) samples, tests, and analyzes the wine before it undergoes blending and aging. Wines that meet the Institute's established standards are awarded a Designacao de Origen (Certificate of Origin). For export, they receive a Vinho do Porto Garantia designation, which includes an individual testing number that appears on a sticker affixed to the cork.

Estate-bottling, known as *Engarragado na Origen*, is not commonly practiced in Portugal. (The best wines carry a regional or a brand name rather than a vineyard name.) *Garrafeira*, which translates as "Best Wine" or "Private Stock," refers to a premium wine which has undergone a degree of aging.

🍇 🍇 🍇

Madeira Labels

Madeira's wines usually carry the name of their predominant grape. These traditionally, were sercial, bual, verdelho and malmsey, but other varieties are also included now. Since the wines usually represent several years, the date on the label does not indicate the vintage, but the year that blending began. Wines aged at least three years are labeled Choice, Selected, or Finest. Those labeled Reserve are aged for five years; Old Reserves are ten years old, and Special or Extra Reserves are fifteen. Vintage Madeiras —considered the best wines of a single year— use only traditional grapes and spend at least twenty years in wood and another two in glass.

GERMAN LABELS

Germany labels its wines in a consistent and highly structured way, with the growing units for the entire country comprehensively demarcated. For quality wines, the labels provide the following information in uniform order: vintage, growing region, commune or town, vineyard, grape variety, quality level, and producer. (Regional blends, involving lesser grapes, generally use brand names.)

Before 1971, there were about twenty-five thousand wine names in Germany and almost as many vineyard sites. Reform legislation that year reduced the unwieldy number to less than three hundred sites by setting a minimum size of twelve-and-a-half acres for each vineyard. The reforms also specified that a site or a district name could be used only if the wine was actually grown there. These changes resulted in the incorporation of many secondary sites in each town into two or three highly regarded vineyards. The famous Bernkasteler Doktor label, for example, previously confined to about three acres, was expanded to include some eighty other sites within a five-mile radius of the town of Bernkastel. (The best wines continue to be grown at or very near the original site, however.) Piesporter Goldtröpfchen, once referred to as the wine of a single vineyard, now includes wines drawn from a number of Piesport vineyards.

The 1971 reforms also replaced three earlier wine categories (General Blends, Village Wines, and Quality Wines) with four new ones (Gebiet, Bereich, Grosslage, and Einzellage). Each of the newer categories represents areas that narrow down from the largest region to the smallest parcel of land. The Gebiet represents an entire growing region, such as the Rheingau; the Bereich is a subregion within a Gebiet, such as Johannisberg. Each Bereich is then divided into a number of Grosslagen (collective or composite neighboring vineyards), which share a similar soil and climate and bear the name of their best-known village. The

Einzellage is an individual vineyard that is at least twelve-and-a half acres in size.

To merit a Bereich (subregion) designation, at least 75 percent of the wine must be grown in the area named. The wines of the Grosslage (collective vineyard) may come from the named village or from several others in the vicinity. For example, a Niersteiner wine may not only come from the village of Nierstein itself but from any or all of the twenty or more vineyards located in fourteen nearby villages.

An "er" added to the village name converts it to a possessive, as in Niersteiner (from around Nierstein), Hattenheimer (from around Hattenheim), Piesporter (from around Piesport), etc. For Einzellage (individual vineyard) wines, the village name is followed by the vineyard name; as in Hattenheimer Hinterhaus, Oppenheimer Herrenberg, Wehlener Klosterberg, etc. Some Einzellage wines are so famous that only their vineyard names need to appear. In the Rheingau, they are Marcobrunn (in Erbach), Schloss Johannisberg (in Johannisberg) and Schloss Vollrads (in Winkel). In the Mosel-Saar-Ruwer, they are Josephshof (in Graach) and Scharzhofberg (in Wiltingen).

To summarize: If a German label reads "Hattenheimer Wisselbrunnen, Schloss Rheinhartshausen," Hattenheim with an "er" is the Grosslage (village), Wisselbrunnen is the Einzellage (individual vineyard) while Schloss Rhein-hartshausen is the specific site. Should the label read "Johannisberger, Schloss Johannisberg, Fürst von Metternich," Johannisberg with an "er" represents the Grosslage, Schloss Johannisberg the Einzellage, and the proprietor is a member of the von Metternich family. (*Fürst* translates as "prince.")

Although the same vineyard name may appear on more than one label, the village name preceding it will eliminate any confusion. The towns of Wehlen and Zeltingen may both have Sonnenuhr (Sun Dial) vineyards, but one is a Wehlener Sonnenuhr and the other a Zeltinger Sonnenuhr. And while the towns of Graach and Zeltingen both have Himmelreich (Kingdom of Heaven) vineyards, the wine of one is a Graacher Himmelreich while the other is a Zeltinger Himmelreich.

Nevertheless the similarities can be confusing. In the Saar region, for example, Scharzhofberg is the wine of an Einzellage (individual vineyard), but Scharzberg is the wine of a Grosslage (composite vineyard) and Wiltinger Scharzberg is a generic blend whose components may be drawn from anywhere in the Saar region.

NOTE: Further efforts to simplify German wine names and classifications have encountered the country's strict wine laws. The labels for a number of lesser wines, however, feature only the name of their town and their shipper.

The 1971 reform legislation also set up three quality levels for German wines: 1) Deutscher Tafelwein, 2) Qualitätswein Bestimmter Angaugebiete or QBA, and 3) Qualitätswein mit Prädikat or QMP.

Deutscher Tafelwein (German Table Wine), the broadest category —also known as Tischwein— covers the simple, light, pleasant wines best consumed directly from the cask. These carry the name of one of the country's five general regions: Rhein, Mosel, Oberrhein, Neckar, or Main. (At least 75 percent of the wine must come from the designated region.) Tafelweins need not involve any particular grape, however, nor attain any specific level of alcohol.

NOTE: In 1982, a new regional category known as Deutscher Landwein (German Country Wine) was created. A step above Tafelwein, it too covers the light, uncomplicated wines primarily intended for domestic consumption.

At the next level is Qualitätswein, further broken down into two categories: Qualitätswein Bestimmter Anbaugebiete or QBA (Quality Wine from a Designated Region), and Qualitätswein mit Prädikat or QMP (Quality Wine of Special Distinction).

The QBAs come from approved quality regions known as Anbaugebieters (Wine Regions under Cultivation) These are the Rheingau, Rheinhessen, the Pfalz, Mosel-Saar-Ruwer, Nahe, Franconia, Ahr, Baden, Hessiche Bergstrasse, Mittelrhein, and Württemberg. Their grapes must have ripened sufficiently so that their wines exhibit the taste and style associated with their particular regions.

The QMPs or Qualitätsweins mit Prädikat are grown in individual vineyards within the subregions. In addition to meeting the basic QBA requirements as to origin and legal approval, these are the highest quality wines. Elegant and long-lived, they represent the best concentration of such attributes as brilliance and breed. (In poor years, no QMPs are made.)

The QMP category is further divided into six quality levels, each denoting a higher degree of ripeness, an increased fullness of body, and a greater concentration of flavor and sweetness. In their ascending order, these are: Kabinett, Spätlese, Auslese, Beerenauslese (BA), Eiswein, and Trockenbeerenauslese (TBA).

Kabinett, the driest premium wine, is pressed from the first gathering of fully ripened grapes in a normal harvest. Slightly fruitier than a QBA, the wine is light, delicate, and low in alcohol. Kabinetts range from *trocken* (dry) to *halb-trocken* (half-dry).

NOTE: Kabinett wines acquired their name in the eighteenth century when vineyard owners locked away the wines of superior vintages in special cabinets for their own use.

Spätlese (Late-picked Berries) is made from more fully ripened grapes, picked at least a week after the main harvest. Riper and more intense, more concentrated in their depth and flavor, these wines average 10 percent alcohol by volume and may be vinified dry, medium dry, or sweet.

Auslese (Specially Selected Late-picked Berries) is made from a still-later gathering of extraripe grapes. (The blemished, unripe, or otherwise defective berries are removed from the clusters.) Produced only in excellent vintages, these wines are more intense in their bouquet and flavor than the Spätleses and are usually sweeter as well. They are often served as dessert wines.

Beerenauslese or BA (Selected Picked-off Berries) is made from fully ripened, specially selected, hand-picked clusters, often affected by noble rot. Produced only two or three times in a decade, these are sweet, luscious wines which display honeyed, nectarlike flavors, flowery aromas, and a superb concentration of fruit.

Trockenbeerenauslese or TBA (Selected, Dried, Picked-off Berries) the rarest of German wines, is produced only once or twice in a decade. Its botrytized berries, left to shrivel on the vine until November, are individually hand picked. Each grape yields a concentrated and syrupy drop of must; its sugars are so dense that they cannot ferment out fully. The resulting wine is intensely sweet and rich, yet relatively low in alcohol (only about 7 or 8 percent). Phenomenally complex, the Trockenbeerenauslese wines feature a fruity scent intermingled with a subtle suggestion of herbs and spices.

Between the BAs and TBAs are the Eisweins (ice wines). These are made from extremely late-ripened grapes, which have been left on the vine until the first frost of winter. Containing about 30 percent sugar, the grapes are gathered berry by berry, and pressed while still frozen. The water in their must —now ice— is discarded, concentrating the sugars further. Eisweins are extremely sweet with a ripe acidity which balances out their rich fruit sugars.

Geographical Classification	Quality Level
Gebiet (Region)	Tafelwein
Bereich (Subregion)	Landwein
Grosslage (Wine District)	Qualitätswein (QBA)
Einzellage (Vineyard)	Qualitätswein mit Prädikat (QMP)
	Kabinett
	Auslese
	Spätlese
	Beerenauslese
	Eiswein
	Trockenbeerenauslese

Note: Some vineyards indicate their quality grades (Kabinett, Spätlese, Auslese, etc.) by using different colored foil capsules covering their corks: blue, green, pink, gold, white, etc. The practice is not official, however, and can vary from maker to maker.

Chaptalization —or sugaring to bring up the level of alcohol— is permitted for some German wines but not for others. Even in good years, it is allowed for Tafelweins and Deutscher Landweins. (In poor years, these wines may also be balanced out with wines imported from other countries.) Bereich and Grosslage wines can be chaptalized too, to bring their alcohol levels up to the desired minimum. QBA wines can be sugared if necessary, but QMP wines cannot; they must attain at least 9.5 percent alcohol on their own. The Einzellage (single-vineyard) wines are not chaptalized either.

For German estate-bottled wines, the labels read:
• *Erzeugerabfüllung* (estate-bottled)
• *Erzeugerabfüllung aus eigenem lesegut* (estate-bottled by the producer from his own harvest)

Equivalent terms are *Gutabfüllung, Schlossabzug,* or *Schlossabfüllung* (bottled at the castle.) The Schloss designation, similar to that of a château in Bordeaux, refers to the entire wine-making property, including the buildings as well as the vineyards. (Some of the larger Rheingau estates feature actual castles or at least manor houses.)

German quality wines receive an official testing number, known as the Amtliche Prüfungsnummer (Official Testing Control and Registration Number), abbreviated to A.P. Nr. or Pruf. Nr., or simply P.R. The number, which appears on the label, indicates that the wine has passed an objective three-part appraisal administered by an official government panel. The appraisal involves inspection of the applicant's vineyard and cellar, chemical analysis of his wine, and a sensory evaluation of the wine's taste, color, clarity, and bouquet.

The German label terms, Wachstum, Kreszenz, Gewächs and Eigenegewächs, all refer to growth. When followed by a specific name, they indicate the vineyard's ownership. Erben, which translates as "heir," refers to wines sold under the name of the vineyard's original owners. When preceded by a proper name, it indicates that the vineyard is managed by the current generation of the family.

Bestes is the owner's best barrel. Fass, Fuder and Stück all refer to the cask. Since the Germans treat each day's pressings separately for their best wines, a number is used to indicate the specific cask from which the wine was bottled. For example, "Fuder" followed by "109" indicates the 109th barrel put down that year. (This enables the consumer to purchase more of a given wine if he wishes.)

Other label terms include Weinbauort, referring to a wine community, and Weingut (wine estate), referring to a specific winery, including its cellars or vineyards. A Staatsweingut (state-owned vineyard) is the property of the German government, although operating autonomously. A crest on its label features a stylized eagle. Weinkellerei refers to a wine cellar, Zentralkellerei to a central cellar. (The latter, combined with "Staatsweingut" indicates a quality wine produced in a state-owned vineyard.) Abfüller (bottler) refers to a winery or a bottler. Winzerverein is a wine producers' association or a growers' cooperative. Verband Deutscher Prädikat Weinguter or VDP (German Association of Vineyardists of Distinction) is a wine growers' group. Deutsches Weinsiegal refers to a wine seal.

Germany's sparkling wines are known as *sekts* or *schaumweins;* the finest examples are labeled with a specific place of origin. Qualitätsschaumwein indicates that the grapes were grown in a designated area. Prädikat Sekt signifies that at least 60 percent of the wine is of German origin. (The remainder may come from Italy or France.) Sekt alone indicates that the wine is most likely an import.

Despite Germany's tight labeling laws, certain well-known wines seem to have geographic names but in fact do not. Zeller Schwartze Katz (Zell's Black Cat), which takes its name from the town of Zell, may once have come from a number of vineyards there, but is now an undistinguished blend drawn from unknown sources. (It's usually classified as a Bereich or subregional wine.) The origins of Krover Nacktarsch are somewhat vaguer. Moselblümchen (Little Mosel Flower) is the trade name of a wine drawn from lesser Mosel vineyards. A regional blend, it does not merit a specific geographic designation.

Liebfraumilch is the generic name for a number of extensively blended Tafelweins. A generally haphazard heavy and sweetish blend of low-acid wines drawn from various regions, Liebfraumilch can range from decent to poor. First grown in a monastery vineyard on the outskirts of the Rheinhessen town of Worms, the wine was known as Liebfrauenstift (The Church's Endowment). In the fifteenth century, the monastery chapel was replaced by a Gothic church, the Liebfrauenkirche (Church of the Beloved Lady or Holy Virgin). A nearby vineyard decided to call its wine Liebfraumilch (Milk of the Beloved Lady). The change of name increased the popularity of the wine and soon other vineyards nearby were following suit.

Initially pressed from the riesling grape, Liebfraumilch is now made from the müller-thurgau or sylvaner. When sold in Europe, the wine is fairly certain to be of German origin, usually from the Rhineland. When sold in the United States, Canada, South Africa and Australia, it may not be of German origin at all.

❦ ❦ ❦

AMERICAN LABELS

Regulating wine labeling in the United States is a federal agency, the Bureau of Alcohol, Tobacco, and Firearms (BATF). A division of the Treasury Department, it is primarily responsible for overseeing the taxation of wines and spirits. (In individual states, agricultural inspectors may measure grape-sugar levels and set the minimum alcohol requirements for the wines.)

American wines are usually generics or varietals. (Sometimes generic and geographic names are combined, as in New York State Champagne and California port.) As a rule, winery names predominate; in effect serving as brand names. American wines are classified as table or dinner wines when their alcohol level is below 14 percent. Between 14 and 24 percent alcohol, they are known as dessert wines although they may not be sweet at all.

NOTE: The term "fortified" is not employed because after the repeal of Prohibition, some wines were promoted for their high alcohol levels. Government officials decided to ban the term to discourage excessive consumption; concerned that "fortified" on the label might imply the wine's potential to intoxicate.

The United States generally recognizes two quality grades: standard and premium wines; both largely defined by price. Premium —also known as Special or Select— refers to wines in the higher price range; while the Superpremium and Ultrapremium wines are priced progressively higher. Wines aged longer than usual may be labeled as "Reserve."

NOTE: These various terms are not applied consistently and may differ from winery to winery.

In recent years, the BATF has created a number of American Viticultural Appellations or AVAs, basing them generally on the region's geographic features, its climate, and history of grape production. In some cases, the AVAs formalize existing place-names. In others, the growers petitioned to have their areas named.

The first AVA was approved in 1983; there have since been more than a hundred others. In California, they include Napa Valley, Howell Mountain, Santa Ynez, and Los Carneros, along with Amador in the Sierra foothills; Edna Valley and Paso Robles; also York Mountain in San Luis Obispo, and Cuenoc Valley in Lake Country; plus Shenandoah, Santa Cruz Mountain, Yolo, and Pope Valley. (Napa also has a number of sub-AVAs; a recent addition is Stag's Leap.)

AVAs in the northeast include the Finger Lakes district, Martha's Vineyard, and the North Fork of Long Island. A widely dispersed Hudson River AVA covers Westchester, Dutchess, Orange, and Ulster counties. The Lake Erie appellation cuts across several states, encompassing Ohio, Pennsylvania, and New York. A

Southeastern New England appellation covers Connecticut, Rhode Island, and southern Massachusetts.

NOTE: In the West, winery owners have requested a Pacific Coast appellation to cover tristate blends from California, Oregon, and Washington State. At present, such wines can only use a general "American Wine" designation.

Critics point out that although the AVAs aim to define quality areas, they are vulnerable to political pressures. They note that a viticultural area may be highly regarded because it includes one or two prominent wineries while its overall wines are generally mediocre. Some believe that the AVAs should be defined by soil characteristics and weather patterns and not —as a number of them are— by roads or other readily identifiable physical boundaries which have nothing to do with wine growing. The critics also note that while the European appellation laws usually specify the grape varieties that can be planted, as well as the yield per vine or per acre and the style of the wine, American AVAs carry no such requirements.

When the term "estate-bottled" is used on the label, the grapes must come from a vineyard owned or controlled by a winery located in an AVA. When a vineyard name is specified, 95 percent of the grapes must derive from that source.

American Estate-bottling is indicated by the following:

• Grown, produced, and bottled by so-and-so
• Produced and bottled by so-and-so

If the label reads:

• Perfected and bottled by so-and-so
• Perfected and bottled in our cellar
• Blended and bottled by so-and-so
• Made and bottled by so-and-so
• Cellared and bottled by so-and-so

it means that 10 percent of the wine need come from the maker's own production; the rest can be drawn from other sources. The producer here may have given the wine cursory treatment or only arranged for its final blending. He may even have contracted for others to make the finished product. Or he may have bought the wines in bulk and not separated them from other lots fermented in his cellars. (Large wineries have been known to exchange wines with one another, as a way to balance out their inventories.)

A label reading "Produced by so-and-so" indicates the wine was probably not made from grapes grown in the vineyard listed on the label. A label that reads "Bottled by so-and-so" gives no indication as to the origins of the wine. (The winery may have purchased the grapes, then finished and bottled the wine; or the winery may only have bottled it.)

On American sparkling-wine labels, "Fermented in the Bottle" indicates the *méthode champenoise*, "Fermented in this Bottle" refers to the transfer method, while "Charmat Process" or "Cuvée Close" indicates that the wine was made sparkling by the bulk fermentation method.

LABELING IN OTHER COUNTRIES

In 1959, Argentina's Congress set up the Instituto Nacional de Vitivinicultura, or INV and gave that agency jurisdiction over the country's grape-derived products. Australia does not have an appellation system as such but indicates the wine's general origin with such geographic abbreviations as VIC (Victoria), NSW (New South Wales), SA (South Australia), and WA (West Australia).

For its quality wines, Austria's labels are about as detailed as the German labels are. These include regional, village, and vineyard names and employ terms such as Qualitätswein, Kabinett, Spätlese, Auslese, Beerenauslese (BA), and Trockenbeerenauslese (TBA). A uniquely Austrian category, Ausbruch — somewhere between a BA and a TBA— covers wines made in years with a high incidence of noble rot. Austrian wines that meet established prerequisites and are true to type, receive a Weingutessiegel Osterreich (Austrian Quality Seal). Those that pass an official tasting examination —somewhat like the German P.R. appraisal— receive a Wein aus Osterreich (Austrian Wine) seal.

Canada's best wines carry a Vinters' Quality Alliance (VQA) designation, indicating that the grapes came from a specific area and that the quality of the wine has been attested to by a panel of vintners and sommeliers. (This designation appears on the label or on the neck capsule.)

In Chile, quality wine labels carry both a brand name and a place of origin. Also specified may be the grape variety, vineyard name, and vintage year. Four government-controlled categories indicate the wine's age here: Courant, Especial, Reservado, and Grand Vino, referring respectively to wines aged one, two, four, and six years.

The appellation control system, established in Greece in 1969, created twenty-eight official wine regions. These represented about 11 percent of the country's vineyards. Typically, Greek wines were blends drawn from sizable areas and involved different regions of the country. The practice is now banned. While some wines were initially named for their general place of origin (Crete, Sámos, etc.) they now carry more specific place-names such as Peza and Archanes in

Crete. Greek labels generally are not very informative, however. Some employ the French phrase "Produit de Region Determinée" (Product of a Selected Region) or the equally vague English phrase, "Appellation of Origin of High Quality."

Hungary usually names its wines for the districts in which they are grown; seventeen of these districts have been officially classified. Adding an "i" to the place-name here converts it to an adjective as in Balatoni for Lake Balaton, Tokaji for Tokay and Egri for Eger. The grape name (kadarka, furmint, rizling) often follows the place-name. For noble-rot Tokays, a special neck band indicates the number of puttonyos in the blend. Wines designated for export bear a seal of authenticity issued by Monimpex, an agency run by the state.

In Israel, generic names have been phased out in favor of varietal ones and the country now markets most of its wines under their winery names.

In South Africa, its Origin of Wine law requires that, to bear a place-name, the wine must be drawn 80 percent from the defined area. To carry a varietal name, it must derive 75 percent from the given grape variety. Exercising considerable power over which wines are made and who makes them is a wine growers' cooperative association, commonly known as KWV (an abbreviation of its Afrikaans' name). In the 1930s, as part of a deal struck with the French government, the association banned the use of French wine names on South African labels. France in turn agreed to import South African lobsters.

Wines in the former Yugoslavia are usually named for their town, district, or grape variety. *Sortno* on the label followed by a year indicates the vintage, while *stolno* refers to a blend —most likely of lesser wines.

LABEL DECEPTIONS

Despite varying degrees of official and semiofficial control, no country is immune to deceptive labeling. Since ancient times, rogue wine makers have tried to pass off cheap wines as good ones, claiming that their products were of specific origin when their blends included wines from elsewhere. Some have also created the impression that their wines came from desirable geographic sectors or even from particular vineyards, when they were regional blends. And they have used elegant names to suggest certain wine styles and qualities. Wineries in France have appropriated in part the names of famous Bordeaux estates as in Mâitre d'Estournel (reminiscent of the highly ranked Cos d'Estournel) and Mouton Cadet (which echoes the estimable Mouton Rothschild). Wine makers have also copied the label styles of prestigious wines or they've claimed a wine was from a vintage other than its own. Labels have been forged; a practice made easier by photocopying. (To prevent such forgeries, vineyard owners are experimenting with water marks or electronic marks.) And grape names have been falsely incorporated into brand names to deceive the unwary. (A California wine called Domaine Chardonnay contained none of that grape variety at all.)

Another form of deception is "baptizing" or transferring a prestigious name from a small quantity of good wine to a larger quantity of cheap wine. Trainloads of wine from the south of France were rebaptized as "Burgundy" as they passed through the railroad station at Beaune. Wine makers have tampered as well with documentation for export. In the 1970s, French government inspectors, checking a Bordeaux cellar, discovered vats of red wine that carried the notation "Can be used as a Beaujolais in America."

One complicated scheme involving a lesser French product called for shipping the wine in bulk to the Netherlands, bottling it there, then sending it on to England, where it was labeled "Pouilly-Fuissé", and finally shipping the wine to the United States for sale. Early in the twentieth century, producers were pasting Bordeaux labels on bottles of largely Mediterranean wines. More recently, a Burgundy shipper tried to pass off some five thousand bottles of a simple red wine as an elegant example from the Côte d'Or. And Californians have been known to present South American wines as their own. (In fact, some wines from Italy, Chile, and the South of France have appeared in bottles bearing well–known California labels.)

NOTE: Wineries have also withdrawn wines that did not sell, renaming them, then putting them back on the market.

Vintners have been known to sell more wine under certain labels than their vineyards could possibly produce. Great quantities of Chablis are put on the market each year despite the region's limited acreage and problematic weather. (It has been said that although Chablis is a white Burgundy, a white Burgundy claiming to be a Chablis may not always be one.) The same phenomenon has been observed with the Pommards and Beaujolais of France, the Chiantis, Barolos, Barbarescos, and Frascatis of Italy. When grape supplies ran short in Champagne, a number of famous houses purchased already–made and bottled wines from that region's big producers and cooperatives, then labeled and marketed them as their own.

Unscrupulous vintners have also "stretched" or extended their wines by blending them with wines from other regions or even from other countries. Burgundy shippers, unable to find good inexpensive wines locally, have added mediocre bulk wines to otherwise prestigious blends. And less–than–honest Burgundians have stretched their local harvests with grapes from the Midi and Algeria or have bolstered weaker wines with stronger ones from the Rhône Valley. The popularity of Pouilly–Fuissé has prompted its makers to seek out anonymous components increasingly —in one case, a Beaujolais Blanc. In California, some North Coast wineries have trucked in cheaper products from the state's more prolific regions for blending with their quality wines. Some of the stretching combinations are quite curious. A German riesling —an aristocratic grape in its own right— was blended into a white French Bordeaux from Graves.

Weak wines have also been made more robust. Two hundred years ago, red wines from the Rhône Valley or Cahors were regularly used to bolster some pale, thin Bordeaux wines, while an undistinguished Beaujolais was trucked to the Côte d'Or in the dead of night to strengthen the wine of a poor vintage. High–alcohol wines from the Rhône Valley, the Midi, Algeria, Morocco, Corsica, Italy, and Portugal, added to pale, thin Burgundies have made them full flavored and uncharacteristically big and coarse. In Germany, high–alcohol imports have compensated for a wine's shortcomings in poor vintages. In the northeastern United States, in certain years, vintners have bolstered their blends with inexpensive wines or wine concentrates from California, Spain, and other warm–climate regions.

Notoriously difficult to monitor are the "improved" wines of lesser years. Monitoring is always difficult in Burgundy because of the vineyards' characteristic fragmentation. (Vintners there usually produce their wines away from their small plots of land.) Also difficult to monitor is chaptalization, which adds cane or beet sugar during fermentation to boost the wine's alcohol level. Although the law permits Beaujolais producers to increase alcohol levels by 2 percentage points in wines designated for export, some producers have increased these levels by 4 percent and more.

Wine can be altered in other ways. Adding a cheap white wine to a heavier red can simulate the color, body, and bouquet of a premium product. Coloring agents can brighten a wine, while charcoal filtering will render a white wine disarmingly pale. Overly acid wines can be buried in other blends to salvage them. And chemicals have been illegally used to sweeten wines or to sharpen them.

SOME CAVEATS

When reading the labels, it might be helpful to keep certain considerations in mind. Some examples follow:

APPELLATION CONTRÔLÉE: In France and elsewhere, an appellation usually guarantees the origin of a wine, not its quality or character. (The AOC does not govern its bouquet, flavor, or any of a wine's finer characteristics.) As a result, inconsequential wines may carry a distinguished AOC and command higher prices, while wines from lower-ranked areas may be higher in quality if made by more skilled vintners and treated with greater care. In Italy, critics have charged that the DOCG classification, supposedly reserved for the finest wines, has been awarded too widely and now includes a number of mediocre products. And in the United States, a California appellation means that the grapes can come from different locations, scattered all over the state.

ESTATE-BOTTLED: Estate-bottling indicates that a wine was made from grapes grown in the winery's own vineyard, rather than from grapes purchased from outside sources. Although theoretically reserved for the unblended wines of great vineyards, the designation in itself is not a guarantee of excellence. Estate-bottled wines may include grapes grown in the vicinity of the named vineyard as long as the proprietor of record has finished and bottled them. Even when the wine maker uses only his own grapes —if his approach is casual rather than dedicated— he may still turn out a mediocre product. The reverse is also possible; fine wines can be produced by those who don't own any vineyards and so don't qualify for an "Estate-bottled" designation. Such producers may buy their grapes or wines from good outside sources, then finish them with great skill, devotion, and care.

"Château-bottled" in Bordeaux is an assurance of a wine's authenticity, not necessarily an indication of its quality. A Bordeaux grower can register a château name for any piece of land he owns and label his wine "Château-bottled" whether it's good, bad, or indifferent. And any establishment in Bordeaux can call itself a château, even when it blends and bottles imported wines. Producers have also been known to incorporate "Château" into their trade names, or to sell wines under the names of nonexistent châteaus.

SECOND LABELS: Second Labels were originally applied to the products of younger vines grown in prestigious vineyards. They came into prominence in the 1980s when —after a series of successful vintages— the top châteaus became more selective about their blends. The designation has now been applied as well to wines that do not meet the first label standards, although in some cases those wines may be very fine indeed. Second Labels have also become a way for wine producers to market their overproduction. Included as well in this category may be the wines from "rejected" vats that the great French estates don't wish to sell off to shippers or to discard. (In poor years, the estates may offer less than half their output under their own name and the remainder under a Second Label.)

PLACE OF BUSINESS: A French label can state that a wine was bottled in a given village while it supplies no information as to where the grapes themselves were grown. An American winery can indicate as its principal place of business a location where the wine was only bottled. For example, a number of establishments in northern California have left their original vineyard sites, while still retaining their offices and bottling plants there. Their labels may imply that the source of the wine is the more prestigious address although the grapes have in fact been drawn from elsewhere. (To prevent such deceptions, a local Napa Valley ordinance requires that wines bottled in Napa include in their blends at least 75 percent of grapes that were grown there.)

VARIETAL LABELING: In the United States, a wine is permitted to carry a varietal label provided it is pressed 75 percent from the given grape. (The remaining 25 percent is unspecified and can be whatever variety the wine maker chooses.) In itself, a grape name is no guarantee of quality. Even when 90 or 100 percent of the variety named is employed, the grapes can still be grown anywhere in the country. (They need not meet any particular vineyard standards or soil requirements.) As a result, grape names can mean little and geographic names mean everything.

VINTAGE DATING: A vintage-dated wine need not be made 100 percent from grapes of the indicated year. Vintners are always permitted to top off their casks or tanks with a small amount of wine from other years. The required minimums differ from country to country and from wine to wine. For a French vintage Champagne, at least 80 percent of the wine must come from a single year. Germany sets a 75 percent minimum for its vintage wines; while to carry a vintage date, an American wine must be at least 95 percent from the specified year.

NOTE: Because of the public's demand for vintage dating, wine makers have taken a variety of measures in poor years to bring their products up to par. In Bordeaux in bad vintages, grapes that might have been left to rot on the vines are now harvested selectively. (Modern equipment has made it possible to produce drinkable wines every year.) And chaptalization, a common "improvement," can increase a wine's alcohol and general viability despite a mediocre harvest.

OVERPRODUCTION: In the Champagne region, overproduction has been legalized to a degree. In certain years, the vintners are permitted to use the excess production, which is known as "blocked stock" in their nonvintage blends.

SUPERIOR: The term Supérieure in French or Superiore in Italian is not an indication of excellence in itself, but indicates a wine whose alcohol content exceeds the minimum required by local standards. (A mass-produced wine from a lesser district can be called "Superior" as long as its alcohol level is higher than usual.)

❧ ❧ ❧

OTHER CONSIDERATIONS

Wine making has involved forty or so chemicals, including sulfiting agents, fungicides, preservatives, food colorings, etc. Some are the natural products of fermentation while others are added to stimulate fermentation, aid clarification, improve bouquet, or preserve the wine.

Most widely used as a preservative or stabilizer is sulfur dioxide or SO_2, an agent that keeps down the unwanted yeasts and bacteria. Sulfur dioxide protects the newly picked grapes from mold during shipment and destroys spoilage microbes during the wine's transportation, storage, and aging. (The SO_2 can also be used to keep a wine sweet by halting fermentation before all the sugar has been converted to alcohol.)

The majority of wines contain sulfites in one form or another. (Even so-called organic wines generate some sulfites naturally.) Although the sulfites are generally harmless in the amounts normally employed, they can produce severe reactions in individuals allergic to them, particularly in people with asthma. Since 1987, warning labels have been mandatory in the United States for wines containing more than 100 parts of SO_2 per million. (The legal limit is 350 parts.) The labels here must read: "Contains Sulfites." Wine makers who don't employ any SO_2 can carry the statement, "No Added Sulfites."

For some time now, American consumer groups have requested full label disclosure of the ingredients or substances in wine. The Food and Drug Administration (FDA) has also sought such disclosure but wine-industry representatives have resisted, maintaining that fermentation substantially transforms the wine's basic ingredients and its additives. They also state that FDA involvement is not necessary since wines and other alcoholic beverages are not consumed for nutritional purposes.

6

BUYING, STORING, AND AGING

An estimated four thousand wines —domestic and imported— are currently on the market. The choices are overwhelming; the array of bottles, styles, and labels often bewildering. Trying to distinguish between the excellent and the commonplace can certainly be daunting.

BUYING WINE

Some suggest that when buying wine, you look for a shop with a friendly, helpful staff, and that you seek out those with both the knowledge and the patience to assist you in your purchases. More than four decades ago, a British wine enthusiast described the ideal merchant as one who would offer you selected wines of good quality to suit your palate and your pocket, take back a wine that didn't satisfy, and provide you with something else in its place. That merchant, he said, would always be glad to taste a wine with you before you bought it and discuss its particular characteristics as well as its virtues or defects. Moreover, such a merchant would provide a carefully selected and yet moderately inexpensive wine collection on which you could depend with confidence for all occasions and he would also replenish your supply of wine as you required.

If such merchants exist anymore, they are few and far between. Usually, little assistance is available in learning to purchase wine. Often it's a matter of trial and error. Only by experimenting and tasting over a period of years can you acquire a deep and practical knowledge of wine. But if you approach the subject in the spirit of adventure, if you leave yourself open to discovery and surprise, you will gradually find out where your own personal preferences lie. An eminent wine collector once likened the process to the princess who went around kissing frogs. "Kiss enough of them," he said, "and you will find a prince."

In making their selections, some people look for a clue, any clue. Perhaps a name enchants or a fragment of advertising comes to mind. Maybe they're responding to the shape of the bottle, the color of the wine, the name of the grape. Perhaps their choice is based on the wine's place of origin or its price. (One shop, wishing to be helpful, classifies its wines by taste.) Some people find a few wines they can count on and stick with them. Others are willing to sample the less known examples along with the more publicized ones.

There are a number of ways to learn about wine: you can look through newspaper ads and wine-shop catalogues. You can read specialized publications and books on wine. Browsing in the wine shops is always of major importance. The best times to check them out are on Mondays through Thursdays, when they are less crowded and the salespeople are more readily accessible. The ideal time is in summer, the quietest buying season of the year. The worst time is in late fall and early winter, between Thanksgiving and New Year's Eve.

When browsing in the shops, you can see if the table wines are presented horizontally (as they should be) or stood upright (as they should not). And you can observe whether the bottles are displayed in the window, exposed to the light and heat (as they should not be). After several visits to a given shop, you can get some idea of the stock on hand, as well as a sense of its turnover. And if you deal with more than one shop, you will have the chance to ask more questions and compare the prices and the inventories.

Common sense is the key to intelligent buying. Before embarking on costlier wines, it is best to sample the more affordable ones in the same general category and to become accustomed to them. After becoming familiar with the modest wines, one is better able to appreciate the nuances of the more expensive examples. Best for everyday drinking are the moderately priced wines, and plenty of good, honest, straightforward examples drawn from all over the world can be found at reasonable prices. (When wines from one part of the world have become too expensive, others from elsewhere are always available.)

Wine pricing is as much an art as a science, based as it is on image, ego, and tradition, as well as on market conditions. High prices in themselves are not always a clue to quality and should not be equated with merit. (Some wines owe their fame and fortune to skillful salesmanship.) In tasting competitions, lower-priced wines have sometimes tied for first place with the more costly ones.

Although making a good wine doesn't come cheap, the prices of premium wines often have little to do with their actual cost. Owners of prestige wineries acknowledge that their prices are based primarily on what the market will bear. Those established for the most famous Bordeaux wines exert an influence on premium prices elsewhere. They are considered a benchmark in California. (The state's top producers believe that their best Cabernets equal or surpass the best Bordeaux.) As one California wine maker stated, "I always believed that buyers would take us more seriously if we priced our wines the way the French do."

NOTE: In Europe, the traditional formula for propping up wine prices is having the wine makers bulldoze some of the vineyard land or else by distilling their excess wines into industrial alcohol. (Each year, the Europeans convert literally millions of gallons this way.)

Also driving up wine prices is the demand for wine as well as the scarcity brought on by poor vintages or by vineyard diseases. (The scarcer the wine, the more people would like to acquire it.) On the other hand, wine bargains should be approached with caution. When the price seems too good to be true, the wine is best avoided. It may have been mishandled in shipping, stored too long in an over-heated warehouse, or exposed to freezing temperatures while sitting on a landing dock. Or the wine may simply be too old. Even when specially priced, last year's Beaujolais Nouveau still is no bargain.

Some consumers like to buy their wines in quantity. Purchasing wine by the case can prevent the frustration of seeing it disappear from the shelves of the wine shop. And since all the bottles in the case are likely to be much the same, there is the assurance of a greater consistency. Buying by the case also means being eligible for a discount. The discount on a twelve-bottle case is customarily 10 percent. (Some shops offer a 5 percent discount on a six-bottle purchase.)

NOTE: A number of serious collectors rarely buy in quantity, believing this reduces the adventure and the risk of the true wine experience.

In order to recoup their costs, producers usually sell their quality red wines long before they reach their peaks; generally releasing them at about age two. (Aging the wines themselves is an expensive proposition which does nothing to ease their cash flow.) Top Bordeaux vintners realized, however, that if they sold off their entire vintage at once and then wine prices rose, the middlemen —and not they themselves— would benefit. So each year, these vintners hold back a certain percentage of their wine, gradually releasing it in small lots, perhaps a fourth of the vintage at a time. Each lot is called a *tranche* or slice. (If the *première tranche* does well, the second batch can be offered at a somewhat higher price.)

Wine is generally distributed through a three-tier system involving the winery, wholesaler, and retailer (or restaurant). The producers sell to the wholesalers or distributors (shippers, importers, exporters) who then supply the retailers. The wholesalers and retailers, like the wineries, usually sell their red wines young, not wanting to tie up their capital while waiting for them to mature.) As one retailer said, "If you're not selling them, you're not getting paid for them." So the fine red wines, which would command high prices at maturity, are relatively inexpensive when released. (Later on they may be too costly or no longer available.)

NOTE: When buying a mature red wine, it is important to know your retailer. A few years of inept handling can age a wine too quickly and hasten its demise.

In the past, rare wines were bought as investments —purchased while still young and modestly priced— then held until they had appreciated in value. Because the first-growth Bordeaux wines were rarely ready to drink when released, British connoisseurs and collectors would age them in their own cellars. Then, selling off part of their purchase, they would keep the rest for their personal use. In effect, they acquired their drinking wines free and clear. Nowadays, such wines are often bought up by speculators, who cellar them for a few years, then cash them in. These investors rarely drink the wines themselves.

NOTE: The wines considered investment grade include less than a dozen top Bordeaux châteaus and some leading vintage ports. Also considered "trophy" wines are some top red Burgundies along with A-list California Cabernets.

Not all those who collect these expensive products are seriously interested in wine. The growth of discretionary income in the industrialized nations has created an increased demand for luxury items, including high-priced wines. The growing taste for such wines has been driving up their cost and creating shortages. Premium bottles of red Bordeaux are often snapped up by those who know little about wine but can afford to buy what they have been told is the best. What counts most for such consumers is the cost of the wine, and to some degree, its provenance. Their collecting impulse is more about the pride and prestige of ownership. What matters is their status, not the wine. For some who have amassed impressive cellars, the interest in enjoying their treasures is peripheral at best. In many instances they will hoard and trade their wines and never drink them at all.

Wine Futures

Wine Futures are another way to buy wine. These Futures are contracts to purchase a wine before it matures. The customer pays for the right to acquire bottles at a fixed price, regardless of what they will cost when they come to market. The purchase amounts to a wager that the wine will increase in value at maturity. Most of the Futures market is in first-growth red Bordeaux, but contracts have also been offered for French Burgundies, premium Italian red wines, and some California Cabernets. Initially purchased by wine merchants to ensure their supply, Futures are now offered to the general public as well. (Dabbling in Wine Futures has become a form of prestige for those with discretionary income; they like to tell their friends they are laying down some claret.)

In the Futures contract, the wine is usually sold by the case. (A rare prestigious few are available only by the bottle.) The price is announced six to nine months after the harvest. After keeping the wine in wood for about two years, the winery then bottles and ships it out. (Further aging by the consumer is always required; the wine may not be drinkable for a decade or so.) Wineries sell these contracts for future delivery to shippers, who sell them to importers. They finally reach the consumer by way of the retailer. On signing the contract, the purchaser usually pays in full, making a long-term commitment to finance the maturation of a wine that he will not receive for some time. The seller in the meantime receives an interest-free advance on the developing wine.

NOTE: In vintages producing early-maturing and light wines, there isn't any Futures market.

Although Futures have been promoted as a way of locking in advantageous prices, the value of the wine can remain unchanged or can even drop. This happens if the wine doesn't live up to the early predictions or if the supply exceeds the demand. It happens if serious fluctuations occur in international currencies; or if a spectacular vintage intervenes, dampening the interest in that particular year.

And if the economy is depressed, a mature wine might sell for less than its original cost, leaving the contract holder committed to a wine he could have bought locally at a much lower price. Or the contract holder might have used the money to buy another good wine at a more attractive price. Or if he had put his money into a conservative short-term investment of some sort, he might have accrued enough interest to cover the cost of the mature wine if he still wanted to acquire it.

Wine Futures seem to suggest that there are regulators to enforce the guarantees that the purchaser receives on signing the contract. But no such legal safeguards exist; security laws do not cover these investments. Should the firm become insolvent, the customer has little recourse in getting his money back. (It is always a good idea to check out the stability of the source offering the Wine Future.)

Wine Auctions

Wine can also be purchased at auctions, which create a lively secondary market outside the normal commercial channels for wine distribution. Auctions serve those who wish to sell off their excess inventory or those looking for unusual opportunities to buy. (In the years after World War II, old British families would sell off most of their wine cellars to pay their estate taxes.)

Wine auctions are conducted in London, Paris, and elsewhere. In the United States, they have been generally restricted because of the concern of the wine-and-spirits trade that importers and other distributors might use the sales to move their excess stock and so unfairly compete with the retail establishment. New York now permits such auctions, provided they offer the consumer already-matured wines from private collections and that the sales have been cleared by a licensed retailer of long standing. (The retailer is paid a fee for his participation.)

NOTE: When the wines at auction are sold anonymously from a private cellar, one cannot know if the bottles were moved from owner to owner or what their previous storage conditions were.

American auctions, long permitted as charity events, have not been true auctions at all. Many of the wines offered were donated. The high prices such bottles brought were more often a reflection of the bidder's generosity than of the actual value of the wines. Such auctions have sometimes featured ancient wines whose significance lies in their labels and provenance. (The chances of their being drinkable are usually quite remote.) Yet bidders eagerly spend thousands of dollars on such bottles. Some of the purchasers are restaurateurs or people in the wine trade, seeking to generate publicity for their own enterprises. These buyers may hold the wines for a few years, then auction them off again. The wines themselves are rarely uncorked and consumed. They may in fact have faded away.

STORING THE WINE

A wine cellar is both a collection of bottles and the place where those bottles are stored. The cellar can be either short-term, meant for day-to-day drinking, or long-term, meant for aging the wines as well as storing them.

For the short-term cellar, no more wine should be acquired than can be consumed in a few months. Virtually any space can do: a shelf in a cupboard, a cabinet, or a bookcase. It might be a file drawer, countertop, or even a corner of the floor. The collection itself might include a dozen or so relatively uncomplicated wines: eight table (red and white), three fortified (dry and sweet), and one sparkling wine. The fluctuating nature of such a cellar encourages variety and experimentation. Its nicest feature is convenience; you don't have to dash out at the last minute to find a bottle for an evening's meal or a spontaneous celebration.

A long-term cellar takes years of buying, culling, and tasting to assemble a collection which reflects one's personal tastes and interests. In creating such a cellar, it is best to begin with a few bottles and then to gradually increase its scope. (The designated space should not be too cramped to allow for its expansion.) The collection might include wines from various countries, or perhaps concentrate on one country, one region, or even on one town. (The most specialized cellars have concentrated on a single vineyard.)

Long-term storage requires thoughtful care. The better the wine, the more sensitive it is to its environment. Red wines need storage temperatures of about 55°F. When stored at sustained high temperatures, they lose their freshness and vitality and become brownish, flat, and unpleasant. White and sparkling wines, being more delicate, require slightly lower temperatures. When stored under sustained warm conditions, they darken and take on the taste of overripe grapes and caramel. Temperatures holding at 65 to 70°F are acceptable for soon-to-be consumed wines. (Seasonal fluctuations that are neither too abrupt nor too drastic should not cause serious concern.) On the other hand, storage at exceedingly low and sustained temperatures, will numb the wine and damage its taste.

NOTE: It is essential that wines be kept away from boilers, hot water heaters, and the like. Hardest on them are the furnaces that turn on during the day, building up the heat, and then turn off at night, causing the temperatures to fall sharply.

Red table wines, set aside for aging, develop best at relatively low and constant temperatures. Their long-term storage should not be considered if the wines will be exposed to high temperatures or to marked fluctuations in temperature. Such conditions speed up the wine's aging process by increasing its reaction rate. They also expand the bottle microscopically, creating a bellowslike effect that draws in the unwanted outside air.

For its proper development in long-term storage, a wine needs to remain serene, to be kept safe from vibrations and shock. Any sustained jostling or similar disruption can alter its breathing pace and cause it to throw off its sediment prematurely, thus accelerating the aging process. (Some of the best-preserved wines have not been moved in years.) For example, heavy street traffic or nearby construction can stir up a wine. When the Paris subway was under construction, an elderly gentleman living in the vicinity of l'Étoile stopped storing his clarets at home. He feared they might become too "bubbly."

Wine should also be kept away from the vibrations produced by frequently run washing machines, humming refrigerators, noisy air conditioners, and loud-playing stereos, as well as from perpetually slammed doors and heavy foot traffic. Storing the bottles under the stairs is not a good idea. They're subject to frequent footfalls there.

Darkness is also a necessity for wine. Exposure to bright light over an extended period will accelerate its aging and generally damage the wine. (Although the bottle's tinted glass offers some protection against the harmful ultraviolet rays, it doesn't filter them all out.) Particularly destructive is any direct, sustained fluorescent light, which can discolor the wine and make it dull and cloudy, while also producing an unattractive musty or off-taste. Wine needs a fairly stable humidity as well: about 60 percent. (Too little moisture will dry out the corks while too much will encourage the growth of destructive mold and fungi.)

Wine Cellars

Winery cellars provide the most ideal conditions for the storage of wine. Some are natural caves with never-changing temperatures. Other cellars have been dug deep into rock or chalky subsoil, with the surrounding tons of earth and stone serving as insulation. In the Champagne region, cellars are located in limestone quarries, dating back to Roman times. Some descend seven levels below the street; elevators link them to the surface. (Such cellars are so extensive that trains run through them.) In Rioja, vaults have been carved into the chalky subsoil seventy feet down. In Vouvray, the vineyards are sited atop a great limestone cliff, while a deep honeycomb of caves is cut into the chalk below. Some of California's oldest cellars were dug by Chinese laborers using picks and shovels. (They had come to America to help build the transcontinental railroad.)

Other winery cellars are located above ground. These include the long, low shippers' lodges of Oporto, whose earthen floors and few windows help maintain reasonable interior temperatures all year round. In Andalusia, the whitewashed sherry bodegas shield their tiny windows with straw mats, which keep out the heat and light, while allowing cooler air to circulate. Modern aboveground cellars rely on air conditioning and special insulation to stabilize their temperatures and help control their humidity.

In private homes, a section of the basement can serve as a long-term cellar if its temperature is cool and fairly even, and if there is sufficient humidity and a general serenity. If not, air conditioning can stabilize the temperature, while special insulation can cushion the wines stored there against excessive vibration.

NOTE: The decision whether or not to store wine in an apartment depends on the specific circumstances. A reasonably quiet hall closet can prove suitable, provided it is well ventilated with a relatively consistent temperature and if there are no excessive vibrations in the vicinity.

Despite the kitchen's convenience for serving wine, it is too bright and busy a place for extended storage. The stove continually creates extreme fluctuations in temperature. The various appliances and general household activity produce too many vibrations. A wine there can lose its freshness in a matter of weeks. And unless the storage space is fairly large and well ventilated, the wine can also absorb the unsavory fumes and sharp penetrating odors that float about in the air.

Note: Any bottles of wine kept in the kitchen should be rotated frequently and not kept near bottles of vinegar under any circumstances. (Its bacterial agents can quickly convert the alcohol in the wine into the astringent acetic acid that is itself known as vinegar.)

Some people store their wines in ready-made cellars, which are self-contained units, ranging from cabinets that hold three dozen bottles to walk-in chambers with a capacity of a thousand or more bottles. Refrigeration enables these units to maintain a basic temperature of 52 to 55°F. (Some cabinets provide additional compartments for chilling and for keeping the wines at room temperature.) The more elaborate units feature absorption systems designed to minimize vibrations and carbon filters which absorb extraneous odors.

Available for wine storage in some large cities are warehouses, which provide special temperature-controlled vaults. (These are maintained at an optimal 55°F.) A monthly fee is charged for each of the cases stored. Restaurateurs, retailers, and serious collectors avail themselves of these facilities, but their rental costs are prohibitive for the more modest collector.

Caring for the Wine

Good wines demand thoughtful care. When treated with respect, they can last for a long time. When stored carelessly or indifferently, they may peak too soon or or else turn to vinegar and be undrinkable.

It was once believed that the corks were porous enough to let tiny quantities of air enter the bottle and that this limited oxidation —enabling the wines to breathe gradually— enhanced the aging process. It was subsequently learned that the cork's cellular structure actually sealed out the air. Yet the wine in the bottle does breathe and develop because some air is already present. (It is inevitably introduced in the form of a bubble at the time of bottling.)

The cork is the wine's primary defense against deterioration. To do its job properly, the cork must remain moist, supple, and expansive. Horizontal storage —placing the bottle on its side— makes this possible. Shifting the bubble of air from the top of the bottle to the center puts the cork in direct contact with the liquid and so keeps it moist.

Storing the bottle upright would cause the bubble to float to the top, creating an air space between the cork and the wine. The cork would then dry out and shrink away from the sides of the neck, not only creating the danger of leakage but more significantly permitting the entrance of outside air. Even in minuscule amounts, the air would overoxidize the wine, rob it of its character, benumb its vitality, age it prematurely, and encourage the proliferation of the vinegar makers. For a sparkling wine, the shrinking cork would not only speed up the wine's deterioration but cause its effervescence to dissipate, leaving behind a flat, insipid liquid.

Employed for horizontal storage can be the wooden crate or cardboard carton in which the wine was shipped. The box is simply set on its side and the bottles arranged cork-side out so that any signs of shrinkage or other deviations can be noted. Individuals with large collections often use diamond-shaped bins to stack their bottles one atop the other in staggered rows. Others have custom-made racks designed to fit a given space in their homes. Still others use free-standing, ready-made racks of wood, bamboo, metal or plastic. Available in modular or stackable units, these come in various sizes and shapes. Whatever the rack's style or material, it should be at least fourteen inches deep to accommodate the bottles comfortably, with the compartments high enough to let air circulate around the bottles, making them less susceptible to temperature changes.

Because heat rises, the most delicate wines should be stored closest to the floor; with the lowest tiers reserved for the sparkling wines. Positioned directly above these are the white table wines, then the rosés and the lighter reds, and finally the sturdier reds. Fortified wines do not need horizontal storage; their higher alcohol content protects them against spoilage so they can be stored upright. Nor do such wines need lower temperatures; they do best when stored at 60 to 65°F.

For extensive cellars, the wines can be organized according to their country of origin, their grape variety, vintage and so on. Marked accordingly should be the racks, shelves, or compartments. One can also keep a cellar book which spells out the location of the bottles. It might take the form of a simple loose-leaf binder, an elegant leather-bound volume, or a computer disk. Columns on the left-hand page would include the name of the wine, date of purchase, location in the cellar, country of origin, vintage, shipper, retailer, quantity purchased, and price paid for the bottle. On the right-hand page, the columns would include the date of uncorking, tasting notes, and perhaps the menu for the meal at which the wine was served (along with a list of the guests who attended).

Some people incorporate wine labels into their cellar books; others paste them in special scrapbooks organized country by country, somewhat like a postage-stamp collection. Most of the labels peel off after a bit of soaking. Should they prove recalcitrant, the bottle can be filled with warm water and placed in a narrow cylindrical container to which ordinary household ammonia is added. (Rubber gloves should always be worn for this.) After about an hour, the label will generally come loose; a razor blade can assist if necessary.

A bottle stored away in a large cellar with its label not readily visible can easily be forgotten and the wine can lose its charm, if not its life. To make the contents known at a glance, a plastic tag —marked with the wine's name and vintage— can be placed over the neck of the bottle. (Sold in some wine shops, these tags come with pens featuring erasable ink.)

Monitoring the bottles from time to time can prevent their overlong storage and a resulting decline in quality. The wine's color should be checked periodically for brownish traces of maderization; the corks should be inspected for shrinkage and other deviations. A bulging cork generally indicates excessive heat or cold. Wine bleeding through the cork indicates that too much air has seeped in. (Such corks are called "weepers.") A loose cork is usually an indication that the bottle was stored too long in an upright position.

Even under the best of conditions, a cork's cellular structure will eventually break down and the cork will shrink. The life expectancy of a good cork is about twenty-five years. (Most major châteaus recork their wines every fifteen or twenty years.) To prevent overoxidation, some collectors —when recorking— top off their bottles with additional wine, preferably of the same vintage or at least of the same decade. A number of experts, however, object to such refilling and recorking.

They note that opening the bottles exposes fragile old wines to too much air, putting them at risk. They point out that bottles of very old wines —still sealed with their original corks— have often been found in excellent condition.

The bottle's fill level can also be reduced by slow evaporation over time. This condition, however, need not damage the wine. Wines, at age fifteen or so, are often perfectly good even when they reach only midway to the shoulder of the bottle. (For young wines, the liquid level should reach the neck or be close to it.) A recent catalogue announcing the sale of a restaurant's wine cellar listed bottles of red Bordeaux that had never been refilled. These were described as "HSF," "MSF" and "LSF," referring to their high-, mid-and low-shoulder fill levels.

Vintage Charts

Vintage charts are designed to rate certain wines and to provide an overall sense of how they fared in specific years. The farther north one travels, the more important the vintages become. They are most significant in areas of unpredictable weather, where no two crops are alike and where the wines are most susceptible to broad swings in quality. (In some places, splendid back-to-back years are rare and only one year in three may be good.) In years of volatile weather, the differences can be spectacular. (Even minor variations can produce markedly different wines.) In the more southerly regions, where the climate is generally consistent and sunny, vintages are of little consequence.

A vintage is considered great when all the wine's elements come together, when its color, personality, and character cannot be improved upon. In good years the grapes will develop higher sugars; while in poor years they don't mature properly and yield coarse and overly tart wines.

Tannin levels also rise in good years, while in poor years, even quality grapes may not acquire enough tannin to hold the wines together. Red wines, with their higher levels of tannin, are more dependent on the character of their vintages than white wines are.

NOTE: Technological advances have narrowed the differences between vintages. The vintner, employing modern grape-growing and wine-making techniques, can compensate for nature's shortcomings and produce reasonably good wines in all but the most disastrous years.

At the start, vintage charts were concerned with certain French wines; they have long been influential in Bordeaux, in the Côte d'Or and in the Chablis region of Burgundy, as well as in Champagne. Now such charts are also considered significant in northern Italy and Germany's Rhineland. Although the variable weather of California's North Coast does not begin to compare with the volatility of northern Europe, the state has begun keeping its own vintage charts. (These generally cover Napa, Sonoma, and Mendocino, along with Santa Clara to the south.) Yet even when frost, rain, and excessive heat damage some California grapes, the overall crop is usually abundant enough to compensate for the loss.

Vintage charts are neither uniform nor consistent in their ratings. Their scales range from 1 to 10 or 1 to 20, all the way up to 1 to 100. Yet all the systems are based on the premise that the wines were in good condition when purchased and that the bottles were stored in relatively cool, vibration-free and odor-free cellars with sufficient humidity to keep their corks from drying out.

One 10-point chart calls wines rated 1-2 acceptable, 3 inoffensive, 4 fair, 5 average, 6 good, 7 very good, 8 excellent, 9 outstanding, and 10 extraordinary. In another chart, 1-2 represents a less-than-average vintage, 3-4 average, 5-6 good, 7-8 very good, and 9-10 exceptional. And in still another, a defective wine is rated 0-1, a clean but not a special wine is 2-5, a good and harmonious wine is 6-9, while a ripe, noble wine is rated 9-10.

Generally associated with France is a 20-point system, which some experts say is sufficiently comprehensive to cover all of a wine's nuances and gradations. One such system rates poor wines 0-9, and fair ones 10-12, while 13-15 signifies good, 16-18 very good, and 19-20 are the best. Another system uses 1-10 to indicate an outright failure to barely passing, 10-11 is considered a sound and acceptable wine with no defects, 12-13 is fair, 13-16 is sound with some personality, 16-17 is memorable, while 18-20 represents a great wine.

Often employed in the United States is a 100-point system, which in effect is a 50-point system, since the bottom half indicates only the worst ratings. One such chart ranks poor wines as below 60, while average wines are 70-79, good to very good wines are 80-89 and excellent wines are 90-100. Another 100-point chart uses 75-79 to signify average wines and 96-100 to indicate the extraordinary ones.

NOTE: There are also the charts which don't use numbers, but letters to indicate the wine's quality levels. One such chart lists the top wines as AAA, followed by those rated AA, A, B, C, and D.

Many vintage charts add letters to the numbers to track the development of a wine and the pace of its aging. These indicate when the wine is not ready to drink, when it is drinkable but with its potential still unrealized, and when it is fully ready to drink. In one system, A indicates the wine would be best with more bottle age, B it can improve with additional aging, and C it is now ready to drink, while D advises caution about further aging, and E indicates the wine may already be over the hill. In another system, C represents caution (the wine may be too old), E is for early maturing (the wine may be drunk now but has not yet reached its peak), T is for tannic (the wine needs further aging), and R (the wine is ready to drink). In yet another chart, D signifies that the wines are ready to drink, A that they are still immature, and U that the wines are unavailable since they're still aging in the winery cellars.

NOTE: Given the differences in wine quality not only from year to year but from region to region, vineyard to vineyard, cellar to cellar, grape variety to grape variety and even bottle to bottle, some people think it is presumptuous to try spelling out the drinkability of a given wine.

If the limitations are understood, a vintage chart can serve as a rough guide to buying and storing wine. Since the charts are essentially a collection of generalities, they tend to oversimplify. Although they single out the bad years and give general advice on the good ones, they cannot encompass all the wine-producing countries, or even the varied regions within each country. Nor can they cover the various conditions affecting the wine's taste, color, bouquet, and longevity. The charts cannot deal with the variations in microclimates, soil types, elevations, grape varieties, wine-making skills, etc. And because they lump all of a region's wines together for a single year, they cannot acknowledge that natural cataclysms such as heavy rain, hail, and drought rarely affect each growing area equally, that one sector can encounter devastating weather while another in the same region might be experiencing good conditions. Nor can the charts deal with a stormy spring which damages early-ripening grapes while leaving the later-flowering varieties largely untouched. They cannot recognize that a vintage will be mixed if some grapes are gathered before a rain and some after. In short, no vintage chart can capture the many variations possible in many places in a single growing season.

It should also be noted that even in good years, indifferent or poor wines are inevitably made. (There will always be incompetent or greedy producers, who turn out thin, dull wines with little character.) Yet in lower-rated years, skilled wine makers may produce decent enough wines and secondary vineyards may yield better wines than their more distinguished neighbors.

Assessments of a wine's potential are also subject to change. A vintage, sandwiched between two highly regarded years, may be overlooked in its youth, then discovered years later. Or a good wine may lapse into dullness for several years and then recover its initial attractiveness.

Vintages are a significant factor in the marketing of wines. A wholesaler may deliberately understate the quality of a better vintage and exaggerate the virtues of a lesser one to even out his income from the good years to the bad. Or to create more receptivity to the wine of a relatively unimpressive year, he may keep it off the market until the more popular vintages are gone. A series of good vintages create their own problems, making it difficult for the wholesaler to sell the inventory from lesser years at a profit.

The relationship between the wholesaler, middleman, and retailer also comes into play when certain wines are allotted. The retailer wants to make sure that he will be included in the distribution channel when a high-quality vintage is released, so if the wholesaler asks him to accept a certain number of other wines as well, including those of a bad vintage, he will usually put those bottles on his shelves. The same is true with a rare bottle of wine. For an importer to qualify for a single bottle from the prestigious Domaine de La Romanée, for example, the shipper might demand that he buy large quantities of other wines as well.

AGING WINE

Although site and soil remain the same, variations in the weather from year to year cause the grapes to mature at different rates and their wines to differ in their potential for aging. Some vintages hit their peaks sooner and others later. (As a result, the wine of one year may be better for immediate drinking while that of a previous year is best consumed at a later date.) Red wines from relatively light vintages are low in tannin and are best consumed before the wines of heavier years.

Fine wines are alive and constantly changing. Although the dynamics of their aging process are not fully understood, their development has been likened to the stages of human growth; the wines evolve from childhood and adolescence to maturity and old age. A young wine is one that has not reached its peak and is still improving. A mature wine has developed its richness, softness, and refinement, while an old wine has passed its peak and is declining.

The more slowly a fine wine develops, the longer-lived it can be. Red wines of unmistakable concentration and depth are rarely drinkable early on. Closed-in, rough, and unfocused at first, they need time to open up and express their subtleties. With bottle age, they can develop finesse and complexity, and demonstrate a range of tastes and aromas that a younger wine cannot match. Wines that need time to tame their tannins, that call for long-term cellaring, include the best French red Bordeaux and Burgundies, premium Italian wines, and some California Cabernet Sauvignons, among others.

Only by tasting a slowly developing wine can we determine how it is coming along. Some collectors, who purchase wine by the case, buy an extra bottle so they can judge the wine's progress after a number of years. Others open a few bottles to determine the wine's maturity. (If one bottle and then another shows signs of excessive age, this is a warning to drink up the rest as soon as possible.)

There are some who keep their wines too long; who save them as a comfort for their old age, or treat them as cherished objets d'art. Wines past their prime become brown and dried out, acquiring a dry-leaf odor and an oxidized taste. Some ancient red wines that were drinkable when first uncorked proved so fragile that they faded within minutes. A century-old bottle of Lafite yielded a pale brown liquid tinged with scarlet and exuding a dim bouquet of violets. Tasting vaguely of grapes, the wine was so thin on the palate as to be almost watery. Jonathan Swift once refused a venerable wine, saying, "Sir, I drink no memories."

NOTE: Ninety percent of all wines are bottled within months of the harvest and are meant to be consumed within a year or two. (Beginning to deteriorate soon, they lose their color and bouquet and become flat and dull.) The remaining 10 percent age gracefully and can gain in value with time.

It has been estimated that about 95 percent of the wines purchased are consumed within a day or so of leaving the shop; most of them within a week. People assume the wines are ready to drink when purchased. In our impatient times, most of the better reds are consumed prematurely. Although the wines may need further aging, many people cannot resist the temptation of uncorking them immediately. Drinking a good wine too soon has been described as a kind of "infanticide." As one wine maker noted, "The average person has never aged a wine and so he doesn't know the difference."

It was once believed that to be truly great, a red wine had to be undrinkable for the first decade of its life. The rich, tannic reds, made in an older, slower-developing style, often took years to come around. Perhaps they were more capricious and erratic, but they could develop more pronounced personalities. Today, few red wines are vinified to mature for the length of time of which they're capable. They are made ready to drink in five years or less; some of the finest peak after about ten years. And the rush is currently on to produce lighter, fruitier, quicker-maturing wines which become "friendlier" sooner. Such speeded-up wines are ready for consumption two or three years after the harvest. They may be charming in youth but fade quickly. (Most languish and die within a couple of years.)

White wines, quite negligible in their tannins, require little aging. (As soon as they are bright and stable, the wineries generally bottle and ship them out.) Most are meant for consumption when released and keep only a year or two. The greatest charm of a white wine is its engaging freshness. Only a rare few have the potential to age gracefully; these include the noble-rot Sauternes, the great white Côte d'Or Burgundies, and the finest German Rieslings. As the youthful fruit abates in these unusual whites, they become more complex and rounded, acquiring deeper flavors and a more desirable bouquet.

As a rule, blush wines and rosés are best enjoyed in the freshness of their youth and should be consumed within two years of the vintage. (They generally turn dangerous by age three and are pretty much over the hill by age four.) Nor are sparkling wines meant for aging; their freshness and vivacity diminishes with time. Champagne is already bottle-aged and ready to drink when released. (Vintage Champagnes, once made in a richer, fuller style, could remain bubbly for a decade or more.) Sparkling wines sold in larger-than-standard bottles —i.e., magnums, jeroboams, etc.— should be consumed as soon as possible. (The transfer to these oversized bottles increases their oxidation and reduces their staying power.)

Fortified wines generally benefit little from bottle aging but, because of their higher alcohol levels, can be stored away for extended periods. Best soon after bottling, however, are the lighter and drier sherries —the finos and manzanillas— along with the ruby and tawny ports. Vintage ports need to evolve for years in the bottle and demonstrate great keeping powers; the finest improve for thirty, forty, and even fifty years. (The current trend is to make them drinkable in fifteen or twenty years.) Madeiras are the longest-lived of the fortified wines; the rarest among them have retained their fruit and vitality for sixty years or more.

The factors that determine when a wine will reach its peak and how long it will remain there include its source, grape variety, quality of the vintage, size of cask or tank, and extent of oxidation. Significant too is the style of vinification, the wine's condition when purchased, and how the bottles were stored.

The following is a general guide to the keeping and aging of wines, assuming that they were properly cellared before and after their purchase.

French Wines

Bordeaux

Médoc wines of good provenance and vintage are characteristically firm and hard in their youth. Once needing decades to reach their peaks, they could survive a quarter century or more. Reflecting the current trend toward earlier drinkability, the French have come to prefer their Médocs, even the greatest among them, relatively young. The average aging time for the finest examples had been up to fifteen years, but some now reach their peaks in eight to ten years, hold that level for another five years or so, and then begin a slow decline.

Other good Médocs, once ready to drink in five to ten years may now be drinkable in three to seven years. Gascony wines, in general, usually take two to three years to soften up; most from the Petit Châteaus are at their best soon after bottling. (Second-Label Bordeaux are also meant to be taken young.) St.-Émilion and Pomerol wines, generally less tannic than the Médocs, are ready to drink in five to eight years at their finest. (Some rare examples can be aged for ten to twelve years.) The long-lived St.-Éstephes once needed more than five years to become smooth and attractive; some are now drinkable at age two or three. Among the white Bordeaux, Château d'Yquem ages beautifully. (Some examples have lasted more than five decades and shown no deterioration even at the age of eighty.) Most of the other white Bordeaux wines are meant for immediate consumption.

Burgundy

Red Burgundies, pressed from the pinot noir grape, usually mature faster than the Cabernet Sauvignons from Bordeaux and are not generally expected to last as long. A few rare Côte d'Or wines once reached their peaks in eight to ten years, with some surviving for two decades. Most are now ready to drink by age five. Lesser red Burgundies ripen in about eighteen months.

Among the Beaujolais crus, Moulin-à-Vent generally ages best, with the finest examples improving for eight to ten years. Morgon, Fleurie, and Chénas can last five years or more. Most other crus usually ripen in three to four years, while some St. Amours can usually be drunk within two years of the vintage. Ordinary Beaujolais wines soon lose their attractive grapy color, flavor, and fragrance. It is said in the region, "Drink the wine of the preceding year, no older." Beaujolais Nouveaus usually crumble in about six months and are best taken by Christmas of the vintage year. They should generally be avoided after the following March or April. (Preservatives, however, may prolong the life of the Nouveau exports.)

Among the white Burgundies, the most magnificent from the Côte d'Or can remain at their peaks for four to six years, while the more typical examples go off in about three. A Grand Cru Chablis is usually at its best by age four or so. Other good Chablis generally retain their youth and fragrance for two or three years; the lesser examples last only a year or two. The better Côte de Beaune whites usually run their course in a year or so. As for the regional Bourgogne Blancs, the sooner they are consumed, the better.

Rhône Valley

Some of the finest Hermitage wines needed decades to reach maturity and proved to be longer lasting than the famous red Bordeaux. Now some of the best are made drinkable by about age ten. (A number need only six years of bottle aging.) Cornas and Gigondas reds can benefit from five to ten years of aging, while the Crozes-Hermitage need only three or four. The better reds of St. Joseph can improve in the bottle for about five years but most are ready to drink in two to three. The best Côte Roties once needed six years or so to blossom but can now reach their heights after three or four years. The good Syrahs, needing at least five years to open up, may be better at ten years of age or more.

The red wines of the southern Rhône are generally softer and faster maturing than their northern counterparts. The best Châteauneufs once needed a decade to reach their peaks but can now be taken at age five or less; the lightest can be consumed within a year or two. The Côtes du Rhône can be drunk on their release and for the next two or three years. (Some are best taken within a year or so.)

Among the Rhône white wines, the top-ranking Château Grillet with the greatest potential for aging, reaches its maximum drinking level by about age five. The region's other whites, such as Condrieu, are best taken young. Muscat Beaumes-de-Venise can be drunk after a year or so, but with a degree of bottle age the wine becomes more subtle as certain complex secondary aromas replace its initial fresh and flowery, youthful appeal.

Loire Valley

Most Loire Valley reds are ready to drink when released. (In superior vintages, those from Chinon, Bourgueil, and St. Nicholas may improve for a few years in the bottle.) Among the Loire whites, the finest Vouvrays can take long cellaring without any loss of their verve, while the most extraordinary examples have been known to remain fresh and youthful for as long as five decades. (Noble-rot wines from Bonnezeaux and Quarts de Chaume have also survived for half a century.) Sweet luscious Anjous can take a few years of aging, while some highly acid Savennières are not worth considering until age five or so. The Loire whites (Pouilly-Fumé, Sancerre, Quincy, and Muscadet) are best taken within a year of their release, and no more than two. By age three or four, these wines can become tired and disappointing.

Alsace

The finest Alsatian whites need some bottle aging to achieve their fullest depth and complexity. Special Reserve Selections need several years, while the greatest VTs (Vendange Tardives) don't reach their peaks for five or six years. The latter can last for ten to fifteen years, as can the SGNs (Selections des Grains Noble). Most other Alsatian wines are ready to drink on their release.

Other French Wines

Champagnes are ready to drink when sold but some people prefer a Champagne of greater age. Cahors, once dark, harsh, and unyielding, needed a decade or more to develop its potential. Vinified for earlier maturity now, it can be drinkable in about five years. Moulis reds are generally ready to drink around age five and are capable of improvement for about a decade. Some of the best Bandols, along with the reds of Rully and Givry, are ready to drink in two or three years. Among the Mâconnais white wines, Pouilly-Fuissé is best taken by age two or three and should be avoided after age five. Other white Mâcon wines are meant for immediate consumption since they fade within a year or so.

Italian Wines

The great Barolos, once robust, tannic, and long-lived, did not reach their peaks for two decades or more. (A rare few survived for nearly a century.) The best are now generally drinkable after about ten years. Most other Barolos, currently made in a fruitier, softer style, are ready in six to eight years. (A few may mature even sooner.) The most extraordinary Barberas possess ten to fifteen years of life, while others are ready to drink within four to eight years; and some by age three. A Barbaresco can mature in six to ten years, while a good Gattinara needs about five years to develop.

Amarone once needed a decade or two to reach its peak, but is now vinified to be drinkable by about age five. Brunello di Montalcino, famed for its intensity, once needed more than two decades to achieve its balance and finesse. (Some aged well for half a century.) Made less tannic and more accessible now, the Brunello wine can mature in six to ten years. The lighter Rosso di Montalcino, known as Brunello's younger brother, is ready to drink when released.

The classic Chiantis from great vintages once needed a decade or two to work off their tannins. Some can now be enjoyed after five or six years. Simple fruity Chiantis are meant to be taken within a couple of years of the vintage while they remain light and fresh. Rubesco is ready to drink on its release but can keep for several years.

Valpolicellas are drinkable in about three years. The lighter-bodied, earlier-maturing Bardolinos and Dolcettos are best taken by age one or two, since they will soon fade. (For the most part, these wines are over the hill by age three.) Freisa di Chieri is ready to drink when released, but can shed its rough tartness after a couple of years and acquire quite a remarkable bouquet. The best Taurasis are relatively long-lived, reaching their maturity at about age ten. (Some examples have aged well up to fifteen or twenty years.) Montepulciano d'Abruzzo can age well for about a decade.

Most of the Italian white wines —Soave, Verdicchio, Vernaccia di San Gimignano, Cortese, Pinot Grigio, etc.— are best taken as young as possible, preferably within a year of the vintage. Good examples of the Lacryma Christi, however, have aged up to fifteen or twenty years.

Spanish Wines

Rioja's outstanding red Riservas are capable of aging gracefully. Those from exceptional vintages can come into their own at about age ten and reach their peaks at ages fifteen or twenty. (A rare few have survived for thirty and forty years.) The more typical Riojas and other Spanish reds are generally ready to drink when released (at age four or five). Vega Sicilia's Gran Riservas are ready after ten years, as are the finest Ribera del Dueros. (Ribera wines from light vintages can be taken around age five.) The Spanish white wines are meant for immediate consumption.

Portuguese Wines

The highly tannic red wines from Colares need a decade or more to mature. The Reserva Dãos from top vintages are also fairly tannic and can last two decades or more. Other Dão reds usually mature in five to ten years. The white Dãos are best consumed within a year. Also meant to be taken young and sprightly are the Portuguese vinho verdes, which should be drunk within a year or so.

German Wines

Good German Rieslings are ready to drink on their release but can age superbly because of their excellent acid balance. Those from the richest vintages can develop their subtleties and nuances until about age ten. By their fifteenth year, however, they become dull and murky.

QBA and Kabinett wines reach their fullest flavor within five years. Spätleses are enjoyable when young and generally peak in five to ten years. Ausleses, requiring two to three years of bottle age, continue to develop in glass for at least a decade. Although the BAs, TBAs, and Eisweins peak in seven to ten years, they usually remain fresh and intriguing for decades. The more modest German wines are ready to drink when shipped and are best consumed by age two.

American Wines

Most Napa Valley Cabernet Sauvignons are at their best between the ages of five and eight; superior examples can continue to improve until about age fifteen or twenty. Many, however, are vinified for earlier consumption and are ready to drink on their release. (When aged another two or three years, they may acquire additional complexity.) The finest California Merlot wines can be laid down for seven to eight years, the lesser examples for four to six or less. The more robust petite sirah varietals can be aged for five years or more.

Zinfandels may be taken either youthful or mature, depending on where they were grown and how they were vinified. The richer, fuller examples can be profitably aged for a decade; the most tannic among them need ten to fifteen years in the bottle. Other red Zinfandels are ready to drink by age seven or eight, while some are made approachable by about age two. The finest California Chardonnays are ready for consumption on their release, but demonstrate a more complex bouquet and flavor after three or four years. Some can be aged for eight to fifteen years. (One thirty-year-old Chardonnay was still in superb condition when tasted.) Most, however, should be consumed within a year or two.

In the Pacific Northwest, Cabernet Sauvignons from good years have lasted as long as a decade. In Oregon's Willamette Valley, the Pinot Noir wines are generally meant for consumption within three or four years of the vintage. Other northwestern reds are usually ready to drink on their release, as are the red table wines from New York State.

Other Countries

Many Australian red wines are ready to drink when bottled. Particularly good Shiraz-Cabernet blends, however, can be cellared for fifteen to twenty years. (Although most of the tannic Australian reds can age well and acquire a rounder finish, their true potential is often sacrificed for the softness of early maturity.)

Swiss white wines are intended for immediate drinking and generally should be consumed within three years of the vintage.

7

SERVING

When served at the proper temperature,
a wine will demonstrate the finest qualities
for its type and its style.

WINE TEMPERATURES

Room temperature is ideal for some wines while others need cooling or chilling. Generally speaking, the better the wine, the less chilling it requires; the more substantial, the warmer it should be served. Also the sweeter the wine, the cooler it should be served. Another consideration is the time of year. In summer, a wine can be served a few degrees cooler than in winter. (Warm weather makes a Cabernet Sauvignon taste flabby.) Still another consideration is the point in the meal at which the wine is served. Taken as an apéritif, it should be served a bit cooler than when accompanying the main course.

There are four basic serving temperatures for wine: room temperature, cellar temperature, light chilling, and sharp chilling.

Room Temperature

The room-temperature concept originated in Europe before the introduction of central heating. Indoor temperatures in cool weather then were usually 60 to 65°F. (Since house and apartment interiors are now about 10 degrees warmer, a wine literally served at "room temperature" tends to be warmer than it should be.)

For tannic red wines, about 60°F is best. At that temperature, the elements responsible for their taste, aroma, and bouquet are most active. At 70°F or more, a robust red wine will lack the necessary astringency so that the alcohol dominates its taste. Losing its vigor, the wine will take on a semistewed flavor and become formless, flabby, and oppressively heavy. (A few minutes in the refrigerator should cool it down sufficiently). On the other hand a sturdy tannic red, when served too cool, will be deprived of its taste, aroma, and most of its bouquet. At about 50°F, it seems much more astringent than it actually is.

Best served at room temperature are the more substantial red wines: the Bordeaux and Burgundies; the Hermitage and Côte Rôties from the Rhône; the Barolos, Barbarescos, and Riserva Chiantis from Italy; along with the heavier California Cabernet Sauvignons, Zinfandels, etc. Room temperature is also suitable for fortified wines which are medium-rich. These include sherries, ports, Madeiras, and Marsalas.

Cellar Temperature

Cellar temperature ranges from 50 to 60°F, as if the wine had just emerged from a cool cellar. This is best for uncomplicated wines characterized by irrepressible fruit, such as the lighter reds, blush wines, and rosés. A slight cooling will enhance their freshness and remove their typically sharp edges, while letting their flavor and crisp acidity come through. (Room temperature would throw their sweetness and acidity out of balance, making such wines seem dull and flat.)

Best served at cellar temperature are most Beaujolais. (The heavier Grand Crus —Moulin-à-Vent and Morgon— are more pleasant when served a bit below room temperature.) Cellar temperature is also appropriate for the lighter red wines from the Rhône's Côtes du Ventoux, the Chinons and Bourgueils from the Loire, and the Italian Bardolinos, Valpolicellas and Dolcettos; along with the Spanish Valdepeñas and the lighter California Zinfandels. Cellar temperatures are suitable for the generic Burgundies and clarets as well as the sweeter fortified wines.

Light Chilling

Light chilling, which ranges from 45 to 55°F, can enhance the crisp flavor of a white wine, accentuate the delicacy of a rosé, and refresh an unpretentious young red. It can also reveal the lovely subtleties of a drier fortified wine (served as an apéritif) and show a sweeter, heavier-bodied dessert wine to its greater advantage.

Light chilling is generally appropriate for most white wines, including the fine white Burgundies and top-quality German and Alsatian Rieslings, as well as the fuller-bodied, fuller-flavored Chardonnays from California and Australia. It is also suitable for the light-bodied, sometimes slightly sweet red wines meant to be drunk young, such as rosés, Beaujolais Nouveaus, Côtes du Rhônes, Cabernet Francs from the Loire Valley, and the lighter Italian Chiantis and Spanish Riojas.

Light chilling is suitable too for the lighter fortified wines served as apéritifs; among these are the fino and manzanilla sherries, light tawny ports, and dry vermouths, along with the sercial and verdelho Madeiras. Light chilling is appropriate as well for the richer Madeiras and oloroso sherries, and for the Málaga, Muscatel, and Tokay wines.

Sharp Chilling

Sharp chilling, which ranges from 35 to 45°F, is best for sparkling wines. This not only accentuates their crisp taste and tingle and brings out their flavor but reduces the bottle's internal pressure as well. Sharp chilling also keeps their CO_2 in solution, prolonging the life of their bubbles. (Higher temperatures would stimulate the molecular activity of the sparkling wine and expand its CO_2, creating a greater propulsive force behind the cork and making the wine go flat much sooner.)

Sharp chilling serves to counteract the assertive sweetness of luscious white wines and to offset their possible cloying. It is particularly suited to botrytized wines, including the French Sauternes and Barsacs. (Bottles of Sauternes have been encased in blocks of ice, chilling them almost to the freezing point.) Other wines that can also benefit from such sharp chilling are the French Beaumes-de-Venise, the Italian vin santos, and the German Ausleses, Beerenausleses, Eisweins, and Trockenbeerenausleses.

NOTE: Since cold can mask a wine's subtle qualities, overchilling should generally be avoided. For most wines, too much cold will damage their quality, impair their bouquet, dull their flavor nuances and even paralyze them. Freezing

the taste out of a wine makes it the equivalent of ice water. Warming up during the meal, the wine will lose whatever remains of its sprightliness, freshness, and charm. Rarely does the last glass taste as good as the first.

Warming and Cooling

Whether a wine is to be warmed or cooled, it should always be brought to its proper temperature gradually. Red wines carried up from cool cellars were once set aside on a sideboard to let them reach room temperature slowly. (This was known as *chambrer, chambre* being French for "room.") Permitted to warm itself naturally, the wine can open up fully, displaying all its bouquet and lingering flavor. Raising the temperature too abruptly would throw the wine off balance. Plunging a bottle into hot water, setting it in front of an open fire, or placing it near a radiator would cause the wine to breathe off most of its bouquet.

NOTE: If time is short and the wine is too cool, a hand cupped around the glass together with the ambient temperature of the room should be sufficient to warm it in a few minutes.

Nor should chilling be hastened. Placing a bottle in the freezer, subjecting the wine to a sharp, swift drop in temperature, would shock it and dull its personality. Extreme cold can also expel the cork or crack the bottle. Nor is it a good idea to place ice cubes in the glass. They would dilute the wine and damage its flavor beyond recall. (Ice should never be added to a good wine.) Nor is it wise to place the glasses themselves in the refrigerator, fill them temporarily with ice cubes, or to set them upside down in an ice bucket. The moisture that's introduced would inhibit the evaporation the wine needs to release its bouquet and aroma. For a sparkling wine, it would destroy the effervescence. (If the glasses are chilled and then dried beforehand, the heat of the hand will only rewarm them.)

Assuming that a red wine is reasonably cool to begin with, about twenty minutes in the refrigerator is sufficient for light chilling. A white wine will need about an hour; for sharp chilling, it needs several hours. (Champagnes and other sparklers, bottled in thicker, more stress-resistant glass, need about two hours.) Those in oversized bottles —magnums and jeroboams— require even more time.

NOTE: If the bottles are too large or too numerous for the refrigerator, they can be placed in sturdy plastic bags filled with ice. Or they can be arranged horizontally in the bathtub and topped with a layer of ice cubes. Adding enough cold tap water to immerse the bottles will encourage the ice cubes to melt and cool the wine more efficiently.

A wine should be chilled no more than a few hours in advance. If left in the refrigerator overnight, it will never again regain its earlier charms. (Champagne, in particular, develops an odd flat, unpleasant smell and taste.) Table wines stored in the refrigerator for an extended period enter a state of suspended animation and do not evolve naturally. Bottles that were chilled but not uncorked are better returned to the cellar, then chilled again before serving.

Casual wines meant to slake the thirst can be cooled more casually. A jug wine, taken "on the rocks," may in fact taste better since a colder temperature will mask its imperfections. For picnics, the wine can be chilled in the refrigerator, then transferred to a thermos jug or an ice chest. In places, such as southern France, Italy, Spain, and Greece, ordinary red table wines are often diluted with water in the summer. Inexpensive white wines and rosés may also be cut with water in the summertime or else combined with club soda and ice cubes in a cool, refreshing drink known as a "spritzer."

Wines can also be chilled in ice buckets. Cracked or crushed ice is more efficient here than ice cubes. Even better is a half-ice, half-water mixture, which makes more surface contact with the bottle. (If the wine bucket in a restaurant contains only ice, you can ask the waiter to add water to chill the wine more efficiently, or you can simply add the water yourself.) After about twenty minutes the bottle should be fairly icy to the touch. Sparkling wines, bottled in thicker glass, need about thirty minutes. Although the wine bottles should be immersed up to their necks, most buckets are not deep enough to accommodate the long-necked flute-style bottles from Germany, Austria and Alsace. Upending them in their buckets for a few minutes will make their necks feel as icy as the rest.

Ice buckets are also useful for red wines which seem too warm on the tongue. (Chilling them lightly for ten or fifteen minutes will make them taste livelier.) Adding very cold water to the bucket without ice can also cool them down sufficiently in about half an hour or so.

Note: Although an ice bucket is useful for retaining the chill of a white wine during a long leisurely meal or for prolonging the bubbles of a sparkling wine, it is generally superfluous for wines that have already been chilled in the refrigerator.

Uncorking the Bottle

When a wine has been brought to its proper serving temperature, the bottle can be uncorked. Some people prefer doing this in the kitchen beforehand in order to sample the wine before serving it to others. Trying a quarter glassful allows you to check on the wine's soundness and to remove any stray particles of cork. You can then securely recork the bottle until serving time.

When opening the bottle, it's best to have a corkscrew with which you are familiar. (The better the wine, the more carefully its bottle should be opened.)

These are the steps in uncorking a bottle of wine:

1. First remove the capsule or foil covering the cork and the bottle neck. Using the point of a corkscrew or a knife, score the capsule all the way around the first ridge, about one and a half inches from the top; then strip off the foil to expose the cork. (Some corks are protected by a coating of hard wax rather than a capsule.) Wipe the cork, neck, and rim with a dampened cloth or paper toweling to remove any traces of mold or residue.

2. Holding the bottle firmly by the neck, insert the corkscrew. Turn until it penetrates the length of the cork almost fully. For corks that are balky and difficult to extract, set the bottle on the floor and press down with one hand for greater leverage, while pulling up steadily on the corkscrew with the other hand. Should the cork break off midway, reinsert the corkscrew at a slightly different and a more diagonal angle, and begin again.

3. Ease the cork out and inspect it. It should be moist, firm, and clean smelling. It should not be discolored or emit a musty or otherwise objectionable odor.

4. With the dampened cloth or paper toweling, carefully wipe the lip of the bottle inside and out to remove any traces of mold or residue.

5. While pouring the wine, do not rest the bottle on the rim of the glass. (Stemmed wineglasses, with their high centers of gravity, are susceptible to spills.)

6. When the pouring is done, a slight clockwise twist of your wrist will send the last few drops of wine back into the neck of the bottle and prevent dripping.

Wine is served clockwise around the table. (Port is traditionally served counterclockwise.) If you'd like your guests to serve themselves, place the bottle in the center of the table or simply ask them to pass it along. When more than one bottle is served, pour wine from the second bottle into fresh or at least empty glasses in case the second wine differs substantially from the first. Do not discard the cork; you might need it. Recorking the bottle at slow, leisurely meals will prevent the wine's overoxidation. The cork may also be needed for a leftover wine.

NOTE: Never fill the glass to the brim, but allow the wine's volatile substances and evaporating ethers to collect at the top so the bouquet and aroma can develop. If the cork is inadvertently pushed into the bottle, don't try to retrieve it. If it crumbles, push the remaining section into the bottle. In both cases, strain the wine at once into a clean container through a cheesecloth-lined sieve.

Corkscrews

Before corkscrews were invented, wine corks projected over the rims of the bottles. (A strong set of teeth was needed for their removal.) The introduction of the corkscrew made possible straight-sided corks, with their tops set flush with the top of the bottles. (Previously, the corks were tapered in shape.)

Traditional corkscrews feature a metal shaft or worm and some form of leverage. The worm is preferably helix shaped with an outside diameter of three-eighths of an inch and about six spirals. Short worms can't extract long corks. (Solid augers with straight shafts which look like wood screws do not get a good grip and their sharp edges can split or shatter the cork.) The crossbar provides the necessary leverage by intensifying the twisting action of the worm. A modern corkscrew features a plastic sleeve which both grips the bottle neck and centers the worm precisely. Its extralong stainless-steel helix has an antifriction coating, making the extraction virtually effortless. (This device is particularly good for extracting broken or dried-out corks, or for corks set in place too tightly.)

A variant of the traditional corkscrew, called the "swimmer," features a pair of vertical wings which raise up laterally as the worm penetrates. Returning the wings to their vertical position exerts a strong pull upward. Another variant is a compact folding corkscrew which looks like a penknife. Known as the "waiter's friend," it features a lever at one end, which is braced against the lip of the bottle and acts as a fulcrum for the helical screw. Seen in restaurants and wine bars is a heavy-duty corkscrew installed on the bar itself. This device features a pair of hinged arms that grip the bottle firmly, along with a wooden lever, a sharply pointed worm, and a stainless-steel barrel. Here, the cork is removed with two smooth, swift motions: the first, a twist of the wrist, activates the lever, forcing the worm into the cork; the second reverses the lever, extracting the cork and ejecting it out the other end of the stainless-steel barrel.

Nontraditional cork extractors dispense with the worm entirely, leaving the cork unpierced and intact. One is a two-pronged cork puller, featuring a pair of tines attached to a small handle. The tines are inserted on either side of the cork and the handle is gently and steadily twisted to bring out the cork intact. (This is particularly useful for soggy or crumbly corks, which would be demolished by conventional corkscrews.) Another nontraditional device is the cork popper, which injects neutral nitrogen gas through a hollow steel needle inserted in the cork. The nitrogen builds up in the space between the cork and the wine, replacing the oxygen bubble and pushing the cork upward until it exits. (This device is not recommended for bottles made of thin or uneven glass, since the gas pressure generated inside the bottle might cause it to shatter.)

Opening the Champagne Bottle

Champagnes and other sparkling wines should be well chilled before uncorking, not only to bring out their inherent flavor but to reduce the propulsive pressure behind their corks. Such bottles should be opened at the last moment and the glasses set out well in advance to preserve as much of their active and lively effervescence as possible.

Particular care must be taken when opening a bottle of Champagne. Any undue shaking or agitation might cause the mushroom-shaped cork to be expelled prematurely. Flying out suddenly, the cork can careen around the room at high speed or ricochet dangerously off the walls. Its likely trajectory should always be kept in mind, with the neck of the bottle always pointed away from your body, face, and eyes, as well as from those of others in the vicinity. The bottle should also be pointed away from such breakable objects in the room, as mirrors, lamps, clocks, glass-framed pictures, window panes, etc.

NOTE: The safest instrument for extracting the mushroom-shaped cork is the human hand, which can exercise the greatest degree of control. (A corkscrew, knife, or similar implement should not be used, except to remove the foil capsule.)

These are the steps in uncorking a bottle of Champagne:

1. With the point of a knife, incise the foil capsule, scoring it about one and one-half inches from the top all the way around. Strip away the foil, exposing the cork that is anchored in place by a wire hood.

2. Untwist the wire's bottom loop and lift off the hood. Remove any remaining scraps of metal which might taint the wine when it is poured.

3. Tilt the bottle at a 45-degree angle away from your body. Then grasp the mushroom-shaped dome of the cork firmly between the thumb and forefinger of one hand. With the other hand, rotate the bottle slowly by its base in one direction, a quarter of a turn at a time. Always rotate the Champagne bottle, *not* the cork. (You always turn the bottle out from under the cork, rather than twisting the cork out of the bottle.)

4. With thumb and forefinger, guide and control the cork's emergence, rocking it gently to let some of the CO_2 escape and so dissipate some of the propulsive pressure behind the cork.

5. When two-thirds of the cork has emerged, ease the rest out smoothly. (The cork

should exit with a muted sound, accompanied by a slight wisp of vapor. The louder and more explosively the cork departs, the faster the CO_2 will rush out, taking some valuable wine with it.)

6. To prevent any foaming over, pour each glass one-third full; then a moment later, pour the wine two-thirds to the top. (Filling the glass more fully than that only invites spilling.)

NOTE: If the cork does not move out on its own, continue rotating the bottle by the base. (Should the cork remain stubborn, run a stream of hot water over the neck for a few seconds.) If the cork breaks, cover it with a cloth and hold the bottle neck under tepid water until the cork works itself loose. If the cork does not emerge, do not try to remove the remaining stem with a corkscrew or any other implement. Instead, lay the pressure-filled bottle on its side until it can be returned to its place of purchase. (A reputable wine shop should replace the bottle.)

BREATHING

A wine's breathing is simply its exposure to air. This calls for uncorking the bottle in advance to aerate the wine. (If time is short, the aeration can be hastened by pouring the wine into a glass beforehand and exposing more of its surface to air.) Breathing is essential for some wines and unnecessary for others. For still others, the results can be disastrous.

Tannic red wines benefit most from breathing. Aeration can make harsh and closed-in wines heady and delicious. Contact with the oxygen in the atmosphere brings these wines to life and releases more of their subtle flavors. Wines that benefit most from breathing include the best Bordeaux and other good Cabernet Sauvignons; high-caliber Burgundies, many Spanish and Portuguese reds, and Italian Barolos, Gattinaras, and Spannas, as well as the classic Chiantis and the Brunellos di Montalcino, among others.

Breathing is also especially beneficial for the tight and seemingly unyielding young red wines. Such oxidation will soften their tannins, modify their inner hardness, and round off their rough edges. The more sharply tannic the wines, the more positively they will respond. After an hour or so, they will become softer, fuller, and more generous. (Some tannic young California Cabernets are able to benefit from several hours of breathing.)

Since most mature reds have already resolved their tannins during bottle aging, about half an hour of breathing is usually sufficient for them. Additional exposure risks a loss of their fruit and much of their character. After an hour or so, they are not as fresh and vigorous as they once were. After two or three hours of breathing, they are likely to deteriorate. (There are some exceptions. In Italy, certain sturdy Barolos have been uncorked up to twenty-four hours in advance.)

NOTE: To intensify the oxidation further, the wine is gently swirled or rotated in its glass. And transferring inexpensive red wines back and forth several times between their glasses and another container enables them to absorb still more oxygen from the air.

Although aeration seems to speed up a wine's maturation, it is not a substitute for the normal aging process. A well-made red wine will achieve its highest potential only by its slow and gradual development in both the cask and the bottle. (If the bottle is opened five years too soon, the wine may need twice as much breathing as its properly matured counterpart.)

For venerable and delicate old red wines, to breathe is to die. Whatever aeration they need best occurs in the glass where they can be monitored and consumed before they fall apart. Such wines should not be opened until the last moment. The older and more fragile they are, the shorter their life expectancy once they have been uncorked. Such wines may taste fine when first sipped, but can rapidly fade away. Some will crumble on contact with air and literally disintegrate in a few minutes. (Tragic tales have been told of uncorking old wines in advance only to find that their long-developed flavors have floated away.)

Nor is advance aeration advisable for those wines which possess fewer tannins: the lighter reds, rosés, and whites. Uncorking their bottles ahead of time would cause such wines to lose the fresh, fruity character and aroma which constitute their greatest charm. Breathing is also inappropriate for sparkling wines, whose lively bubbles would escape into the air and vanish. And it is unnecessary as well for fortified wines, with the exception of some vintage ports. A fifteen-to twenty-year-old vintage port may benefit from some aeration, but the older examples should not be opened in advance of their serving time.

DECANTING

Most fine wines throw a degree of deposit as they age in glass. Their sediment although harmless, would muddy the wine, obscure its color, and produce an odd, somewhat furry sensation on the palate were it permitted to float free. To leave it behind, the wine is decanted or transferred from its bottle to another container. Known as the decanter, this might be a vessel with a stopper, an open-necked carafe, a pitcher, a jug, or another (recycled and well-washed and dried) wine bottle.

Most in need of decanting are mature, well-made tannic red wines which throw a considerable deposit in the bottle. These include high-caliber reds from Bordeaux and Burgundy's Côte d'Or, Hermitage wines from the Rhône, and such full-bodied Italian wines as the Barolos, among others.

During its extensive aging in glass, vintage Port also throws a heavy sedimentary crust inside the bottle. If that crust becomes dislodged, the unopened bottle should be stood upright for about twenty-four hours to let the loose particles drift downward to the bottom. (After the bottle is uncorked, the wine is then immediately strained into a decanter through a cheesecloth-lined sieve.)

Red wines, aged primarily in wood, rarely need decanting since frequent racking has removed most of their sediment before bottling. Lighter red and rosé wines also need no decanting since they throw only a negligible deposit in the bottle. Many speeded-up modern wines need no decanting either. (They have already been clarified by filtration.) Nor do the fortified wines —other than vintage port— need decanting. Since they are generally stored upright, their deposit will settle to the bottom where it can be easily left behind when the wine is poured.

For proper decanting, the bottle must be handled gently. (Any twisting, jiggling, or jerky up-and-down motions can stir up the sediment.) When done slowly and carefully, decanting can draw off all but half an inch or so of the clear bright wine. When done poorly, it can leave as much as two or three inches of a sediment-laden —and not a very drinkable— wine behind.

The decanting process can be vertical or horizontal. Vertical decanting stands the unopened bottle upright for a while to let the sediment drift slowly down to the bottom. (Depending on the degree of deposit, this may take several hours or several days.) The foil capsule covering the cork is then completely stripped away, to allow an unobstructed view of the bottle neck. To illuminate the neck, a light source is set up three or four inches away. (This might be a candle, a not-too-glaring flashlight, or perhaps a lightbulb.) Pouring begins with the light concentrated on the neck while the bottle itself rests lightly on the rim of the decanter. As the first trace of sediment begins to appear in the neck, pouring stops and the clear wine is ready to serve.

For horizontal decanting, the bottle is gently transferred from its horizontal rack in the cellar to a wine basket. The wine, still reclining in its basket, is then carried to the table and the bottle is tilted slightly so that the cork can be extracted. The uncorked bottle is then carefully lifted to enough of an angle so that the slow, smooth pouring may proceed.

NOTE: Some people miss the point of horizontal decanting entirely. They carry the bottle to the table horizontally in a basket, then stand it upright to pour, distributing the sediment throughout the wine. Or they use the basket for a white or a rosé wine, whose sediment is either negligible or nonexistent.

One can also decant by setting out the glasses beforehand in a neat row and smoothly pouring the wine in an unbroken stream. Particular deftness is required here since any abrupt interruption can rouse up the sediment in the wine.

Since decanting involves the transfer of wine from one container to another, some exposure to air is inevitable. The aeration may be beneficial or hazardous depending on the wine. Tight, tannic young red wines can be decanted well in advance to accelerate their breathing and soften their rough edges. Well-made mature reds should be decanted no more than an hour ahead. And venerable old red wines are best poured directly into the glass just before serving so as to retain their desirable qualities.

GLASSWARE

A wine glass that pleases the eye and feels good in the hand can enhance the wine's loveliest qualities and stimulate the anticipation of sipping. Clear, unadorned glass is best for showing off to advantage the wine's color and highlights. (Etched, frosted, or extravagantly decorated glass tends to detract.) When the wine is poured, the glass should feel well balanced in the hand, neither awkward nor top-heavy.

The glass itself should be uniform, with no distracting bubbles, striations, or irregularities. Thinner, more delicate glass with a smooth, finely polished rim and little or no bead (thickness) around the edge, seems to make the wine taste better. Coarser glass with a thickly rounded, obtrusive rim interferes with the pleasures of sipping. As a French restaurateur once said, "A grand Bordeaux in a bad glass is no longer a grand Bordeaux."

The components of the wine glass are the bowl, stem, and base. The bowl should have about a twelve-ounce capacity to provide enough breathing space for the wine's bouquet and aroma to develop. Huge, oversized bowls may look dramatic but they tend to distort the bouquet, while small bowls allow little breathing space and are usually overfilled so they're prone to spillage.

Best are the bowls shaped like partially opened tulips, ballooning out in the middle and tapering gently inward at the top. Their narrower diameter at the top concentrates the bouquet and aroma at the point where the nose meets the glass. As one vintner noted, "When wine is served in a water glass, it's pretty hard to catch a noseful."

The stem raises the bowl up and isolates the wine from the hand. (A hand on the bowl would obscure the view and warm a wine meant to be taken cool.) The stem also makes twirling and swirling possible, further releasing the bouquet. However, the stem creates a higher center of gravity, making the goblet inherently unstable so that spillage is always a possibility.

NOTE: When a white wine is spilled, club soda should be poured on the tablecloth as soon as possible. When a red wine is spilled, the spot should be daubed with some white wine or sprinkled with salt. In either case, the cloth is rinsed in cold water, then laundered normally.

Specially designed glasses, varying in shape, size, and height are available for Burgundies, Bordeaux, Rieslings, Chardonnays, Chiantis, and other wines. Simplifying matters is an all-purpose wineglass, which stands six to eight inches tall, with about a three-inch stem. Its bowl is about three inches in diameter with a capacity of twelve ounces or so. For red wines, the glass is filled about half full since they need the most aeration. For white and sparkling wines and rosés, the glass is filled two-thirds to the top since these wines need no breathing.

NOTE: For casual table wines with straightforward fruity flavors, ordinary water glasses will do. (Such wines include light Zinfandels, light Chiantis, lesser Beaujolais, some Chenin Blancs, and jug wines in general.) For picnics and other large informal gatherings, where not-very-high-caliber wines are served, knock-about plastic wineglasses might be made available.

Sherries are traditionally served in copitas, which are narrow, distinctive tulip-shaped, and short-stemmed glasses, with a three-or four-ounce capacity. Other fortified wines are served in short-stemmed chimney-style glasses whose capacity is four-to six-ounces. Port is often served in good-sized brandy snifters; the wine poured about a third full.

Preferable for Champagne and other sparkling wines are the tapering, narrow V-shaped glasses, known as flutes. Their narrow tops not only concentrate the bouquet but provide less surface area for the wine's evaporation. Tall enough for the energetic bubbles to rise, they prevent their quick dissipation and prolong the lively sparkle. (The bubbles in a good Champagne poured into a good glass, may continue to rise for half an hour or more.)

NOTE: Not recommended but often used for Champagne and other sparkling wines are squat, short-stemmed, wide-mouthed glasses, called coupes. With their small bowls and long stems, these glasses are generally unwieldy. They also let the wine warm too quickly diminishing its bouquet. And exposing too much of the wine's surface to air, they increase the flow of bubbles, making the wine go flat quickly. Moreover, their shallowness can often encourage spilling.

Caring for Glassware

Stemmed wineglasses are best stored by suspending them upside down by their bases in slotted racks. (Air circulates around the bowls, while their interiors remain free from dust.) Otherwise, the glasses should be stored on their bases, not on their fragile rims. (Storing them on the rims can also trap stale air inside the bowls. And the rim —in direct contact with a wooden shelf— can pick up the wood's distracting odors.)

Wineglasses are best rinsed in very hot water, swabbed with a brush, set in a rack to dry, then polished with a lint-free cloth. Soap or detergent may leave a microscopic residue, creating an off-flavor, and impairing a sparkling wine's effervescence. The decanters are washed and dried in the same manner.

MISCELLANY

The best ice buckets are made of such metals as stainless steel, silver, aluminum, or copper; all of which conduct the cold. Ice buckets made of crystal or glass are not as effective but allow the bottles and their labels to be seen.

Various artifacts, gadgets, and paraphernalia are available for serving the wine. There are decanters with built-in ice compartments for chilling; terra-cotta coolers, which must first be soaked in water; iceless chillers with insulated sides; and reusable gel packs kept in the freezer, then slipped sleevelike over the bottles.

There are also the wine cradles meant to ensure more precise control in decanting. And gadgets that pump out or vacuum out most of the air in a half-used bottle to slow down spoilage. In addition, there are special pouring spouts which prevent the wine's dripping by sending the last few drops back into the neck of the bottle. And there are the special coasters meant to keep the bottles from leaving untidy rings on the tablecloth.

The secret to a long life is to stay busy, get plenty of exercise and don't drink too much. Then again, don't drink too little.

—Hermann Smith-Johannson

8

TASTING

The finer the wine, the more deliberately it should be tasted.
When we approach a wine with our senses alert, we become aware not only
of its appearance and aroma but of its tactile quality, its "feel" or its texture.
We also sense the wine's inner structure, its very "bones," as it were.

To determine how a wine measures up, we look at it, sniff it, and sip it. The wine should meet certain basic requirements: it should be attractive to look at and pleasant to smell, while demonstrating fruit and roundness along with a reasonable degree of acidity.

Looking at the Wine

One of the loveliest attributes of a wine is its color, which can also tell us about its health and age. To observe the color, we pour the wine into an unadorned glass and hold the glass against a white background (a tablecloth, napkin, or even a sheet of white paper). We tilt the bowl at a 45-degree angle so that the liquid will form a neat oval pool.

We look down into —not up at— the wine, noting its color from the shallower edge to the center. In a young red wine, the color is bright, even, and consistent; in an older red, it is more tawny. A rosé should be pinkish. (The presence of a yellowish cast or an overly pronounced orange tinge may indicate a defect.) White wines range in color from pale ash to amber, sometimes with a tint of green or silver. In either a red or a white wine, a slight brown edge implies too much oxidation, while a stronger brown indicates excessive age.

Clarity is another key to a wine's soundness; the wine should be clear and even throughout. Any hint of haziness, cloudiness, or murkiness indicates a problem. (If the bottle has been agitated and its sediment roused up, the condition may only be temporary.) Before any final judgments are made, the wine should be given a chance to rest and to settle down.

NOTE: Clarity was once a reliable clue to a wine's stability and health, but filtering can now produce a startling clarity in almost any wine.

After observing the wine's color, we consider its body or substance. Holding the stem of the glass between thumb and forefinger, we tilt the bowl slightly and spin the glass gently. The wine will swish up the sides, then trickle back down, forming streaks or paths known as "legs." Fairly uniform legs indicate a thicker wine; unevenly spaced legs mean a thinner one. The more slowly the legs descend, the fuller the wine's body. In wines of considerable viscosity or thickness, the slow, graceful, trickle-down patterns create nearly perfect arches, which the Germans call *kirchenfenster* or "church windows."

Sniffing the Wine

Sniffing is an integral part of tasting. To bring out the innate vapors of a wine, we fill the glass half-full to allow the aromatic compounds —the essences and ethers— to collect in the space above the liquid. (Filling the glass to the brim would cause the bouquet to float off in all directions.) To speed up the release of these volatile elements, we aerate the wine by spinning or swirling the glass. This opens up the aromatic constituents, thrusting them upward toward the nose for a fuller appreciation. Swirling, the French say, makes the wine "waltz."

Wines that benefit most from swirling are the red wines, richest in aromatic compounds. Lesser reds, rosés, and white wines, possessing fewer of these compounds, need little or no swirling. Champagne and other sparkling wines are never swirled; spinning the glass would destroy their already fragile effervescence.

Although most people believe the sense of taste is confined to the mouth, it is intrinsically linked to the sense of smell. Most experts agree that smell can tell us much more about a wine than its taste. Seventy-five percent of our enjoyment comes from the wine's aroma and bouquet. And no instrument is as sensitive to its nuances as the human nose. (To understand the role of the nose, take a sip of wine and hold it in your mouth for a moment. When you pinch your nostrils shut, the flavor will disappear. When you release your nostrils, the flavor returns.)

As we sniff, the wine's aromatic vapors travel up behind the soft palate at the back of the mouth, entering a narrow cavity high in the nostrils, There, they encounter the olfactory receptor cells, whose nerve endings pick up the aromatic message of the vapors and transfer it directly to the olfactory bulb of the brain. The brain then converts that message into electrical signals, which are interpreted as they are received.

To sniff the wine, we lower the nose into the glass, inhaling quickly and rather sharply to carry the fragrance to the nerve endings high in the nostrils. Then we swirl and sniff the wine once more. (By sniffing when the wine is first poured, then sniffing again after a few seconds of swirling, we can detect a world of difference in the aroma and bouquet.)

In considering the aroma and bouquet, we ask ourselves: Is the odor fresh and clean? Is the scent aromatic or flowery? Does it suggest herbs, earth, or fresh hay? Is the fragrance spicy, smoky, woody, or musky? Does the wine smell of fruit as it should? If it's a varietal, can we recognize the character of the predominant grape?

NOTE: Sniffing can also reveal such defects as corkiness, moldiness, or mustiness in the wine, along with a vinegary characteristic or another unpleasantness.

Sipping the Wine

After sniffing, we pause for a few moments to let the nose recover. Then we sip and hold the wine briefly in the mouth. We note its general shape and temperature. We consider its viscosity along with its texture, weight, and consistency. To reach as many taste buds as possible, we roll the wine slowly around in the mouth, turning it over and over. (Our taste buds are sensitive to four basic tastes: sweet, sour, bitter, and salty. Tasting a wine generally involves only the first three.) We can perceive the sweetness at the tip of the tongue, the acidity in the middle, and the bitterness at the back. In a good red wine, the sensation might be soft and nearly sweet at first, followed by some acidity; then we can discern the slightly bitter taste of its characteristic tannins.

As we sip, we ask ourselves: What is the wine like to taste and drink? Does it feel good in the mouth? Is the taste simple or complex? Dull or stimulating? Does the wine's flavor confirm what the aroma has indicated? We also think about the sugar-acid balance. A tart wine needs a bit of sweetness for balance; a sweet wine needs a degree of acidity to keep it from beoming cloying.

We consider the wine's flavor. Simplest and most immediately appealing are the fruit flavors which reflect the grape's character. Some wines actually taste grapy, while others suggest cherries, raspberries, peaches, etc. A definite grapiness indicates extreme youth. A more vinous taste suggests greater maturity. Some wines taste of eucalyptus, mint, or peppers. Others reflect the flavor of their soil (as evidenced in the earthiness of a Burgundy or the tanginess of a Chablis). And wines aged extensively in wood may carry an oaky flavor. After swallowing, we pause and note the aftertaste (the length of time the bouquet remains on the palate). Most desirable is an aftertaste that is long, lingering, and memorably flavored.

Although the tasting ritual can intensify a wine's charms, the sequence of looking, sniffing, and sipping can be varied in any way we choose. (After sniffing, we might reappraise the wine's color, then spin the glass again to take another sniff.) The emphasis should always be on the sensory rather than the cerebral. (Too much analysis only diminishes the here-and-now pleasures of a wine.) Some people dispense with the ritual entirely. As one fellow declared, "I don't care much about a wine's nose or its legs or even its full body, I just like the taste."

GOOD, GREAT, AND POOR WINES

Fine wines begin in the vineyard. Some claim that the key to a wine's greatness lies in its climate and weather. Others maintain that the "soil speaks," that the distinctiveness of a wine comes from the plot of land on which its grapes are grown. As one vintner said: "We seek to find harmony between the grape and its soil, so we can create the best aromatic expression of the wine." Yet paradoxically, great wines are almost always made under very difficult conditions. Those that demonstrate the greatest complexity and depth are associated with harsh climates and barren soils. It seems that whenever the vine's existence is challenged, it is able to develop a greater tenacity and stamina. The harder the vines have to struggle, the more likely they are to produce splendid wines. Grapes that are "stressed" often yield some of the greatest wines in the world.

Wine quality begins with the choice of the grape. The grapes must be selected judiciously; mediocre varieties can never make great wines. The grapes associated with excellence are the cabernet sauvignons, pinot noirs, chardonnays, and rieslings. The basic equipment of the winery is a stemmer-crusher, press, fermenting tank, and a number of oak casks. The establishment's design is secondary. As one distinguished wine maker noted, "You don't need fancy equipment. It just needs to be good and clean."

The refinement of a wine comes from the talent, judgment, and skills of the vintner and from his or her intense desire to create something fine and enduring. Quintessential wines have always been made by small wine makers with a passion for detail. These are the men and women who give their wines the close personal attention they demand. Such vintners have been unstinting in their dedication to every aspect of the wine-making process.

In a great wine, all the elements come together; their components are in the right proportion. In a beautifully balanced wine, no one component predominates. The wine's color, personality, and character cannot be improved upon. The wine displays extraordinary finesse, a tremendous concentration of ripe fruit, a lovely bouquet, and wonderful nuances of style. Such wines are meant to be savored. Impressive and memorable, they differ subtly from bottle to bottle, glass to glass, sip to sip. Each is fascinating and alive. The flavor lingers on. "So much is happening," one oenophile said, "you practically have to pick your way through." Great wines are endowed with the strength for a long life as well; they are able to combine the splendid freshness of youth with the grandeur of age.

NOTE: Although many of today's wines have become standardized products, the enjoyment of others revolves around the unexpected, the element of risk so there is always the possibility that the wine may be inconsistent. At times, even the biggest names or the rarest wines may disappoint.

Some wines may initially look good, smell good and taste good, while lacking the necessary internal structure, firmness, and texture. Such wines do not hold our interest for long. Exhibiting little bouquet, breed, or subtlety, they are meant for casual consumption. Then there are the wines that weren't very good to begin with. (They may have been made from immature vines or from overcropped grapes.) Excessive character makes some of these wines too assertive, while too little character makes others dull and monotonous.

Finally, there are the definitely out-of-balance and the outright poor wines. They may be too bland or bitter, excessively earthy or musty. For some, too much acidity makes them thin and tart, or sharp and unpalatable. Too little acidity makes others fat and flabby. Some wines with too little alcohol are watery and meager, while those with too much are clumsy and heavy.

An incorrectly made wine may be cloudy and short-lived; disagreeable in taste, unpleasant in bouquet, and unclean or "off" in its odor. A wine supposed to be dry may be almost sickeningly sweet. An overly oxidized wine may prove to be undrinkable, as may a wine long past its prime. A wine ruined by a bad cork will develop a moldy smell.

Another problem is an overdose of sulfur dioxide, the agent widely used in wine making both as a preservative and as an antioxidant. Employed in moderation, it imparts no smell or taste of its own. At higher levels, its presence may be felt as a light prickly sensation in the nose or as a faintly pasty, dried-out impression at the tip of the tongue. In excess the SO_2 overstimulates the nerve endings, anesthetizes the nose, and induces sneezing or a scratchy throat. It may also produce an acrid metallic odor and an unpleasant taste. (Sparkling wines are particularly susceptible to SO_2 since their bubbles quickly carry its odor to the nose.)

Judging a Sparkling Wine

In evaluating a sparkling wine, the key consideration is the base wine, not the bubbles. No amount of effervescence can improve a mediocre sparkling wine. And making an inferior wine sparkling only worsens it since the bubbles emphasize its flaws and make its defects more apparent. (The driest sparklers need the best base wines since there isn't any sweetness to mask their flaws.)

Sparkling wines range from light and delicate to full-bodied and strongly flavored. Some exhibit a dry elegance and finesse, while others are on the luscious and creamy side. Good Champagnes are characterized by a pronounced acidity and a delicate bouquet. (Since red and pink sparklers are by nature fuller in body and stronger in flavor, a delicate bouquet is of less importance to them.)

After evaluating the taste and aftertaste of the sparkling wine, we consider the character of its bubbles. They should be neither too few, making the wine flat, nor too many, making it frothy. We look for tiny persistent bubbles which gently prick the tongue. (Bigger bubbles burst out too explosively and quickly disappear.) Much more than a visual delight, the effervescence plays a significant role in our appreciation of the wine. Carrying the aroma and bouquet quickly to the nose, it clearly reveals the wine's flavor and enhances its desirable characteristics.

PROFESSIONAL TASTINGS

Tasting is an essential tool for people in the wine business, for the wine makers, shippers, wholesalers, wine merchants, restaurateurs, and those who regulate labeling, not to mention wine writers and critics. Brokers in Bordeaux taste the new wines in the spring —before wood extracts from the casks start to permeate— as they decide which wines they will buy or not buy.

Wine makers need to taste their still-fermenting wines at intervals. As one said, "I taste the wine every fourteen days to see how it is coming along. I wait until the sweetness and the acidity are in harmonious balance." The vintner, sampling a six-week-old wine, can tell if it has the staying power needed for special aging. And he tastes representative samples periodically to see if the wine is spending enough time in wood and glass.

Tasting is also an indispensable tool for the blender. In Beaujolais, one shipper tastes hundreds of wines in order to create his own distinctive blends. Sherry-makers sample and grade their wines to see which will be designated for a solera system and which will go into the general blends. For Champagnes, the secret of the great ones is in selecting the best batches for the wine's final assemblage.

Professional tasters seldom swallow the wine. Since alcohol releases the mechanisms that inhibit those parts of the brain responsible for recording new information and for exercising judgment, any excessive intake would numb the olfactory sense and upset the brain's delicate balance. The tasters need objectivity to do their job properly so they don't swallow the wine. Their ability to make distinctions is the key to their work.

Professional tasting involves swirling, sniffing, sipping, "chewing," and spitting. After swirling, the judge holds his nose four or five inches away from the rim of the glass to inhale the fragrance. Swirling again, he lowers his nose into the glass to take a second sniff. He paces his sniffs about half a minute apart so as not to dull the olfactory nerves. Taking a good mouthful of wine —at least half an ounce— he rolls it around in his mouth to analyze the flavor and other characteristics. Swishing the wine over his gums, teeth, and palate while pressing his tongue intermittently upward against his hard palate; he seems to be chewing it. As he balances the wine in his mouth, he sucks in a little air through slightly pursed lips as though whistling inward. (This aeration releases the flavor further.) As the warmth of the mouth brings out the wine's aromas and volatile compounds, he intensifies the experience by breathing down his nose. (This enables the vapors to pass through the olfactory bulb once more, extending the moment when the wine, air, nose, and palate come together.)

Some experts can identify a wine by its place of origin, vintage, and grape variety, but professionals who taste the product of a grower or a shipper every day, evaluate the wine not in relation to other wines but as to how it measures up to its own specific type. Particularly sensitive to the wine's aromas and flavors, they acquire a built-in memory of its bouquet and its body. Concentrating on a relatively narrow range, such professionals may know little about wines produced outside their own area of expertise. (When presented with a wine out of context in a blind tasting, they may be unable to distinguish a Pomerol from a Médoc, a California wine from a French wine or even an unfamiliar red wine from a white.)

A blind tasting is required as part of an examination given annually by the Company of Vintners, a London guild for a "Master of Wine" certificate. The examination, which lasts four days, includes written tests, essays, and an oral examination on enology, viticulture, marketing, and retailing. (Candidates must have five years of experience in working with wines and spirits.) For the tasting, each candidate is presented with a group of wines arranged in pairs: three reds, two whites, and a rosé. He or she is informed that one wine in each pair is from a known French district while the other is not French at all. After identifying the French wine and its district, the candidate must accurately describe its quality, area of production, vintage, state of maturity, and the grape variety or varieties in the blend. For each non-French wine, the candidate must name its country of origin. Participants who pass this complex and demanding examination are awarded the prestigious Master of Wine certificate.

WINE THIEVES AND BARREL TASTINGS

Wine thieves are devices designed to withdraw small quantities of wine for sampling from barrels, vats, or tanks. The earliest example was most likely a hollow reed inserted into the bunghole of a cask. (A finger placed over the reed's upper end held the wine inside. Lifting the finger released the wine.) Currently in use are siphons, pipettes, etc. Sherry makers employ a unique device called a *venencia*, which is a long flexible shaft with a cup at one end. The operator, the *venenciado,* dips the cup into the cask, fills it, and then with a flourish raises the shaft high in the air, pouring an accurate and steady stream of wine into the several small glasses he holds in his other hand. This gives the sherry, which thrives on oxidation, maximum exposure to air in a minimum amount of time. Barrel tastings are used to sample still-developing and unfined wines, which tend to be rough and murky. One wine merchant described these tastings as "a lonely dirty business," adding that, "someone has to do it."

NOTE: Professional tasters, who spend much of their time in the semidarkness of bone-chilling cellars, are subject to various occupational hazards. These include deadened palates, swollen tongues, and mouths that feel like sandpaper from their prolonged exposure to the tannins in red wines.

TASTING COMPETITIONS

Tasting competitions and awards are designed to evaluate and promote certain wines. Retailers, restaurateurs, wine consultants, wine writers, etc. serve as the judges. These tastings are generally blind so that the wines may be judged on their own merits. (Knowing what one is drinking inevitably affects his or her response.)

In a blind tasting, the label is masked by covering it with a paper rectangle, or by wrapping the bottle in foil. If the bottle's shape is a giveaway, it might be covered with a corrugated cardboard cylinder or a paper or plastic bag taped shut at the neck. (The coverings should always be uniform in appearance.) A number is then assigned to identify each bottle. (If the wines are to be poured beforehand, the glasses may be numbered to correlate with the numbers on the bottles.) Since tasting competitions usually involve many wines, they are generally divided into more manageable groups of ten or so, which are known as "flights."

The judges first evaluate the wines for their overall quality, rarely needing to sample them all since they can eliminate those that are inadequate in bouquet and aroma by simply sniffing them. Then they rate the remaining wines according to their strengths and weaknesses. (The judges take no food during these sessions, although wine is generally meant to be served with food.)

NOTE: In the competitions, wines with lush, rich, fruity qualities and an intensity of alcohol often push the more elegant and subdued examples into the background. Those that take the prizes are not necessarily desirable for drinking however, nor do they always go well with food. As one observer noted, "Too much wine is being made these days to be tasted, not to be drunk."

A wine judging is at best an inexact exercise, a series of fleeting impressions. There are few objective criteria; the individual responses of the judges are essentially subjective. Those judges vary in their ability to taste the diverse compounds in a wine. Their responses are also highly ephemeral. A wine can taste one way in the morning and another way in the afternoon. Even professionals may contradict themselves if asked to judge the same group of wines two weeks apart.

The judges all have different approaches, temperaments, and perceptions, and also different thresholds of sensitivity. Some are more aware than others as to how the wine opens in the glass, and are generally more receptive to its subtleties and nuances. A wine that seems dry to one person may seem sweet to another. One judge may find the acids crisp and delicious while another considers them sour and painful. One person may find the tannins obnoxious, while another sees them as important and profound. One might find a high-alcohol wine rich and lush while another considers it harsh and unbalanced. One taster, sampling a wine, described it as "heavy and meaty, with earthy flavors," while another called the same wine "superbly elegant." Reviewing a Napa Valley Chardonnay, one wine publication called it "smooth, concentrated, and well behaved [with] deep fruit flavors and a sense of intensity;" another publication described the wine as "bitterly acid, austere, and lean… [with] no character and no soul."

Judges also have their good and bad days. A number of factors can affect their responses: the time of day, their physical condition, what they ate or drank earlier. Judges are also susceptible to sensory overload and palate fatigue. Although they taste only tiny quantities and seldom swallow, the number of wines they can deal with effectively is limited. (Two or three hours of concentrated tasting can numb even the finest palate.) Yet the judges are often called on to sample more than a hundred wines in four hours with only brief intervals of rest. (They may however be able to eliminate half the wines by the smell alone.)

PLANNING A TASTING

Group tastings are a fine way to learn about grape varieties, vintages, and wine-producing countries. They also make it possible to sample many wines in a short period of time. And when the wines are considered side by side, their similarities and differences can become more apparent. The subtle distinctions between them can be observed as well.

A tasting can be held to instruct or entertain. The first generally does not involve swallowing, while the second does. To keep matters manageable, the number of participants should be limited to six or eight. To prevent sensory overload, the number of wines should be kept to five or six. The wines may be red or white, sparkling or fortified, but should all be in the same category or of somewhat equal quality since there isn't much point in comparing a French Burgundy with a German Mosel or a fortified sherry with a Bordeaux table wine.

NOTE: The tasting may also be horizontal (comparing wines from the same vintage) or vertical (comparing the same wine from a number of vintages).

To keep the nose and taste buds undistracted by other tastes and smells, the wine tasting should be held after a stretch without food. Avoided beforehand should be anything that might inhibit the ability to taste, such as acidy juices and highly seasoned or other palate-numbing foods. Also to be avoided is anything that might detract from or interfere with the wine's bouquet, aroma, and flavor such as cooking odors, the smell of flowers, heavy perfumes, colognes, aftershave lotions, cigarettes, pipes, etc. (Serious tasters have even been known to sniff the inside of the glass before the wine is poured to check for any lingering detergent odors.)

At a serious tasting, the participants say little and speak only in moderate tones to exclude as many distractions as possible. To eliminate the power of suggestion, they will avoid frowning, smiling, or showing similar responses until all the wines have been sampled.

Each guest can pour his or her own wine or there can be someone to do it for them. The wines themselves should be set out in the sequence in which they will be tasted: white wines preceding the reds, dry wines before the sweet, the light bodied before the heavier bodied. The position of each wine in the sequence is important, since one set of impressions can distort the next: a hard wine can make one that follows seem softer than it is; a concentrated wine will not only overshadow a more delicate one but might dull the palate as well.

Younger wines should generally be tasted before older ones. (The younger's assertive nature and stronger taste can overwhelm its older, smoother counterpart.) When wines are the same age, the least expensive should be tasted first. (However, there are some exceptions: an elegant wine, sampled earlier in the session, will more likely create a better impression.)

NOTE: All the bottles should be uncorked at the same time so that all the wines can be aerated evenly.

A wine tasting generally lasts two or three hours. Professional tasters find midmornings —at about ten o'clock or so— best since the palate is then at its freshest. A social tasting can be scheduled as a lengthened cocktail hour running from five-thirty to seven-thirty, or as an after-dinner event. The earlier tastings might be preceded by a bowl of bland soup and some plain crackers so as not to startle the empty stomach with a succession of wines. Accompanying the tasting itself can be neutral breads or crackers and bland, palate-cleansing cheeses, such as a Gruyère cheese or a mild Cheddar, which leave no significant aftertaste.

NOTE: When the participants have gone without substantial food for some time, an assortment of hors d'oeuvres, pâtés, cheeses, and nuts can be served afterward. Sessions held later in the evening might be followed by cups of tea or coffee and a good, rich cake.

Tasting Themes

The tasting needs a unifying theme to create some sort of focus. When wines of different countries are tasted together, it is better as a rule to concentrate on those pressed from the same grape variety so that the variations produced by their climate, soil, and style of vinification can be detected more readily.

The tasting possibilities are countless. A few themes follow:

1. Compare red or white table wines from several countries, made from the same grape and within the same price range, such as Cabernet Sauvignons from California, Romania, Israel, and Australia, or Rieslings from Germany, Alsace, Chile, and New York State.
2. Compare a group of white wines from a single country, such as Italy (Orvieto, Soave, Verdicchio, Frascati, Lacryma Christi) or France (an Alsatian Sylvaner, a Muscadet, a Pouilly-Fumé, a white Bordeaux). Or compare a group of red wines from Italy (Valpolicella, Barbera, Barolo, Chianti, etc).
3. Compare several wines from one geographic region such as the Chiantis of Tuscany, the Riojas of Spain, the Zinfandels of northern California, or the Rieslings of the Rheingau.
4. Compare three or four red or white French Burgundies from the same vintage but from different communes.
5. Compare a group of red California varietals, such as Zinfandels, Pinot Noirs, or Cabernet Sauvignons, made by different producers. Or similarly compare a group of California white varietals, such as Chenin Blancs, Sauvignon Blancs, Chardonnays, and Johannisberg Rieslings.
6. Compare three New York varietals, red or white, with three of its generics.
7. Compare three or four California sparkling wines with three or four French Champagnes.
8. Compare several vintage Champagnes, made by different producers, with several nonvintage Champagnes.
9. Compare a group of white wines representing different German regions (Rhine, Mosel, Nahe, etc.).
10. Compare the Bordeaux wines of one region, such as the Médoc, with those of another, such as St.-Estèphe, Pauillac, St.-Julien, or Margaux.
11. Compare a varietal such as a Cabernet Sauvignon from different California counties in the north (Napa, Sonoma, Mendocino and Santa Clara).
12. Compare the wines of a single vintage from several vineyards in a major Bordeaux commune, such as St.-Émilion, Pomerol, Graves, St.-Julien, St.-Estèphe, or Pauillac.

13. Compare three Auslese wines from the same region in Germany, but from three different growers.
14. Compare two or three white Burgundies from the same vintage and the same vineyard or commune, but produced by different shippers.

Rating Systems

Various wine rating systems have been devised to tabulate the judgments of the eye, nose, and palate. Listed on a tally sheet, they assign a specific number of points to each of the wine's characteristics. The sheet may also provide space for jotting down a descriptive word or two, which can heighten one's perceptions and make his or her responses more precise. (See the Vocabulary of Taste.)

The rating systems employed are based on either a 10-point or a 20-point scale, with the latter allowing for the recognition of more nuances in the wine. One 10-point scale assigns 1 point to each of the following characteristics: appearance, color, aroma, volatile acidity, total acid, sugar-acid balance, body, flavor, bitterness, and general impression.

A 20-point tally allows up to 2 points for color, 2 for appearance, 6 for the olfactory characteristics (aroma and bouquet), 2 for flavor, 5 for gustatory characteristics (sweetness, bitterness, acidity), 2 for overall quality, and 1 for "feel" or texture. A wine scoring 9 to 12 points is considered acceptable here, while 13 to 16 is an average score, and 17 to 20 is outstanding. Another 20-point system allows up to 5 points for flavor, 4 for bouquet, 4 for general quality, 3 for balance, 2 for clarity, and 2 for acidity.

One specific 20-point scorecard reads:

Appearance: Brilliant—2, Clear—1, Cloudy—0
Color: Correct—2, Somewhat off—1, Distinctly off—0
Aroma and Bouquet: Varietal—3, Distinct but not varietal —2, Vinous—1 (One point can be added for bottle bouquet and 2 points can be subtracted for any odd or off-odors.)
Sweetness: Normal for wine type—1, Too much or too little—0
Total Acidity: Normal for wine type—2, Somewhat high or low—1, Too high or too low—0
Flavor: Desirable for type—2, Deficient or slightly off—1, Distinctly off—0
Astringency and Bitterness: Normal—2, Slightly high—1, Distinctly high—0
Body: Normal for wine type—1, Too much or too little—0
Texture: Satisfactory—1, Unsatisfactory—0
Overall Quality: Impressive—2, Slight—1, Undistinguished—0

NOTE: Although these rating systems seem to suggest that a wine's quality is precisely identifiable, the conversion of sensuous experience into quantifiable data is usually more personal than scientific.

The primary purpose of a tasting is to decide which wines are liked most and which are liked least. At the end of the session, the group can be polled by a show of hands to discover which were its favorites and which were the least preferred. Or else the participants might vote for their favorites in order of preference; with 3 points for first place, 2 for second and 1 for third.

At a blind tasting, the voting should be done when the wines have been sampled, but not yet identified. The coverings are then removed to reveal the labels. (A list of the wines tasted, keyed to the numbers on the bottles, may be distributed after all the wines have been rated.)

Ingredients and Supplies

The following items are needed for a wine tasting:

1. The wines to be sampled.
2. A good-sized table or a series of smaller tables to hold the bottles.
3. White cloths to cover the tables.
4. One or more reliable corkscrews.
5. Stemmed wineglasses.
6. Glasses and pitchers of drinking water, or bottles of mineral water (to clear the palate between sips and help to relieve palate fatigue).
7. Pitchers of water to rinse out the glasses and a large bucket for discarding the rinse water.
8. Paper napkins for drying the rinsed glasses and a trash basket for discarding them. (An ample supply of paper napkins is needed in case of spills.)
9. A spittoon bucket if the wine is not to be swallowed.
10. Neutral bread, bread sticks, melba toast, or water crackers.
11. A bland cheese (If it isn't presliced or diced, knives and cutting boards should be provided.)
12. For early sessions, a bland soup to serve with crackers before the tasting. For later sessions, hors d'oeuvres, pâtés, cheeses, and nuts along with coffee and cake to serve after the tasting.
13. Pencils and tally sheets or small pads of paper for note taking (to be distributed before the tasting begins).
14. A list of the wines presented, providing such pertinent information as the wine's full name, its producer, shipper, vintage year, shop where purchased, and the amount paid (to be distributed after the tasting).

NOTE: If the tasting is blind, the supplies should include paper rectangles to mask the labels and aluminum foil, corrugated cardboard cylinders, or uniform plastic or paper bags to cover the bottles, as well as the tape to fasten these in place, along with felt-tipped pens for numbering the bottles.

To determine the amount of wine needed for the tasting, count on six to twelve samples in each bottle, depending on the type of wine and whether or not it's to be swallowed. An ounce of wine is just enough for a few swallows although two ounces may be better. (Some suggest providing half a bottle per person of all the wines combined.)

Glass stemware is best for tastings. (It can be borrowed, rented, or purchased.) The glasses themselves should be uniform in size and shape so as not to introduce extraneous elements into the comparisons. (If the glasses do vary, the larger ones can be used for red wines and the smaller ones for white wines.) It's a good idea to provide a glass for each participant or two glasses if both red and white wines are to be sampled. (Each glass can be labeled at its base with the name of the guest to avoid any confusion.)

To defray the cost of the tasting, a BYOB (bring your own bottle) event can be organized. Here, the host or hostess sets the theme and asks each participant to bring one or two bottles which represent a given country, vintage, or price range. (To avoid duplication, a list is made of the individuals responsible for each wine.) Participants must then deliver the bottles in sufficient time for the red wines to settle down and the white wines to be chilled.

In a BYOB variation, each participant contributes to a dinner by preparing a dish and providing the accompanying wine. To round out the meal, the host or hostess provides a dessert wine or some vintage port. (Variety is ensured and duplication avoided by working out the menu and the choice of the wines in advance.)

NOTE: People have also organized themselves into wine-tasting clubs which meet regularly on a rotating basis at one another's homes, either once a month or once every other month.

THE DEVELOPMENT OF TASTE

Wine has inspired a wide range of personal preferences. Some people like their wines red, others white; some prefer them dry, others sweet. Some seek out the more assertive examples, while others like them milder.

Habit and culture also play their part. The Spaniards, who take sherries with their food, prefer them light and dry. The sweet sherries are produced mainly for export (brown and cream sherries were created specifically for the Anglo-Saxon market.) As the Spanish say, "We ship them sweet, but drink them dry." The Italians, on the other hand, vinify their Orvietos dry for export, but take them semisweet at home. The French drink their luscious Beaumes-de-Venise as an apéritif while others consider it an after-dinner drink.

The development of individual taste is an evolutionary process. Fine wines are subtle and demanding; they take time to appreciate. The beginner needs to work his way up to them gradually. At first, he wants his wines immediately accessible, preferring his reds robust, full-bodied, and slightly sweet, and his whites and rosés fresh and fruity. (Softness in a wine is much appreciated in the United States, accounting for the current success of the Merlots.) As our palate develops, we become more accustomed to the idea of complexity. We begin to find that a degree of dryness is necessary and desirable in a wine. As we move on from the simpler to the more intricate examples, we come to appreciate the tartness and the moderate bitterness produced by the tannins and the other compounds.

NOTE: A wine needn't be dry to be good. In Germany and France, a wine's sweetness is considered a valuable asset. The Germans base their quality ratings on ripeness and sugar levels; the sweeter the wines, the more costly they are. And among the most expensive French wines are the sweet and celebrated noble rots.

There are also different kinds of sweetness. Harvesting the grapes later than usual concentrates their sugars and produces richer and more intense wines. The extraordinary botrytized wines, made in a number of countries, are notable for their intriguing interplay of intense sweetness and balancing acidity. Lesser wines may be sweetened artificially; these often create an unpleasant, sticky feeling in the mouth. And what is perceived as sweet can differ from what is actually sweet. A wine with 1.5 percent residual sugar may not seem sweet if its sugars are balanced out by its acidity.

Tastes in wine can be contradictory. In the United States, people talk dry but often drink sweet. Accustomed to the taste of soda pop, they prefer a degree of sweetness in their wine. (The most popular examples all contain some residual sugar.) At the same time, many Americans turn away from openly sweet wines, equating sweetness with self-indulgence and a lack of character. In an attempt to accommodate this contradiction, French vintners have begun to reduce the sugars in some of their wines. In Entre-Deux-Mers, Monbazillac, and Jurançon, they often pick their grapes prematurely to produce lighter, crisper wines. The Germans, also trying to appeal to the large American market, are vinifying some of their wines *trocken* (dry) or *halb-trocken* (half-dry). They ferment out all the sugar for the former, and retain an almost imperceptible degree of sweetness for the latter. The finest German wines, however, continue to stress sweetness.

In the United States, before the 1980s, red wines were more popular than white wines. A preoccupation with fitness and health then generated an interest in lighter beverages leading to an increased emphasis on white wines. Taking advantage of this trend, various countries have increased their white wine production in areas normally known for their red wines. (Current reports citing the cardiac and the general health benefits of red wines seem to be reversing the trend.)

Although white wines appear to be lighter than red wines, they can in fact be more fattening. A wine's calories come primarily from its alcohol content, not its pigmentation. The calorie count is established by multiplying the alcohol by two. Since 0.5 percent alcohol represents one calorie, an ounce of table wine with 12.5 percent alcohol contains twenty-five calories; a three and a half-ounce glass adds up to some eighty calories. Fortified wines, higher in their alcohol, average forty-four to fifty-five calories an ounce. Depending on the fortified wine, a 3-ounce serving can range from one hundred twenty to one hundred seventy calories. (These wines, however, are usually consumed in smaller quantities.)

NOTE: Developed for the diet-conscious have been wines which are lighter in calories. The grapes here are harvested early while their sugars remain low, or else they are allowed to ripen fully and then some of their wine alcohol is processed out. In either case, these modifications compromise the wine's character and flavor. People, who wish to lower their caloric intake would do better by eliminating the extra fats, sugars, and starches from their daily diets, than by seeking out wines that are lower in calories.

🍇 🍇 🍇

9

MATCHING WINE WITH FOOD

Wine and food are a great combination; each brings out the best in the other.
But in matching them, certain considerations apply. Dry wines are generally
more appropriate with food; their higher acidity stimulates the palate and
cleanses it between bites. Sweet wines appease the appetite and are usually
best with desserts or on their own. There are always exceptions. Only through
experience can we discover which combinations work best. After all, the most
suitable wine is the one we feel like drinking with the food we feel like eating.

Wine and food need a balanced relationship so they can complement rather than
compete with one another. In matching the two, common sense is the main
requirement. Light wines call for light dishes; delicately styled wines call for
delicately flavored dishes. The heavier the food, the heavier the wine. (Full-bodied
wines hold their own with assertively flavored foods by cutting across their richness and robustness.) Delicate sauces require light-bodied wines, while richer
sauces need more assertive ones. And, as a general rule, lighter wines are best
served at the beginning of the meal and heavier ones at the end.

Although conventional wisdom calls for pairing white wines with white meat,
poultry, or fish, and for pairing red wines with beef or lamb, this narrows the
options too much and does not always work. Compatibility with food is based on
the character of the wine, not its color. A delicately nuanced light red would be
overwhelmed by a platter of barbecued ribs, while it would go well with a lobster
dish. And although a white wine is usually undone by a dark, pungent pot roast,
such a wine —if sturdy and full-bodied— might be just right with a robust game
bird, or even a thick, juicy steak.

Red wines range in character from the light and fruity to the medium-bodied
and on to the full-bodied, strong, robust, and assertive. Lighter bodied reds,
minimal in their tannins, go best with the blander meats such as pork and veal.
Medium bodied and more elegant reds are suitable for most meat dishes, but can
also accompany sauced poultry, rich vegetable dishes, and fresh-tasting cheeses.

While moderate to robust red wines are best suited to beef and lamb; they also go well with duck and goose, casseroles, ragouts, and cassoulets. As for the rich, concentrated, intensely flavored reds, their assertiveness calls for such substantial foods as steaks, roasts, and game dishes.

White wines are generally thought of as lively and light, with a freshness and an acidity meant to enhance light meals. But white wines run the gamut from the simple, light, and refreshing to the medium dry with a moderate acidity, on to the subtle and multifaceted and the big, robust, and powerful, as well as the full-bodied and sweet. Light dry white wines with delicate flavors can be enjoyed on their own, either as apéritifs or as sipping wines. Crisp and pleasantly acid whites go well with light fish preparations, light pastas, and other light dishes. Whites with good acidity can freshen the flavors of pork or veal while fuller-bodied examples are meant for richer pastas, sauced or grilled fish, and simply seasoned poultry. The fruitier, sweeter white wines meanwhile are generally compatible with highly seasoned or spicy foods. (The delicate nuances of a subtle dry white wine would be destroyed by such foods.) Most white wines tend to lose their charms when paired with robust foods, but those with a more pronounced character and a fair amount of body can stand up to and enhance a fairly heavy or a highly seasoned dish. (Best for spicy Mexican and Indian dishes and for the slight sweetness of certain Chinese and Thai dishes are off-dry white wines such as Rieslings, Gewürztraminers, and Chenin Blancs. Another good accompaniment for these is a fino sherry.)

Luscious white wines, too sweet and intense for food, are best served with desserts or on their own. These wines include Sauternes, late-harvest German and California Rieslings, Italian vin santos, and Alsatian VTs and SGNs. Yet the balancing acidity of a luscious noble rot makes it more versatile than one might expect. When served at the start of a meal, its botrytized sweetness can complement the richness of a pâté de foie gras.

Areas producing primarily red wines have served these not only with rich meats, game, and sausage, but with fish and seafood. In Bordeaux, where red wine is king, red wines often accompany fish-based meals. The French are well known for using them in sauces for salmon, tuna, and halibut; in St.-Émilion, a robust red wine is a key ingredient in a typical sturgeon dish. On the coast of Spain, red wines are taken with fish and shellfish; while in Portugal, robust reds are paired with sturdy, freshly cooked sardines. And the Corsicans like to accompany their highly seasoned fish dishes with local rosé wines.

In areas where white wines predominate, these are often matched with heartier meats and game. Rhône Valley residents pair their robust full-flavored white wines with spicy dishes and pungent cheeses. In Burgundy, a rich Meursault has been served with beef. In Germany, white wines are taken with lamb chops, bacon, ham, and sausage. In Alsace, full-bodied Gewürztraminers often accompany its typically strong, savory platters of ham and roast goose. And in Reims and Épernay, it is not unusual for Champagne to accompany every course of the meal.

Regional dishes are often developed with local wines in mind. In Sancerre, an innkeeper says, "We make very light sauces for our meat and fish dishes so that our light local wines go with everything." In Greece, the piquancy of a retsina is a perfect foil for the richness and spiciness of its food. In Spain, the brisk nutty flavor of a fino or a manzanilla sherry combines well with tapas, seafood, and other local specialties. (Americans take such wines chilled as apéritifs.) Well suited to Mediterranean dishes, which characteristically feature garlic, herbs, and olive oil are the sunny wines from southern Italy, France, and Spain.

In pairing a dish with a wine, other considerations are the seasoning, sauce, marinade, or stuffing. A chicken prepared with mushrooms can be matched with an earthy Pinot Noir; a chicken prepared with dill can take a herbal Sauvignon Blanc. A robust dish with an intense, spicy brown sauce calls for a fuller bodied wine. A highly acid tomato sauce needs a wine that is relatively high in acid. A heavy cream sauce requires a strong, dry wine, while a slightly sweet sauce (made from a meat stock or a butter-and-cream reduction) does best with a wine that is not austerely dry.

NOTE: A dish cooked with wine should be accompanied by a wine of a similar style: a red Burgundy served with boeuf bourguignon, a Madeira with a sauce madère, a red Bordeaux or other Cabernet Sauvignon with a dish featuring a bordelaise sauce.

Still other considerations in matching wines with food are the cooking method, time of the year, and character of the meal. Lighter wines are best served with steamed foods; fuller wines with grilled or barbecued foods. The characteristically light food of summer can be accompanied by a tart white wine or a rosé. The bigger, richer meals of winter call for the heartier reds. Formal occasions require more splendid and complex wines, while best for picnics and other casual get-togethers are the simple, ingenuous and easy-to-drink wines.

NONFRIENDLY FOODS

A number of foods don't lend themselves readily to pairing with wine. Artichokes, asparagus, and citrus fruits can interfere with one's sense of taste. Artichokes can make a wine taste metallic or cloying; asparagus tends to dull the palate while the high acidity of citrus fruits and fruit cocktails can create a deadening effect. Some have also suggested that any foods involving chocolate should also be avoided since chocolate interferes with the taste of most wines. (Yet sweet fortified wines, sweet Champagnes and sweet California Muscats have accompanied cakes and desserts featuring chocolate.)

To be avoided generally as well are the uncommonly strong-flavored or highly seasoned foods, which can overpower a wine. These include foods pickled in vinegar or seasoned with horseradish, cloves, mints, certain mustards and hot peppers. Also to be shunned are pungent cocktail sauces and dips containing Tabasco or Worcestershire sauce, along with hot curries and spicy salsas.

NOTE: It is generally risky to serve a delicate sparkling wine with dishes prepared with considerable amounts of garlic, forceful spices, or other aromatics. Yet a robust everyday table wine can hold its own with such assertive dishes.

BEFORE THE MEAL

There are two schools of thought about serving spirits before a meal featuring wine. One school maintains that a cocktail before dinner can give the diners a lift and make them more receptive to the food that follows and also to one another. (Cocktails laden with fruit and sugar, however, can take away the desire for food and can make a dry wine served later seem harsh and bitter.)

The other school of thought holds that grape juice and malt spirits are incompatible, that hard liquor numbs the palate, dulls the senses, and impedes the appreciation of the wine. As a noted French restaurateur once observed, "After a cocktail or two, one couldn't possibly tell a great Bordeaux from a bottle of red ink."

To prime the palate and prepare it for the foods to follow, a more appropriate introduction to the meal might be a well-chilled, low-alcohol table wine (dry or medium dry), a dry sparkling wine; or a crisp fortified wine with a lively assertiveness, such as a dry vermouth or a fino sherry. Other possibilities are a not-too-sweet rosé or a wine-based apéritif, characterized by a certain tanginess and zest.

THE ALL–PURPOSE WINE

Although rosés and sparkling wines are often thought of as "all–purpose," they are not quite flexible enough to be served throughout the meal. Rosés are often selected by those reluctant to choose between a white wine and a red. Yet rosé wines are more of a compromise than a solution. The easy–to–drink rosés, which are lighter colored, lighter bodied, and attractive to look at, can be taken with hors d'oeuvres, fish dishes, lightly flavored foods, and the generally lighter meals. And while the richer, fruitier rosés go well with lighter meats, they do not do very much for the heavier ones.

As for sparkling wines, their specific character will determine their suitability for the dish. While the crisp clean dryness of a brut Champagne brings out the brininess of oysters and goes well with canapés, it is generally too acid for most dishes and hardly suitable for roasts or game. And while a medium–dry sparkler with a fresh lively taste and crisp fruit can complement fish and shellfish (as well as ham, turkey, lamb, duck and chicken dishes with rich but delicate sauces), it doesn't work well with the meat dishes of a greater richness and gravity. (These call for sparkling wines with big, weighty flavors, such as a fuller–bodied Blanc de Noirs.) Most appropriate for light desserts and delicate cheeses are the smooth, aromatic extra dry Champagnes which demonstrate a degree of sweetness. And while the more substantial pink Champagnes (sparkling rosés) can be paired with such heavier dishes as a rack of lamb, the lighter ones are best served at the end of the meal. (They're particularly good with fresh fruit and light creamy cheeses.)

With the Meal

Hors d'Oeuvres

Appropriate accompaniments for hors d'oeuvres are the appetite-whetting wines, the light-bodied Champagnes and other sparklers. When crisp and dry but not too fruity, they can complement the savory appetizers without overshadowing them. Their fresh acidity goes particularly well with the smoky, salty foods which are often served before dinner; they set off the richness of caviar quite nicely. Appropriate at the start of the meal as well are the dry, crisply acid white wines, characterized by a certain steeliness or a bone-dry tanginess.

The specific nature of the hors d'oeuvres will determine their most suitable accompaniments. Raw vegetables can take a light white wine, such as a Chenin Blanc or a Pinot Grigio. Fish-based appetizers generally call for crisp and fruity dry whites, while meat-based appetizers go well with a light red such as a dryish or moderately sweet rosé. Stuffed mushrooms, salami, salted almonds, and ripe olives harmonize well with dry vermouths and Madeiras. A fino or amontillado sherry goes well with Spanish tapas which feature tidbits of sausage, ham, prawns, and mussels, while an oloroso sherry can be taken with the more aggressively flavored tapas such as smoked squid.

The First Course

Suitable for countering the salinity of oysters on the half shell and for rounding out their acidity are the full but dry white wines. The stony flavor and flinty bite of a fine Chablis provides a wonderful contrast to the brininess of the oysters. Other good accompaniments for raw shellfish are a brut Champagne, musky Muscadet, a St. Véran, crisp white Graves, or Sauvignon Blanc, Sémillon, Aligoté, or a Pinot Gris. Refreshing with steamed mussels or clams are the Portuguese vinho verdes, Italian Vernaccias, or manzanilla sherries. Paired with smoked salmon might be a dry white wine, a light red, a dry sherry, a Madeira, or a Marsala. (Some people even prefer a rich Sauternes with their smoked salmon.)

Suitable for rich pâtés are the dry to fullish white wines of moderate acidity. Good with duck and rabbit pâtés are dry white Swiss wines as well as light-bodied reds and rosés. Pâtés also respond to the intensity of an older, sweeter German Riesling (a Spätlese or an Auslese). Also providing the necessary counterpoint to foie gras is a sweet French Beaumes-de-Venise. (And some maintain that only the intense sweetness of a luscious Sauternes can moderate the excesses of a pâté.)

Soup

Since soups run the full gamut from light broths to almost stews, they can be accompanied by a wide variety of wines. A wonderful partner for consommés and most clear light soups is a medium-dry Champagne. Also appropriate are dryish fortified wines, such as fino or amontillado sherries or sercial Madeiras, served at cellar temperatures. A light white wine might accompany pumpkin soup, a medium-dry white matched with a rich oyster-spinach broth, while a medium sherry or tawny port is fine with onion soup. For a rich bouillabaisse (fisherman's stew), it might be a weighty white wine, a light to medium red, or a dry rosé. Other fish-soup possibilities are fino or amontillado sherries and verdelho Madeiras. Paired with a lobster consommé or a cream-based soup might be a not-too-dry sparkling wine or a medium-bodied white, such as a Chardonnay. And appropriate with a thick, hearty soup might be Pinot Noir or other dry red wine.

Fish and Seafood

Generally needed to cut through the oiliness of fish dishes is a wine with some acidity. White wines —usually more acid than the reds— have a special affinity for seafood. Most suitable are those that are crisp, clean, and tangy or somewhat flinty, with a degree of fruitiness. Other good accompaniments are light-or medium-bodied sparkling wines, dry finos, or manzanilla sherries. (A fino served ice cold can add a bracing bite to the taste of the fish.) Although the tannins that characterize red wines and rosés clash with delicate fish and seafood dishes, a fruity red wine can accompany the more strongly flavored ones.

Depending on the specific character of the fish and how it's prepared, the accompanying wine might be light and delicate or full-bodied and vigorous. For a light fish —simply broiled, baked, grilled or steamed— the wine might be a crisp dry Aligoté, Sauvignon Blanc, Chardonnay, Sancerre, Riesling, or Chenin Blanc. It might be a Swiss Chasselas, a Seyval Blanc, vinho verde, or Muscadet. Or it might be a Verdicchio, Sancerre, Chablis, Champagne, Pouilly-Fuissé or German Spätlese. Big-flavored saltwater fish such as salmon, swordfish, halibut, monkfish and bluefish require flavorful wines on the mellow but not the sweet side. These include such fruity young reds as a light Pinot Noir, Sangiovese, or Beaujolais and sturdy white wines such as a Chablis or a Pinot Gris. Baked or grilled salmon can be paired with a Pinot Noir. Rich seafood dishes with thick sauces and the more complex seafood stews call for assertive wines exhibiting a fair amount of fruit and body. A fish in cream sauce can find a perfect partner in a high-alcohol Chardonnay with plenty of body and flavor. A grilled salmon in a béarnaise sauce can be paired with a big-bodied white or a lighter red wine.

For oyster and shellfish dishes, a fine accompaniment might be a Sauvignon Blanc, a Sémillon or Pinot Gris, a Chablis, Sancerre, or white Graves. Mussels, clams, and shrimp can take a French Muscadet or an Aligoté, as well as an Italian Verdicchio. Grilled shrimp and vegetables go well with an Italian Soave or a Greek retsina. Shellfish prepared with tomato-based sauces are best with red wines and rosés. Full-bodied, high-acid wines are needed to bring out a lobster's rich, subtle sweetness and buttery flavor. A California Chardonnay, German Riesling, or an Italian Gavi dei Gavi might be suitable here, or a French Chablis or other fine white Burgundy. (Lobster ravioli has been served with a Soave.) Or perhaps the lobster might be accompanied by a light red wine with some degree of substance.

With Pasta

For pasta, the components of the dish and the seasonings in the sauce will determine its appropriate wines. Those suitable here can range from medium-dry whites to lighter or fuller reds and even include a medium-bodied sparkling wine. Seafood pastas and pastas topped with light cream or cheese sauces can take dry to medium-dry white wines and medium-to full-bodied reds. For linguine with a tomato-based seafood sauce, a Lacryma Christi offers a fine combination of dryness and acidity. Savory pastas, topped with rich, pungently flavored meat sauces call for robust, assertive reds such as a Barbera or a Chianti Classico.

With Poultry

Grilled or roast chicken can take anything from a crisp dry white wine to a light red or sturdy rosé, on to a fuller and moderately luscious, even a robust red wine. Other good companions are white wines with smoky flinty flavors, such as a Pouilly-Fumé from the Loire, a white Burgundy, a lean American Chardonnay, or a German Riesling. Roast poultry with a fairly simple stuffing calls for a light red wine, while a more richly stuffed bird needs a weightier red. For poultry prepared with cream or fruit sauces, the wine might be a full-bodied white such as a gently fruited Vouvray or a Chenin Blanc. Poultry served with tomato sauces or with spicy brown sauces can be accompanied by a fruity young red such as a Beaujolais. And Cornish game hens can be paired with a white Riesling or Chardonnay, or a red Pinot Noir, among a number of other possibilities.

Suitable for fuller-flavored, more pungent poultry such as turkeys, ducks, geese and game birds are red and white wines, exhibiting a pronounced taste, good body, and a complex personality. Turkey can be accompanied by a medium-rich to full-ish white wine with good fruit and low acidity, such as a California Chardonnay, a Riesling or Gewürztraminer from Alsace, a Pouilly-Fumé, a white Burgundy, or a white Hermitage from the Rhône. Turkey with a rich spicy stuffing might be complemented by a robust, flavorful red wine from the Rhône, Beaujolais, or Provence; also an intense French Bordeaux or other Cabernet Sauvignon, a Spanish Rioja, an American Zinfandel or Merlot, a California or an Australian Syrah. Possible here too are earthy Burgundies, dark muscular Barolos, Pinot Noirs from Oregon, or perhaps a fino or a medium-dry amontillado sherry.

Duck can be partnered with either a red or a white wine such as a medium-bodied dry red or a fruity, flowery white which is intense and fruity enough to cut through its richness. For duck prepared with oranges or cherries, it might be a red wine such as a California Merlot, a Bordeaux or a Rioja, or a white wine such as a German Spätlese, a vin jaune, or even a luscious Sauternes. Admirably holding their own with assertive turkey and game bird dishes are German wines of appreciable sweetness. The more concentrated examples can harmonize beautifully with the full flavors of roast goose as well. Roast goose can also be matched with a gutsy red wine such as a Châteauneuf-du-Pape, a St.-Émilion or Pomerol, or a Burgundy from the Côte de Nuits, a Chianti or a Barolo. Lightly smoked goose breast can be paired with a Muscat Beaumes-de-Venise. Suitable for roast goose with an apple-sausage stuffing would be an Alsatian Tokay or Pinot Gris. The richness of squab calls for a mellow wine such as a white Riesling, possibly a Chardonnay or perhaps a red Barolo. Generally best for richer-tasting game birds such as pheasant, partridge, grouse, guinea hen, quail, and wild duck are the more robust and assertive red wines: the big Burgundies, Amarones, and Zinfandels.

Meats

Lighter, fairly delicate meats such as veal and pork are best paired with wines that are neither too acid nor overly sweet. They may be reds, whites, or rosés. Depending on the dish, the wine may be light or medium-bodied, and semidry or moderately luscious. Full-bodied reds can accompany highly or richly seasoned meats. (Some people prefer a medium-bodied sparkler that will let the taste of the veal or the pork come through.)

For veal in a light cream sauce, the wine might be a fresh young Swiss white. For veal in a spicy brown or tomato sauce, it might be a fruity young red such as a Merlot. Richly roasted or braised veal calls for a more concentrated red wine such as a Rioja, a Cabernet Sauvignon, or a Pinot Noir, while a veal cutlet Milanese or veal medallions can be paired with a Chianti or a Sangiovese. Ossobuco needs a full-flavored red wine with enough acidity to cut through its richness and with enough body to match its weightiness.

Fresh ham, pork chops, pork loins, and simple pork roasts go well with fruity young red wines and with deep-bodied, not-too-dry whites. The red wine might be a Beaujolais, or a Bandol from Provence, the white from Switzerland or Germany. Wines of bright acidity such as rosés and light reds can balance out the saltiness of smoked hams. Smoked pork chops might be paired with a drier Gewürztraminer. Glazed hams can take a sweeter white, such as a German Spätlese or a rosé wine.

Although it is customary to recommend a claret (red Bordeaux) with lamb, a white wine can accompany this meat as well. Either a white Fumé Blanc or a red Côtes-du-Rhône might be served with a roast rack of lamb seasoned with tarragon. For tender young lamb, a medium-bodied red or a richer white is best, while for a more pungently flavored older lamb a more mature and complex red wine is called for. Suitable for grilled lamb chops, crown roast, a rack of lamb, or a leg of lamb are medium-to full-bodied red wines with substantial alcohol, such as a Médoc or a Pomerol, a Fitou, Hermitage, Rioja, or Barolo, as well as a Cabernet Sauvignon, Merlot, or Pinot Noir varietal. Lamb stews do well with fresh lively red wines such as Italian Dolcettos. And roast leg of lamb has even been paired with a light or medium-light sherry.

Beef dishes —steak tartare, baby ribs, and calf's liver— call for the medium-bodied red wines and rosés. Heavier red meats —steaks, chops, prime ribs, or roast beef— require somewhat fuller-bodied, more robust red wines with sufficient tannins to hold their own. Suitable for grilled steaks are good earthy Burgundies, forceful Bordeaux, Portuguese Dãos, as well as solid red wines from the Rhône Valley or northern Italy, and Petite Sirahs from California. The robustness of a roast beef might be matched by an Amarone, a Rubesco, a Hermitage, a Cahors, or else a Pinot Noir.

Although an entrecôte of beef is usually paired with red wine, it has on occasion been served with a luscious Sauternes. Beef stew can take a Zinfandel, a Beaujolais, or a Côtes-du-Rhône, a red Rioja or a Bandol, or a full-bodied Italian Dolcetto. Recommended for roasts and other hearty fare are sturdy red Portuguese wines. And served with pot roast might be a full-bodied Zinfandel, a Petite Sirah from California, a French Châteauneuf-du-Pape, an Italian Barolo, or any other robust red.

Heavy, dark game meats, such as venison and boar — which are pronounced in taste, robust in texture and powerful in their intensity— demand complex, high-alcohol wines. Included here might be rich Riojas, Rubescos, Amarones, full-bodied Rhône reds (Hermitage or Châteauneuf-du-Pape), Barolos, Petite Sirahs, and certain Zinfandels. And depending on the sauces and seasonings, a perfect match for a game dish might be a full-bodied Riesling (Spätlese or Auslese) or a late-harvest Pinot Gris from Alsace.

Salads

Traditional wine-oriented meals rarely include a salad course. The vinegar in the dressing would bring out latent acids in the wine, distorting its flavor, and lingering disturbingly on the palate. (At formal dinners, the salad course is often accompanied by a glass of water.) When wine accompanies the salad, some people substitute lemon juice, lime juice, or mustard for the vinegar in the dress-ing. Others maintain that a fairly light dressing —made up of 1 part vinegar to 5 or 6 parts oil— would hardly affect the taste of the wine. Some suggest a spicy wine such as a Gewürztraminer as a good accompaniment to the salad. (A combination of arrugula and radicchio has been served with a Lacryma Christi.)

With Cheese

Cheese and wine go well together, the alkalinity of the cheese complementing the acidity of the wine. As a rule, the milder and more delicate the cheese, the more delicate and fruity the wine should be; the more assertive and sharp-flavored the cheese, the more assertive and full-bodied the appropriate wine. Harder, more neutral cheeses find a good match in fruity, low-alcohol wines, while softer cheeses generally call for richer and riper wines.

Most suitable for the simple, everyday, unassertively flavored cheeses such as provolone, Muenster, Monterey Jack, and Bel Paese are fruity wines, either red or white, which are light to medium in body. A Chenin Blanc can go with a mild white cheese, a dry Gewürztraminer with a Muenster. Slightly sweet unripened cheeses such as a mozzarella can take a dry, fuller-bodied white wine or a light red or rosé wine. Savory soft, creamy cheeses —Camembert and Brie— pair well with medium-dry white wines with body such as a Chardonnay, or accompanying them might be a light-to medium-bodied red wine, such as a Dolcetto or a Beaujolais.

NOTE: Any inexpensive red wine can do for the lesser, ripe-flavored cheeses, such as Limburger or Liederkrantz.

Various wines are appropriate with mild, semifirm cheeses such as Swiss, Jarlsberg, Emmentaler, or Gruyère. These include light dry white wines, fruity, aromatic, full-bodied red wines and medium-bodied sherries. Other semifirm cheeses —Edam, Gouda, fontina, cheddar— call for weightier wines. Accompanying a rich sharp cheddar might be a fruity, dry, medium-bodied red or rosé, a medium-bodied white wine, or a fortified port or sherry.

Strong brash, brawny, and pungent cheeses —Danish blues, Roqueforts, Gorgonzolas and Stiltons— go well with young fruity, medium-bodied reds (Zinfandels, Merlots, Petite Sirahs). Sweet white wines are also good. A great Sauternes provides an intriguing contrast to a strong Roquefort, the sweetness of the wine balancing out the powerful taste of the cheese. Bigger wines —German Ausleses and Beerenausleses— are splendid with richer blue-veined cheeses, their appreciable sweetness blending well with the pungent character of the cheese. Also paired with Gorgonzola and strong blue cheeses can be a Recioto della Valpolicella, a Barolo, or a Barbaresco. Good with pungent cheeses as well are amontillado and oloroso sherries, port wines, Madeiras, and Marsalas. In England, vintage port is traditionally paired with Stilton, as are the ruby and LBV ports.

NOTE: Some Bordeaux vintners have suggested that their oldest red wines be taken with goat cheeses and blue-veined cheeses, while other makers maintain that such cheeses are too sharp tasting to show off a high-caliber wine to advantage. They recommend instead that milder, less competitive cheeses be served with their old red table wines.

Desserts

Served with the dessert course can be still, sparkling, or fortified wines. The desserts, however, should be a little less sweet than the accompanying wines since sweet foods can make the wines taste relatively bitter.

Rich, sweet wines match well with the tartness of fruits such as apples, plums, pears, apricots, peaches, etc. Particularly good with fresh-fruit desserts are Muscat wines, Asti Spumantes, Alsatian Gewürztraminers, and the less concentrated noble rots. Accompanying fresh strawberries and poached fruit might be a sparkling wine, somewhat on the sweet side. Poached pears filled with mascarpone have been served with a Moscat d'Asti.

Lighter desserts call for lighter wines, while the more substantial cream-based confections require richer, heavier ones. Paired with light desserts can be full-bodied rosés or pink Champagnes. Fine with ice creams, sherbets, fruit tarts, and light cakes are sweet sparklers. Also suitable with cakes, tarts, pastries, flans, custards, mousses, crêpes, rich creamy desserts and puddings, etc. are the late-harvest and noble-rot wines. (Custards, baked fruit soufflés, fruit tarts, mince pies and pumpkin pies can highlight the power and elegance of a rich Sauternes.)

Served with the dessert course as well can be a port, Marsala, Madeira (bual or malmsey), or an oloroso sherry (amoroso or cream). Sweet sherries have accompanied fresh fruit, banana tarts, mince pies, and cheesecakes. Supersweet, superdark pedro ximénez sherries have been paired with rich ice creams and caramel desserts. A dry fino or amontillado sherry or a sercial Madeira has been served with nutmeats at the end of the meal.

Wine for Other Occasions

Casual, light-bodied wines are suitable for light lunches, brunches, and summer picnics, as well as for lawn and beach parties. More elegant buffets featuring quiches, fondues, cold cuts, pasta salads, smoked fish, lobster and seafood salads call for rich but somewhat dry white wines (a Sauvignon Blanc, Vouvray, or Savennières from the Loire, a German or an Alsatian Riesling).

Appropriate for assorted cold cuts and cheeses are the uncomplicated light- to medium-bodied reds such as the Italian Barberas, as well as the semidry rosés. Traditionally taken with brunches or buffets of cold meat and fowl are delicate Champagnes and other sparkling wines, although some people like to serve such meals with a fino, or a medium-bodied sherry with a sweetish tang.

While omelets and quiches can take a white wine, a more heartily seasoned egg dish responds best to a light fruity red such as a Beaujolais or a rosé. Accompanying grilled hamburgers might be a Chilean Merlot, a modest California Cabernet Sauvignon, or a Beaujolais. Suitable for pungently barbecued meats might be a Petite Sirah or a Zinfandel with rich spicy fruit. Other possible wines here are a Côtes-du-Rhône, Chianti, Valpolicella, or a Barbera. And holding their own with chilis and pizzas are the lesser Chiantis and Petite Sirahs.

Wine Taken After Dinner or Alone

Some wines are so rich, intense, and complex that any food would be a distraction. These are the ones that are best enjoyed alone so they can be given the full attention they deserve. Known as meditation wines, they are meant to be sipped and savored in a slow, leisurely and relaxed manner, accompanied only perhaps by a biscuit or a sweet cracker.

Among these are certain fortified wines (semisweet sherries and Malmsey Madeiras along with tawny and vintage ports) as well as luscious, late-harvest wines (great Hungarian Tokays and the highest-caliber French Sauternes, German Eisweins, Beerenausleses and Trockenbeerenausleses). Also included here are rich Gewürztraminers and vins de paille, along with great full-bodied Italian reds such as Barolos and Brunellos di Montalcino in their prime. Often more suitable as sipping wines are the bigger, more full-bodied California Chardonnays, which are sometimes a bit overwhelming with food.

Great Wines

A great wine should be the centerpiece of, not an accessory to, the meal. The more serious the wine, the less fussy the food paired with it should be. To show off its subtleties, the dishes accompanying the wine should be kept simple and their sauces lightly seasoned.

Served with the finest red wines might be a simple roast chicken, game bird, lamb chops, grilled steak, or roast beef. Served with the finest white wines might be a steamed or a simply prepared fish with a delicate hollandaise sauce. Accompanying such meals might be a few modest vegetables and a loaf of good bread. Presented at the conclusion might be a wedge of cheese that is neither too bland nor too sharp.

NOTE: On such an occasion, flowers should be omitted from the table since their aroma might interfere with the wine's memorable and lingering bouquet.

Serving Several Wines

Several wines might be served at a dinner party or at another formal event. A dry sparkler can be presented as the apéritif, a red wine can accompany the meat course and an even better red paired with the cheese. When two main courses are involved, a lighter red can accompany the poultry and a heavier red the roast. After dinner, an oloroso sherry may provide the comfort and solace of a brandy, although some maintain that a vintage port is the only fitting conclusion to a special meal.

When serving several wines, as much thought should go into their sequence as their selection. Ideally, each wine should build up to the next one, a white wine should be followed by a red, a dry wine followed by a sweet, a young wine by an old, a lighter-bodied wine by a fuller-bodied one, a cool wine by a wine at room temperature, and an inexpensive wine by a more costly one.

NOTE: Wines served at either end of the meal need not follow this pattern; the apéritif and the dessert wine can be older or younger than the wines that follow or precede them.

Some say that the last wine should be the finest to provide a fitting climax to the meal. Others don't believe in saving the best for last. One oenophile says, "I like to drink the rare wines while my palate is still sharp enough to appreciate them." And others share this point of view. The host at a special Bordeaux luncheon told his guests, "We are going to drink what I consider the good wines first and then drink the younger wines afterwards."

Here are some examples of multiwine meals:

❖ At a French-oriented dinner, Champagne accompanied the terrine de foie gras, a red Burgundy was served with the red snapper in a red wine sauce, and a red Bordeaux was paired with the saddle of venison with wild mushrooms. The salad course was served alone. For dessert, a rhubarb tart, topped with a scoop of vanilla ice cream, accompanied a sweet Beaumes-de-Venise from the southern Rhone.

❖ At another French-oriented meal, Corton-Charlemagne was served with the oysters and Château Cheval Blanc accompanied the capon stuffed with sausage and steamed morels. Taken after various cheeses was a Grand Cuvée Champagne, accompanied by a rich *feuilles d'automne* dessert.

❖ At an all-Champagne dinner, the wines increased progressively in sweetness as they accompanied the hors d'oeuvres, salmon fettucine, goat cheese salad and red snapper. The sweetest wine of all was served with the crème brûlée at the end of the meal. Another all-Champagne dinner began with a Blanc de Blancs, moved on to a nonvintage brut, then to a vintage brut, and finished with a sparkling rosé (pink Champagne).

❖ At an all-Bordeaux meal, a white Graves was served with the poached salmon, a St.-Émilion was paired with the stuffed guinea hen, while a luscious Barsac accompanied the dessert. Another all-Bordeaux dinner featured wines from the same St.-Émilion estate but from several vintages. These increased progressively in age as they accompanied the pâté, coq au vin, and Stilton cheese.

❖ At a meal featuring Italian wines from Tuscany, a Vernaccia di San Gimignano served as the apéritif, a Chianti Classico accompanied the pappardelle with dried tomatoes, a Chianti Classico Riserva was paired with the seared tuna, and a Brunello di Montalcino accompanied the grilled sirloin steak.

❖ At an all-Chilean meal, a Chilean Chablis was served with the shellfish and a Chilean Cabernet Sauvignon accompanied the steak and potatoes.

❖ At an American state dinner featuring California wines, a Chardonnay was paired with the medallions of Maine lobster; a Cabernet Sauvignon accompanied a roast fillet of beef. Concluding the meal was a sparkling Blanc de Noirs served with a dish of lime sherbet and fresh raspberries.

Other multiwine meals have been international in their style:

❖ At a spring dinner at a private New York club, a sparkling Alsatian Crémant accompanied the oysters, a verdelho Madeira the curried soup of mussels and shrimp, a white Burgundy the carpaccio served with green mustard and red caviar, a red Burgundy the pheasant served with morels, while a late-harvest Gewürztraminer from Alsace accompanied the dessert of sherbet and caramelized pears.

❖ At a London banquet, a German Auslese Riesling was served with the poached salmon, a French red Bordeaux with the lamb-and-chicken mousse, and a moderately sweet Champagne with the peaches and coffee ice cream.

❖ At an even more international dinner, an amontillado sherry accompanied the consommé, a dry American Chardonnay was served with the poached salmon, an Italian Barolo was paired with the cheese course, while a French Beaumes-de-Venise and a rich fruit pie concluded the meal.

LEFTOVER WINES

Once uncorked, a table or a sparkling wine should ideally be consumed in its entirety. (The wine begins to decline when exposed to air.) The more quickly and securely the bottle is recorked, the better the wine's chances for short-term survival. A properly cared-for table wine can remain drinkable for about twenty-four hours, although it won't taste quite as good the second time around.

To keep the flavors and aromas from deteriorating too rapidly, leftover wines should be refrigerated. (Leaving them in a fairly warm place would encourage microbial action and speed up their spoilage.) About two hours before serving, a leftover red can be taken out of the refrigerator and allowed to return to room temperature gradually. A white wine or a rosé, normally taken chilled, is best served directly from the refrigerator.

NOTE: A wine refrigerated more than a day or so can become discolored and acquire a musty aroma and a flat taste. Although some people claim that most leftover red wines can last three or four days in the refrigerator and the white wines can survive a week or so, the sooner they are consumed the better.

Since fortified wines are meant to be taken in smaller quantities, they are invariably left unfinished, but —because of their higher alcohol content— they are in less danger of spoilage. Nevertheless such wines will also oxidize and evaporate. The finer the fortified wine, the sooner it should be consumed. Lighter, drier sherries go off rapidly and are best refrigerated and finished within the week. (A fine fino should be consumed in a day or two.) Sturdier, sweeter sherries will generally keep somewhat longer, as will the Màlaga wines. (The optimum time for preserving their flavor in the refrigerator is about a month.) Ruby ports soon lose their freshness. True tawny ports, having spent their formative years in wood where they were exposed to a slow oxidation, can keep for weeks. Vintage ports, aged in glass, should be decanted and consumed in a day or two. (Some decanted Madeiras have remained noble for months.)

The ancient Romans protected their wines by pouring a thin layer of vegetable oil over the surface, then flicking that oil off just before serving. The outside air can be excluded in various other ways as well. For example, leftover table wines and sparkling wines have been decanted into smaller bottles. (The bottles must be thoroughly washed and rinsed so that no traces of their previous contents remain, then the bottles are air-dried or dried in a slow oven for about half an hour and allowed to cool.)

A leftover wine can also have its ullage displaced by adding glass marbles to the bottle —the kind that children play with. The marbles must first be sterilized in boiling water. (When pouring the wine, care must be taken so these marbles won't chip the goblets.)

More elaborate protective methods call for blanketing the leftover wine with an inert gas; vacuuming out the air with a special hand pump; or suspending a balloonlike pouch inside the bottle. The pouch will expand and fill the ullage when the wine is poured.

Unfinished wines have various uses. Some people keep a special vinegar keg on hand into which they toss the odds and ends of their leftover wines. Or such wines can go into other beverages, into fresh fruit concoctions, or desserts. A leftover Champagne, combined with orange juice, then corked well and refrigerated, can serve as an apéritif the next day. The tail ends of sparkling and/or table wines, left over after a party, can be combined the following day as a wine punch that's topped off with a fresh fruit garnish.

Leftover wines also can serve as marinades, as meat tenderizers, and sauce ingredients. Tannic reds are good for marinades, while the not-too-acid red and white wines are suitable for sauces. (Wine, after all, is an integral part of a number of dishes such as coq au vin and boeuf bourguignon.) For cooking, the left-over red wines should be young and full-bodied and the leftover whites dry and preferably strong. Such wines should be tasted first; if they are not any good on the palate, they will not be improved by cooking. They might even spoil the dish.

NOTE: Wines are used for their flavor in cooking, not for their alcohol. The heat of the stove, however, does not evaporate out their alcohol entirely. Anywhere from 5 to 45 percent may remain, depending on the cooking method, the cooking time, the heat applied, and other factors. (A sparkling wine, when heated, will lose its bubbles but not its ability to flavor the food.)

IN A RESTAURANT

The Wine List

In a restaurant, most people choose their food first, then look at the wine list. Others choose the entrée only after selecting the wine. Before deciding, the diner should look around to see if the restaurant stores its bottles in the dining room. Lesser wines or those with a quick turnover may not be harmed if kept in a too-warm place, but serious wines should not be treated this way.

Many people find the wine list intimidating; they fear they might make a mistake. So they settle for something familiar, like a rosé, a Beaujolais, a Merlot, or a Chardonnay. Some, who do not wish to appear cheap, are hesitant about choosing the lowest priced wine. (It has been slyly suggested that you order the third least expensive bottle to avoid the problem.) Some diners may ask the waiter for his recommendations. (It is always best to indicate the price range up front to avoid any misunderstandings.) And it should be noted that in some situations, the management may direct the waiters to "push" certain wines.

Wine lists run the gamut from handwritten slips of paper to computer printouts. (Some are bound "books" with thick covers that include the actual labels.) In one Bordeaux establishment, the list is a notebook, whose hand-written entries resembled those of a journal kept by wine makers. Some establishments offer two lists: a shorter, abridged version for most customers featuring lower-priced wines, and a special list offering generally higher-priced selections for the wine enthusi-ast. There have also been computerized lists that allow the diner to type in his or her main course. (The computer then indicates the appropriate wine.) One restaurant even faxes the wine list to its customers, so that they can think about their choices well in advance.

Depending on the restaurateur's temperament and expertise, the wine list can be cautious or daring, classic or innovative. Some proprietors let wine salesmen draw them up. Others invest in a few expensive Bordeaux or Burgundies to dress up their lists and to serve as conversation pieces.

A wine list can be short or long. (Some contain over five hundred items.) Good lists offer small but meaningful selections appropriate to the menu and the setting. They are also frequently revised to reflect the changes in the menu, the inventory on hand, and the wine market in general. For the most part, the best lists are seen in restaurants with a large enough and knowledgeable enough clientele to make worthwhile the considerable investment that is required for the storing and aging of quality wines.

Many of the wine lists leave much to be desired. They may include vintages too young for consumption or they may depend on speeded-up products or faster-maturing regional wines. Other lists may omit the vintage year so one can't know if the wines are too young or too old; or come from a good year or a poor one.

Traditionally, the lists have been organized by geography, wine color or grape variety, and sometimes by price. A number of restaurants try to make the selection process less stressful by using the menu itself to suggest specific wines to go with its entrées. Some places pair a wine with each main course, while others list a wine or two after each dish. (A *menu de dégustation*, or tasting menu, matches the food with the wine.) Some restaurants list four red wines suitable for steaks and chops and five white wines for fish, oysters, and other shellfish. Others offer a wine of the week and suggest the dishes that can accompany it.

One place offers a prix-fixe dinner, including four wines: a Champagne, a

California Chardonnay, a white Burgundy, and a red Bordeaux. (The diner can sample one or all and pour as much wine as he pleases.) Other restaurants sponsor special dinners —often in conjunction with a wine maker, importer or distributor— providing a wine with each course. (The wines may include everything from the apéritif to the digestif.) Some menus include two or three wine choices at different price levels. One restaurant breaks the choices down into red-and white-wine categories, and then divides them further into the light-medium and full-bodied. One place separates its wines into sensory or flavor categories with such descriptions as full-bodied, floral, or spicy. And some establishments treat their dessert wines separately, combining these with the dessert list.

Before the diners are seated, the restaurant may place a bottle on the table to encourage them to sample the wine. (The diners here pay only for what they drink, or they can purchase the entire bottle.) Wine may also be ordered by the half bottle, carafe, or glass. Ordering wine by the glass permits greater experimentation, but it is not more economical. (A full bottle holds about six glasses.) Ordering a wine in lesser quantities, however, may be more appropriate when a number of people are involved and the food they select is so varied that a single wine might not suit them all.

NOTE: Offering wine by the glass may be the restaurant's way of selling wines that carry a high profit margin. Or it may be their way of unloading some dying inventory. (When ordering a house wine by the glass or carafe, it's always a good idea to ask what the wine is and where it comes from.)

On occasion, one may wish to bring a special bottle of wine to the restaurant. Establishments without a liquor license generally allow this, but may charge a corkage fee. Other places usually discourage the practice since it cuts into their profits, but may be obliging if the request is made well in advance. (They will most likely charge a corkage fee for permitting this.)

Restaurant Wine Pricing

There is a strong psychological factor in restaurant wine pricing. (Some proprietors believe a wine should bring whatever the traffic will bear). Restaurants mark their wines up a minimum of two and one half times the wholesale price, and more often three, four, and even five times. Reinforcing this approach are the customers, who equate wine prices with merit. High prices have contributed to the aura of elitism surrounding wine; those prices are largely responsible for the commonly held belief that wine is the sole province of connoisseurs and gourmets.

Great wines are often ordered by those who are more exhilarated by the notion of drinking something expensive than by the wines themselves. Believing that only the most costly wines are worth drinking, they select them as much for their cachet as for their taste. According to one restaurateur, "They miss the point entirely. If you drink only the best," he says, "you have no way of knowing that it is the best." And another proprietor declares, "It's not necessarily the most famous wine that is the best."

At the other end of the spectrum are those diners who will not choose the least-expensive wines, no matter how highly recommended they may be. One proprietor says, "I have to push people to drink the inexpensive wines. They always want to pay more." Other restaurateurs have stories to tell of the good but inexpensive wines that did not sell until their prices were raised.

The Ritual

When the waiter presents the bottle, there is usually the ritual of showing the label, extracting the cork, pouring a little wine, waiting for a response, and finally serving the wine itself. Before the bottle is uncorked, the diner should have the chance to inspect the label and the vintage date to see if this is indeed the wine he or she has ordered. (Wines that have been completely decanted and are presented only in their decanters may not always be the wines that were selected.) If the bottle arrives covered with a napkin, the diner should ask to have it temporarily removed so that the label is visible.

NOTE: If the diner selects the wine of one vintage and the waiter uncorks the wine of another year, he or she has the right to protest. If the diner hasn't been informed of the change in the wine list, the restaurant owes him the opportunity to choose another bottle.

Some restaurants employ a sommelier or a wine steward to look after the wine cellar and to assist the diners in making their selections. His symbol of office is a silver chain worn around the neck with a *tastevin*, or tasting cup, attached. (The sommelier may also wear a cellar apron.) An attentive wine steward will select the wine, decant, or chill it, then see that it is properly served. (Since decanting provides the opportunity to impress the diner, some sommeliers tend to overdo the flourishes.)

NOTE: For a genuinely helpful wine steward, the rule of thumb is to tip at least 10 percent of the cost of the bottle. If the sommelier has done nothing more than hand the diner the wine list, pour the first round, and then vanish for the rest of the evening, he merits no special gratuity.

❦ ❦ ❦

Sending the Bottle Back

Being served a bad bottle in a restaurant is a rarity. When it does happen, a degree of courage is needed to send it back. Even those who are knowledgeable about wine hesitate to complain. Yet a wine that is cloudy, or emits an off-odor is not acceptable, nor is a table wine so oxidized that it tastes more like a sherry or a Madeira. Unacceptable too are moldy wines and those that smell or taste of vinegar.

When served a bad bottle, the diners can enlist the assistance of the sommelier, the captain, or the waiter. He might say, "It took me a moment to realize it, but I think that something is not right with this wine." He might add, "Try this wine, I think it may be off." If that doesn't get the desired results, he might say, "I'm sorry but I must ask to try another bottle." Or perhaps, "I want this bottle of wine replaced even if I have to pay for it." (A responsible restaurateur will replace the bottle and probably send it back to the distributor or wholesaler, who will have to take the loss himself.)

More commonplace is a wine that disappoints. One proprietor says that when a customer is not pleased with a relatively inexpensive wine, "We bring him something else that is similar in price and character, but never the same wine." As for the diner who orders an expensive old wine that has been resting for many years in the restaurant's cellar, he or she may be told that the bottle will be opened at the diner's own risk. Rare is the restaurateur willing to assume responsibility for a long-stored, ancient bottle of wine.

10

CONCERNING ALCOHOL

Because wine is an alcoholic beverage,
it needs to be considered as such.

The positive effects of wine are enormously appealing. Taken in moderation, wine offers a form of mental and physical relaxation. It can induce feelings of conviviality and enhance life in general. Long before the development of pharmaceutical tranquilizers, wine was seen as a vital restorative, providing an antidote against tension, stress, and anxiety, and serving as a tonic against fatigue. Since wine's acidity resembles that of the gastric juices, it can also stimulate the salivary glands, whet the appetite, and improve digestion. Summing up its many attributes, an eighteenth-century man of science noted that wine "stimulates the stomach, cheers the spirits, warms the body, raises the pulse, and quickens the circulation."

Wine has provided a psychological lift and lent interest and flavor to the diets of convalescents and the aged, the weak, and the irritable. In European hospitals, many older patients are given small rations of wine with their meals. And physicians have been known to prescribe Champagne after surgery.

The accumulating evidence of long-term studies suggests a link between moderate alcohol consumption and reduced coronary disease. Mainstream authorities have cautiously endorsed the idea that moderate drinkers experience fewer cardiovascular problems than teetotalers, that they suffer fewer heart attacks and have less risk of a stroke. (Those who enjoy a drink or two a day have only about half as much heart disease as the teetotalers.) One large study, covering a nine-year period, found that moderate drinkers had a lower death rate than non-drinkers. Alcohol, the cardiologists say, relaxes the drinker by reducing the stress that contributes to obstructing the arteries that feed the heart. Alcohol also reduces the likelihood of blood clots, which can trigger heart attacks. (Blood clots are considered a major factor in heart disease.)

NOTE: Diet is also a significant factor here. The coronary death rate is higher in countries where more animal fats and fewer fruits and vegetables are consumed.

Temperate drinkers also appear to have higher levels of protective HDL (high-density lipoprotein), the so-called good cholesterol that helps to keep the coronary arteries free of the fatty deposits that can cause heart attacks. Alcohol in modest amounts has been found to raise HDL levels about 10 percent, while blocking the accumulation of the LDL (lower-density lipoprotein). The latter is considered the dangerous cholesterol because of its artery-clogging properties.

Various studies have indicated the benefits of red wines. One in France has shown that taking red wine as part of a regular diet helps to keep down the incidence of heart disease. Red wine is known to raise HDL levels. Other research has indicated that it also inhibits the oxidation of the LDLs, and so reduces the accumulation of cholesterol on arterial walls. It is also believed that the tannins in a red wine slow down the formation of blood clots. Red wines are said to contain antioxidants as well, (phenolic compounds, or flavinoids) which may have a positive effect on the cardiovascular system. Research has shown too that a substance prominent in grape skins may interfere with the development of cancer cells. And another study showed that only wine —not beer or hard liquor— was associated with longevity. This apparent protective effect seemed to be far greater in wine than in any other alcoholic beverages.

Alcohol does not need to be digested. On entering the digestive tract, it goes directly to the stomach where a special enzyme neutralizes about 20 percent, breaking it down into intermediate acids and toxins. The remaining alcohol passes through the stomach wall and is filtered and metabolized by the liver. It then enters the bloodstream, which transports it to the parts of the body containing water. As the alcohol travels through the body, it affects every biological pathway and every cell.

The rate at which the alcohol is absorbed into the bloodstream largely determines one's feelings of intoxication. A slower rate is most desirable. (It is believed that the alcohol in wine is absorbed more slowly than the alcohol in distilled spirits, perhaps because of the buffering effect of elements in the grapes.) Food further slows down its absorption. (A full stomach delays complete absorption of the alcohol). Most effective here are foods dense in carbohydrates, which also replenish some of the blood sugars that the alcohol depletes. However, when too much alcohol is consumed, food cannot prevent intoxication.

NOTE: Champagnes and other sparkling wines increase the alcohol's absorption rate because their CO_2 causes some vasodilation or widening of the blood vessels.

Alcohol is a mind-altering drug. The more alcohol in the bloodstream, the more reaches the brain and affects its natural functioning. Excessive intake will slow down reaction times, cause drowsiness and a loss of alertness and concentration. It can also disrupt visual ability by reducing peripheral vision, blurring the eyesight, and causing double or multiple vision.

Excessive intake also interferes with one's reflex responses and coordination and affects one's muscular actions. It makes voluntary movements clumsy, staggering the walk, and slurring the speech. Even more significantly, alcohol dulls the areas of the brain that enable people to make sensible decisions; it impairs their judgment. Under normal conditions, however, the impact of alcohol on the psychomotor and other systems is only temporary.

The individual's response to alcohol varies according to age, body weight, metabolism, and gender. Weight is a key factor in determining how quickly the body can metabolize and clear the alcohol from the bloodstream. The heavier the individual, the greater his or her capacity. (The same amount of alcohol is proportionately greater in potency when the body mass is smaller.) Men can handle relatively more alcohol than women because their bodies are generally characterized by more muscle and less fat. Women have less water per pound of body weight and weigh less on average. Studies have suggested that most women can safely drink only about half as much alcohol as the men. (One drink for a woman can have the effect of two drinks for a man.)

Women can also become intoxicated faster than men for other reasons. They seem to have less of the special stomach enzyme that processes and helps neutralize the alcohol, allowing more of it to pass directly into the bloodstream. And alcohol has ramifications during pregnancy as well. Freely crossing the placenta, it can affect the developing fetus. Although some experts maintain that the mother's blood alcohol needs to reach a certain threshold before the fetus is at risk, many physicians recommend that women abstain from drinking entirely during pregnancy. They say that drinking, even at a social level, during the first month or two can affect the developing child, impair its intellectual ability and its ability to concentrate. Heavy drinking, they point out, can cause the fetal alcohol syndrome, whose symptoms include mental retardation, abnormal facial features, central nervous system problems, deficiencies in growth, and difficulties in behavior.

A standard drink is defined as the equivalent of one-half ounce (twelve grams) of pure alcohol. This can take the form of five ounces of wine, twelve ounces of beer, or one and one half ounces of a distilled spirit at 80-proof. Light drinking involves the consumption of one to ten drinks a week. Moderate drinking has been defined as from ten to twenty-nine drinks a week. (This generally accepted definition of moderate drinking is based on the daily amount of alcohol an average, healthy adult can consume without untoward effect.) Heavy drinking involves thirty or more drinks a week, while binge drinking means downing five consecutive drinks or more at a single sitting.

American health experts generally recommend that consumption be kept to one to two drinks a day; one drink a day for women and no more than two drinks a day for men. The evidence shows that those who consume this quantity have a lower risk of mortality. Other studies suggest that even more ideal is two to six drinks a week for men and one to three drinks a week for women.

The amount of alcohol in a given volume of blood is known as the BAC (blood alcohol concentration). This is measured by the number of grams of alcohol in each ten liters of blood. The BAC varies according to the individual's sex and weight. It also depends on how much and how often the person drinks, how much food is in the stomach and how fast his or her metabolism works. (It takes at least twenty minutes for the BAC to reach its peak after the last drink is consumed.)

The BAC is measured by testing a person's breath. In the United States, the legal definition of intoxication is the point at which the BAC reaches 0.10 or one-tenth of one percent. In many states, the driver of an automobile is considered legally drunk when his or her blood alcohol level registers this amount. Some states have lowered the permissible BAC level for motorists to 0.08 percent, while more restrictive states have set it at 0.05 percent.

Studies have shown that drivers with a BAC level of only 0.04 percent are more likely to have accidents and that, even at 0.05 percent, the ability to drive a car is questionable. Recognizing these hazards, U.S. federal regulations require that a warning statement appear on wine labels to the effect that the consumption of alcoholic beverages impairs one's ability to drive.

The body generally needs about an hour to metabolize the alcohol in a drink. If one sips slowly and waits that length of time before taking a second drink, this will allow for the return of normal concentration and muscular coordination. (Time is the only effective remedy for clearing the blood.) In excessive consumption, the drop is slower although the effects eventually taper off. A period of about eight hours is generally needed for the body to eliminate the alcohol intake entirely.

When too much alcohol is consumed, a hangover can result. According to popular theory, a hangover is a form of withdrawal, a rebound phenomenon. Over the course of heavy drinking, the brain apparently becomes somewhat tolerant of the alcohol. Then about eight hours later, when the alcohol leaves the brain, the rebound occurs and withdrawal symptoms are experienced. Among others, these symptoms include a headache and an acid stomach. The recommended treatment is aspirin and a mild antacid along with some physical activity to produce more adrenaline and increase the body's circulation. Some suggest that spicy and peppery foods can help the body rid itself of the intermediate acids and toxins by increasing its metabolism. There is also some dehydration, but water or plain soda can help to replace the body's fluids.

The rate at which the body breaks down the alcohol varies from individual to individual. Even within the same age and weight range, many variations in the speed of the processing are possible. The rates are based on the individual's chemistry, his previous drinking experience, physical health, whether or not he has eaten, how fast he drinks in a given period, and how much he consumes. People who are tired, anxious, or depressed may have an exaggerated response to the alcohol that they consume.

The ability to absorb alcohol decreases with age. As one grows older, total body water diminishes, while body fat increases. And older people metabolize the alcohol at a slower rate because the liver does not process it as efficiently as before. According to scientists and other experts concerned with the effect of alcohol on the health of the elderly, alcohol may be helpful in small amounts, but heavier consumption can lead to physical and mental impairment and to a worsening of chronic ailments. Also affected can be the liver, pancreas, and intestines, as well as the blood and nervous systems. Experts recommend that older people limit their intake to one drink a day. (The actual signs of alcoholism, such as problems with memory, balance, or sleep are often incorrectly assumed to be a natural consequence of the aging process or the effect of chronic illness.)

NOTE: Since the elderly often take various medications, they need to be aware of possible interactions between the alcohol they are consuming and the prescription drugs that they're taking.

The line that divides drinking and problem drinking is often blurred. Drinking to excess has been described as drinking to get drunk, or as being unable to remember what happened after one has been drinking. A problem drinker has been defined as anyone who drinks enough for it to interfere with his or her physical or social functioning. He or she has also been described as someone who has been drunk at least six times during the previous year or has had serious difficulties during that time as a result of their drinking. According to one expert, the central questions are: How much and how often does the person drink? When does he drink? Is his drinking accompanied by difficulties on the job or with his family?

An alcoholic has been described as someone whose behavior is determined by alcohol, for whom alcohol has become a physiological or a psychological necessity, whose dependency overwhelms his or her judgment, and yet who nevertheless continues to drink. In other words, alcoholism is characterized by impaired control over drinking, either on a continuous or a periodic basis, and by a preoccupation with and the use of alcohol despite its adverse consequences. In 1966, the American Medical Association classified alcoholism as a disease.

NOTE: Experts who treat alcoholism say that those closest to the alcoholic are often the last to acknowledge the existence of the problem. Family, friends, and co-workers tend to minimize the serious repercussions of alcohol abuse and of alcoholism, perhaps preferring not to confront the situation because of the general climate of denial surrounding the subject.

The physiology of the alcoholic differs from that of the social drinker. Excessive intake over an extended period can cause anemia and other blood abnormalities, such as low white cell or platelet counts. It can also promote malnutrition. (Although alcohol contains small amounts of carbohydrates that provide the elements necessary for quick energy, alcohol in itself is not sufficiently nutritious to substitute for food.) And alcoholics not only tend to eat less but experience an impaired ability to absorb the food they do consume.

Commonly associated with alcohol abuse and alcoholism is cirrhosis of the liver. The liver, which clears the body of many toxic substances —including the alcohol itself— burns fat as fuel under normal circumstances. But when alcohol is present in the bloodstream, the liver burns the alcohol instead, causing the fat to accumulate in the liver. Cirrhosis refers to a fatty, thickened, and scarred liver that cannot perform its usual filtering function as effectively as before. Since the liver can no longer remove as much alcohol from the bloodstream, more alcohol reaches the brain and the other organs. Moreover, there's a buildup of acetaldehyde, the toxin produced by the normal breakdown of alcohol. This creates a decreased tolerance for alcohol and finally leads to a general loss of the various control mechanisms in the body.

The special stomach enzyme that neutralizes alcohol works even less in alcoholics, so they cannot properly process the alcohol they do consume. Alcoholic women may be so lacking in this enzyme that even when they consume less alcohol than men, they are more likely to develop liver disease. (Women who drink heavily are also more prone to gynecological problems.)

On a more superficial level, alcohol dilates the subcutaneous blood vessels, causing blood to rush to the skin. In excessive and long-term drinking, the blood vessels feeding the facial skin dilate and contract so frequently that the smaller ones become fragile and rupture, appearing as blotchy red spots. (The dilation causes the eyes to puff up as well.)

Alcohol may protect the heart when consumed in small quantities, but in large quantities does nothing to prolong life. Studies have indicated that alcohol abuse can raise the risk of high blood pressure, and act as a major contributor in cardiovascular disease and strokes. (Among the dangers of chronic overuse is muscle weakness, including a weakness of the heart muscle, leading to heart failure.) Heavy drinkers are also subject to an increased risk of gastrointestinal ailments, and to cancers of the liver, pancreas, mouth, and throat. Excessive use can cause other organic complications, sometimes involving the brain. Alcohol abuse increases the chance of an early death from cirrhosis as well, or from accidents caused by diminished coordination and impaired judgment.

Scientists generally accept the notion that alcoholism is a multifaceted disorder based on complex genetic, social, and cultural factors. They have discovered that the blood chemistries of some individuals make them especially vulnerable to the side effects of alcohol and more prone to addiction. One study involving male twins found a strong genetic influence in those who developed drinking problems before age twenty, while environmental factors seemed to be the stronger influence on those who developed their drinking problems later in adulthood.

NOTE: Researchers have also found that women share the same genetic susceptibilities to alcohol as men.

The predisposition to alcohol seems to run in families. It has been estimated that the children of alcoholics have three to four times a greater risk of developing alcoholism than the offspring of nonalcoholics. (Generally the children of alcoholics are also at a greater risk than their peers of having physical, mental, and emotional problems.) Counselors recommend that people with a family history of problem drinking avoid drinking alcohol on a daily basis, that they avoid it when they are alone or depressed, and perhaps that they even avoid the consumption of alcohol altogether.

Wine drinkers are more likely than other drinkers to drink moderately. (They are generally not binge drinkers since they usually take the alcohol with their meals.) Wine also tends to work best in a social or family setting. As one oenophile pointed out, "Wine is a drink that simply does not work if you sit down and try to drink a bottle all by yourself." Researchers have found that alcoholism is less of a problem in cultures that encourage the responsible consumption of wine. Such cultures seem to find a balance between the advantages of moderation and the problems of overconsumption. As one researcher stated, "It may in fact be better to have a culture that views alcohol as part of daily life than one that prohibits it, because forbidding children to have any experience with alcohol may leave them unable to control their drinking as teenagers." Abstention, he points out, gives children the message that "drinking is a kind of evil," making it virtually impossible for them to deal with alcohol in moderation.

Children tend to follow the drinking patterns of their parents. According to most findings, parents play a major role either directly or indirectly in determining the patterns of their children's alcohol use. Apparently, it isn't what the parents say but what they do that influences whether or not the children will become misusers of alcohol. When parents drink every evening to relieve feelings of stress, children learn that lesson. "Youngsters do what parents do," one observer notes, "and if the parents drink a lot, the kids do too." (Experts have found that children exposed to alcohol abuse early in their lives are more likely to become alcoholics themselves.)

The best parental role models are those who treat wine as a natural component of a meal, who present it in an unglamorized family setting, and who demonstrate in their own lives that moderate consumption is the key to the pleasures and benefits of wine. Children who have never been taught moderation at home, or who consider drinking an indulgence often tend to view alcohol consumption as a rite of passage into adulthood. (Binge drinking is most often seen among those just emerging from their teens.) "The message young people need to receive," another observer said, "is that while alcohol should be drunk only by adults, drinking does not make you an adult."

NOTE: Researchers have also found that while peer group influences on behavior predominate during the midteen years, parental influences tend to be longer lasting. These influences dominate earlier and then assert themselves again as the children become older.

Wine is constant proof that God loves us and loves to see us happy.

—Benjamin Franklin

11

ADDITIONAL INFORMATION

THE VOCABULARY OF TASTE

Describing the taste of a wine is no simple matter, although some aspects of this sensory experience are easier to define than others. We can characterize sweet, sour, and bitter more readily than we can describe fruity or flowery.

Without any clear-cut terminology available, wine descriptions have often been overblown or precious. Wines are said to be "racy," to "exhibit a savage, primordial character," to display a "bricky taste," "a whiff of tar," to suggest "new leather" or possess the "lacy nose of licorice." Writing about a group of wines, one critic, said, "They grab you by the palate, swing you around, give you a bone-cracking massage and leave you limp with an almost silly grin on your face." A Frenchman, encountering a fulsome description, said, "Delicate and elegant I can swallow, but when I read that a wine is also coaxing, purring, and tender, I'm not sure whether to drink it or marry it."

For years, wine professionals have been trying to establish a standardized terminology but have been unable to agree on the fine points. Until they come up with such definitions, the following terms may prove useful in registering our responses to the wines that we drink.

ACIDITY: A wine's natural tartness or bite, produced by its nonvolatile acids, and felt lightly on the tongue. Properly balanced by the grape's sugars, it will provide a refreshing and necessary piquancy. (Acidity should not be confused with the sour pungency caused by acetic acid or vinegar in the wine.)

AFTERTASTE: The sensation that lingers on the palate after the wine has been swallowed, the echo of its flavor and bouquet. (The aftertaste in a great wine may persist for fifteen minutes or more.) Depending on its length, a wine is said to be long or short.

AROMA: A wine's unique fragrance, the characteristic smell of its grapes. Associated with fresh, young wines, it is less apparent in the light, dry ones.

ASTRINGENT: A rough, coarse quality, more related to the wine's feel than to its taste. Produced by the tannins, it is detected as a puckery sensation in the mouth, similar to that produced by a cup of strong tea. Cleansing the palate, it makes the last sip taste as good as the first. (Astringency can be an indication that the wine will be long-lived. Red wines require tannins in moderation, but taste bitter when they are excessive.)

ATTACK: The vivid first impression created by a wine; a term used by British wine writers.

AUSTERE: A dry crispness seen in wines that are restrained and subtle. Primarily associated with high-caliber Cabernet Sauvignons, it is also evident in some white wines, such as a fine Chablis. Can also refer to the sharp, excessive tightness of a red wine in need of breathing. (Also see Closed-in.)

BALANCE: The proper proportions and harmonious relationship of a wine's various components as they complement rather than overwhelm one another. These include the physical elements (body and color), the taste elements (sweetness and acidity), and such less tangible qualities as character and finesse.

BARNYARD: A wine that smells unpleasantly like wet hay.

BIG: A wine's unusual strength and power. Refers to the intensity of its flavor and the assertiveness of its bouquet and aroma. Generally applies to highly tannic red wines, possessing more body and alcohol than most others. Is often a code word for a wine higher in alcohol. (Since a wine's upper limit is normally about 13 percent, a big wine would be anywhere from 14 to 17 percent.) Can also refer to a heavy wine, lacking in subtlety and refinement.

BITTER: A wine's harshness related to its tannins. Is usually perceived in the aftertaste and tends to disappear with age.

BODY: A wine's substance or degree of concentration, reflecting the nonsugar solids in solution. Red wines tend to be medium to full in body, while white wines are typically lighter.

BOUQUET: A wine's enhancing fragrance or scent, the distinctive and subtle mingling of its diverse odors. Originating in the deepest levels of the earth to which the vine roots penetrate, bouquet is more complex than aroma; developing largely during bottle aging when slow oxidation modifies the wine's various components. (While aroma is seen in young wines, bouquet is a characteristic of the older ones.)

BREED: The obvious superiority of a wine as demonstrated by the harmonious balance of its bouquet, flavor, and complexity. It is the hallmark of wines pressed from aristocratic grapes, grown in the finer viticultural districts.

BRUT: A mark of extreme dryness, indicating the wine's negligible retention of grape sugar. Although initially used to describe Champagne, it can now refer to table wines as well.

BUTTERY: A wine's richness of flavor, its creamy lusciousness. Is primarily associated with Chardonnays in California.

CHARACTER: The definite, unmistakable quality of a wine that possesses the color, taste, and bouquet associated with its type in full degree.

CHEWY: The full-bodied texture that makes a wine feel good and rich in the mouth; a characteristic associated with fine red wines.

CLEAN: A wine's pleasing palatability and soundness. Is sensed as a refreshing purity in the mouth after the wine has been swallowed.

CLOSED-IN: A tightness indicating the wine has not matured sufficiently to express its flavor or bouquet. Is also associated with tannic young red wines that can be improved by breathing.

CLOUDY: A wine's lack of clarity; its haziness or muddiness. May be due to poor fermentation, agitation of the bottle, or bottle sickness. If the condition does not clear up with rest, the wine may prove undrinkable.

COARSE: A wine's heavy heartiness, a lack of depth and finesse. Is generally seen in full-bodied, but otherwise ordinary, red wines.

COMPLEX: A multiplicity of stimulating and pleasing flavors and aromas, a characteristic of high-caliber wines.

CORKY (Corked): A wine tainted by a dried-out, moldy, or defective cork and characterized by a generally stale, disagreeable moldlike smell and taste suggesting rotting wood or damp basements. Is generally is attributed to the chemical compound created when the cork is processed. Can first be detected by sniffing the moist end of the cork. If the condition doesn't quickly dissipate, the wine should be tasted before serving to see if it's still palatable.

CRISP: A clear-cut briskness produced by the wine's acidity. Is primarily seen in white wines, which tend to be higher in acid than red wines.

DELICATE: A light elegance, sometimes a fragility, associated with good white wines. The opposite of sturdy, big, or coarse.

DRY: The absence of residual grape sugar in a wine, the opposite of sweet. (Also see Brut and Residual Sugar.)

DUMB: A young wine, lacking the characteristic taste or smell of its type.

EARTHY: The unmistakable character of the warm, sweet-smelling earth, perceived as an attractive taste and aroma in a wine. A characteristic of wines grown in alluvial or predominantly clay soils. Is seen in the sturdy, no-nonsense reds from the Rhône and Loire valleys. When too pronounced, the characteristic can be disagreeable. (Also see Goût de Terroir.)

ELEGANT: The finesse and balance that give high-caliber red and white wines their complexity and interest.

FAT: A wine's heaviness. Is considered a positive attribute in big, generous red wines and in rich, luscious white wines.

FINESSE: A wine's style and polish. The successful and harmonious combination of a wine's delicacy, strength, and body.

FINISH: The taste that lingers after the wine has been swallowed. Is most desirable when it creates a pleasant feeling of warmth in the mouth. (Also see Aftertaste.)

FIRM: A wine's sturdiness or backbone. Produced by high tannin levels, it is an indication of the wine's keeping qualities. (Can also be a polite way of saying the wine is harsh.)

FLABBY: A wine's lack of firmness or structure, caused by insufficient acidity.

FLAVOR: The actual taste of the wine. Along with aroma and bouquet, it reveals the wine's complexity or the lack of it.

FLINTY: A clean, sharp, almost austere attractiveness. A characteristic of fine, dry white wines grown on chalky soils. Is seen in Champagnes and in Chablis wines.

FLOWERY: A bouquet that evokes the soft scent of violets, honeysuckle, lilacs, etc. Associated with white wines grown on stony soils in cooler districts, it is seen in German Rieslings from the Mosel Valley and in some northern Italian white wines.

FORWARD: A wine that has become soft and pleasant before its time. Is seen in the red wines of lesser vintages, which lack the potential for much aging.

FOXY: A strong pungent flavor, a rich distinctive muskiness and a fruity tang. Is evident in wines pressed from labrusca grapes. (The labruscas have been called "fox grapes.")

FRAGRANT: A wine's pronounced and agreeable bouquet or aroma.

FRESH: A liveliness of fragrance and taste seen in young wines; is often their most charming and appealing characteristic. It usually disappears with bottle age although mature, high-caliber wines can retain this attractive characteristic to a considerable degree.

FRUITY: A wine's unmistakable grapy aroma and flavor; a combination of its tartness and sweetness. Suggesting the taste of ripe fruit, it may be reminiscent of apples, pears, apricots, peaches, blackberries, black currants, etc.

GENEROUS: A rich, hearty quality that is associated with full-bodied, full-flavored red wines.

GOÛT DE TERROIR (Taste of the Soil): An elusive, almost rustic earthiness, evident as a fairly high acidity dominating the wine's fruit elements. Is related not only to the soil in which the wine was grown but to the total environment that nurtured it. A characteristic associated primarily with fine red Burgundies.

GRAPY: A sweet wine aroma and pronounced fruit flavor, imparted by certain grapes varieties, particularly the muscat and concord. Is not highly regarded as a rule since it tends to diminish the subtlety of a wine.

GRASSY: See Herbaceous.

GREEN: The generally disagreeable acidity of a wine pressed from unripe fruit. Can also refer to the appealing freshness of wines pressed from prematurely picked grapes, as in Portuguese vinho verdes and French Muscadets.

GRIP: Refers to a full-bodied wine with a good combination of tannin and acidity, as opposed to a soft, bland wine; a term used mainly by British wine writers.

HARD: A lack of suppleness due to a wine's excessive tannins. An indication of potential longevity, it can change to firmness with age. Is generally seen in austere red wines and is also evident in the high-acid extremely dry white wines from Chablis and the Saar Valley.

HARSH: A roughness or overastringency associated with immature red wines; it usually disappears with age.

HEAVY: A wine's fullness of body and high degree of alcohol, without a corresponding richness of flavor. Is often seen in chaptalized or sugared wines.

HERBACEOUS: A wine's vegetablelike flavors and odors; agreeable when grassy and evoking tea or eucalyptus, but harsh when suggesting bell peppers, artichokes, or asparagus. (The harshness may be caused by improper trellising, inadequate ripening, or vinification problems.)

INTENSE: A concentrated and well-defined taste and texture that sets the best wines apart from the others.

LIGHT: A wine low in body and alcohol; a physical characteristic, not an indication of quality. (Some light wines are charming, while others are quite dull.)

LIQUOREUX: The luscious viscosity of a fine rich, wine; a characteristic associated with noble rots and other good dessert wines. Refers more to the wine's unctuous and velvety body than to its sweetness.

LONG: A wine's ability to persist on the palate for some time after it has been swallowed. (Also see Aftertaste and Finish.)

MADERIZED: A wine's chemical deterioration caused by its prolonged aging or its exposure to heat. Acquiring a hint of burned taste, the wine may be palatable at first but then becomes flat and musty. Before finally turning to vinegar, it emits a distinctly "rancio" odor or the smell of rotting hay. Also affected is the color; maderization causes red wines to fade and white wines to turn brown. (Also see Oxidized and Rancio.)

MELLOW: A wine's soft, ripe lusciousness that also implies a degree of sweetness. Is generally associated with mature red wines, but can be seen in chaptalized or sugared wines as well.

MOLDY: An unpleasant flavor and a fetid odor caused by a wine's excessive aging or a defect in the cork. (Also see Corky.)

NOSE: The scent of a wine, a composite of all its fragrances, ranging from light and delicate to deep and complex. May reflect the wine's predominant grape or suggest almonds, cloves, black pepper, cherries, vanilla, or a hint of the salt sea. Experts talk about nosing a wine or sniffing it as they seek to unearth the mysteries of a young wine's aroma and an older wine's bouquet. A good nose refers to a wine with considerable aroma and a pleasing flowery bouquet. A big nose refers to a wine with a rich complex bouquet that fills the room when the bottle is uncorked. A sophisticated nose indicates a layered complexity, produced by years of bottle aging. An off-nose refers to a wine that does not smell right.

NUTTY: A wine's pleasant, pungent aftertaste that is reminiscent of almonds, walnuts, hazelnuts, etc. It is generally associated with such fortified wines as sherries and Madeiras.

OAKY: A wine's attractive, vanillalike aroma and taste imparted by its aging in oak. Is at its best when it's remarkably restrained and does not mask the fruit on the palate or in the bouquet. (The oakiness of some American Chardonnays can be so overwhelming that they taste more like wood than like wine.)

OXIDIZED: An overexposure to air that increases the wine's volatile acidity, causing it to lose freshness and color, and sometimes to develop a cooked taste. Is most prevalent in old wines, but can also be responsible for the premature aging and deterioration of other wines.

PAPERY: The odor of dry leaves; a characteristic of old wines that have shed most of their tannins during aging.

RAISINY: A sweetish flavor associated with hot-climate wines that are pressed from overripe or shriveled grapes.

RANCIO: A gently bitter, nutlike taste and odor caused by a wine's partial oxidation. While desirable in fortified wines such as sherries, Madeiras, and Marsalas, it is unpleasant in table wines.

RESIDUAL SUGAR: The natural sugar that remains in a wine after the fermentation process, accounting for its sweetness.

RICH: A wine's fullness of body, density of flavor and generosity of bouquet.

RIPE: A wine's mellowness. Refers to wines with no trace of harshness or greenness in their character.

ROBUST: A wine's sound and sturdy heartiness; refers to its well-developed body and flavor.

SCENT: A wine's aroma. In young wines, the flowery scent of roses, violets, and magnolias is not uncommon. In older red wines, the scent may suggest chocolate, cloves, cinnamon, wood smoke, toast, or truffles.

SHARP: See Acidity.

SOFT: An ingratiating sensation related to the wine's maturity. (Can also refer to wines that are lacking in character.)

SHORT: Refers to wines that do not linger on the palate because they lack the necessary firmness and acidity. (Also see Aftertaste and Finish.)

SOUR: A disagreeable acidity seen in wines that are turning to vinegar. (They may have been poorly made, improperly stored, or sealed with defective corks.)

SPICY: A piquant, attractive flavor, suggesting nuances of mint, herbs, pepper, and so on. Is seen in fruity young wines.

STALKY: A somewhat unpleasant odor suggesting twigs or green wood. Is seen in tannic but underripe red wines and usually diminishes with age.

STEELY: A wine's austere tartness, even an extreme hardness that produces a fresh, attractive, metallic sensation on the tongue. Is associated with well-made white wines from the Saar Valley and Chablis. (Also see Flinty.)

STEMMY: A harsh greenness, generally associated with those wines fermented on their stems. Is considered a desirable characteristic in some wines, such as the grassy whites of Sancerre in France.

STRUCTURE: A wine's armature or backbone based on its tannins. Largely associated with red wines, it is an assurance of their longevity and strength.

SWEET: The presence of discernible sugar in a wine. (Also see Residual Sugar.)

TANNIC: A wine's slight astringency or bitterness, sensed in the mouth as a stimulating puckery feeling, similar to that produced by a strong cup of tea. (Derives from an assortment of organic compounds that are found in grape skins, seeds, and stalks.) Is associated with full-bodied red wines that have become rich and mouth- filling with age.

TART: A wine's somewhat sharp, refreshing quality, reflecting a high degree of fruit acids. (Should not be confused with either a harsh greenness or a vinegary sourness in the wine.)

TEXTURE: A wine's tactile quality or feel in the mouth; a reflection of its grape solids. Is associated with red wines that are invariably fermented on their skins.

THIN: A somewhat watery quality seen in wines deficient in body or alcohol.

TIRED: A wine whose charm has passed; a wine that should have been consumed young but wasn't.

UNCTUOUS: A wine's great full-bodied fatness, produced by high levels of glycerin; a characteristic of noble-rot wines. (Also see Liquoreux.)

VANILLA: A mild flavor produced by vanillin (a substance found in oak) and imparted during wood aging. Apparent in the wine's nose and aftertaste, it is associated with mature red wines from Bordeaux and Burgundy and with some Chardonnay wines.

VEGETAL: A wine's negative herbaceous smell and taste that suggests rotting vegetables at its worst. Caused by excessive irrigation or improper trellising, it is sometimes seen in red Bordeaux wines and in the California Cabernets. (Also see Herbaceous.)

VINOUS: The concentration or essence of a wine's good qualities. Can refer to its alcoholic strength as well.

WITHERED: A wine's desiccation or loss of its freshness, caused by excessive oxidation. Is seen in wines left in poorly corked bottles or too long in their casks. (Also see Woody.)

WOODY: A musty, overbearing flavor and aroma, caused by storing the wine in wood too long, or by a defect in its cask.

YEASTY: The taste and odor of a wine that has just emerged from fermentation. Obscuring the nose at first, it generally disappears with age. Is considered desirable in wines bottled soon after their fermentation, such as some Swiss wines, Muscadets, and Champagnes. (In other wines, its persistence may indicate an improper vinification.)

GRAPE VARIETIES

Some grapes are grown throughout the world; others are cultivated in restricted areas. The more northerly regions, experiencing briefer growing seasons, need the earlier-ripening varieties. (Predominant here are the red cabernet sauvignon and pinot noir and the white riesling and chardonnay.) Warmer regions need grapes that are able to resist sunburn and shatter while retaining a fair degree of acidity. (Varieties here include the red syrah, carignan, grenache, and zinfandel and the white muscat, trebbiano, french colombard, and green hungarian.)

Wine makers once showed little interest in grapes grown outside their own areas. A number still use indigenous berries as much as possible to preserve the unique characteristics of their locales. Others, however, have uprooted the vines adapted over the centuries to specific sites and replaced them with grapes of distant origin. In many countries, the cabernet sauvignon and chardonnay have become particularly ubiquitous. Most recently, the merlot has emerged as a popular grape.

Traditionalists view these developments with alarm, considering them a first step in the eventual homogenization of wine. They warn that consumers —seeing the varietal name— will come to expect the wines always to taste the same, regardless of where the grapes were grown. Yet the source of the grape is always significant. Modifying each variety is its immediate environment, its specific combination of site, soil, sunshine, and rainfall. Although certain grapes are adaptable to a wide range of conditions, their wines can never be quite the same from one place to the next. (A noble grape may yield a mediocre wine in one location, while a less respected grape can produce a good one there.) Even when the methods of cultivation, harvesting, and cellar care are identical, transplanting a grape not only from country to country and region to region but sometimes from vineyard to vineyard can produce markedly different wines.

NOTE: Different countries and even different sectors of the same country have named the same grape differently. And some varieties have been misnamed, being called pinots or rieslings when they aren't those grapes at all.

Recent DNA research is clarifying the relationship between some varieties. The following is a sampling of some of the grapes now grown:

ALBANA: Italian white grape grown in Emilia-Romagna. Yields a high alcohol wine with a distinctive aroma. Vinified dry and sweet, it is also made sparkling.

ALBARIÑO: White grape grown in northwestern Spain and Galicia's most important variety. Yields a rich, floral, white wine that is often naturally pétillant. Is similar to the riesling and said to be of Rhine Valley origin although some believe the grape originally came from Portugal. (Monks making a pilgrimage to the shrine of Santiago de Campostela brought it to Galicia in the twelfth century.)

AGLIANICO: Red grape grown in southern Italy; said to be of Greek origin. Yields an intense, well-structured wine that shares some of the longevity and elegance of the wines made from Italy's better-known varieties. Flourishing in Basilicata, on the slopes of a now-extinct volcano, it's employed in Campania for Taurasi wines.

ALEATICO: Italian red grape from Elba. Yields a fairly sweet wine with a pronounced spicy flavor. (Much prized is the Aleatico di Portoferraio.) Cultivated all over Italy, the grape is most successful in Tuscany, Umbria, and on the island of Corsica. Brought to California nearly a century ago, it's employed there in blending and as a dessert wine. (California also makes a dry, off-white wine with the grape by removing its skins.)

ALICANTE: See Grenache.

ALICANTE BOUSCHET: High-yielding red hybrid, widely grown in California's Central Valley. Produces a sturdy, somewhat coarse wine, high in sugar and best suited to bulk blending. Also serves as a varietal. Is often employed as a teinturier (dyer), whose intensely colored pulp and juice is used to darken paler red wines.

ALIGOTÉ: French white grape cultivated on the lower slopes of the Côte d'Or. Once scorned as a second-class variety in Burgundy, it came into its own when the chardonnay was in short supply there. Employed now as a varietal, it yields a fresh, crisp, medium-bodied wine with good fruit. (When overcropped, its generally thin, acidic wines are used in the region's lesser blends, including a white Beaujolais.) Is also grown in California, the Russian Federation, Bulgaria, and other countries, where it's employed both as a varietal and in blending.

AURORA: White hybrid grape, which does well in a short growing season. Cultivated extensively in New York State's Finger Lakes region, it yields a light, crisp, fragrant white wine, made both dry and semidry. Also serves as a component in sparkling wines there. Is cultivated in Switzerland as well.

AUXERROIS: See Malbec.

AZAL: Indigenous Portuguese white grape; a component of vinho verde.

BACCHUS: White hybrid grape, grown in Germany; a combination of the riesling, sylvaner, and müller-thurgau. Is similar to, but more prolific than, the müller-thurgau grape.

BACO NOIR: Red hybrid, cultivated primarily in the American Northeast. Early bearing and moderately frost resistant, its wines are light- to full-bodied; some are young and fruity like a Beaujolais, while others show some potential for aging. Is also grown in France.

BARBERA: Red grape widely cultivated in northern Italy and elsewhere in that country. (It may have originated in the Piedmont.) Its dark, tannic, full-bodied, and somewhat astringent wine displays a robust bouquet, good fruit flavors, and a woodsy aroma. In northern Italy it serves as a varietal, and in the central and southern sectors and Sardinia, it's employed as a blending grape. Because of its high acidity and its resistance to sunburn and shatter, the grape is also widely grown in California's Central Valley. Once considered a second-rate variety, best suited to blending, it now enjoys popularity there as a rich, hearty varietal. Is also cultivated in South America, particularly in Argentina.

BEAUNOIS: See Chardonnay.

BLANC FUMÉ: See Sauvignon Blanc.

BLAUBURGUNDER: See Pinot Noir.

BLAUFRÄNKISH: Austrian red grape related to the gamay.

BOUSCHET (Gros Bouschet): See Cabernet Franc.

BRETON: See Cabernet Franc.

BRUNELLO: Italian red grape, a subvariety of the sangiovese, Cultivated in Tuscany, it's responsible for the Brunello di Montalcino, one of Italy's finest reds. (Also see Sangiovese.)

BUAL (Boal): White grape cultivated in Madeira. Yields a luscious, somewhat sweet wine that bears its name.

BURGER: Productive but poor quality white grape, used in Germany's lesser blends. (Its cultivation is no longer permitted in the better French vineyards.) Serves as a blending wine in California and in the bulk production of sparkling wines there.

BURGUNDER: See Pinot Noir.

CABERNET D'ANJOU: See Cabernet Franc.

CABERNET FRANC: French red grape, closely related to the cabernet sauvignon but more productive and less tannic. Yields a rounder, faster-maturing wine, whose fruitiness is reminiscent of cherries, blackberries, or blueberries. Widely cultivated in the Médoc and Graves, it's used there in blends to soften and balance out the more astringent cabernet sauvignon. Known as the bouschet in St.-Émilion, where it's the predominant grape, it reaches its peak in the estimable wine of Cheval Blanc. Is also grown in Pomerol and in the Loire Valley. Known as the breton in the Loire, it's responsible for the crunchy wines of Chinon and Bourgueil and is also employed in Cabernet d'Anjou and Cabernet de Touraine blends there as well as in various rosés, including the Cabernet Rosé de Saumur. It's cultivated in northeastern Italy too and on the East and West Coasts of the United States. Serving as a California varietal, it's also used there in high-level proprietary wines.

CABERNET SAUVIGNON: The classic red grape of France and the aristocrat of Bordeaux. Yields a wine celebrated for its depth and structure. Known to have been grown in Bordeaux in the seventeenth century, it is now the world's most widely planted top-quality red grape. In the Médoc, its lean, complex, full-bodied wines display a hardness, even an astringency in youth, becoming soft, velvety, aromatic, and complex with sufficient age. At their finest its wines demonstrate strength, character, elegance, longevity, and an incomparable balance. In France, the cabernet sauvignon is also grown in the Loire Valley and Provence.

Increasing in popularity in Italy, the grape is cultivated in Tuscany, the Piedmont, and other regions, either blended with traditional Italian varieties or vinified as a claret-style wine. Considered America's most popular red varietal, it is now grown extensively in California, where its wines —developing more rapidly than the French— are generally characterized by a fruity and fleshy style that tends to show off well in youth. Some examples are rich and robust, others are less tannic and lighter bodied, while still others are soft and flabby. The finest examples come from the Napa Valley; other good Cabernets come from Sonoma and Santa Clara counties. The grape is also grown in Australia, Chile, and Spain. In Rioja, where it's called the clarete, its wines are generally softer and easier drinking than in France. The grape is cultivated as well in Bulgaria, Hungary, Israel, Romania, the Russian Federation, South Africa, and the former Yugoslavia.

NOTE: The cabernet sauvignon is believed to be the result of a spontaneous cross-pollination that occurred centuries ago. Recent DNA research indicates that its genetic parents are the cabernet franc and sauvignon blanc.

CANAIOLO: Italian red grape whose soft, fragrant, and somewhat sweetish wine is made as a varietal. Is also used in Chiantis and in other blends.

CANNONAU: See Grenache.

CARIGNAN: High-yielding French grape, best suited to warm-climate cultivation. Produces a sturdy, agreeable, high-alcohol wine known for its firmness and color. Serves as a varietal in the Rhône Valley and Provence and is also used in blending there. In Italy, it's called the gragnano, and in Spain the cariñeno. (In Rioja, it is known as the mazuelo.) In California, where it's called the kerrigan or carignane with an "e," the grape was initially dismissed as a lesser variety, but now —along with other Rhône varieties— has found greater favor there. Serves in the state as a robust varietal and also in generic Burgundies and fortified wines.

CARMENÈRE: French red grape, employed in various Bordeaux blends. (It may be related to the cabernet sauvignon.)

CARNELIAN: Red hybrid grape; a combination of the grenache, cabernet sauvignon, and carignane. Grown primarily in California's Central Valley, it yields light-colored, quick-maturing wines there.

CATAWBA: Hardy, productive, and vigorous American red hybrid; discovered in

North Carolina on the banks of the Catawba River. (Believed to be the result of a chance pollination between labrusca and vinifera vines.) One of the first commercially developed grapes in America, it's widely cultivated in New York State, Ohio, and California, and is employed in various red and white blends that range from dry to sweet. Also serves as a component in sparkling wines.

CHARBONO: Red grape grown in California and believed to be of Italian origin. Yields an extremely dark, full-bodied, and flavorful wine, similar in style to a Barbera, but somewhat rougher. Is employed as an inexpensive varietal and also in generic Burgundies.

CHARDONEL: White hybrid, a cross between the chardonnay and the seyval blanc, but more cold resistant than the chardonnay. Grown in New York's Finger Lakes region, it yields a light, fruity, and delicate wine that is vinified both dry and sweet. Also serves as a component in sparkling wines.

CHARDONNAY: Premium French white grape; believed by some to have originated in Asia Minor. One of the easiest of the noble grape varieties to grow since the vine is particularly vigorous and its berries ripen early. Yields clean, fresh, crisply dry, fine-textured, and intensely flavored wines, characterized by a certain flintiness. Is used in virtually all the best French white wines, including those from the Côte d'Or, the Rhône and Loire valleys. Is employed exclusively in the great white Burgundies, with the wines ranging from the finest steely Chablis (where the grape is called the beaunois) to the soft, delicate, flowery, aromatic Meursaults and the big, chewy Montrachets. Is also the basic white grape of Champagne, where its firm, full, strong, yet unbelievably light wine displays extraordinary delicacy and finesse. Is associated with Mâconnais wines as well, such as the Pouilly-Fuissé and the St. Véran. Has recently become a fixture in the vast vineyards of the Midi, serving both as a varietal and a blending grape there.

Thriving under a wide range of climatic and geographic conditions, the chardonnay has been planted all over the world: in Italy, Spain, Portugal, Germany, Russia, Bulgaria, and the Czech Republic, as well as in Australia, New Zealand, South America, South Africa, and the United States. Italy grows the grape mostly in the northern provinces although its cultivation has also recently moved south. (In the Piedmont, the grape is known as the pinot d'alba; in Alto Aidge, it's called the weissburgunder or white burgundian). The chardonnay has enjoyed considerable success in Spain too, especially in the Penedés region. In Australia, where it's known as the morillon, the grape has been edging out the sémillon in popularity. Australian chardonnays —depending on their growing region— range from big, fruity, and often high-alcohol wines with a rich buttery texture to more austere examples. New Zealand's wines tend to be leaner and more acidic.

Considered America's most successful white varietal —supplanting the chenin blanc, colombard, and others— the chardonnay is the grape of choice in at least fifteen states, including California, Oregon, Washington, and New York. In the United States, its wines run the gamut from fruity and uncomplicated to rich and complex. They range from the leaner, lighter, more delicate and elegantly styled to the big, mouth-filling, and opulent; displaying a delicate fragrant bouquet and a lightly toasted creamy flavor at their finest. (Many, however, are flawed by too much body and oak, making them seem more like dessert wines than like table wines. In the more rigorous growing conditions of the Pacific Northwest, New York's Finger Lakes, and Long Island, its wines are more acidic, taut, and lean; sharing some of the intensity and fragrance of those grown in France. In the United States, the chardonnay is also used for generic wines and in various blends.

NOTE: Initially known as the pinot blanc chardonnay, the grape was believed to be a white-fruited version of the pinot noir. When subsequently found to be a separate and distinct variety, the "pinot" designation was dropped. although the French still occasionally refer to it as the pinot blanc.

CHASSELAS: Productive, early-ripening white grape, the dominant grape variety in Switzerland. Yields a mild, fresh, sturdy wine that is lively at its finest and often slightly pétillant. Appearing under different names in the various Swiss districts, the grape is known as the fendant in western Valais, the dorin near Lake Geneva, and the markgrafler in the east. Is also cultivated widely in France, where it produces light, attractive wines, such as the Pouilly-sur-Loire and the Crépy of Savoie. Was the traditional grape in Alsace until superseded by the gewürztraminer and other varieties. Is still used in ordinary blends there and as a carafe wine. Is also grown in Germany, where it is called the gutedal.

CHASSELAS DORÉ: See Palomino.

CHAUCHE GRIS: See Gray Riesling.

CHELOIS: Red hybrid grown in the Finger Lakes region of New York and in the midwestern United States and Canada. Yields a dry, full-bodied, vinous wine, displaying a pleasant flavor and a subtle bouquet.

CHENIN BLANC: The principal white grape of the Middle Loire. (Originating in Hungary, it was introduced into France in the twelfth century by the monks of Angers.) A productive and easy-growing variety, it yields a soft, flowery, and fragrant wine with a melonlike succulence. It's responsible for the finest Vouvrays, the wines of Touraine, Anjou, and Savennières and the sparkling wines of Saumur. Its wines at their finest retain some natural sweetness, while their excellent acidity produces a clean, crisp, lively finish.

The chenin blanc is the predominant variety in South Africa, where it's known as the steen and is used in table wines, dessert wines, generic sherries and ports. In California's Napa Valley, it yields a fresh, full, fruity wine, displaying an agreeable sweetness and a nice touch of acidity. In the Central Valley, its wines are generally bland and undistinguished, but they exhibit a touch of sweetness. In California, the grape also serves as a component in sparkling wines.

NOTE: Although sometimes called the pineau blanc and pineau de la Loire in France and known as the pinot bianco in Argentina and Chile, the chenin blanc isn't related to the pinot blanc and is not a true pinot at all.

CINSAULT: Red grape grown in warmer climates and thriving in southern France, South Africa, and California, where it yields robust wines characterized by a certain spiciness and intensity. Is used to add warmth, fullness, scent, and color to various blends. Cultivated extensively in the southern Rhône, it serves there as a component in Châteauneuf-du-Pape wines. California uses it in Rhône-style blends. In South Africa, where it's known as the hermitage, the grape is responsible for some of the country's best red wines.

CLAIRETTE: French white grape planted extensively in the Rhône Valley and in the south of France. Is employed in various blends there and also in the sparkling Clairette de Die.

CLEVNER: See Gewürztraminer.

CLINTON: Red hybrid grape brought to Italy from the United States about a century ago. Yields an aromatic and popular wine in eastern Veneto.

COLOMBARD: White grape grown in France. Yields a pale, fresh, lively wine with a touch of sweetness balancing out its acidity. In the Cognac region, its rather acid wine is best suited to distillation and made into a brandy. (The United States also employs it in brandy making.) In California's Central Valley, where the grape is known as the French colombard, it yields a neutral, rather dry wine, used in inexpensive table wines, lesser sparkling wine blends, and generic jug wines. A few California wineries now feature the colombard grape as a varietal.

COLORINO: A highly pigmented Italian red grape grown in Tuscany, where it is used primarily to heighten the color of some Chiantis.

CONCORD: Hardy, productive, early-ripening labrusca grape, initially cultivated in Concord, Massachusetts. Its dark purple, full-bodied, aromatic, high-sugar wine, characterized by a distinctive foxy flavor, is employed as a varietal and in various blends, including generic Burgundies and Champagnes. Also serves as a component in semisweet and sweet fortified wines. Tolerant of a wide range of growing conditions, the concord is cultivated extensively: in Arkansas, Missouri, North and South Carolina, Kansas, Nebraska, Iowa, New York, California, the Pacific Northwest, and elsewhere. (Extremely versatile, it is employed in wine concentrates, grape juice, jams and jellies, and serves as an eating grape as well.)

CORTESE: White grape grown in Italy's Piedmont region. Yields a light, fresh, dry wine with a mild fruity bouquet. Best known is the Cortese di Gavi whose sharp, but balanced acidity makes the wine reminiscent of a crisp and dry Chablis.

COT: See Malbec.

CRIOLLA: See Mission.

DE CHAUNAC: French-American red hybrid, grown in New York's Finger Lakes region and on the Niagara Peninsula. Yields a wine, characterized by considerable color and substance. Rich, soft, and claretlike, it's employed in various blends.

DELAWARE: Sturdy, productive red grape; thought to be a complex hybrid resulting from chance pollination between labrusca and vinifera vines of German and Italian ancestry. Discovered in New Jersey in the nineteenth century, it was transplanted to Delaware, Ohio. Yields a pale, well-balanced wine characterized by a fresh, clean, fruity taste, a pleasing flowery bouquet, and a definite but not-too-strong foxy flavor. Used in various red and white blends, it adds body, richness, and bouquet to them. Also serves as a medium-dry varietal and as a component in sparkling wines.

DIAMOND (Moore's Diamond): American white grape, developed by Jacob Moore in the nineteenth century and believed to possess some European ancestry. A vigorous grower with excellent cold-weather hardiness, it yields a pale, tart, delicate, almost austere wine which combinies fruitiness and piquancy with great subtlety and a pronounced aromatic bouquet. Cultivated primarily in the northeastern United States, it is employed as a varietal and in still and sparkling blends.

DOLCETTO: Productive red grape grown in northwestern Italy; the quickest-maturing of the Piedmont reds. Yields a fragrant, flavorful, medium-bodied wine with good color and plenty of fruit. (Dolcetto translates roughly as "sweet little thing" although the wine itself is dry.) Its best-known example, Dolcetto d'Alba, is grown in the hilly country around the city of Alba.

DORIN: See Chasselas.

DURIFF: Red grape, named for the nurseryman who propagated it late in the nineteenth century. Yields a full-bodied but undistinguished wine, used primarily in blending. Was once planted widely in the Rhône Valley and is now also cultivated in California, where it's called the petite sirah.

DUTCHESS: Red hybrid grown in the northeastern United States. Developed in the nineteenth century on the west bank of the Hudson River, it's believed to be a cross between vinifera and labrusca grapes, involving the concord and delaware varieties. Yields a light, dry, rather clean wine with a generous bouquet and no trace of foxiness. It's employed both as a varietal and in blending.

EHRENFELSER: White hybrid grown in Germany, a cross between the riesling and the sylvaner. Is popular in the cooler districts there because it produces high yields of quality fruit in a relatively short growing season. Is employed in blending.

ELVIRA: American white grape, discovered in Missouri and now also grown in New York State. Relatively low in sugar and medium in acidity, it yields a fresh, spicy, somewhat foxy wine which is used in various blends.

EMERALD RIESLING: White hybrid, a cross between the johannisberg riesling and the muscadelle. Developed for California's warm climates, the grape has been increasingly cultivated in its Central Valley region. Yielding a rather soft, light, semisweet wine which displays an agreeable bouquet, it is employed as a varietal and in various blends there. Also grown in Israel, it produces a charming and flavorful wine in that country.

FENDANT: See Chasselas.

FLORA: White hybrid grape developed at the University of California; a cross between the gewürztraminer and the sémillon. Its spicy wine is somewhat similar to a Gewürztraminer and is employed as a varietal and in various blends. Also serves as a component in sparkling wines.

FOLLE BLANCHE: White grape widely cultivated in France. Known as the gros plant in the Nantes region of the Loire Valley, it yields a light, dry wine there which is thinner and sharper than a Muscadet. (The Germans import it for use in their lesser sparkling blends.) In the Cognac region, it yields a light-bodied, high-acid wine, best suited to distillation. In Armagnac, where the grape is called the picpoul, its wine is also distilled into a brandy. Grown in California's North Coast counties as well, the folle blanche serves as a varietal and in generic Chablis blends.

FRANKEN RIESLING: White hybrid grape grown in California, a cross between the sylvaner and the mainriesling. Yields a pale, dry, delicate, and fairly fruity wine, employed as a varietal and in generic Rhine wines.

FREISA: Italian red grape, whose wine —somewhat tart when young— is vinified both dry and semisweet. The best known examples are the Freisa di Chiera and the Freisa d'Asti. Also serves as a sparkling wine component in Italy. Grown in California, it's employed there as a blending grape.

FRENCH COLOMBARD: See Colombard.

FURMINT: White grape, grown extensively in southeastern and central Europe (including Hungary, Germany, and Italy). Its wine displays an almost herblike aroma. The best-known example is the legendary sweet, golden and luscious Hungarian Tokay .

GAMAY: French red grape prized for its easy-growing, quick-maturing qualities. Cultivated extensively in Beaujolais, it yields a medium-bodied wine there with a distinctive fruitiness, a fresh, light, enticing flavor, and a wonderful sprightliness. Elsewhere in Burgundy, its wines are commonplace and used primarily in regional blends. (The gamay is barred from the best Burgundian vineyards.) Also is grown throughout the Loire Valley, and in certain sectors of the northern Rhône. Is cultivated in Switzerland as well, and as a varietal grape in California.

GAMAY BEAUJOLAIS: Red hybrid, initially thought to be a gamay, but now believed to be a lesser pinot noir clone or perhaps an obscure grape variety from the south of France. Grown widely in California's North Coast counties, it yields a generally fruity wine, which is employed as a varietal, in rosé wines, and in generic Burgundy blends.

GARGANEGA: Italian white grape grown in Lombardy and Veneto. Serves as a component in Soave wines and in other white-wine blends.

GARNACHA: See Grenache.

GEWÜRZTRAMINER: White grape, a selected strain or clone of the traminer; named for Tramin or Termano, its village of origin in the Italian Tyrol. (Although the terms *traminer* and *gewürztraminer* are technically interchangeable, the latter, translating as "spicy traminer," supposedly yields a more intense and flavorful wine.) The gewürztraminer is grown in Alsace, Austria, Eastern Europe, and the United States. In Alsace, its distinctive wine displays an infectious floral bouquet, an intensely fruity taste, a slight sweetness, and a concentrated pungent flavor evocative of herbs and spices. (Outside Alsace, its spiciness is muted.) Despite a rich, flowery bouquet, the wine is quite dry. The grape is also cultivated in Germany, where it's known as the clevner, and in Switzerland, where it's called the traminer aromatico. (In the Italian Tyrol, it's also known as the traminer aromatico.) In California, the grape yields a heavier and more alcoholic wine.

GRAGNANO: See Carignan.

GRAUERBURGUNDER: See Pinot Gris.

GRAY RIESLING: French white grape, grown in Alsace. Also known as the chauche gris, it yields a fresh, clean wine with a flowery fragrance. (Despite its name, this grape is not a true riesling.)

GRECHETTO: Italian white grape, the basic component of Orvieto. Is also blended with the chardonnay to create an earthy white wine.

GRENACHE: French red grape, a principal variety of the Rhône Valley. Lightly pigmented and high yielding, its fairly assertive and occasionally hard wine serves as a traditional component in the Châteauneuf-du-Papes and the region's heavier blends. Is also grown in the Loire Valley. In the South of France, where it's known as the alicante, the grape yields a good dessert wine in Banyuls, adds strength and fruitiness to Provençal blends, and is responsible for some of the best rosés of Tavel and Lirac. Called the garnacha in Spain, it serves principally as a blending grape in Rioja and is also grown in Sardinia, where it's called the cannonau. In California the grape, which is redolent of fruit and spices at its finest, serves a varietal. In the Central Valley, it's a workaday variety, yielding large quantities of light-colored, full-bodied, and generally undistinguished wines that are used in table-wine blends and generic ports. Is cultivated in Australia as well.

GRIGNOLINO: Italian red grape grown in the Piedmont, particularly in Asti. Its dry, light-to medium-bodied wine is rather high in alcohol with a flowerlike aroma, and an almost imperceptible touch of bitterness. Is also used there in sparkling wines. In California, it yields a pleasant varietal and is also employed in rosé wines.

GROS LOT (Grolleau): Productive French grape grown in the Loire Valley. Yields a fair-quality wine that is often vinified to retain a degree of grape sugar. Is also employed in ordinary Anjou rosés and other lesser blends.

GROS PLANT: See Folle Blanche.

GRÜNER VELTLINER: Austrian white grape yielding a fruity, delicate, and lively wine. Is also cultivated extensively in Italy and grown in California as well.

GUTEDEL: See Chasselas.

HEIDE: See Gewürztraminer.

HERMITAGE: Australian red grape, an offspring of the cinsault that yields a sturdy red wine with great staying power. Is named for a famous Rhône Valley vineyard (whose primary grape is the syrah, not the cinsault.)

HUNTER VALLEY RIESLING: White grape grown in Australia. Despite its name, it is not a riesling grape at all but a sémillon. (Also see Sémillon.)

IONA: American red grape named for an island in the upper Hudson River where it was first cultivated. Grown now extensively in the Finger Lakes region of New York, it serves as a component in white-wine blends there.

ISABELLA: American red grape, one of the country's first to be commercially cultivated. Its full-bodied, slightly dry wine with a distinctive foxy flavor was variously employed as a varietal, in red and rosé blends, and in generic Champagnes. Considered an inferior variety now, it is no longer much grown.

IVES: American red grape, believed to be an accidental hybrid related to the concord. Is named for Henry Ives, who grew it from seed on the banks of the Ohio River. Yields a coarse, heavy wine with a strong foxy flavor, which is particularly valued for its deep red color. Is employed in generic Burgundies, in still and sparkling wines, and in sweet fortified wine blends.

JAQUEZ: White grape grown in Madeira and more disease resistant than other local varieties. Is frequently included in blends bearing the names of Madeira's better-known grapes.

JOHANNISBERGER: See Sylvaner.

JOHANNISBERG RIESLING: See Riesling.

KADARKA: Hungarian red grape, similar in style and color to the Italian grignolino, and believed to be of Albanian origin. Now serves as the principal grape in Egri Bikavér (Bull's Blood).

KERRIGAN: See Carignan.

KLEVNER: See Pinot Noir.

KNIPPERLÉ: Alsatian white peasant grape. Yields a generally undistinguished wine which is used in lesser blends.

LAGREIN (Lagarino): Red grape grown in the Italian Tyrol and used in light red and rosé blends. A particularly good example of its rosés comes from Bolzano.

LAMBRUSCO: Italian red grape grown in Emilia-Romagna. Yields a light-colored and somewhat fizzy wine which is not entirely dry. Is also employed in blush wines and in white wine blends.

MAINRIESLING: White hybrid grape, a cross between a riesling and a sylvaner. Is now employed in various wine blends.

MÁLAGA: Prolific red California grape, used in various blends. (Is not related to the Málaga wines of Spain.)

MALBEC: French red grape, whose wine is rich, full, moderately tannic, and relatively quick-maturing. Was once widely planted in Bordeaux, where it softened the more astringent Cabernet Sauvignons. Is primarily the grape of choice in Cahors, where it's known as the cot or the auxerrois. (Is also called the cot in the Loire Valley.) In the south of France, the grape is known as the pressac. In Argentina —where its name is sometimes spelled "malbeck"— it yields a popular medium-bodied and supple varietal wine. Is also cultivated in California's Napa Valley and on New York's Long Island. (The malbec has recently become a rising star in the Long Island vineyards.)

MALVASIA (Malmsey): White grape, originating in Crete and now grown principally in the south of France, most notably in Banyuls and Roussillon. Blended with the grenache and other varieties, it produces both apéritif and sweet dessert wines. The grape is also widely grown in Italy, where it adds a slightly broad style and aroma to Est! Est! Est! and Frascati wines. Is employed in Verdicchio and Chianti blends as well. Made in Sicily as a rich liquoroso, it's responsible for one of the country's best dessert wines, the sweet, golden Malvasia di Lipari. In Madeira, its rich, sweet, aromatic wine is called Malmsey. In California, its wines are undistinguished and employed in various still, sparkling, and dessert wine blends.

MALVOISIE: See Pinot Gris.

MARÉCHAL FOCH: Winter-hardy red hybrid, requiring only a brief growing season. Cultivated in the northeastern United States, it yields a dry, fairly sturdy, berrylike wine, which is somewhat reminiscent of a Burgundy.

MARKGRÄFLER: See Chasselas.

MARSANNE: White grape of the northern Rhône, employed in Hermitage Blanc wines. Has become an increasingly important grape variety in California.

MATARO: See Mourvèdre.

MAZUELO: See Carignan.

MELON DE BOURGOGNE: See Muscadet.

MERLOT: Early-maturing French grape, yielding a round, supple, and medium bodied wine with accessible tannins and a berrylike taste. (Its name, translating as "little blackbird," refers to the wine's dark color.) Widely planted in Bordeaux, the grape is routinely used there to soften the region's more astringent Cabernet Sauvignon wines. In St.-Émilion and Pomerol, the merlot constitutes about 80 percent of the blend. At Château Pétrus, where the grape is used exclusively, the wine is full-bodied and unmatched in its excellence.

A faster ripening grape than the cabernet sauvignon and harvested earlier, the merlot generally yields more approachable and less demanding wines. Increasing in worldwide popularity, the grape is now planted more extensively in Bordeaux, and also cultivated in the south of France, Italy, Spain, Switzerland, Hungary, Romania, Bulgaria, the former Yugoslavia, Argentina, Chile, Australia, New Zealand, and the United States.

Grown from the Alps to the tip of the boot in Italy, the merlot ranges in use from jug wines to rare and expensive examples. It does extremely well in northern Italy, particularly in Veneto, where it yields a rich and chewy wine with good fruit and a seductive aroma. (Elsewhere in Italy, its wine tends to be soft and bland.) The merlot also serves as a key component in Hungary's Egri Bikavér and in Spain's Vega Sicilia. In Australia, it's used as a varietal and in blending. In the United States, where the merlot is the fastest-growing wine category, the grape makes for a soft, plummy varietal in Napa and Sonoma and softens the Cabernet Sauvignons there as well. Has also been successfully cultivated in Washington State and in the vineyards of Long Island.

MEUNIER: Productive French red grape traditionally combined in Champagne blends with the pinot noir and the chardonnay. Also yields pleasant rosé wines in Alsace and the Loire. In California, it serves as a blending grape, and is also fermented away from its skins to produce a white wine there.

MISSION: Red grape, the first vinifera to be cultivated in America, and believed to be of Spanish origin. Initially called the criolla, it was brought to California from Mexico in the eighteenth century by Franciscan monks. Its wine is fruitful and vigorous but lacks color and acidity. Although no longer highly regarded, it is still used by bulk producers for table wine blends, generic ports and sherries, as well as for sweet dessert wines in southern California.

MISSOURI RIESLING: Indigenous white American grape, resembling the elvira. (Is not a true riesling despite its name.)

MOORE'S DIAMOND: See Diamond.

MOURVÈDRE: Warm-climate grape, yielding a dry, astringent wine with hard tannins. Originating in Spain, where it's called the mataro, it is now also grown in France, particularly in the southern Rhône. Primarily employed in blending there, it adds finesse to Châteauneuf and Côtes du Rhône wines. In combination with the grenache and cinsault, it produces the fine red wine of Bandol in the south of France. In California where it is known as the mataro, it's employed in a dry and flavorful vin gris.

MÜLLER-THURGAU: Prolific, hardy, and early-ripening white hybrid grape, developed in the nineteenth century by a Swiss scientist who left no written record of his work. Initially believed to be a cross between a riesling and a sylvaner, it is now thought to combine two riesling clones. Designed for difficult climates, the grape is able to withstand harsh winters and to achieve highly reliable yields in a relatively short growing season. Less acid than the riesling —and the most widely planted German grape variety— it is responsible for vast quantities of mild, soft-scented middle-range wines, which display a flowery bouquet and a slight muscat flavor. (Some examples, however, are undistinguished and flabby.) Serves as a component in various wine blends including Moselblümchens and sparkling sekts. Is cultivated in Austria and in central Europe as well.

MUSCADELLE: French white grape grown in the sweet-wine districts of Bordeaux (Sauternes and Barsac). Generally blended with the sémillon and the sauvignon blanc, the grape imparts a faint, agreeable muscat flavor to the resulting wine.

MUSCADET (Melon de Bourgogne): French white grape, initially grown in Burgundy, where its wines were of little quality or interest. Transplanted to Brittany —where it was called the melon— it yielded a light wine with a faint muscat flavor which made the region famous. Is now cultivated extensively in the lower Loire. In California, where the grape is known as the pinot blanc, it yields a heavier, fruitier wine.

MUSCADINE: A subgenus of the *Vitis rotundfolia*. (Also see Scuppernong.)

MUSCAT: One of the oldest grape families; experts believe that the Vitis viniferas are its direct descendants. Is thought to have been grown by the Phoenicians, Greeks, and Romans in what is now southern France, or perhaps transplanted there by the Crusaders on their return from Corinth and Cyprus. More widely cultivated than any other species now its grapes are variously called muscatel, muscadelle, moscatel, moscat, muskat, moscat ottonel, etc. Its wines are characteristically rich, high in sugar, and low in acid; exhibiting a pronounced flavor and scent and a powerful fruity bouquet. Displaying a distinctive honeysuckle taste and a certain muskiness, they usually show to best advantage in dessert wines. (Some, however, are served as apéritifs.) The muscat has also proved particularly useful in blending because of its ability to knit other wines together.

There are perhaps hundreds of subvarieties, ranging in color from pale yellow to reddish amber, on to almost black. These are grown in Italy, France, Spain, Portugal, Greece, Hungary, the United States, Australia, and the islands of Cyprus and Sardinia. Muscat wines vary in style from country to country, ranging from light to heavy and from completely dry to intensely sweet. One of the best examples, is the Muscat d'Alsace, a dry, full-bodied, aromatic wine with a spicy bouquet which is served as an apéritif. From the Mediterranean region of France comes the sweet fortified Muscat Doré de Frontignan. Italy is known for its sweet Muscats: the Moscato d'Asti, Moscato di Canelli, Moscato del Trentino, Moscato Siracusa, and so on. The United States produces a Muscat blanc and a Muscat Canelli, among others, while Australia is known for its Brown Muscat.

MUSCATEL: See Muscat.

MUSKAT: See Muscat.

NAGYBURGUNDI: See Pinot Noir.

NAPA GAMAY: See Gamay Beaujolais.

NEBBIOLO: Italian red grape, whose name derives from *nebbia,* translating as "fog" and referring to the early-morning mist that clings to the Alban hills during the harvest season. Yields a sturdy, chewy, full-bodied, fairly high-alcohol, and intensely flavored wine, which exudes an aroma of dried fruit. Is associated with the Piedmont's greatest wines: its most powerful Barolos, its most refined Barbarescos, its Gattinaras, Infernos, Sassellas, and Grumellos, along with various other still and sparkling blends. In parts of the Piedmont, the nebbiolo is known as the spanna and in Valtellina, as the chiavennasca. Has also become an increasingly popular grape variety in California, particularly in the Central Valley.

NIAGARA: Versatile white hybrid grape grown on the Niagara Peninsula (a stretch of land shared by Canada and the Finger Lakes region of New York). Yields fruity wines which range from the fresh and clean with a distinctive foxy flavor to the rather sweet and bland. Is sometimes used as a semidry varietal and in various fortified blends, including generic sherries.

PALOMINO: Spanish white grape, the great grape of sherry. Is cultivated on the chalky soil of Jerez. Is also grown in California's Central Valley, where it serves as a component in dry table wines and in sweet fortified blends, including generic sherries. (In California, the grape is called the chasselas doré or the golden chasselas, although it isn't a chasselas at all.)

PARELLADA: Spanish white grape from Catalonia. Is employed in California in chardonnay blends .

PEDRO XIMÉNEZ (PX): Spanish white grape, grown widely in Jerez. Yields a thick, highly aromatic wine whose concentrated flavor suggests prunes, coffee, or chocolate. Is employed to add depth, color, and sweetness to sherry blends.

PETITE ARVINE: Swiss white grape, said to trace its lineage back to the Roman legions.

PETITE SIRAH: Red grape, first propagated in the nineteenth century. Was believed to be related to the Rhône Valley syrah, and later said to be the duriff. Has now been found to be neither. Yields a big, rough, tannic, full-bodied wine, better known for its strength and vigor than for its elegance. (Was brought to California because of its resistance to downy mildew.) Popular there as a sturdy blending grape, it's used to add color and body to generic Burgundies and clarets and to various jug wine blends. Is also made in California as a full-bodied, robust, and intensely colored varietal with soft, fruity flavors. (When oak aging smoothes out its tannins, the wine becomes rich and generous.)

PETIT VERDOT: French red grape, whose characteristically assertive and acid wine is used to add body to the Bordeaux blends. Some California wine makers are also blending it with the cabernet sauvignon.

PICPOULE: See Folle Blanche

PINEAU DE LA LOIRE: See Chenin Blanc.

PINOT: Noble grape family, whose name derives from pine cone; a reference to the shape of its clusters. Known for producing wines with breed, the pinot is widely planted in many of the world's best growing regions. Its subvarieties include the red pinot noir and pinot meunier, and the white pinot blanc and pinot gris.

PINOTAGE: Red hybrid grape, a cross between Burgundy's pinot noir and the Rhône Valley's cinsault. Yields soft, round, fruity wines of some refinement which resemble the wines of the Rhône. Was developed in South Africa in the 1920s and is now grown there almost exclusively.

PINOT BLANC: French white grape, a distant cousin of the pinot noir. Grown widely in Burgundy, it yields light-textured, agreeably dry, fruity, and lively wines of some character and class. One of its best examples, produced in Alsace, exhibits at its finest intense flavors, a beautiful bouquet, and a touch of spiciness. In the Loire, the grape is called the melon de bourgogne, better known as the muscadet. (Once an important component in Champagnes and in other French blends, the pinot blanc has now been largely supplanted there by the chardonnay.) Is also grown in Italy, Germany, Austria and the United States. Made in California as a crisp, dry, fruity varietal, it also serves there in still and sparkling wine blends.

PINOT GRIGIO: Italian white grape that is almost identical to the French pinot gris. The country's most popular white grape, it is grown mainly in the northeast. Yields a pleasant, dry, fruit-scented wine which is vinified both light, fruity, and crisp, and richer and more full-bodied. The best examples, made in the Friuli region, are soft, fruity, and fragrant. The wine it yields in the United States is also popular, but somewhat undistinguished.

PINOT GRIS: French white grape, a mutation of the pinot noir. Grown in cool climates, it yields a crisp dry wine with attractive fruit, characteristically displaying a sturdy fullness together with a slight fragrance. Initially a Burgundian grape, it now flourishes in Alsace, where —known as the tokay d'alsace— it yields an austerely dry, high-alcohol wine with very round flavors.

Grown in various other countries, the pinot gris is called the pinot grigio in Italy, the malvoisie in Switzerland, and the rülander and grauerburgunder (gray burgundian) in Germany. The grape also thrives in the American Northwest, particularly in Oregon, where it yields a wonderfully fruity, yet a quite dry wine.

PINOT MEUNIER: See Meunier.

PINOT NOIR: Extremely dark purple —almost black— grape, believed to have been brought to Gaul by the Greeks. Finicky, troublesome, and hard to grow, it does best in a cool climate with a longer growing season. The principal red grape of Burgundy, it yields wines ranging from light and charming to big and mouth-filling. Is responsible for the great, subtle, splendid reds of the Côte d'Or, rich in their alcohol and strength, and intensely flavored without being full-bodied. Its earthy yet delicate wines are also characterized by a distinctive velvety quality, an elegant deep bouquet and the ability to age well. The pinot noir also produces excellent full-bodied rosés with a lovely pinkish hue. (When transported south to Beaujolais, its wine, however, disappoints.) The pinot noir is also a key component in Champagne blends. It makes for light, pleasant red wines in Alsace and is grown in the Loire Valley as well.

Hundreds of pinot noir clones are now cultivated throughout the world: in Germany, Austria, Italy, Switzerland, Hungary, and the former Yugoslavia, as well as South America (Chile), Australia, New Zealand, South Africa, and the United States. Known in Germany as the spätburgunder, it produces the country's best red wines, characterized by a fine bouquet and a piquant spiciness. Is responsible for good German rosés as well. In Switzerland, where the grape is called the bourgogne or burgunder in one district and the klevner in another, it yields a deep-colored, full-bodied varietal with a good potential for aging. (Blended with the gamay in Valais, it produces the fine red wine called Dole.) In Hungary, where it's called the nagyburgundi, it yields a highly valued wine. But in Austria, where it's called the spätburgunder or blauburgunder (blue burgundian), its wines are often thin and commonplace. In northern Italy, the grape —known as the pinot nero— yields smooth, full-bodied, full-flavored wines and also serves as a component in Asti Spumante blends. Has been increasingly cultivated in California, where it is employed in the better sparkling blends and as a varietal. Some of its wines there are lush and opulent, while others are drier and less complex than the French. (Many are relatively light bodied.) The grape does particularly well in Oregon, where its varietals are closer in character and style to their Burgundian prototypes. Also cultivated on Long Island, the pinot noir is employed in various red wine blends, some of them made sparkling.

PINOT ST. GEORGE: Red grape grown in California's North Coast counties. Yields a thin, somewhat astringent wine, employed in various generic and other table-wine blends. (Is not a true pinot, but a lesser grape.)

PLANT D'ARBOIS: See Poulsard.

PORTUGIESER: Prolific, early-ripening red grape, the mainstay of Germany's red table wines. Widely planted in Rheinhessen and in the Pfalz, it yields light-colored, somewhat sweeter wines with less body than the Spätburgunders. Is also grown in Austria, where it's known as the blauer portugieser.

POULSARD: French red grape grown in the Jura, where it's also known as the plant d'arbois. Its light-colored wines are considered the best reds of the Jura.

PRESSAC: See Malbec.

PROCANICO: See Trebbiano.

PROSECCO: Italian white grape grown in Veneto. Yields a light, dry, pleasant wine that is sometimes made semisweet. Is also employed as a component in sparkling wine blends.

RAMISCO: Hardy Portuguese red grape, yielding a dry and fruity wine. Grown in Colares near the coast, it is able to withstand the ravages of salt water and wind. And, planted deep in sandy soil, it has proved resistant to the phylloxera aphid.

RAVAT: See Vignoles.

RED PINOT: Lesser California grape, whose wine is used in blending. (Despite the name, it is not a true pinot.)

RIESLANER: German white hybrid, a cross between the riesling and the sylvaner. Grown in the Pfalz, it's used in various blends there.

RIESLING (Johannisberg Riesling): Hardy, frost-resistant German white grape, believed to derive from a wild Teutonic vine. One of the noble and classic grape varieties, it can ripen steadily to high levels of sugar while retaining enough acidity to extend the life expectancy of its wine. A modest bearer, it combines the highest possible quality with the smallest yield. Particularly well suited to late harvesting, it is one of the few grape varieties susceptible to noble rot. Flourishing in Germany's northernmost vineyards, the riesling is the source of virtually all the fine Rhine and Mosel wines. These range from the light, bone-dry, and crisply acid to the sweet and unctuous. The wines at their finest are distinguished by a harmony of tartness and sweetness, a sharp, crisp taste and a flowery bouquet. Demonstrating breed, character, and uncommon depth, they combine a touch of dryness with an elegance and a discreetly perfumed fragrance.

The grape is also grown elsewhere in Europe —in France, Switzerland, Portugal, Italy, Austria, the former Yugoslavia, Bulgaria, etc.— as well as in the United States, South America, Australia and New Zealand. In Alsace, the wine is dry and well structured with a steely flavor, firm fruit, and an usually excellent balance. In Austria and Eastern Europe, where it's called the wälschriesling, the grape is more productive and yields a lighter, slightly coarser wine. In South Africa, where it's called the weisser riesling, it is responsible for a steely, dry wine, resembling a Muscadet. In Chile, its light, crisp, attractive wine serves both as a varietal and as a component in sparkling wine blends. Is also grown extensively in Russia and in the Ukraine. In California, where the grape is known as the johannisberg riesling or the white riesling, its wines range from dry and refreshing to somewhat flowery and not too dry. They're generally characterized by a fruity aroma combined with a mild bouquet. The riesling grape also thrives in the coolness of the Pacific Northwest.

NOTE: A number of varieties that bear the riesling name are not rieslings at all. Among these are the gray riesling, missouri riesling, paarl riesling, emerald riesling, franken riesling, mainriesling, and hunter valley riesling.

RIESLING-VIDAL: White grape grown in Virginia. A combination of the riesling and a hybrid, it yields a semisweet wine.

ROUSSANNE: French white grape grown extensively in the Rhône. Yields fresh, fragrant wines, some full in body with a rather pronounced character. Is used in various blends along with the viognier and the marsanne. Is also employed in the St. Peray and other sparkling wines, the Seysall, and the regional Roussette de Savoie. Is grown in California as well, producing Rhône-style wines there.

RUBY CABERNET: Red hybrid grape; a cross between the carignan and the cabernet sauvignon; designed to withstand a hot climate. Grown extensively in California's Central Valley, it's used mainly as a blending wine there, but also yields a fruity, dry varietal characterized by good color, acidity, and flavor.

RULANDER: See Pinot Gris.

ST.-ÉMILION: See Trebbiano.

SANGIOVESE: Italian red grape; second only in popularity to the barbera. Yields a tannic, full-bodied, lively, and somewhat astringent wine that's combined in Chianti blends with the trebbiano and the malvasia. Made as a varietal in Emilia-Romagna, the wine is somewhat harsh in youth but its bouquet can intensify with age. Serving initially as a blending grape in California, it's now made as a varietal there as well. (In the Napa Valley, its wine is less sharply defined than in Italy and also is bigger, fruitier, and softer.)

  Note: The sangioveto, a smaller, more intense version of the sangiovese, yields richer and longer-lasting wines.

SANGIOVESE GROSSO: Italian red grape, a clone of the sangiovese. Is responsible for one of Italy's prized red wines, the Brunello di Montalcino. Is also grown in California, where it's blended with the cabernet sauvignon.

SAUVIGNON BLANC: French white grape; the principal grape of the Loire Valley, where it's known as the blanc fumé. The grape of Pouilly-Fumé, Sancerre, Quincy, and Reuilly, it yields a sprightly, fragrant, fruity, flinty, lean, and austerely dry wine, with a slightly herbaceous or grassy taste and a long-lasting finish. (Increasing in popularity in the Loire, the sauvignon blanc has superseded the formerly dominant chenin blanc.) Vinified as a sweet wine in Bordeaux, it is responsible for the luscious and memorable Sauternes and Barsacs, while in Graves, it is better suited to the production of dry wines.

  The sauvignon blanc is also grown in Italy, Cyprus, Austria, Australia, New Zealand, Chile, Argentina, and the United States. In the cooler regions, its wines are intensely flavored; and in the warmer regions, they tend to be softer and flabbier. A mainstay of the California vineyards, the sauvignon blanc has been vinified in a variety of styles, ranging from light and fruity to rich and oaky. When made as a drier-style varietal (similar to a Pouilly-Fumé), it's generally called a Fumé Blanc. When vinified in a somewhat sweeter style, it is known as a

Sauvignon Blanc. California also uses the grape in its generic Sauternes.

SAUVIGNON VERT: California white grape, grown in the North Coast counties. Yields a harsh, bitter wine there that is used to offset the blandness of generic Sauternes and Chablis blends.

SAVAGNIN: French white grape, a component in vin jaune and vin de paille blends. (Believed to be of Hungarian lineage, the grape may have been transported to France by the returning Crusaders.)

SCHEUREBE: Sturdy white German hybrid grape, grown in the Pfalz and in Rheinhessen. A cross between the sylvaner and the riesling, it is more prolific and easier to cultivate than the riesling, and also resistant to cold and disease. Its wines when young, may be hard and acidic, but can acquire fruit and finesse after a few years. When very ripe, the grape yields semidry and sweet dessert wines with a lush black currant flavor. Also receptive to noble rot, the scheurebe has been used in making German Beerenausleses. It is now cultivated as well in California's Napa Valley, in Washington State, and in Oregon.

SCHIAVA: Italian red grape grown in the Tyrol and on the western shore of Lake Garda. Yields a light red wine, used in Caldaro and Santa Maddalena blends.

SCUPPERNONG: American white grape, the best-known variety of the muscadine species. Thrives in the warm, humid climate of the southeastern United States, where it yields an amber-colored, rather full-bodied, and usually quite sweet and aromatic wine. Is also grown in the midwestern United States.

SÉMILLON: French white grape, whose rather rounded and velvety wines are known for their fragrance. Cultivated extensively in Bordeaux, it serves there as the base of its great white wines; is traditionally blended with the sauvignon blanc and, to a lesser extent, with the muscadelle. Susceptible to noble rot, the grape is a major component in the luscious wines of Sauternes and Barsac. In Graves, where it's blended with the sauvignon blanc, the wine is soft bodied, with a clean, crisp grassiness balanced by a fruity bouquet. Is also used in the drier white wines of Entre-Deux-Mers and Monbazillac. Cultivated throughout the world, the sémillon is grown in the United States, South America, and Australia. An important Australian varietal, it's known there as the hunter valley riesling. In California and Washington State, it appears both as a light dry wine and as a sweet varietal. Is also used in various American blends, including among them the best generic Sauternes.

SERCIAL: White grape grown in Madeira and employed in a dry white wine that bears its name there. (The grape's origins are unclear although it's believed to be a descendant of the riesling.)

SEYVAL BLANC: French-American white hybrid, developed to survive the harsh growing conditions of the northeastern and midwestern United States. (The grape also lends itself to late harvesting.) Yields a high-quality, full-bodied, well-balanced wine, exhibiting a delightful bouquet and a clear crisp finish. (Is similar in style to the Sancerres and other French wines based on the sauvignon blanc.) Responsible for some of New York State's best white wines, it also serves as a component in sparkling blends there. Is cultivated in France and in Canada as well.

SHIRAZ: See Syrah.

SPANNA: See Nebbiolo.

SPÄTBURGUNDER: See Pinot Noir.

STEEN: South African white grape, initially thought to be a cross between a riesling and an indigenous variety, but has now been identified as the chenin blanc. Yields a sweet, light, fragrant, and fruity wine. Is sometimes late harvested.

STEUBEN: American red grape, serving as a component in various wine blends. Its wine is more delicately flavored than that of the concord grape.

SYLVANER: German white grape, planted principally in Rheinhessen and in the Pfalz. Faster ripening and more productive than the riesling, it's responsible for a large proportion of Germany's fair to ordinary wines. Considered a superior variety in Franconia, it yields a light, fresh, and unusually mild wine there, with a slight touch of acidity. The sylvaner is cultivated in many parts of Europe as well; in France, Switzerland, Austria, the Italian Tyrol, and Hungary; also in the United States and Chile. In the Valais district of Switzerland, it's known as the johannisberger, and in Austria, as the osterreicher. Its wine in Alsace is charming with a clean, refreshing bouquet.

SYMPHONY: White hybrid grape, developed in California and involving the muscat of Alexandria. Yields a wine similar to a Gewürztraminer, with flavors and aromas that recall flowers, oranges, and spices.

SYRAH: Slow-maturing red grape, initially believed to have been introduced to France in the thirteenth century by Crusaders returning from the city of Shiraz in Persia, now Iran. Scholars now believe that the grape arrived in France much earlier and that it was brought in from Asia Minor around 600 B.C. by the Phoenician seamen who founded Marseilles.

The syrah yields a powerful, intense, tannic, and deep-colored wine, displaying a smoky, licorice-like quality and a memorable bouquet reminiscent of blackberries. Responsible for the great reds of the Rhône, it's associated with Hermitage, Châteauneuf-du-Pape, and Côte Rôtie wines. (The white viognier and marsanne may be included in these blends.) Also provides the structure and backbone for other Rhône wines and adds robustness, color, and bouquet to the wines of Provence. Has become an important grape in California as well, serving as a varietal and in Rhône-style wines. Planted widely in Australia in the nineteenth century and called the shiraz, it has become that country's dominant red grape, yielding a fruity, full-bodied tannic wine, with a rough spicy character, sometimes blended with the cabernet sauvignon. Is also cultivated in South Africa.

TEMPRANILLO: Red grape, believed to be a strain of the pinot noir. Was brought to Spain centuries ago by the monks of Cluny. Now the principal grape of Rioja, it is employed there as a varietal and in blending. Yields a soft, spicy, moderately acid wine with a full rich quality, a chewy texture, and a lingering finish. Is also grown in La Mancha, where it's called the cencibel, and in the Duero, where it's called the tinto fino. (Elsewhere in Spain, the grape is known as the tinto del pais.) Called the ugni blanc in France, it's an important grape in the Cognac region. The tempranillo is also cultivated in Italy, Portugal, and California. (It is called the valdepeñas in California.)

THOMPSON SEEDLESS: White grape, grown in California. Yields a rather neutral, nondescript low-acid wine, used in generic Rieslings and in various table and jug-wine blends. Is extensively cultivated by the bulk wine producers in California. Also serves as an eating grape and as a source of raisins.

TINTA: Portuguese red grape whose deep-colored, full-bodied wine is employed mainly in port and Dão blends. Is also grown in Madeira, and cultivated in California's Central Valley as well where it is generally used in sweet fortified blends, including some of the better generic ports.

TOCAI: Italian white grape. Yields a fairly full-bodied, dry wine with a delicate aroma and a slightly bitter aftertaste.

TOKAY: California red grape, said to have originated in Algeria. Is used for eating rather than for wine making. (Is not related to the Tokay wines of Hungary, which are made with the furmint grape.)

TOKAY D'ALSACE: See Pinot Gris.

TORRANTES: Algerian white grape whose spicy, dry wine is somewhat reminiscent of an Alsatian Gewürztraminer.

TRAMINER: See Gewürztraminer.

TREBBIANO: Widely cultivated Italian grape; the source of most of the country's white wines. (The grape is known as the procanico in Umbria.) Made as a varietal in Tuscany, it yields a luscious, fruity, definitely scented and fairly assertive wine. Elsewhere in Italy, its wines are generally bland and unimpressive. Also serves as a component in Orvieto, Frascati, and Chianti blends. A subvariety, trebbiano di soave, yields a wine with some character. (It's used in the best Soave blends.) A coarser, more prolific variant is the trebbiano toscano, yielding a blander wine.

Cultivated in other parts of Europe, the trebbiano is known in the south of France as the ugni blanc and produces generally uninteresting wines there except for the fresh white wines of Cassis. In the Charente region, where it's known as the St.-Émilion, it yields a high-acid, low-alcohol wine that achieves greatness when it's distilled as Cognac. In California, the trebbiano yields an agreeable but neutral wine that is almost always employed in blending, although occasionally it is made as a varietal wine.

UGNI BLANC: See Trebbiano.

VALDEPEÑAS: See Tempranillo.

VALPANTENA: Red Italian grape, named for a region in Verona. Is employed in Valpolicella blends.

VELTLINER: See Grüner Veltliner.

VERDEJO: Spanish white grape, believed to derive from the pedro ximénez. Cultivated extensively in Madeira, it is employed there in the somewhat sweet fortified wine which bears its name. In Portugal, the grape serves as a component in white port wines.

VERDICCHIO: Italian white grape grown in Marches on the Adriatic coast. Yields a pleasant, dry varietal wine.

VERDOT: French red grape grown in Bordeaux. Yields a deep-colored, full-bodied, fruity, tannic wine which serves as a component in claret blends.

VERGENNES: American white grape grown in New York State. Yields a very dry, exquisitely flavored wine, employed both as a varietal and in various blends.

VERNACCIA: Italian white grape grown in Tuscany. Its fresh, full-bodied wine exhibits a good acidity and sometimes earthy nuances. It is vinified both dry and sweet. The best known example is Vernaccia di San Gimignano, grown around the ancient town of that name. In Sardinia, the grape yields a very dry wine with an intense almond-like aroma, resembling an unfortified sherry.

VIDAL: American white hybrid, grown in New York's Finger Lakes region; a cross between a vinifera and a labrusca. A relatively early ripener, the grape yields a naturally sweet wine.

VIGNOLES: French-American white hybrid grape (also known as the ravat), grown in the Finger Lakes region of New York. Winter-hardy and rapidly maturing, it yields a fairly full wine with a distinctive bouquet which serves as a base for sparkling wines. The grape is sometimes late harvested as well.

VIOGNIER: A once obscure French white grape, originally brought to Marseilles by the Greeks, then transported north to the Rhône Valley. Yields a full-bodied wine which displays a flowery perfume and a crisp but fruity flavor redolent of apricots and peaches. Is responsible for the rare white wine of Condrieu, which reaches its peak in Château Grillet. When added in small quantities to the Côte Rôtie's red wines, the viognier softens them and makes them less astringent. Is also grown in the Ardèche and Languedoc-Roussillon regions of France. Now cultivated in California as well, the grape yields an intensely fruity and spicy wine used mainly in blending. Is also grown in a number of other American states. Experimental plantings are now underway in Italy and Australia.

VIURA: Spanish white grape grown in Rioja. Yields a light, aromatic wine with an excellent crisp quality.

WÄLSCHRIESLING: See Riesling.

WEISSBURGUNDER: See Chardonnay.

ZINFANDEL (Zin): Reliable, sturdy, tough-skinned and prolific red grape characterized by high sugar and high tannins. Grown in the United States at least since the mid-nineteenth century, it has been called a truly "American" grape, although its actual origins are unknown. Resembling the primitivo of the Apulia region of southern Italy, it is also genetically similar to some grape varieties from Hungary and the former Yugoslavia. (It has been traced to Croatia and the Dalmatian coast.) The zinfandel may have been brought to California by Agoston Haraszthy, who imported thousands of cuttings from Europe. Or it may have arrived with the waves of European immigration at the time of the Gold Rush. Early in the twentieth century, it was the favorite of eastern wine makers because it could survive the long cross-country train trip by boxcar better than most other California varieties.

Was initially a workaday blending grape and the source of California's mostly rough, mass-produced wines, giving body and color to generic, low-acid clarets, Chiantis, and Burgundies, in addition to serving as a component in sparkling wines and as an inexpensive varietal. Marvelously adaptable, the zinfandel has come into its own in recent years and is now made in a multitude of styles and strengths, ranging from the soft and unassuming to the tannic and assertive, and from the smooth and silky to the big, powerful, and rough-edged. Some of the wines are fresh, fruity, and light like a Beaujolais; while others are medium-bodied, later-maturing, and elegant like a Cabernet Sauvignon. Still others are rich and heavy, full of spice and fruit flavors, with a touch of earthiness. The best examples are produced in the North Coast California counties, particularly in Sonoma. Full-bodied and rich but not too heavy, these are open textured, lively, and agreeable wines with a rich berrylike fruitiness, a slightly tart quality, a distinctive — almost spicy— bouquet, and a long lasting finish. (When late harvested, their wine is robust and intensely sweet like an after-dinner port.) Often high in alcohol, the wines range from more than 14 percent to over 17 percent.

A white Zinfandel has been made by separating the color-laden skins from the clear juice early in the fermentation process. Pale pink or salmon in color, it's actually a blush wine. Generally light, bland, and low in alcohol, the wine may be blended with the chenin blanc and other varieties to increase its flavor. A touch of sugar may be added for a slight sweetness and a bit of carbon dioxide injected to make the wine slightly fizzy. (The result is often more like a soft drink.)

🍇 🍇 🍇

There was a man who once said he liked his wines
and his women
at room temperature

GLOSSARY

AMARONE: See Recioto.

ANGELICA: Amber-colored, fruity, and somewhat sweet fortified wine, pressed from mission, grenache, and other grapes. The better examples are blended and aged like sherries; the lesser are little more than grape juice bolstered with brandy.

AQUATA: See Piquette.

ARMAGNAC: Brandy produced in southwestern France in Gascony. Made by the single-distillation method, the spirit retains more of its sturdy grape elements, making it more robust than Cognac.

BOURGOGNE PASSE-TOUT-GRAINS: See Passe-Tout-Grains.

BRANDY: A spirit distilled from high-acid wines, then aged in oak.

BYRRH: Proprietary brand of a fortified aromatic wine, made in France. Is characterized by the appetite-whetting taste of quinine and served as an apéritif.

CLARET: British name for the red wines of Bordeaux. Originated in the twelfth century when Gascony was a possession of the British crown and these mostly pale-colored wines were called clairet or clarret, deriving from clair (light or clear) "Clarret wines," it was said, "be fair coloured and bright as a rubie, not deepe as an ametist." Claret has since become the generic name for red table wines.

COGNAC: A double-distilled brandy produced by individual grape growers and cooperatives in the Charente region of France. They distill the spirit in small quantities, then sell it to the major producers who do the actual blending and aging.

COLD DUCK: A combination of red and white sparkling wines. Initially known as *Kalte Ende* (Cold Ending), the drink grew out of the thrifty German custom of serving wines left over after a party as a chilled punch. Because of either a deliberate pun or a typographical error, the punch came to be called *Kalte Ente* (Cold Duck). Made available in bottles, some versions combine generic sparkling Burgundies and generic Champagnes while others involve carbonated wines.

COOKING WINE: Wine made unsuitable for drinking by the addition of salt (to exempt it from taxes on alcoholic beverages). Somewhat acrid in taste, it's not as good for cooking as ordinary wines are.

DUBONNET: Proprietary red semisweet wine; made somewhat astringent with quinine and aromatic with herbs. Serves both as an apéritif and as a component in cocktails. Produced initially in France, it's now licensed for production in the United States and in other countries. (Each uses a domestic wine as the base.) Is also made in a somewhat drier white wine version, known as Dubonnet Blonde.

FOLK WINES (Specialty Wines): Wines made from ingredients other than grapes and generally produced in regions unable to grow their own grapes. These wines have involved various fruits, including cherries, peaches, blackberries, currants, elderberries, plums, gooseberries, loganberries, strawberries, apples, rhubarb, apricots, pineapple, cranberries, etc. Also employed have been vegetables and such other unusual ingredients as parsnips, potatoes, dandelions, and even the sap of the silver birch tree.

GRAPPA: Clear, colorless Italian brandy distilled from pomace. (The name may be the shortened form of the Italian *grappolo di uva,* which translates as a "bunch of grapes.") Described as the last element of wine, grappa was initially a harsh, raw, potent, and generally fiery spirit, coarse in texture and smelling of earth and hay. It's now made in several styles: some grappas are distilled directly from grapes, others are also flavored with fruit, flowers, or herbs. The best examples are made from a single grape variety; their delicate and discreet flavors are then rounded out by wood aging. (Also see Marc.)

JUG WINES: Generally inexpensive and unobtrusive wine blends, which undergo shorter fermentations and briefer aging times than most other wines. Bottled in gallon jugs or magnums, they are produced in France, Italy, Spain, the United States, and various other countries.

KIR: An apéritif combining a white table wine (originally a Burgundy) with crème de cassis (black currant liqueur) in a ratio of 3 or 4 parts to 1. The white wine often used now is an inexpensive Aligoté or a Muscadet. Introduced in Burgundy and initially known as Vin Blanc de Cassis, it was renamed after World War II to honor Felix Kir, the mayor of Dijon and a hero of the French Resistance.

A number of variants have been developed: Kir Cardinal, replaces the crème de cassis with Beaujolais; Kir Rabelais replaces the white wine with the sturdy red wine of Cahors, and Kir Royal replaces the still wine with Champagne or another sparkling wine.

KOSHER WINE: Wines originally intended for sacramental use and made in conformity with Jewish dietary laws. (The entire wine-making process, from crushing to bottling, is carried out by observant Jews working under rabbinical supervision and following exacting standards.) Products that meet these require-ments carry a "U" inside a circle on their labels, standing for the Union of Orthodox Jewish Congregations, or have Hebrew lettering to that effect printed on their corks and capsules. Such wines are now produced in Israel, Italy, France, the United States, and elsewhere.

The traditional kosher wines —made principally from concord or malaga grapes— were red, heavy, and cloying. Now they may be red or white, still or sparkling, varietal or generic. They may also be pressed from vinifera, labrusca, or hybrid grapes. (The varieties employed have included the gamay, gewürztraminer, merlot, petite sirah, pinot blanc, pinot noir, riesling, shiraz, and zinfandel.) Some of the wines are bone-dry, others are honey sweet. Among the most popular are the blush wines and rosés, which represent a transition between the traditional sweet wines and the drier examples more suitable for accompanying food.

LIGHT WINES: Wines subjected to special processing to reduce their alcohol content. (Also see Nonalcoholic Wines.)

LILLET: Proprietary French wine, flavored with herbs and fortified with brandy. Served as an apéritif, it is available in both red and white versions.

MÁLAGA: Dark amber and generally sweet fortified wine, characterized by an unusually fragrant bouquet. Produced in southern Spain, it's named for the port from which it was first shipped. Pressed principally from sun-dried muscat and PX grapes, the wine is blended and aged in a solera.

MARC: Clear, colorless brandy, distilled from pomace in the Burgundy and Champagne regions of France. It's a somewhat coarse, rough spirit with a woody, strawlike taste and a pungent aroma. A notable example is Burgundy's Marc de Bourgogne, flavored with oranges, lemons, and herbs. Also known as burning water, marc is called *trinkbrandtwein* in Germany, *aguardiente* in Spain and a*gurdente* in Portugal. (Also see Grappa.)

MAY WINE: German white wine flavored with the sweet, aromatic leaves of the woodruff plant and traditionally served as a punch, garnished with fruit. Has been marketed in bottles in Germany and the United States.

MEAD: An ancient beverage produced by the fermentation of honey. It is not a wine although sometimes considered as one.

MUSCATEL: A wine pressed from muscat grapes in California, and generally of poor quality.

NONALCOHOLIC WINES (Soft Wines): Wines —red, white, or rosé, still or sparkling— whose alcohol has been removed by special processing. As much as 0.5 percent, however, may remain. (The wines that retain no alcohol are labeled "Alcohol Free.")

ORDINAIRE: See Vin Ordinaire.

ORGANIC WINES: Wines made from grapes grown without the use of chemical fertilizers, fungicides, or pesticides. Fully organic wines are extremely rare. A wine made from organic grapes may still not be completely organic because of its processing method. (As yet, there is no universally accepted definition as to what constitutes an organic wine.)

PASSE-TOUT-GRAINS: A light red Burgundy, a blend of pinot noir and gamay grapes, designed to stretch the region's limited supply of the pinot noir. Only 30 percent of this variety is required and it is generally drawn from the lesser Côte d'Or communes. (Since a red Burgundy must by law be pressed exclusively from the pinot noir, Passe-Tout-Grains is technically not a Burgundy wine.)

PIQUETTE: Thin, tart, low-grade wine, made from pomace in France and containing only 3 to 4 percent alcohol. Is generally served free to winery workers. (Its commercial sale is illegal.) The Italian version is known as Aquata.

POMACE: The pressings left over after wine making; they consist of grape seeds, stems, and skins.

POP WINES: Wines or wine-based beverages, bottled and marketed under brand names. Usually transient in popularity, these have included wine coolers, Cold Duck, Kir, sangria, apple wine, May wine, etc.

PUNT É MES: Italian proprietary wine; a sweetened vermouth, served as an apéritif. Originating near the Milan stock exchange, its name comes from the stock-broker's term which translates as a "Point and a Half."

RAKI: A grape-based distillate, produced in Turkey. Flavored with anise, it is generally taken with water in a one-to-one ratio. Is similar to, although somewhat drier than, the Greek ouzo and the French pastis.

RECIOTO: Red or white Italian wine, made from rich ripe grapes picked from the uppermost part of the cluster, then raisined to concentrate their sugars further. The resulting wine is full-bodied, high in alcohol, sweet, spicy, and unctuous, with great depth and complexity. The best-known example, the red Amarone of Veneto, is characterized by a full, warm taste and a delicate aroma. (Its grapes are dried for up to six months and the wine itself is aged for about three years.) Recioto della Valpolicella is a sweeter version. A sparkling Recioto is also made.

ROSÉ WINES (Vins Rosé): Wines pressed from red grapes whose skins are withdrawn when the desired shade of pink is achieved. True rosés are made by leaving the pigmented skins of red grapes briefly in contact with their fermenting juice, allowing a certain amount of color to leach out. (The cheap versions add a little bit of red wine to a large quantity of white wine.) Rosés are made in every wine-producing country, including France, Italy, Spain, Portugal, Greece, Morocco, Algeria, Israel, Germany, Austria and the United States. Grape varieties employed have included the grenache, gamay, pinot noir, cabernet franc, cabernet sauvignon, petite sirah, grignolino, cinsault, carignan, etc., as well as the pinkish gewürztraminer. (Classic examples are pressed from moderately pigmented grapes such as the grenache and the gamay.) The wines themselves run the gamut from light and pale to more full-bodied and darker. They range in color from light garnet through deep pink to pale coral. The best examples are relatively low in alcohol and exhibit a richness of color, a fine fresh fruitiness, and a bit of residual sugar. Modifying their sweetness is a slight touch of sharpness, which makes them seem drier than they actually are.

The finest rosés come from Tavel and Lirac in the south of France. Also well known is the Rosé d'Anjou from the Loire and Burgundy's pinot noir rosé from Marsannay. The Italians make hundreds of Chiaretto rosés in the south and in Sicily, mostly for local consumption. One of the best examples is the light, fresh Chiaretto grown at the southern end of Lake Garda. Spanish Rosados are pressed from the garnacha (grenache) grape; some are full-bodied, while others are fresh, delicately fruity, and elegant. Germany produces an extremely pale pink Weissherbst, pressed from the pinot noir. The most notable American rosés are grown in California's North Coast. Pressed from the grenache and gamay, these are fairly pale, fruity, and somewhat crisp wines. (Most rosés hover between 11 and 12 percent alcohol, although some muscular examples from California can reach 13 percent alcohol or more.)

SAKE: Japanese beverage made from fermented rice; sometimes with the addition of alcohol, sugar, yeast and other ingredients. (Although appearing to be a white wine, it is in fact an uncarbonated beer, averaging about 6 percent in alcohol.) Various versions are currently produced: some are somewhat sweet, others display a slightly bitter aftertaste. Traditionally taken warm in tiny cups, sake is now served chilled as well.

SANGRIA: Red-wine punch originating in Spain. Its name —deriving from *sangre*, which translates as "blood"— refers to the wine's strong ruby red color. Initially a harsh, dry, wine, it was modified with oranges, lemon juice, sugar, and soda water. Sangria may also be garnished with pineapples, cherries, or berries, or have brandy or cinnamon added. (Bottled versions are produced in California and Spain.) A white-wine variant is also made.

SFURSAT: Concentrated Italian red wine pressed from nebbiolo grapes that are left to dry in airy lofts for up to two weeks after the harvest.

TOKAY: Hungarian white wine named for Tokaji, a village in the Carpathian Mountains. Pressed from furmint grapes, it ranges in color from pale straw to amber and in taste from dry to sweet. Some examples are crisp and dry, while others are fiery and full-bodied.

VIN DE PAILLE (Straw Wine): Gold-colored French wine, produced in the Jura. Pressed from raisined grapes and fermented slowly, it is sweet, thick, strong, and somewhat spicy in character. Inordinately rich, the wine has an unusually high alcohol level. Other versions are made in Switzerland and Italy.

VIN GRIS (Gray Wine): French white wine, pressed from red grapes. Displaying only a slight trace of pinkness, like a blush wine, it is remarkably hardy and refreshingly dry. In Alsace and Burgundy, vin gris generally refers to the pale rosés made from the pinot noir. Other versions are produced in the Jura and Morocco. The term has also been applied to pinkish blends of red and white grapes, made elsewhere in France and in Central Europe.)

VIN JAUNE (Yellow Wine): Deep golden, exceedingly dry, high-alcohol French wine, produced in the Jura. Pressed from late-gathered grapes, it grows a florlike yeast. Aged for five to ten years in small casks, the wine acquires a highly developed and intensely fragrant bouquet with a pleasantly oxidized edge and a vaguely nutlike flavor that is somewhat reminiscent of a sherry. Is served both as an apéritif and as an after-dinner drink.

VIN ORDINAIRE: A commonplace blend of French red or white wines that often is not bottled at all. (The blend may also include wines from North Africa, Greece, or Spain.) In Portugal, ordinary wines are called *vinhos do consumo;* in Spain, *viños do pasto,* and in the United States, jug wines. In Britain, they are known as *plonk,* possibly a corruption of "blanc," as in *vin blanc*.

VIN ROUGE: Undistinguished French red wine, often originating in the Midi and usually strengthened with domestic or foreign wines. May not be French at all unless the label reads "Product of France" or its equivalent.

VIN SANTO: Rich, sherrylike Italian wine, made from late-gathered grapes and served as an after-dinner drink. The grapes are partially dried indoors for some months, then pressed slowly. Their thick concentrated juice, fermenting for three to six years or more in small oak casks (sealed with cement or wax), is kept in an attic or other uninsulated place and subjected to extremes of weather. The resulting wine —sweet, intense, and potent— generally ranges from 14 to 17 percent in alcohol. Some versions combine a spicy, honeyed sweetness with a delicate flavor and a distinct pleasant dryness in the finish. Others are almost dry on the palate and exude an aroma of hazelnuts and almonds. Most notable is Tuscany's vin santo, produced in the vicinity of Florence. A dry version also is made.

VINHO VERDE (Green Wine): Tart, low-alcohol, faintly fizzy wine, made in Portugal from underripe grapes. Is generally fermented in stainless steel or in glass-lined cement vats, rather than in wooden barrels to preserve the wine's fruitiness and to keep it pleasantly refreshing. Vinho verdes may be red or white wines. (The "green" in their name alludes to their bracing acidity and to the fact that they are bottled while still quite young.)

Made from a number of grape varieties, and ranging in style from dry to semidry, vinho verdes generally average 9 percent in alcohol. (Most Portuguese table wines usually average 12 or 13 percent.) For export, some of the wines are injected with carbon dioxide to re-create their youthful fizziness.

WEISSHERBST: See Rosé wines.

WINE: Wine is the fermented juice of grapes. Composed primarily of water, a small percentage of organic solids, and 8 to 14 percent alcohol (although some unusual table wines reach about 17 percent), it is much more than a dilute solution of alcohol. Wine contains hundreds of compounds, including sugars, acids, sulfates, phosphates, mineral salts, esters, aldehydes, etc. Some of these elements derive from the grape itself, while others are created by the fermentation and aging processes. Differing in proportion from one wine to the next, these elements determine the uniqueness of each wine.

WINE COOLERS: Hybrid products, combining nondescript wines with fruit juices and carbonated water. They may also be sweetened and colored. These are usually white wines, although red and rosé versions have also been made. Ranging in alcohol from 4 to 6 percent, wine coolers are sold in small bottles like beer.

Miscellaneous Terminology

ABBOCCATO: Italian for "semisweet." Literally translating as "mouth-filling," it refers to wines that have retained a degree of unfermented sugar —usually 1 to 3 percent. The term is applied to Orvietos and other Italian wines made in a soft and slightly sweet style.

ABOCADO: Spanish for "semisweet."

ADEGA: Portuguese for the "cellar or warehouse of a wine producer," the equivalent of a Spanish bodega.

ALMACENISTAS: Spanish for "storekeeper" or "stockholder." Refers to privately held lots of high-quality sherries purchased by established sherry houses from small growers who cannot afford to bottle and ship their own wines themselves. Labeled "Almacenistas," the wines, are then marketed without further blending and may be identified by a number to indicate their original producer.

AMABILE: Italian for "semisweet," somewhat sweeter than abboccato.

AMPELOGRAPHER: A specialist in grapes and wines.

AMPELOGRAPHY: The study and classification of grape varieties.

APÉRITIF: A light beverage, usually a fortified wine, flavored with herbs and other botanicals and generally displaying both acidity and sweetness. Taken before meals, it stimulates the appetite and prepares the palate for the foods to follow. Apéritifs include dry sherries and vermouths and such proprietary cocktail wines as Cinzano, Dubonnet, Lillet, etc.

APERITIVO: Italian for "apéritif."

ASCIUTTO: Italian for "dry." Refers to a wine that retains up to 1 percent unfermented sugar. (The term is interchangeable with secco.)

ASSEMBLAGE: The wine's final blending; a term generally associated with Champagnes.

BALLON: A large wineglass.

BARREL FERMENTATION: A wine's fermentation in wood, generally in oak.

BENATON: A harvest basket in France.

BISTRO WINES: Light, fruity, and generally undistinguished wines, intended for casual sipping.

BODEGA: Spanish for a "producer's establishment"; it may be a winery, a wine cellar, or a small wine shop.

BROKER: Middleman in Bordeaux, who serves as the liaison between the négociant (shipper) and the château (winery).

BULLETS: Bunches of grapes unsuitable for wine. Hard, acid tasting, and smaller than normal, they are caused by an early spring frost damaging the buds that are about to open.

CANNELINO: Italian for "sweet." Refers to a wine that has retained as much as 3 to 6 percent unfermented sugar.

CANTINA: Italian for a "winery" or "wine cellar."

CARAFE: Wide-necked, clear-glass container used in serving wines. (Can also refer to a wine meant for early consumption.)

CAVE: French for a "winery cellar;" one that is usually located underground. (Can also refer to a wine cellar in a restaurant or a private home.)

CELLAR RATS: Winery workers who lug the hoses and clean the tanks.

CÉPAGE: French for "grape variety." (Cep translates as "rootstock" or as the "individual vine.")

CHAI: French for an "aboveground wine storage space." Associated with Bordeaux, this may be a winery, warehouse, or even a shed.

CHAIR: French for a wine's "body" or its fullness.

CHAPTALIZE: The practice of adding sugar to a wine during fermentation so as to balance out its acidity, mask its coarseness, modify its excessive foxiness, and/or raise its alcohol level. The added sugar, fermenting out at the same time as the natural sugar, does not sweeten the wine itself.

CLARETE: Spanish for a "light red wine." Refers to certain Riojas that have received little wood aging.

CLIMAT: A parcel of land in a Burgundian vineyard, owned by one or by several separate proprietors.

CLONE: A grape subvariety bred to be identical to its parents. (It may vary from them, however, in fruit quality, disease resistance, and longevity.)

CLOS: French for "enclosure." Originally referred to a vineyard surrounded by a stone wall, as was the monastic custom in the Middle Ages. Now refers to a vineyard in Burgundy, often an estate of the highest rank.

CLUSTER SELECTED: The delayed picking of grape clusters for late-harvest wines; a term seen on wine labels.

COMITÉ INTERPROFESSIONEL DU VIN DE CHAMPAGNE: The professional and promotional French organization of the wine industry in Champagne.

COMMUNE: French for "parish." Refers to a town or village and to the land that surrounds it.

CORSÉ: French for "a full-bodied wine."

CÔTE: French for a "slope" or hillside on which the grapes are grown. (The plural of this is côteaux.)

COUNTRY WINES: Anonymous wines made in many wine-producing countries. In France, the term covers not only unknown wines from the more obscure districts but also inexpensive Bordeaux wines and Muscadets.

COURTIERS: Brokers in Bordeaux, who act as middlemen between the château owners and the shippers.

CRU: French for "growth." The term, referring to a particular parcel of land and its wine, implies quality. In Bordeaux, a Grand Cru (Great Growth) represents a high-caliber vineyard or wine. The term is also important in Burgundy and Alsace.

CUVÉE: French for the "contents of a cask or vat." In the Champagne region, it refers to the blending of wines pressed from several varieties of grape. (Also see Assemblage.)

DÉGUSTATION: French for a "sampling of wines," a wine tasting. In a restaurant, a menu de dégustation pairs appropriate wines with the special dishes served.

DIGESTIF: A beverage, usually somewhat sweet, taken at the end of the meal to complement the dessert course. (Is also meant to soothe the stomach and aid in digestion.) Included here are cream sherries, ports, Madeiras, noble-rot wines, etc.

DOLCE: Italian for "sweet." (Also see Cannellino.)

DOMAINE: Holdings that constitute a vineyard property or an estate under one management. In Bordeaux, the term can refer to a single unified property, provided the wine was actually produced there. In Burgundy, the parcels of land involved may be located in different communes and have different names.

EDELWEIN: A late-harvest wine made from botrytized grapes in California.

ÉLEVEUR: See Négociant.

ENCÉPAGEMENT: French for a "blend of grapes." (Also see Cépage.)

ENOLOGIST: A wine scientist or a master wine maker. (The name derives from the Greek *oinos*, translating as "wine.")

ENOLOGY: The science and study of wine and wine making.

ENOTECA: Italian for wine library. The term usually denotes a wine shop, which may include a wine bar. Can also refer to a restaurant that serves local dishes to match local wines.

ENOTECHE: Italian for "wine shop."

FRECCIAROSSO (Red Arrow): Italian term that initially referred to wines grown in a Lombardy village of that name, but is now the proprietary name for certain Lombardy wines.

GEMEINDE: The German name for a delimited township and the land surrounding it; the equivalent of a French commune or parish.

GOULAYANT: French term for a wine's general goodness.

GOÛT D'APPELLATION: French for the "taste of origin." In Burgundy, it refers to the commune where the wine originated.

GOÛT DE GRÊLE: French for "taste of hail." Refers to a wine whose grapes were bruised in a hailstorm, a condition that may be evident as a slight taste of rot appearing in the finished wine.

GRANDE MARQUE: French for a "major label." In Champagne, the term implies quality but has no significance elsewhere.

HALB-TROCKEN: German for half-dry.

HAUT: French for "high" or "elevated." Is meant to suggest wine quality. The Haut-Médoc region in Bordeaux is a particularly high-quality area. Elsewhere the term has been applied somewhat loosely, as in Burgundy, where the Haut-Côte de Nuits and the Haut-Côte de Beaune are minor areas, known for producing light and undistinguished wines.

HOCK: The British name for Rhine wines; a short form of Hochheim, a notable wine village in the Rheingau.

HORIZONTAL BLENDING: The combining of wines from a single vintage but from several vineyards.

LAGE: German for a "vineyard" or a specific parcel of land; the equivalent of a French climat or cru.

LESE: German for "harvest." (Spätlese means "late harvest.")

LIEBLICH: German for a "mild wine with a touch of sweetness;" it is somewhat sweeter than halb-trocken.

LIQUOROSO: Italian for "liqueurlike." Refers to sweet and rich dessert wines.

MÂITRE DE CHAI: French for "cellar master," a term associated with Bordeaux.

MARQUE DEPOSÉ: French for "registered trademark," a term that usually appears on labels accompanied by a trade name or a coined name.

MENU DE DÉGUSTATION: See Dégustation.

MILLÉSIME: French for "vintage."

MONOPOLE: French for a "shipper's private brand." Implies exclusivity but does not indicate a monopoly. (The wine may come from a vineyard owned by a shipper or from other sources.) Generally refers now to diverse wine blends, bottled by the big firms.

NÉGOCIANT: French for "shipper," wholesaler, or wine merchant; refers to a man who buys grapes and wines from others, and then produces his own blends.

OENOLOGIST: See Enologist.

OENOPHILE: A lover of wine; a wine enthusiast.

ORGANOLEPTIC: The application of the senses in evaluating a wine.

PARISH: A commune or township in France.

PASADO: A Spanish term used to describe a superior old sherry.

PASSITO: A sweet raisiny Italian wine made from overripe or sun-dried grapes, usually muscats. It varies in style and flavor according to its region of production. A prime example is Tuscany's vin santo.

PICOLIT: A sweet Italian dessert wine, high in alcohol; a form of grappa.

PIERRE À FUSIL: French for "gunflint." Refers to a wine's flavor or aroma, evoking the sharp smell of flint struck with steel; a term used to describe the bouquet of a fine Chablis wine.

PINEAU DES CHARENTES: A combination of Cognac and fresh grape juice which is taken chilled as an apéritif.

PREMIUM: Refers to wines produced in limited quantities. Is meant to suggest high quality and exclusivity, but has been so loosely applied as to be virtually meaningless.

PROPRIÉTAIRE: French for a "vineyard owner" or grower.

PROPRIÉTAIRE-RECOLTANT: French for a "vineyard owner-manager."

QUINTA: Portuguese for a "farm;" refers to a vineyard estate.

RÉCOLTÉ: French for a "vintage" or "harvest."

REDUCTIVE: The method of retaining a white wine's zesty fruitiness by using stainless steel containers, rather than wood to keep air from getting at the wine.

RÉGISSEUR: A French term, roughly translating as "general manager." Refers to the individual in Bordeaux who supervises a vineyard and the making of its wine.

RESERVE: A reference to a wine's age. Although implying special attributes and some degree of exclusivity —as if the wine were held in reserve until ready to drink— it generally has no official standing and can be defined in any way the producer or shipper wishes to define it.

RHINE WINE: German white wine produced in the Rheingau and in Rheinhessen, the Pfalz, and Mittelrhein. (Has also become a generic name for some white wines produced in California and elsewhere.)

RIPASSO: A wine steeped in sediment to achieve added color and an extra depth of flavor. Refers to ordinary Valpolicellas, stored in casks that contained the rich residue of Amarone wines.

ROSATO: Italian for a "rosé wine."

ROSSO: Italian for "red;" a name generally given to California red wines that are not entirely dry.

ROUTE DES GRAND CRUS: French for "Road of Great Growths," a famous Burgundy wine road, beginning a few miles south of Dijon and winding its way through the important Côte d'Or vineyards. (Also see Weinstrasse.)

ROUTES DU VIN: French for "wine roads." Refers to areas in the Médoc, Burgundy, and Alsace characterized by a high concentration of vineyards.

SACK: The British name for sherry, now a registered trademark for a private brand. (The term once also applied to fortified wines from the Canary Islands, which never quite recovered from the phylloxera invasion in the nineteenth century.)

SEC: French for "dry." When applied to Champagne, it indicates some degree of sweetness.

SECCO: Italian for "dry"; the opposite of abboccato or amabile.

SÉCHÉ: French for "dry"; a reference to a withered or a dessicated wine.

SÉLECTION DU GRAINES NOBLES (SGN): A wine made in Alsace from late-harvest grapes which are individually picked. Characterized by great concentration and aging power and the equivalent of a fine Sauternes, it is usually sold in half bottles.

SINGLE VINEYARD: Wine made from grapes grown on a vineyard plot owned by one wine maker.

SPITZENWEIN: German for a "sweet, luscious wine." Refers to high-quality wines pressed from botrytized grapes.

SPRITZER: A drink combining wine and club soda, often in a one-to-one ratio.

SUPÉRIEUR: French term referring to a wine's higher-than-normal alcohol level, not to its superiority.

SUPERMARKET VINTAGE: Bordeaux term, referring to wines sold through the channels that are not normally used in the distribution of fine wines.

TERROIR: French term for "soil," but signifying much more. Refers to the unique characteristics of the place where the wine was produced, not only to its specific vineyard site but to its entire ecosystem; a term integrating the site, soil, and climate with the vines, rootstocks, and grape varieties. Refers as well to man's role in grape growing and wine making. (In Burgundy, where the focus is primarily on the soil, terroir is usually defined as a vineyard site or a parcel of land.)

TÊTE DE CUVÉE: French term signifying the "top of the line." Once had legal significance, but now is loosely used.

TINTO: Spanish for "red wine."

TONNELIER: French for a "cooper," or a maker of barrels.

TROCKEN: German for "dry"; also refers to a withered or a dessicated wine.

UVA: Spanish for "grape." Refers to a spirit distilled directly from grapes, rather than from pomace.

VDP: A German organization set up to ensure high standards for the country's quality wines.

VENDANGE TARDIVE: French for "late harvest." Is associated with Alsace, whose botrytized wines are rich in fruit although not always sweet. Also refers to French and American wines, whose fermentation has been halted before their sugar is fully converted out.

VERAISON: The start of the grape's maturation; the point at which the berry's initially green color changes and its opacity becomes translucent.

VERJUS: French for "green juice," the unfermented juice of unripe grapes —both red and white— which have been pruned to strengthen the vine. Made in France and in the United States, it's sweet-tart and nonalcoholic, and is used as a cooking product in marinades, sauces, and salad dressings.

VERONESE: Fresh, light jug wines produced in Italy.

VERTICAL BLENDING: The blending of wines of two or more vintages drawn from a single vineyard.

VIELLES VIGNES: French for "old vines." Their grapes generally yield wines that demonstrate a greater complexity.

VIGNERON: French for "grape grower." He may supervise the work of others, but more often is simply a skilled vineyard worker.

VIN DE GLACE: French for "ice wine."

VINICULTURE: The art and science of wine making.

VINS DE CÉPAGE: French term for "varietal wines."

VINTNER: See Wine Maker.

VITICULTURE: The art and science of grape growing; also refers to vineyard management.

WEINGUT: German for a "vineyard property"; can also refer to a winery and the wine that it produces.

WEINSTRASSE: German for "wine street" or "wine road." A notable example extends from the Pfalz, west of Mannheim, south to Schweigen near the French border. (Also see Routes du Vin.)

WINE MAKER: The individual who oversees all phases of wine making, from the cultivation, picking, crushing, and pressing of the grapes to the fermentation, racking, aging, blending, and bottling of the wine.

QUANTITIES AND MEASUREMENTS

Wine bottle sizes are based on the metric system, whose cornerstone is the liter at 33.8 ounces. (The liter is the equivalent of 2.11 pints, 1.06 quarts, or 0.26 of a gallon.) When the United States adopted the metric system in 1979, the conversion of bottle sizes presented no serious problems. Since the quart is 32 ounces or 1.057 liters, the liter at 33.8 ounces is a touch more, and the difference between a fifth at 25.6 ounces and 3/4 of a liter is less than a quarter of an ounce.

The U.S. conversion to the metric system established the following bottle sizes:

- The *split* at 6.4 ounces became 3/16 liter (187 milliliters) or 6.3 ounces.
- The *tenth* (also known as the half-bottle) at 12.8 ounces or 1.10 gallon or 2/5 of a quart, became 3/8 liter (375 milliliters) or 12.7 ounces.
- The *fifth* at 25.6 ounces or 1/5 of a gallon or 4/5 of a quart, became a 3/4 liter (750 milliliters, 75 centiliters) or 25.4 ounces.
- The *quart* at 32 ounces became 1 liter (1,000 milliliters, 100 centiliters) or 33.8 ounces.
- The *magnum* at 51.2 ounces became 1$^{1}/_{2}$ liters (1,500 milliliters, 150 centiliters) or 50.73 ounces.

- The *jeroboam* at 102.4 ounces became 3 liters (3,000 milliliters, 300 centiliters) or 101.46 ounces.

NOTE: Although the quart measurement in the United States is a fourth of a gallon or 0.946 liters, in England it is 1.39 liters.

In the United States, by law, a standard wine bottle is 3/4 of a liter (750 milliliters, 75 centiliters). In Europe, wine bottles have varied in size from country to country and even from region to region. In recent years, some have been reduced from 75 or 80 centiliters down to 73, 72, and even 70 centiliters.

Half bottles (which hold 375 milliliters) have their pros and cons. Some say they are generally adequate for two diners. Others maintain that half-bottles offer too little wine for two people. Advocates would like to see more quality wines made available in half bottles. Although this size is a convenient way of becoming acquainted with different wines, it offers no savings. Its cost is usually more than half the price of a full bottle, because special bottles, corks, bottling lines etc., are needed. So they cost almost as much to produce, fill, label, store, and ship out.

NOTE: Certain wines, meant to be served in smaller quantities, are invariably sold in half bottles; among them are the rich, luscious late-harvest wines, along with various ice wines.

Another bottle size, introduced by the Germans, is somewhere between the traditional bottle and the half bottle. At 500 milliliters or nearly 17 ounces, it can provide two people with two glasses of wine each. Its acceptance by the public has been poor, however. Another size is the 187-milliliter bottle, sealed with a twist-off cap. Used by airlines for their mealtime service, it is now offered in some restaurants.

A single serving of wine averages 4 ounces. A standard 750-milliliter bottle, containing about 25 ounces, is enough for six servings. (Some calculate 5 ounces for a single serving so that there are five drinks in a 750 milliliter bottle; ten drinks in a 1.5 liter bottle and twenty drinks in a 3-liter bottle.)

Determining how much wine will be consumed by a group of people generally depends on the occasion and the type of wine served. At lunch, one or two glasses per person should be sufficient. At dinner, a person will usually drink two or three glasses or 8 to 12 ounces, making the norm about half a bottle per person. A meal featuring several wines should provide about one-fourth bottle of each wine per person. A convivial group can easily put away more if a white wine is served as the apéritif, another white wine accompanies the fish course, followed by a red wine with the meat course, and perhaps a glass of port after the meal. Some suggest allowing at least one bottle per person if you count on a glass or two as an apéritif, or with the first course, and a glass or two with the main course. (At informal dinner parties, the guests will probably consume more than expected because of the casual nature of the event.)

For parties and receptions, the rule of thumb is about two glasses of wine per person per hour. During the first two hours, you can count on eight glasses for four people and twelve glasses for six people. Longer-lasting events require somewhat more wine. For eight to ten serious wine-drinking guests, thirty-two glasses or about a gallon (3.785 liters) should be sufficient. For cocktail parties and sit-down dinners, plan on about two or three glasses of wine per person. (For fifty people, allow about thirty bottles of wine, to provide about three glasses per person.) The serving quantities for Champagnes and other sparkling wines are much the same as for still wines. About six bottles should be allowed for every ten guests. If the wine is to be used only for toasting, a case should be enough for about a hundred people. If it's to be served as a dessert wine, one bottle should be sufficient for every four guests.

NOTE: It's always important to have enough wine on hand. Nothing is more awkward than running short in the midst of the festivities. With enough wine, one can open a few more bottles if necessary. (They should not be uncorked, until required, however.) Some people feel that counting on a whole bottle for each guest is a wise precaution at a social gathering. (Caterers estimate that one hundred guests require six cases of table wine and two of Champagne.)

Because fortified or rich dessert wines are consumed in smaller quantities, they go two or three times as far as table or sparkling wines. (An average serving here is 2 to 2 $\frac{1}{2}$ ounces.) Sauternes and other noble-rot wines are so intense and concentrated that one small glass is sufficient; a bottle can serve eight guests or more. (The half bottles in which many late-harvest wines are sold will generally provide four to six servings.)

For entertaining large groups, the magnum —providing approximately twelve 4-ounce glasses— is more practical, economical and festive than two standard bottles which hold the same amount. Some connoisseurs collect magnums not only for their dramatic impact at a dinner party but because the wine ages more slowly in these larger bottles and also keeps better.

The following information on bottle sizes and the number of servings each provides might prove useful in planning a dinner party or a special celebration:

Size	Fluid Ounces	Servings per Bottle	
		Table or Sparkling	*Fortified*
3/16 liter (split)	4	2	—
3/8 liter (tenth) or half-bottle	12.7	2–3	4
3/4 liter (fifth) or standard bottle	25.4	4–6	8–10
1 liter (quart)	33.8	6–8	10–12
Half gallon	64	12–16	20–30
Gallon	128	24–30	40–60
Magnum (1.5 liters) equivalent of two bottles	50	8–12	—
Double Magnum (3 liters) equivalent of four bottles	101	16–25	—
Jeroboam (5 liters) equivalent of six bottles	169	30–45	—
Imperial (6 liters) equivalent of eight bottles	202	32–58	—

Champagnes are available in a greater variety of bottle sizes than still or table wines, as the following indicates:

Size	Fluid Ounces	Servings
Split or quarter bottle (187 milliliters)	6.3	1 ½ glasses
Half-bottle or pint (375 milliliters)	12.7	3 glasses
Full bottle (750 milliliters)	26	7 glasses
Magnum: 2 bottles (1.5 liters)	52	15 glasses
Jeroboam: 4 bottles (3 liters)	104	30 glasses
Rehoboam: 6 bottles (4.5 liters)	156	45 glasses
Methuselah or Imperial: 8 bottles (6 liters)	208	60 glasses
Salmanazar: 12 bottles (9 liters)	312	90 glasses
Balthazar: 16 bottles (12 liters)	416	120 glasses
Nebuchadnezzar: 20 bottles (15 liters)	520	150 glasses
Sovereign: 36 bottles (27 liters)	936	270 glasses

NOTE: The oversized Champagne bottles are quite heavy, requiring strong arms to lift and a steady hand to pour. The largest are meant primarily for show. The Nebuchadnezzar, holding 15 liters, is rarely seen and usually not exported. The Sovereign, standing three feet tall, was designed as the focal point for the launching of huge ships at sea.

Miscellaneous Measurements

BARREL: A container usually holding 228 liters of wine; the equivalent of twenty cases. (A 50-gallon barrel is the equivalent of nineteen cases.)

BARRICA: An oak barrel with a 225-liter capacity; it's associated with the wines of Rioja.

BARRIQUE: The standard oak cask in Bordeaux; it holds 225 liters.

BUTT: A sherry cask holding 490.68 liters.

CARAFE: An open-necked bottle used in serving; it varies in capacity from one half to a full liter.

CARATELLE: An Italian oak cask holding 50 liters.

CASE: A box made of wood or cardboard, usually holding twelve standard bottles. A case of 1.5-liter bottles holds six, a case of 3-liter bottles holds three, and a case of 6-liter bottles holds one. (For Champagnes, there are six magnums, three double magnums or one imperial to a case.)

CONTAINER: A receptacle used in shipping wine; it holds seven hundred cases.

DEMIJOHN: A squat, round, small-necked oversized bottle, often covered with wicker or straw and set in a supporting wooden frame. Ranging in capacity from 1 to 14 gallons, it most commonly holds 4.9 gallons.

FUDER: A German cask holding 100 liters.

HALBSTÜCK: A German cask holding 600 liters; this is the preferred size in the Rheingau region.

HECTARE: A parcel of land, approximately two and one half acres in size.

HOGSHEAD: A cask holding 225 liters. In Bordeaux, it's called a *barrique;* in Rioja, a barrica and in Burgundy, a pièce. (The casks for ports and sherries are somewhat larger.)

PICHET: A small earthenware pitcher, used for serving wine in France, both at home and in restaurants.

PIÈCE: A Burgundy cask, holding about 225 liters.

PIPE: A cask holding anywhere from 100 to 125 gallons. (For port wines, 550-liter pipes are used.)

POT: A small, heavy-bottomed bottle, used in serving Beaujolais from the cask; its capacity is about half a liter.

QUART: A French carafe whose capacity is about a quarter liter, enough for a single serving. (It's known as a *quartino* in Italy.)

TONNEAU: About a hundred cases or twelve hundred bottles of wine; the equivalent of four barriques.

SUMMARIES

The Vineyard

In the spring, the soil is cultivated; the trellis wires are tightened, and the new canes are tied to them. The vines blossom in April or May.

Cultivation continues through June; the flowering shoots are thinned; the young vines are suckered. In June or July, the grape set occurs.

By late summer, the wine maker has trimmed his vines and is monitoring the shifting balance of sugars and acids in his grapes to determine their ripeness.

In September, the harvest begins. By October or November, most of the fruit has been gathered and wine making gets under way.

In winter, the dormant vines are pruned and cuttings are taken. The wine maker samples his new wines.

In March, when the vines emerge from hibernation, the vineyards are cleared and the weeds and brush are chopped up. The wine maker anxiously monitors his new crop to assess its promise for the coming year.

NOTE: In the Southern Hemisphere, where the seasons are reversed, the grapes are cultivated in autumn and gathered in late winter or early spring.

Wine Making

Port

The crushed grapes are fermented on their skins. Fermentation is then halted while the desired amount of grape sugar remains. (This is done by transferring the still-active must to casks containing a predetermined amount of brandy.)

During the winter months, the wine settles down and precipitates out its gross lees.

Racked into fresh casks in the spring, the wine is transported downriver to the shippers' lodges at Vila Nova de Gaia, where it is tasted, classified, and blended.

After further fortification, the wine is aged in wood and glass for varying lengths of time, depending on the type and style of port of desired.

Sherry

After the harvest, the high-sugar grapes are heaped out-of-doors on mats to raisin in the sun.

Their rich must ferments out completely, leaving the wine bone-dry.

The wine —kept outdoors in loosely stoppered casks—oxidizes and may or may not develop flor.

After its classification as flor or nonflor, the wine is given its preliminary fortification. (Finos receive the least fortification, olorosos the most.)

After spending a number of years passing through a solera system, the sherry emerges fully blended and aged. It may be fortified further, sweetened and colored, according to its type and style.

Madeira

After fermentation, the wine is fortified early or late, depending on the sweetness or dryness desired.

The wine is then baked in an *estufa* to accelerate its oxidation and caramelize its residual sugar. (The baking process creates a richness of color, a smoothness of texture, and a bittersweet taste.)

After passing through a solera system for blending and aging, the Madeira is then bottled and released.

Champagne (The Classic Method)

ÉPLUCHAGE: After the harvest, specially trained workers carefully inspect the grapes, discarding those that are overripe, underripe, or blemished.

BLENDING AND BOTTLING: The wine is fermented, aged briefly in wood, blended into cuvées, and bottled. A precisely measured solution of sugar and yeast (*liqueur de tirage*) is added to restimulate secondary fermentation. A temporary cork (*bouchon de tirage*) seals the bottle. A sturdy metal clamp (*agrafe*) anchors that cork firmly in place.

TIRAGE (Tierage): The bottles are stacked horizontally in cool underground vaults. As secondary fermentation proceeds at a very slow pace in the bottle, the wine matures gradually on its rich, yeasty deposit.

REMUAGE (Riddling): The bottles are placed in slotted racks known as pulpits (*pupitres*) and bottle-turning workmen (*remueurs*) rotate, rap, and tilt the bottles daily over a period of several months until they are positioned neck down (*sur pointe*), with their sediment lodged compactly against the cork.

DÉGORGEMENT (Disgorging): The bottle necks are dipped into a brine solution to chill and congeal the sediment. Then the metal clamp (*agrafe*) is released, ejecting the cork with its icy clump of sediment, along with a bit of the wine.

ADDING THE DOSAGE: To preempt the ullage, the bottles are topped off with a dosage syrup (*liqueur d'expédition*). The dosage, consisting of wine, sugar, and brandy, also establishes the wine's final classification or style.

RECORKING: A mushroom-shaped shipping cork (*bouchon d'expédition*) is inserted and anchored firmly in place with a wire hood or muzzle. The Champagne is then binned away briefly to rest.

Red and White Wines

Red wines, fermented on their skins, are generally more complicated and costly to produce than white wines. They are usually more complex as well since they generate more tannins and acids during their fermentation. At their finest, the red wines acquire richly concentrated fruit, a fine nose, a sturdy backbone, and a greater potential for aging than the white wines. Experts generally consider them more significant as a group.

White wines, which are usually not fermented on their skins, require less processing and tend to be less intricate. At their finest, they generally display a delicate aroma and bouquet and a pleasantly crisp acidity. The exceptions can be quite extraordinary however; the most notable being as complex and nuanced as the finest reds. These include the majestic white Burgundies, the great German

Rieslings, the exquisitely luscious noble rots, and other rare sweet white wines.

This is how the red wines and the white wines differ in their processing:

Red Wines	White Wines
The grapes are gathered and crushed.	The grapes are gathered and crushed.
The must, including the skins and seeds, goes to a vat or tank.	The crushed grapes go to the press; the must is run off into a vat or tank, leaving the skins and seeds behind.
Primary fermentation begins. The skins and solids form a dense floating cap, which must be dispersed.	Primary fermentation begins.
Secondary fermentation begins.	Secondary fermentation begins.
The cap goes to the press.	
Racking and other forms of clarification follow.	Racking and other forms of clarification follow.
The wine is aged in wood.	The wine may be briefly aged in wood.
The wine is blended.	The wine is blended.
The wine may be aged in glass.	The wine is rarely aged in glass.

NOTE: Blending can precede and/or follow aging; it may even precede the fermentation process itself.

Wine Types

Red Wines

LIGHT FRUITY REDS include French Burgundies, such as Beaujolais and Savigny-les-Beaune; Bordeaux's Graves and Juliénas; Côte de Provence reds such as Corbières, Bandol, Roussillon, Minervois, and Fronsac; Loire reds such as Chinon and Bourgueil; Italian Corvos, Valpolicellas, Barberas, Bardolinos, Grignolinos, Lambruscos, lighter Chiantis, Lagreins del Alto-Adige, Gattinaras, Merlots, and Dolcettos; Spain's lighter Riojas and red Penédes; California's Gamays, Merlots, Petite Sirahs, and some Pinot Noirs, Cabernet Sauvignons, and Zinfandels.

MEDIUM-TO FULL-BODIED REDS include Bordeaux from the Médoc and Graves, St.-Émilion and Pomerol; Burgundies from the Côte de Beaune and the Côte de Nuits and southern Burgundies such as Mercurey, Rully, Santenay, and Cahors, along with the more substantial Beaujolais; Côte de Beaune wines such as Volnay; Rhône wines such as Gigondas, Châteauneuf-du-Pape, Hermitage, and Cornas; Italian Barolos, Brunellos di Montalcino, Chiantis, Amarones, Nebbiolos, Corvos, Barberas, Rossos di Montalcino, Rossos Piceno, Sassellas, Ghemmes, Infernos, Dolcettos d'Alba, Valtellinas, Spannas, Taurasis, Barbarescos, and Sangioveses; heavier Spanish Riojas and Penedés reds; American varietals such as the Pinot Noir, Cabernet Sauvignon, Merlot, Ruby Cabernet, Carignane, Petite Sirah, heavier Zinfandels, and northeastern Baco Noirs.

ROBUST, ASSERTIVE REDS include big Burgundies and big Rhône wines; Italy's Amarones della Valpolicella and heavier Brunellos di Montalcino, Barolos, Barbarescos, and Vinos Nobile di Montepulciano; Australia's Cabernet Sauvignons; as well as certain California Cabernets and Zinfandels.

White Wines

LIGHT OR CRISP DRY WHITES include Burgundies such as Chablis; Bordeaux wines from Graves; also Pouilly-Fumé, Muscadets, Sancerres, Pouilly-Fuissés, St. Vérans, Chenin Blancs, Sauvignon Blancs, light Muscats and Pinot Gris; Alsatian Pinot Blancs and Sylvaners; Italian Soaves, Orvietos, Frascatis, Albariños, Verdicchios, Vernaccias di San Gimignano, Trebbianos, Est! Est! Est!, Corteses di Gavi, Lacryma Christis, and Pinot Grigios; Germany's light Rhine Rieslings and Mosels; Swiss Fendants, Neuchatels, and Dézaleys; Chilean Rieslings; Portuguese vinho verdes; and Hungarian Furmint and Szamorodni wines.

MEDIUM DRY WHITES include French Meursaults, Vouvrays, Sancerres, Blanc Fumés de Pouilly, Chenin Blancs, Sauvignon Blancs; Graves from Bordeaux; most Loire wines, including Muscadets and Gros Plants; Alsatian Gewürztraminers and Rieslings; Germany's Rhine and Mosel wines; Italian Corvos, Pinot Grigios, Frascatis, Cinqueterres; Greek retsinas; American Chardonnays, Chenin Blancs, Fumé Blancs, Johannisberg Rieslings, and northeastern Seyval Blancs.

FULLISH WHITES include French Burgundies such as Montrachets, Meursaults, and the better Chablis; Pouilly-Fumés; Hermitages from the Rhône, Monbazillacs, Muscadets; Alsatian Gewürztraminers, Pinot Gris, Sylvaners, and Rieslings; Germany's Rhine and Mosel Rieslings up to and including the Spätleses, also those from the Saar and Franconia; Spanish white wines from Rioja; American Chardonnays and Pouilly-Fumés.

LUSCIOUS WHITES including the sweeter Beaumes-de-Venise, Monbazillacs, Vouvrays and Anjous from the Loire; Sauternes and Barsacs; rich German Rieslings such as Beerenausleses and Trockenbeerenausleses; Italy's richer Asti Spumantes and vin santos; certain Riojas; some American Chardonnays, Chenin Blancs, and sparkling Blancs de Noirs.

*A half–bottle of wine once or twice a week can supply
all the happiness the average person requires without
leaving him in such bliss that he can't do anything
worthwhile for the rest of his life*

Russell Baker

ABOUT THE AUTHOR

Gloria Bley Miller is a writer with a varied background in education and the fine arts. A native New Yorker, she attended schools in New Mexico, Philadelphia, and New York and holds degrees from both Hunter College and the Bank Street College of Education. Food and wine have long been among her major interests.

She is the author of *The Thousand Recipe Chinese Cookbook*, initially published by Atheneum. The book won the first Tastemaker Award in the United States and a Distinguished Award from the German Gastronomic Society. (It was also published in England and Holland as well as Germany.) Praised for its clarity and lucidity, the work was included in Craig Claiborne's Recommended Cookbook Library and selected by Williams-Sonoma as one of their twenty-two Classic Cookbooks.

The New York Times recently included it among a dozen or so cookbooks that have stood the test of time, calling them "comprehensive, with wide perspectives that give a rich sense of the areas of cooking they cover." After selling more than a quarter million copies in hardcover, the book has gone through seventeen printings in paperback; the latter in a Fireside edition, published by Simon & Schuster.

In focusing her attention on wine, Ms. Miller brings to its great diversity her ability to organize and synthesize information. The result is *The Glory of Wine*, a clear, concise, straightforward book which offers an enormously rich introduction to the subject. Its central purpose is to provide the reader with a good, solid foundation, to offer basic yet specific information on wine, while avoiding the dangers of obsolescence.

An early reaction called the book "a marvelous introduction to wine; informative without being dogmatic, interesting without being esoteric." Another reader described it as "the Rosetta Stone of the wine experience."

Ms. Miller lives in Greenwich Village with her husband, sculptor Richard McDermott Miller, whose studio is in the SoHo district of Manhattan. She is a member of the Authors Guild.

INDEX

C

D

O

Oaky 294

Oberemmel 125

Ockfen 125

Oechsle scale 15-16

Oeil de Perdrix 161

Oenologist 329

Oenophile 329

Oestrich 120

Official Testing Number 194

Ohio 141

Olorosos 51-52

Oltrepo Pavese 100

Oporto 117

Oppenheim 122

Oregon 140

Organic wines 322

Organoleptic 329

Ornellaia 105

Ortenau 127

Orvieto 106

Overproduction 203

Oxidized 294

P

Pacific Northwest 140-141

Palate fatigue 250

Palo Cortado 52

Palomino 310

Papery 294

Parellada 310

Parish 329

Pasado 329

Passe-Tout-Grains 322

Passito 329

Pasteur, Louis 21, 23

Pauillac 62

Pays Nantais 90

Pedro Ximénez 310

Peloponnesus 152-153

Pelure d'oignon 33

Penedés 112

Pernand-Vergelesses 75

Perrières 76

Pesquera del Duero 115

Pétillant 45

Petit Chablis 181

Petit Châteaux 176

Petit Verdot 310

Petite Arvine 310

Petite Sirah 310

Pfalz 121-122

PH rating 15

Photosynthesis 1

Phylloxera 4-5

Pichet 337

Pickers 11-12

Picolit 101, 329

Picpoul 311

Pièce 337

Piedmont 96, 98-99

Pierre à Fusil 329

Piesport 124

Piesporter Goldtröpfchen 124

Pineau de la Loire 311

Pineau des Charentes 330

Pinot 311

Pinot Blanc 311

Pinot Grigio 311

Pinot Gris 311

Pinot Meunier 311

Pinot Nero 312

Pinot Noir 311-312

Pinot St. George 312

Pinotage 311

Pipe 337

Piquette 322

Place of business 202-203

Q

R

T

U

V